To Julia and her great-grandchildren, Tyler and Olivia

To my beloved wife, Susan

A M
I
OKAY?

*A Layman's Guide
to the Psychiatrist's Bible*

Allen Frances, M.D.,
and Michael B. First, M.D.

A TOUCHSTONE BOOK
PUBLISHED BY SIMON & SCHUSTER
NEW YORK LONDON TORONTO SYDNEY SINGAPORE

TOUCHSTONE
Rockefeller Center
1230 Avenue of the Americas
New York, NY 10020

First Touchstone Edition 2000
TOUCHSTONE and colophon are registered trademarks of Simon & Schuster, Inc.
DESIGNED BY ERICH HOBBING
Text set in Adobe Garamond
Manufactured in the United States of America

1   3   5   7   9   10   8   6   4   2

"Mini Mental State: A Practical Method for Grading the Cognitive State of Patients for the Clinician."
Journal of Psychiatric Research, 12(3): 189–198, 1975

The copyright in the Mini Mental State Examination is wholly
owned by the Mini Mental LLC, a Massachusetts limited liability company.
For information about how to obtain permission to use or reproduce the Mini Mental
State Examination, please contact John Gonsalves Jr., Administrator of the Mini Mental LLC,
at 31 St. James Avenue, Suite 1, Boston, Massachusetts 02116—1(617) 587-4215

The Library of Congress has cataloged the Scribner edition as follows:
Frances, Allen, 1942–
Your mental health: a layman's guide to the psychiatrist's bible/Allen Frances and Michael B. First.
p.   cm.
Includes index.
1. Psychology, Pathological. 2. Psychotherapy. 3. Diagnosis, Differential.
4. Psychiatry—Differential therapeutics. I. First, Michael B., 1956– . II. Title.
RC454.4.F715   1999
616.89—dc21   98-31154
CIP

ISBN 0-684-83720-X
0-684-85961-0 (Pbk)
Previously published as *Your Mental Health*
The ideas, procedures, and suggestions in this book are intended to supplement, not replace, the medical
advice of trained professionals. All matters regarding your health require medical supervision.
Consult your physician before acting on any information in this book as well as
about any condition that may require diagnosis or medical attention.

CONTENTS

Introduction: How This Book Can Help You   9

Twenty Questions to Get You Started   17

Chapter 1: The "Blues"   31

Chapter 2: Euphoric or Irritable Mood   59

Chapter 3: Anxiety, Fear, and Avoidance   79

Chapter 4: Obsessions or Compulsions   101

Chapter 5: Exposure to Traumatic Events   109

Chapter 6: Alcohol or Substance Use Problems   117

Chapter 7: Abnormal Eating   155

Chapter 8: Sexual or Gender Problems   171

Chapter 9: Sleep-Related Problems   189

Chapter 10: Personality Disorders   207

Chapter 11: Unexplained Physical Complaints   245

Chapter 12: Other Impulse-Control Problems   263

Chapter 13: Dissociative Experiences   281

Chapter 14: Adjustment Disorder   295

Chapter 15: Loss of Reality Testing   303

Chapter 16: Cognitive Difficulties   329

Chapter 17: Delays in Development   355

Chapter 18: Childhood Behavior Problems   375

Chapter 19: Hyperactivity or Distractibility   387

Chapter 20: Other Childhood Problems   399

Conclusion: Ten Take-Home Messages   413

Index   427

INTRODUCTION:

HOW THIS BOOK CAN HELP YOU

People are fascinated by people—especially when they are acting in a way that does not seem to make much sense. Unpredictability in a fellow human is as unsettling as unpredictability in the weather, and almost as dangerous. Our ancestors lived in small, interdependent, wandering tribes. At these close quarters, it was necessarily a case of all for one and one for all. When someone suddenly got manic, or depressed, or phobic, or heard voices, or started behaving strangely, it would throw the world out of joint for the entire group. The spiritual leader of the group (the shaman) had the job of diagnosing and interpreting these illnesses within the tribe's prevailing belief system of ritualized magic. He would then prescribe the appropriate antidotes intended to ward off the problem so that the sufferer and the tribe could return to normal and get on with the difficult business of everyday life.

As the great ancient civilizations emerged in Egypt, India, China, Greece, and Mexico, a division of labor separated the shaman's job into two new professions—a priesthood responsible for spiritual health and a physician group responsible for physical health. The ancient doctors began to study illness from a secular perspective—as a naturally occurring breakdown in body function, not as a curse placed by the spirits, gods, or a malevolent neighbor. For the next three millennia, doctors enjoyed great prestige despite the fact that they had very few real cures for illness. Their power came from the ability to classify symptoms into what appeared to be meaningful categories. The mere act of naming scary things gives us some feeling of control over them. The doctor's knowledge conveyed a comforting sense of order, predictability, and positive expectations in an otherwise terrifying situation. This, along with time, a good bedside manner, and herbal medicine, got a lot of our ancestors better.

Then, as now, any busy medical practice included a large proportion of patients with psychiatric illness and the early classifications in medicine all provided an extensive description of the psychiatric disorders. As medicine developed, its classifications were constantly revised and updated, although the illnesses themselves and the people have probably stayed pretty much the same ever since the dawn of the species. By now, there have been literally hundreds of attempts to explain and classify mental disorders drawn from every era of history and every part of the world. These differ in some details but are remarkably convergent in the descriptions of the various illnesses.

The latest of these classifications is known as DSM-IV—or, more formally, the *Diagnostic and Statistical Manual of Mental Disorders, Fourth Edition,* published in May 1994 by the American Psychiatric Association. DSM-IV has been called the "bible" of psychiatric diagnosis because it provides the official definitions for the mental disorders as these are recognized currently by clinicians from around the world.

DSM-IV has achieved a central role in mental health circles because accurate diagnosis is now more important than ever. For the first time, we have a science, not just an art, of psychiatry. The field has come a long way from the shaman's rattle or the doctor's folk remedies or the alchemist's mercury concoctions. Using powerful imaging devices, we can actually visualize just how the brain works in sickness and in health. We now have very effective tools for treating mental disorders and the future looks even brighter. Getting the right treatment almost always depends on having the right diagnosis.

Our goal is to help people identify their psychiatric problems as soon after they begin as possible. Catching symptoms early makes them easier to treat, less likely to come back, and less able to damage your life. Psychiatric disorders "kindle"—it is always easier to put out the fire before it spreads. Diseases that are dug in are much harder to treat.

The need for a book like this is clear. One in five people has a psychiatric problem at any given moment, and half will have one in a lifetime. But most people who need it never get adequate treatment and there is usually a lag of many years before the right diagnosis is made. This exacts a great toll of personal and family misery and societal cost. The changes in health care delivery make it especially important for you to be an informed consumer. Because managed care has radically reduced the time doctors spend with patients, psychiatric disorders are more likely than ever to fall through the cracks.

Knowledge is still power. You are more likely to get good care if you are educated about your problem, understand its usual course, and know what can be done about it. The more you learn the less alone you will feel, the less helpless, and the less uniquely damned. Most of the psychiatric disorders have been on the planet probably ever since the beginning of mankind. Extensive research effort using the most powerful tools of science is telling us more about these disorders every day and you can almost certainly be helped. It is certainly no fun having a psychiatric disorder, but it is something you can learn to control and manage gracefully.

Before we describe how to use the book, there are a couple of cautions we would like to make about its possible misuses. First off, the book is not intended to provide a menu of "excuses" to relieve people of responsibility for their actions. Being diagnosed with a mental disorder often means that you are, at least temporarily, entitled to the "sick role" and deserve special care, consolation, and time to heal. However, the sick role also brings with it special responsibilities—to learn more about the condition and its treatments and to do everything possible to get well. We are especially troubled by the recent attempts in the courts and in the media to justify virtually all irresponsible or criminal behavior as the product of a mental disorder or victimhood. This is usually done in an exploitative way that adds to the stigmatization of the people who have real psychiatric problems but are responsible in dealing with them.

Many people will read this book not because they are particularly curious about themselves, but rather to learn more about a loved one, a friend, or a colleague who is having symptoms or displaying problematic behavior. We hope that the insights gained will increase your understanding (and tolerance) and will help you to help them. Be mindful, however, that a little knowledge can be a dangerous thing and can cause its own brand of mischief. Please don't use the book to paint your loved one into a corner or to score points in an argument. Psychiatric diagnosis should not become a sophisticated form of name calling.

Finally, don't feel that you or a loved one can go it alone—that reading this book and making a tentative diagnosis is the end of the process. Self-diagnosis is inherently subject to blind spots and to potentially serious errors of both overdiagnosis and underdiagnosis. Your own first impressions must always be checked out with a clinician who has the special expertise, training, objectivity, and experience to determine whether you really have the problem you think you have—and what can be done about it.

This brings us to a few tips on how to use the book. The next section, "Twenty Questions to Get You Started," provides a diagnostic screening questionnaire that covers most of the psychiatric problems a human being is capable of having. Some of you may be reading this book because you are anxious to see if you are "normal." If your answers are "No" to every question in the next chapter, it is a pretty good sign either that you have a clean bill of psychiatric health or else that you have very poor insight into what you are really like. Ask a friend.

The next twenty chapters that comprise the body of the book each expand upon one of the twenty questions. If you are interested only in a fast self-diagnostic run-through, you can figure out which of the twenty questions apply to you and then read only those chapters that are directly pertinent. But this shortcut would, we think, result in a missed opportunity. The psychiatric disorders in aggregate present a wonderful catalog of human thinking, feeling, and behavior, displayed in all of its unusual variety. These are often painful conditions to have, but we can learn a great deal about human nature from them. Seeing how things can sometimes go wrong also helps us to appreciate all the ways they usually go right.

Each chapter describes one or several of the psychiatric disorders described in DSM-IV. They are organized according to the following format:

Some Introductory Remarks: We place each of the psychiatric disorders into its evolutionary context. The psychiatric problems people have are usually an exaggeration or a distortion of a basic human tendency that has fundamental adaptive value when it works well. Many phobias are inborn adaptive fears that have become wildly exaggerated. Binge eating was a great way to store calories when the getting was good in a world without refrigerators and haunted by possible starvation. Mania is the uncontrolled stimulation of pleasure systems built in by nature to reward us for doing the things that are good for us. Depression is part of the price we pay for the mammalian ability to love and be attached. Antisocial personality is an exaggeration of predator skills that had (and have) clear survival value at the right time and in the right place. And so on for all the psychiatric disorders.

The introductions will also place each disorder in its more recent historical context. We will indicate whether there are any controversies about its diagnosis and treatment and discuss public health issues or new research initiatives.

Diagnostic Criteria: DSM-IV provides a set of diagnostic criteria for each of the psychiatric disorders. These are very detailed and explicit decision rules that govern how that diagnosis is to be made. Each criteria set contains a list of the particular symptoms, course, and other features that must be present and that distinguish this disorder from all the others in the manual.

Because of the widespread interest in the diagnostic criteria sets and their value in psychoeducation, we have made them an essential component of this book. However, the DSM-IV criteria sets were developed specifically for use by clinicians and researchers and are written in technical language that is sometimes a far cry from readily understandable English. We have, therefore, rewritten them in a style that we hope to be more accessible. In doing so, however, you should be aware that we have necessarily taken some liberties so that many of the criteria sets in this book no longer conform exactly to the original DSM-IV definitions.

Description: This section is intended to give you a more full-bodied sense of the disorder and what it is like to have it. The individual symptoms are described in some detail and illustrated with actual patient experiences. Our goal whenever possible has been to put you in the mind-set of the person experiencing the problem. We also provide additional information about the condition—when and how it usually starts, its typical course, and its frequency in the general population. Early onsets of psychiatric disorders in childhood and adolescence usually happen when there is a strong family history and suggest that there is likely to be a strong genetic contribution. This makes active and early intervention even more crucial in order to prevent what might otherwise be a long and difficult struggle with the illness. Psychiatric disorders vary dramatically in their course. Some occur only once and disappear forever after successful treatment. Others are chronic and lifelong. Many are episodic, with remissions and relapses. Knowing its likely natural course gives you considerable power over the illness and helps in planning which treatments will work best to keep it in control.

For the most part, the psychiatric disorders are pretty much alike in men and women, in people of different ages, and in people of all the world's races and cultures. There are some few but important variations in the type of the symptoms people have based on gender, developmental, race, and cultural differences—and these are highlighted whenever pertinent.

Differential Diagnosis: Recognizing that you have a psychiatric symptom is only the first step in diagnosis because it can usually be caused by any number of different disorders. For example, difficulty sleeping (see question #9) may result from literally hundreds of different conditions including any of the mood, anxiety, substance use, or psychotic disorders; any number of medical conditions; medication side effects caused by many different drugs; primary insomnia; or it may just reflect that the person is a "normal" restless sleeper. What clinicians call "differential diagnosis" is the process of figuring out which diagnosis makes the most sense.

We certainly do not expect you to become experts in differential diagnosis simply by reading this book. This requires long years of clinical training and experience. However, this section provides clues as to which disorders are most likely to account for your problem and how to distinguish the one that best fits your situation.

Am I Okay? Your biggest risk in reading this book is that you may begin overdiagnosing yourself and the people around you. The DSM-IV disorders are made up of symptoms which, in mild form and in isolation, occur commonly as part of the aches and pains of everyday life. All of us have occasional periods of feeling down in the dumps, being anxious, having a sleepless night, or not feeling in the mood for sex. In this section, we provide you with guidance about whether your problem crosses the line from a normal everyday problem into a clinical condition that warrants further evaluation and treatment. Don't assume you have a diagnosable condition unless the symptoms conform closely to one of the definitions in this book and cause serious distress or interfere with your ability to function in daily activities. We want to help you avoid being an emotional hypochondriac.

Treatment Options: Psychiatric research is providing us with new and more powerful treatments. We can now greatly improve the lives of almost everyone with a psychiatric problem. This is a great time to be a mental health professional and, in this one way at least, a great time to be a patient. This section describes the different medicines and psychotherapy approaches likely to be most helpful for each of the disorders. Sometimes, there is almost an embarrassment of riches and the problem is deciding how to choose from among several different plausible alternatives. The best fit must take into account your own specific preferences, needs, situation, previous experiences, and treatment response patterns.

Suggested Additional Readings: This book is meant to start the process of self-diagnosis, not culminate it. It is important that you keep reading and learning and asking questions. At the end of each chapter, we list additional books that may be helpful in the next stages of your continuing education. Sometimes these have been written by clinicians for a larger audience;

sometimes by people who have gone through what you are going through and have acquired wisdom to share with you.

Where to Go for Help: Each chapter ends with a list of the nationally available self-help, support, and advocacy groups and other information sources—and how to get in touch with them. Patient and family-initiated support and advocacy groups are a remarkably helpful and increasingly powerful force in psychiatry. They are wonderful in many ways and work effectively on both the national and the local level. Perhaps most visible has been their very effective lobbying efforts to extend mental health benefits, achieve equality of coverage, and reduce the discrimination against and stigmatization of those with mental illness. These organizations have great political minds, but always retain a wonderfully generous and open human heart. In virtually every community, there is likely to be a support group for your problem. These are an irreplaceable source of advice, camaraderie, solace, and education. It is also a nice chance to help others. The Internet is bursting with information on mental health and has many friendly chat groups. You need never feel alone.

This book is a kind of summary of our professional lives. We are grateful to everyone who has taught us the things we are now passing on to you—especially our patients, who have always been our best teachers. Living life with a mental illness is not always easy. We have been greatly enriched by the opportunity to share the struggles and triumphs of many people who have confronted their problems often with remarkable courage, wisdom, forbearance, and humor. This is their book as much as ours and we thank them for it.

Twenty Questions
to Get You Started

W hen you go to a doctor for a routine physical checkup, part of the examination will include what is called a "review of systems." The doctor asks you a comprehensive series of questions covering everything about your health from head to toe in order to ensure that nothing important is missed. The following twenty questions are a "review of systems" for your mental health. A positive answer to a particular question will direct you to one (or more) of the subsequent chapters indicating the range of DSM-IV disorders relevant to understanding your symptoms.

Please remember that a "yes" answer does *not* necessarily mean that you have a DSM-IV disorder—these questions are written to cast an especially wide net. Almost everyone has had at least some of the problems mentioned below, but most often these are not severe or persistent enough to be considered a mental disorder. The remaining chapters of the book will help you learn more about your problem and decide whether it is "clinically significant." As we've mentioned before, however, a final confirmation must depend on the clinical judgment of an experienced mental health professional.

If your answer is "no" to each and every one of the following twenty questions, then either you have a clean bill of health, or you may be unaware of (or are denying) problems that do exist; or you may have a problem that is not specifically covered in this book.

If you are reading this book on behalf of a family member or friend, substitute the appropriate pronoun ("Is your spouse depressed . . . ?").

Question #1: Are you depressed? Do you feel sad and blue much of the time? Are you down in the dumps . . . as if nothing feels good . . . as if you don't care about anything?

Do you feel as if you are walking around with a black cloud over your head or falling into a black hole? Does everything seem bleak and gray? Has the fun gone out of your life? Do you find that you just don't care about doing the things that used to matter to you, like hobbies or getting together with friends? Do you just want to crawl into bed and pull the covers over your head? Do you feel as if you no longer have any emotions and don't even care about the people you love? Do you just want to be by yourself and not deal with anyone or anything? Are you a third wheel at work, just occupying space and getting nothing done? Do you find yourself crying frequently, sometimes for apparently no reason? Are you having trouble sleeping or have you found yourself sleeping all the time? Is your appetite not what it used to be and does everything taste like cardboard? Or perhaps you can't keep yourself from eating all day? Do you feel like you are running on half power? Do you feel so agitated and restless that you are jumping out of your skin? Or slowed down as though you are walking in a vat of molasses? Do you feel as if you aren't worth anything to anybody or that you are a burden to everyone around you and that they would be better off if you were dead? Are you unable to concentrate on anything—like watching TV, reading a newspaper, or even following a conversation? Do you feel paralyzed by the prospect of making even a small decision? Are you having thoughts that you should hurt or kill yourself?

We're not talking about just the occasional blues but rather sustained depression that interferes with your life. You feel bad day in and day out for weeks (and sometimes months or years) at a time. Depression has to be distinguished from the aches and pains of everyday life. Everyone has brief periods of unhappiness and disappointment that have little or no impact on daily functioning. A "yes" to these questions means that you have more severe and prolonged periods of depression that really make you miserable, interfere with your functioning, or make everything you do feel like an effort.

If the Answer to This Question Is Yes, Please Refer to Chapter 1.

Question #2: Do you have times when you feel manic? Have you felt so good, "high," hyper, or irritable that you are "not yourself" and have gotten into trouble?

Do you sometimes feel like you are "on top of the world" and "bigger than life"? Do you have times when you suddenly feel especially talented and that you must express your gift—like writing the great American novel or closing the business deal of the century? During these episodes, do you feel as though you have boundless energy, that you can't keep up with your thoughts, that you have more to say than you can fit in, that you need hardly any sleep or any food? Do you become outrageously productive and driven to keep active every minute? Are you on the phone day and night, "catching up" with everyone you have ever known? Do you find yourself going overboard and doing things that are unusual for you (buying expensive clothes you can't afford, traveling all over the place, flooring the accelerator while driving, having sex with people you don't know very well)? Some people who are speeded up have an extremely irritable rather than euphoric mood, especially when they get frustrated.

Everyone (hopefully) has at least occasional outstanding days in which the sun is in the heavens and all is right with the world. Answer "yes" to this question only if your periods of elevated mood cross the line from being wonderful into causing serious problems. We're not talking about normal self-confidence but rather unwarranted grandiosity, impulsivity, and poor judgment that can be of disastrous proportions.

If the Answer to This Question Is Yes, Please Refer to Chapter 2.

Question #3: Are you especially anxious, fearful, or panicky? Do you always feel nervous, on edge, and worry too much? Are you excessively fearful of things you know you shouldn't be that afraid of, so that you have to go out of your way to avoid them?

Do you get an inexplicable terror that seems to come out of nowhere, the sudden feeling that something dreadful is going to happen, that you're about to faint, you don't have enough air, and your heart is beating irregularly or is about to break out of your chest because it is pounding so hard? These panic attacks are usually brief but intense and can come on "out of the blue" or in response to specific triggers that are frightening to you.

Are there situations that you avoid because they make you anxious? Many people react to their anxiety and fears by avoiding the offending situation. Other brave souls stick it out and plow ahead, putting up with the intense anxiety with white knuckles and sweaty palms. Typical situations that people avoid include airplanes, public transportation, bridges, tunnels, heights, elevators, department stores, animals, closed spaces, thunderstorms, and medical procedures. Some people are unreasonably fearful of social situations like taking a class or a job that requires speaking in public, playing a musical instrument or singing in front of others, eating in a restaurant, or using a public bathroom. Do you feel embarrassed to be seen blushing or trembling?

For some, anxiety is a constant companion that is present almost all the time. Are you a worrywart, uptight about everything? Do you find it difficult to concentrate at work because you can't stop worrying about things at home and then can't concentrate at home because you can't stop worrying about things at work? Do you experience a lot of physical symptoms of anxiety such as muscle tension, difficulty sleeping, restlessness, irritability, fatigue, or being keyed up or "on edge"?

It is indeed fortunate that nature has programmed us to experience some degree of fear and avoidance as a way of motivating us to perform and of keeping us out of trouble. People who are completely fearless may be stars on the battlefield (or the football field) but generally get injured in life one way or another. On the other hand, some people have a hair-trigger tendency to experience intense and impairing anxiety that is out of all proportion to the real expectations or dangers of the situation—they are like a smoke detector that goes off in response to burnt toast. Answer "yes" to this question only if your fear and avoidance are excessive, unreasonable, and impairing.

If the Answer to This Question Is Yes, Please Refer to Chapter 3.

Question #4: Do you have obsessions or compulsions?

Obsessions are upsetting or intrusive thoughts or images that don't make any sense to you but keep coming back no matter how hard you try to banish them. People with obsessive thoughts may become preoccupied with the idea that they are contaminated with germs, have run over someone with their car, or have left the stove on even after having already checked it fifteen times. Alternatively, someone might be haunted by the obsessive image of strangling a loved one or doing something obscene or sacrilegious.

Compulsions are thoughts or behaviors that you cannot stop yourself from doing and that lessen the intense anxiety resulting from your obsessions. For example, a person feels driven to repeatedly wash his hands until the skin is raw as a way of counteracting anxiety about being contaminated. Ritualistic praying or counting (for example, from one to eighteen exactly eighteen times forward and then backward) may be performed to atone for having blasphemous or violent preoccupations. Compulsively checking every few minutes that the coffeemaker is turned off or that the front door is locked temporarily allays obsessive doubts concerning safety. And there are people who are compelled to spend hours ensuring that everything in their bedroom is in its own exact "spot" before sleep becomes possible.

Don't answer "yes" to this question if your upsetting thoughts are about realistic concerns (like not having enough money to pay your taxes, getting fired from work, or that your elderly parents may become ill) or if your "compulsions" truly serve you well and are part of your being a careful person.

If the Answer to This Question Is Yes, Please Refer to Chapter 4.

Question #5: Are you haunted by an extremely traumatic event from your past?

When people are exposed to a terribly stressful event, they often cannot get the haunting images of it out of their daytime thoughts or nighttime dreams and may become unhinged by anything that even remotely resembles what happened. The shock of the event also causes a wide range of other symptoms, including being easily startled, having trouble sleeping or concentrating, feeling irritable or angry, or withdrawing from activities and from other people.

Long-lasting psychological effects often occur when someone experiences the threat of serious physical injury or death—as in military combat; severe automobile accidents; violent crime (rape, physical assault, robbery, mugging, torture); natural or man-made disasters (earthquake, tornado, fire, industrial accident); or life-threatening illness. Severe reactions to stress can also be caused by witnessing certain terrible things—seeing people die as a result of violence, accident, war, or disaster; or unexpectedly seeing a dead body or body part. Sometimes learning about a terrible event that has happened to someone you care about causes severe reactions—the sudden, unexpected death or serious injury of a family member or a close friend; or learning that your child has a life-threatening disease.

Of course, even the hardiest soul is shaken up at least to some degree by exposure to an extremely stressful situation. Don't expect to come through a terrible life event completely unscathed. Answer "yes" to this question only if your reaction to the stressor is particularly distressing, severe, prolonged, and interferes with your ability to function.

If the Answer to This Question Is Yes, Please Refer to Chapter 5.

Question #6: Do you have a problem with drinking or substance use? Has your drinking or substance use been excessive; out of control; hazardous to your health; causing problems at home, at work, or with other people; gotten you into trouble with the law; or put you in dangerous situations?

In DSM-IV, the term "substance" is defined broadly to include alcohol and other mind-altering or mood-altering drugs or medicines whether prescribed or obtained illegally. Can you identify with Mark Twain's comment about what it is like to try to let go of an addictive substance (in his case tobacco)—"it's easy to stop smoking . . . I've done it hundreds of times!" Do you crave the substance, think about it all the time? Do you feel as if you can't live without it? Has your husband, wife, or partner told you that they are really worried about your substance use or are becoming so fed up that they are thinking of leaving you? Are your children disappointed in you and embarrassed about the effect the substance is having on you? Does it feel as though your substance use is taking over your life rather than your being in charge of it? You may find that you are spending virtually all of your time thinking about the substance, taking it, experiencing its effects (both good and bad), or making sure you have it regularly available.

Substance use can lead to physical health problems like cancer, stomach ulcers, liver damage, and breathing problems; psychological problems like paranoia, depression, and anxiety; legal problems like arrests for disorderly conduct, and social problems like marital conflicts and physical fights; and occupational problems like missed work, and poor work or school performance. Have you been using a substance in situations where it may be dangerous, like driving while intoxicated, even though so far you may have been lucky enough not to have had an accident? Of course, not everyone who uses substances has a problem with them. Some people are especially vulnerable to substance use problems and some substances are especially likely to cause problems. If you do use substances at all, you should really search your soul before concluding that you do not have a problem since so many people with substance use problems are "in denial." Before saying "no" to this question, be sure that you have no evidence of physical or psychological dependence on a substance, or adverse consequences from using it.

If the Answer to This Question Is Yes, Please Refer to Chapter 6.

Question #7: Do you have an eating disorder? Do you have a problem with binge eating or purging, weigh much less than you should, or are you excessively worried about being or becoming fat?

Do you frequently engage in binge eating behavior? These are distinct episodes of extreme overeating in which you lose control and eat an abnormally large amount of food in a short period of time. A "large amount" is not just two cups of ice cream in one sitting but more in the neighborhood of a half-gallon. After the bingeing, do you frantically do things to get rid of the calories—vomiting, laxatives, fasting, or exercise? Do you feel really bad about yourself after you binge or purge? Depending on how much you compensate for your episodes of binge eating, you might be overweight, normal weight, or underweight.

Are you so terrified of getting fat that you will go to any lengths of starvation, exercise, or purging to remain thin? Has your weight gotten down so low that it is much less than people say it should be? Are you satisfied with the way your body looks (or still feel too fat) even though everyone else says you look emaciated? Are you preoccupied by food, the exact number of calories in everything you eat, and what effect each morsel will have on your weight? Do you find yourself not going to restaurants with other people because you are embarrassed by your strange eating habits? Do you feel you can control your eating only by following strict rules about what you can and cannot have?

We are a society of people obsessed with weight and body image, but most people do not have an eating disorder. You should answer "yes" to this question only if your eating behavior goes well beyond normal dieting to unhealthy weight loss or you are stuck in a disturbing cycle of bingeing and purging.

If the Answer to This Question Is Yes, Please Refer to Chapter 7.

Question #8: Do you have a problem related to sexual functioning or gender identity?
The sexual response cycle has several steps: desire, arousal, orgasm, and resolution. Do you have problems with sexual functioning related to one or more of these steps—lack of sexual fantasies or desire for sex; problems with getting an erection or becoming lubricated; or delayed orgasm or premature ejaculation; or do you have pain or spasms during intercourse? Remember that when it comes to sexual functioning, nobody is perfect and there are no clear-cut standards for what constitutes normal. At a minimum, the problem should be relatively persistent and cause marked distress for you or your partner.

Are your preferred sexual fantasies or situations way out of the ordinary or illegal? For example, are you turned on only by children, by hurting someone else, by being hurt, by exposing yourself, by peeping, or by cross-dressing?

Finally, do you feel that nature made a mistake in the assignment of your gender and that you are a woman in a man's body (or vice versa)? Do you find your own sexual characteristics upsetting or even repulsive? Do you wish you could switch genders?

If the Answer to This Question Is Yes, Please Refer to Chapter 8.

Question #9: Do you have trouble sleeping, sleep too much, or do unusual things happen while you sleep?

There are many different ways in which people have trouble sleeping. Does it take you a long time to fall asleep, tossing and turning while you think about the day's events? Do you wake up many times in the middle of the night? Do you awaken hours earlier than you want to in the morning and feel miserable because you cannot fall back to sleep?

Some people need too much sleep. Do you still feel tired during the day despite getting a full night's sleep? Do you find yourself falling asleep whenever things slow down, like while watching a movie or listening to a lecture?

Is your natural bedtime consistently out of sync with what your schedule requires? Are you a "night owl" who feels like going to sleep at just about the time you are supposed to be getting up for work? Or are you a starling who falls asleep right after dinner and wakes up hours before dawn? Do you work night shifts or have a constantly changing schedule so that you always feel alert or exhausted at the wrong times?

Finally, some people, especially children, have unusual things happen during sleep. Are you (or is your child) a sleepwalker? Do you (or your child) wake up in the middle of the night confused and screaming in terror?

Everyone has an occasional sleepless night and some people are simply restless sleepers. Moreover, the ability to sleep soundly through the night is likely to diminish as you age. You don't have clinically significant insomnia unless your problem with sleeping is severe, persistent, and regularly causes difficulties the following day. Before you diagnose yourself as having hypersomnia, check to see whether you are getting enough sleep. Sleep deprivation has become an ubiquitous feature in our overscheduled lives. Like it or not there are only twenty-four hours in the day. We all require a sufficient amount of sleep and this cannot be dispensed with simply because we are too busy to fit it in.

If the Answer to This Question Is Yes, Please Refer to Chapter 9.

Question #10: Is your personality more of a liability than an asset? Do you have patterns of thinking or behavior that keep you from getting what you want or what you need?

All of us have a personality—a way of viewing the world and ourselves, a style of relating to others, and of pursuing our goals. To a large extent, our personalities determine our fate and create expectations about the world that usually become self-fulfilling prophecies. The way we perceive and act toward others strongly influences the way they perceive and act toward us.

24

The question here is whether one's personality functioning is so inflexible and maladaptive that it can be considered a personality disorder. Do you find that no matter how hard you try to do things differently, you keep falling into the same patterns—the same type of unsatisfying relationship, the same battles with authority figures, the same unfulfilling jobs? Do your personality traits lead to the same vicious cycles? For example, if you are unreasonably suspicious and expect to be disliked, you are indeed likely to act in a way that will turn people against you. If you are excessively dependent and terrified of abandonment, your clinging behavior may well provoke the rejection you so greatly fear. If you excessively control others on the assumption that they will never take the initiative, your micromanagement will itself paralyze their ability to act independently. Finally, excessive demands that people praise you are more likely to result in losing rather than gaining their recognition.

Most people have more difficulty answering this question than any of the other nineteen. Unlike symptoms, which are experienced as unwanted and external to the self, most people remain pretty much unaware of their personality traits because they are experienced as so much an essential part of themselves. It is in the nature of things that your personality traits are probably much more evident to the people you live and work with than they are to you. If you have people in your life whose opinion and good will you trust, it may be helpful to ask them how they experience your personality.

If the Answer to This Question Is Yes, Please Refer to Chapter 10.

Question #11: Have you gone from doctor to doctor with concerns about physical symptoms, your physical health or appearance—without receiving enough help or reassurance?

This question is for people who have recurring physical complaints that cannot be explained by the presence of a medical disorder. This can take several different forms: preoccupation with physical symptoms (e.g., occasional skipped heartbeats, dizziness, pain, or constipation); the belief that one has a serious physical illness; or exaggerated concerns about appearance.

Paying adequate attention to bodily sensations can be an important ingredient in the early identification of illness but some people become hypervigilant about bodily functioning. They spend inordinate and unproductive amounts of time and money in a futile attempt to get to the bottom of every ache or pain. Sometimes visits to multiple doctors may be necessary in the diagnosis of particularly complicated or unusual physical problems.

However, if you have been to many doctors, had dozens of tests, and have been frustrated by being told that there is nothing physically wrong, you should consider that these symptoms may be indicative of mental disorder.

Other people become preoccupied with the idea that they are suffering from a serious illness despite being told that there is no cause for concern. A person may interpret a headache as indicating a brain tumor or that fatigue and frequent colds mean a diagnosis of AIDS. No matter how many doctors say that there is nothing to worry about, the person assumes that the medical workup is incomplete and will not end the search until his or her worst fears are confirmed.

Finally, most people are less than thrilled with their physical appearance but more or less manage to come to terms with how they look. In contrast, some people's lives come to revolve around the conviction that something is really terribly wrong with their appearance. They remain unspeakably hideous in their own eyes, despite reassurances from others that these concerns are exaggerated or completely unfounded.

If the Answer to This Question Is Yes, Please Refer to Chapter 11.

Question #12: Do you have trouble controlling your impulses?
From time to time, even the most disciplined person might have a lapse or two in resisting an impulse. The question here is whether you have a pattern of difficulty controlling your impulses that gets you into trouble. Has gambling become the center of your life, interfering with your work and relationships? Do you have a pattern of destructive violent outbursts that are far out of proportion to any provocation? Do you have impulses you can't resist to steal things you don't really need? Do you get a thrill setting fires? Do you have an impulse you can't control to pull out your hair? Are there other impulses that you are having trouble resisting—drug use, binge eating, sexual desires?

If the Answer to This Question Is Yes, Please Refer to Chapter 12.

Question #13: Do you have the strange experience of feeling disconnected from your memories, from yourself, or from the outside world?
Some people develop amnesia for psychologically traumatic events in their past. Are there particular events or discrete periods of time in your life that you cannot recall anything about? Do you sometimes feel as if you were in a dream or a movie, or as though everything around you is unreal? How about feeling like your body is unreal or that you are like a robot? Have you felt like you don't have a coherent sense of your identity? The

most extreme manifestation of this would be your feeling that you have multiple personalities that take control of your behavior.

Of course, memory is fallible and not everyone feels totally integrated in identity every minute of every day. Do not answer "yes" simply because you cannot remember all of the details of your childhood—nobody can. Moreover, it is perfectly normal to have occasional periods of feeling "spaced out" or feeling so conflicted that you are not sure who the "real you" is.

If the Answer to This Question Is Yes, Please Refer to Chapter 13.

Question #14: Are you unable to handle the stresses you have to face in your life?

Is there something stressful in your life that is really throwing you for a loop? Stress is an unavoidable part of our lives and will inevitably lead to an occasional bad day. This is not what we are talking about in this question. Instead, the issue is whether you are having symptoms in response to a stressful event that are more intense and prolonged than most other people would have in similar circumstances. Is this reaction maladaptive—that is, does it hurt more than help you in dealing with the stressful event? Do you find that you can't just pick yourself up and dust yourself off? The most common problems caused by stress are feeling down and/or anxious, performing poorly at work or at school, developing physical symptoms, and, particularly in children, displaying bad behavior.

If the Answer to This Question Is Yes, Please Refer to Chapter 14.

Question #15: Do you sometimes lose touch with reality?

Have you had any particularly unusual experiences or upsetting beliefs that seem to puzzle other people or make them think you are strange? For example . . . Are you convinced that strangers are talking about you, that you are being followed, that you are being spied on, that there is a plot against you, that you have special supernatural powers, that your spouse is unfaithful, that something is terribly wrong with your body or that it is being poisoned or tampered with, that other people can hear your thoughts, or that someone is controlling your thoughts or actions against your will? Have you ever heard voices of people talking when there was no one around, had visions of things that are not really there, or smelled a foul odor coming from your body that no one else can smell?

A "yes" answer to any of these questions suggests the possibility that the person has lost the ability to distinguish what is real from what is a product of imagination. However, before assuming that there is a severe mental disorder, it is important to determine what is really happening in that person's life. Some people seem to act in a paranoid way because there really is someone out there trying to get them. A "no" answer must also be taken with a grain of salt since it may reflect the denial of illness frequently encountered in those who have lost touch with reality.

If the Answer to This Question Is Yes, Please Refer to Chapter 15.

Question #16: Does your mind seem to be failing you?

This question addresses problems with a number of different mental functions. Do you have trouble with your memory—learning new things and recalling past events? Do you have times in which you lose touch with what's going on around you and have difficulty focusing your attention? Do you sometimes get disoriented—not knowing where you are, what day it is, and who are the people around you? Do you have trouble understanding others when they talk to you or in making sense when you speak? Do you have trouble carrying out the activities of everyday life—washing yourself, dressing, cooking, planning your day?

Most people are more or less dissatisfied with their mental functioning, especially as it begins to decline with age. The question here is whether you are having problems with your mental functioning that are severe enough to interfere with your work or day-to-day activities.

If the Answer to This Question Is Yes, Please Refer to Chapter 16.

The remaining four questions are for those disorders that always have their onset during childhood or adolescence. In some cases, the child will outgrow the problem or have successful treatment for it. In other cases the symptoms persist into adulthood. You may, therefore, be answering these questions either for yourself or for your child. You should be aware that children and adolescents can be afflicted with virtually any of the problems covered in this book.

If you are going through this chapter with your child's problems in mind, be sure to review the first sixteen questions in this chapter as well.

Question #17: Has your child had delays in development of intellectual, academic, motor, communication, or social skills?

Children vary tremendously in the rate at which they develop intellectual, motor, language, and social skills. This question refers to functioning that is significantly below what is normal for your child's age and which causes marked impairment in school or home. Has your child's IQ been measured to be below 70 and, if so, is he having trouble functioning as a result? Has your child been diagnosed with a specific learning disability in reading, writing, or mathematics? Does your child have a severe problem with coordination, speech, or language? Is your child strange in the way he relates to other people—showing no emotion, not maintaining eye contact, treating other people as if they are pieces of furniture? Is your child's behavior rigid, repetitive, or unusual and are his interests and activities quite restricted?

If the Answer to This Question Is Yes, Please Refer to Chapter 17.

Question #18: Has your child had behavior problems?

We cannot expect, and probably would not want, our children to always be perfect little angels. However, some children display patterns of bad conduct or disruptive behavior that are sufficiently severe and persistent to cause major problems for themselves and for the people around them. Is your child unusually aggressive? Does he destroy property? Does he steal things? Does he lie or consistently cut school, stay out overnight, or run away? Does your child have a pattern of hostile and defiant behavior that goes far beyond the usual and consistently causes problems for him?

If the Answer to This Question Is Yes, Please Refer to Chapter 18.

Question #19: Is your child (or were you) hyperactive or easily distracted?

Is your child so overactive and impulsive that he is hard to contain at school and at home? Is your child always on the go, talking incessantly, fidgeting, jumping out of his seat, interrupting others, and generally seeming to get into everything? Is your child so inattentive that he cannot do homework, play games with other children, organize tasks, follow through on instructions, and hold on to his possessions? Is he forgetful, distracted by unimportant stimuli, and reluctant to do things that require sustained attention?

To some degree, overactivity and distractibility define what it is to be a child. No one, and certainly no child, is perfectly calm or attentive all of the time and in all situations, especially if the task is routine or boring. There is also considerable controversy about a possible overdiagnosis of Attention-Deficit/Hyperactivity Disorder in the school system. You should answer "yes" to this question only if your child's hyperactivity and inattention are persistent, occur in many different situations, and lead to severe problems in school and other tasks.

Although hyperactivity and inattentiveness usually improve with maturation, a fair percentage of affected individuals continue to show some symptoms in adulthood. Most typically, the hyperactivity symptoms mellow out, leaving an inattentive adult who is easily distracted and unfocused. *If the Answer to This Question Is Yes, Please Refer to Chapter 19.*

Question #20. Has your child had other problems—difficulty with toilet training, having a hard time separating from you, or having uncontrollable repetitive tic movements or sounds?

This is a miscellaneous question covering a number of unrelated problems that may be seen in children. Does your child continue to have repeated accidents well beyond the time when toilet training is usually completed? Does your child find it so difficult to be away from you that he refuses to go to school or play with other children? Does your child have tics (sudden, rapid, recurrent body movements or vocalizations that he cannot help doing)? *If the Answer to This Question Is Yes, Please Refer to Chapter 20.*

Now you have a choice—either read the book straight through for a picture of the full variety of the human psyche—or just go to those sections that are most pertinent to you or your loved ones.

CHAPTER 1

The "Blues"

There is nothing uniquely human about being depressed—it happens all the time to mammals, both in the wild and in the laboratory. The four major triggers of human depression are the loss of a loved one, a stress that can't be handled, a loss of status, or a feeling of guilt. Animals are definitely able to experience depression in response to the first three of these situations—whether they can also feel guilty depression in the way we do is unknown but at least possible.

The essence of being a mammal is love and attachment. We are born too helpless to survive without the nurturance derived from mutual mother/ child delight. But love offers a hostage to fate. Losing someone precious brings at least temporary heartbreak and sometimes a long-standing depression. Animals in the wild sometimes withdraw from life and die of grief after losing a cherished loved one. In a like way, humans have a much elevated rate of depression and mortality after losing a spouse. What starts out as normal grieving sometimes turns into a depressive illness.

Depressions related to stress have been neatly (if not always kindly) duplicated in laboratory experiments. A mouse or monkey who is unable to succeed in performing a difficult or stressful task will eventually give it up, withdraw, and get demoralized. This is particularly likely to happen if the animal's best efforts have no impact whatever on the outcome. In one particularly telling experiment, two animals are yoked together so that they will receive exactly the same mildly unpleasant shock, but one of the two can take steps that will improve or worsen the outcome for both. Even though both animals receive exactly the same total amount of discomfort, the active animal who can exert some influence experiences much less depression than the totally passive victim. Having some say in our fate, even if it is a difficult fate, helps to prevent demoralization and depression.

The loss of status after losing a dominance struggle can also provoke depression and slinking away—throughout the animal kingdom and in the corporate boardroom. Very often the defeated animal has trouble adjusting to a more submissive role, leaves the group, and quickly perishes. This can also happen to the victim of office politics, country club high jinks, or disgruntled retirement.

If all mammals can experience depression, it is no surprise that it is the most frequently encountered of all the psychiatric disorders in humans. As many as 20 percent of women and 10 percent of men will suffer an episode of depression at some point in their lives. At any given time, 5 to 10 percent of women and 3 percent of men are depressed. The economic consequences are staggering: the cost in lost productivity and increased use of medical services is over thirty billion dollars annually. Having depression on top of another medical condition (like heart disease) can also be dangerous to your health—causing more complications and a much higher risk of death. Unfortunately, however, four out of five cases of depression go undiagnosed and untreated. Most people suffer in silence, and without help. This chapter will help you to determine whether your sad feelings fall within normal mood variation or whether they constitute a clinical condition that deserves diagnosis and treatment. Early identification and treatment helps to tame depression before it can cause serious damage and become a way of life.

There are two forms of Mood Disorder—one called unipolar depression because the person has only downs, and no ups. The other—Bipolar Disorder—describes mood oscillations in both directions. The person with Bipolar Disorder has depressions that are quite similar or even identical to those described here, but also has manic highs. Approximately 15 percent of people with clinical depression will at some point develop a period of elevated mood, resulting in a change in diagnosis from Major Depressive Disorder to Bipolar Disorder. This distinction between unipolar mood disorder and bipolar mood disorder has crucial treatment and prognostic significance that will be a major focus of attention in the next chapter.

In the remainder of this chapter, we discuss the two types of unipolar depression recognized in the DSM-IV: Major Depressive Disorder and Dysthymic Disorder. Most people have the episodic form of depression—called Major Depressive Disorder. In contrast, Dysthymic Disorder is a long-standing, but milder, depression that starts early in life and persists more or less continuously.

MAJOR DEPRESSIVE DISORDER

The severity of an episode of Major Depressive Disorder can range from the equivalent of no more than a bad case of flu to something that more resembles terminal cancer (but fortunately is much more treatable). Even at its mildest, major depression takes the wind out of your sails. You may, or may not, be able to slug through your daily routine of work, family, and social obligations, but everything is burdened by the weight of the illness. At its most severe extreme, you seem to disappear into the illness. The symptoms are so intense, pervasive, and crippling that you can't do much of anything, including thinking straight about getting treatment. You may become virtually unrecognizable to other people and feel as if you have lost yourself.

Perhaps the most dangerous aspect of depression is that most people have little or no insight concerning the enormous influence it has on their self-evaluation and perception of the past and the future. It is as if a sunny summer day has turned into a terrible storm without your noticing the change. Everything becomes gray or black, turbulent, and dreary. Even worse, all your previous sunny days are totally forgotten and the weather forecast promises nothing but an eternity of storms. Depression robs hope and makes everything look much more worse than it really is.

The key step to recovery and gaining control over the illness is being intimately familiar with its particulars. If you can spot the early signs of depression, you can start the process of turning them around before they snowball into something more serious. If you are aware that you are depressed, you will be able to extricate yourself from the distortions in thinking it causes. You can stop blaming yourself for the illness and start doing something about curing it. Know the following symptoms so well that you can spot emerging episodes before they get out of hand. You can't control the weather, but you can control depression.

Handicapping the odds about the future course of your illness can help you in planning how best to deal with it. Major Depressive Disorder is usually, but not always, a recurrent condition. The frequency and severity of episodes can vary greatly. If you have one episode of Major Depressive Disorder, there is about a 50 percent chance that you will never have another. If you are part of the unlucky 50 percent who will go on to have a second episode, it is likely that you will have additional further episodes unless you take certain precautions to prevent them. For instance, if you have already had two episodes, the chances of going on to have a third rise to about 70 percent. If you have had three depressions, the odds of your having a fourth go up to about 90 percent. We, therefore, recommend that you consult a mental health professional and plan a long term, and perhaps lifelong, treatment strategy intended to keep the number of your lifetime episodes of depression to an absolute minimum.

According to the diagnostic manual, you have Major Depressive Disorder if:
- You have had an episode of depression lasting at least two weeks with at least five of the following symptoms:
  (1) You are depressed, sad, blue, tearful.
  (2) You have lost interest or pleasure in things you previously liked to do.
  (3) Your appetite is much less or much greater than usual and you have lost or gained weight.
  (4) You have a lot of trouble sleeping or sleep too much.
  (5) You are so agitated, restless, or slowed down that others have begun to notice.
  (6) You are tired and have no energy.
  (7) You feel worthless or excessively guilty about things you have done or not done.
  (8) You have trouble concentrating, thinking clearly, or making decisions.
  (9) You feel you would be better off dead or have thoughts about killing yourself.
- These symptoms are severe enough to upset your daily routine, or to seriously impair your work, or to interfere with your relationships.
- The depression does not have a specific cause like alcohol, drugs, medication side effect, or physical illness.
- Your depression is not just a normal reaction to the death of a loved one.

DESCRIPTION

Unlike diabetes, cancer, pneumonia, and most other medical conditions, there are no blood tests, X-rays, biopsy results, or sputum cultures that are available to help in making a diagnosis of depression. In the absence of such objective tests, mental health professionals rely instead on identifying a "syndrome" of symptoms that co-occur during the same period of time. As you can see from the diagnostic criteria set, an episode of Major Depressive Disorder is diagnosed if there are at least five characteristic symptoms of depression occurring during the same two-week period of time.

Anyone can have one or two or even three of the above symptoms without being clinically depressed. The average stress and strains we all encounter cause the inevitable emotional aches and pains of everyday life. A major depressive episode goes far beyond this. Many symptoms must congregate together. They have to be consistent from day to day and last for a significant period of time. And the symptoms must cause significant impairment. Judging whether you have a clinically significant depression is sometimes difficult, but always important. Try to get a sense of how many of the following symptoms apply to you.

Depressed Mood: The central feature of depression is the major downward drift in mood. You feel sad, blue, down in the dumps, under a cloud. Any little thing can get you crying and everything seems bleak, dark, dirty, and hopeless. You forget what it was like not to be depressed and start believing that you will never feel right again. You find that your ability to experience and appreciate the pleasures of life is impaired.

Decreased Interest or Pleasure in Things: Life seems gray and boring, without color, taste, or texture. You have little or no desire to work, read the newspaper, watch TV, or even spend time with your friends or family. Everything is a bother and nothing seems worth doing. Kay Jamison, a leading authority on depression and Bipolar Disorder who suffers from Mood Disorder herself, describes being depressed as follows:

> My mind . . . no longer found anything interesting or enjoyable or worthwhile. I was incapable of concentrated thought . . . and [I] was [so] totally exhausted . . . [that I] could scarcely pull myself out of bed in the mornings. It took me twice as long to walk anywhere as it ordinarily did, and I wore the same clothes over and over again, as it was otherwise too much of an effort to make a decision about what to put on. I dreaded having to talk with people, avoided my friends whenever possible, and sat in the school library in the early mornings and late afternoons, virtually inert, with a dead heart and a brain as cold as clay.

At the extreme, you may get so deeply depressed that you lose the capacity to feel anything at all. Your primary experience is a deadening, a complete withdrawal of interest, and the inability to care about anything. You are hollowed out. When things get this bad, it will be a great relief when you are able to cry again. Feeling sad is far better than feeling nothing.

Weight or Appetite Change: Some people lose their taste for food and have to force themselves to eat or may even have to be forced to eat. Others find refuge in food and feel it impossible to stop eating, grabbing just about everything in sight, especially sweets and other high-calorie foods.

Sleep Disturbances: Changes in sleep can also go both ways. Some people can't get a decent night's sleep, whereas others sleep endless extra hours and still feel tired all day. Insomnia can take several forms—difficulty falling asleep, waking up many times throughout the night, or awakening before daylight and then tossing and turning, waiting miserably for dawn to finally arrive. The changes in sleep and eating often go in the same direction. The people who have trouble sleeping usually are the ones who also have no appetite and feel agitated, whereas those who oversleep also tend to overeat and feel slowed down.

Agitation and Lethargy: Mental and physical activity can be either tightly wound up or reduced to a crawl—although some especially unlucky people are condemned simultaneously to feel *both* agitated and slowed down. Agitation is particularly discomforting. You are restless, unable to sit still, wring your hands, pace about, and feel like you're "jumping out of your skin." In contrast, the experience of psychomotor retardation is like being a slow-moving turtle in a world where everyone else seems to be a hummingbird. Your thoughts and actions swim in a slow-motion vat of molasses. People become frustrated with you because you take so long doing things or answering questions or walking down a hallway. Little tasks become Herculean—it may take hours just to get dressed or prepare breakfast or read a newspaper article. Finally, you give up trying.

Fatigue: You feel tired all the time, as if your batteries are all completely drained or that you are running on empty. It is hard to drag yourself out of bed in the morning. Everything is a huge effort; you have no energy, and at the end of the day it seems that nothing has been accomplished. You can't face your work, everything is piling up around you. Your desk, your house, and maybe even your personal hygiene are all a mess, but you don't have the wherewithal to put things right.

Feeling Worthless or Guilty: Your self-esteem has hit rock bottom. You feel like a total "nothing," a burden to everyone, maybe the worst person who has ever lived. You feel guilty about everything, even about getting depressed. You believe it is your fault that you are sick and that you should be trying harder to overcome it. You spend a lot of time adding up your past missteps, convinced that you have ruined your life and the lives of those you love. In the extreme, you may have the guilty delusion that you are the worst person who ever lived or are the ultimate cause of the world's suffering.

Difficulty Concentrating or Making Decisions: Your mind is muddled and foggy. You can't think straight or get your work done. It's hard to focus on any one task because you are preoccupied with worries and your thoughts keep wandering back to how hopeless everything is. It may get so bad that you can't even follow a conversation, let alone pay attention to what's happening on a TV sitcom or in a movie. Making decisions becomes impossible, even the simplest of everyday choices. Deciding what to wear or what to eat seems daunting and fraught with larger significance. You vacillate back and forth, unable to move forward. Your indecisiveness can become so paralyzing and agonizing that you prefer just to lie in bed rather than face the overwhelming complexities of day-to-day living.

Feeling As If Life Is No Longer Worth Living: You feel hopeless about the future and wish you could avoid living it. The mildest forms of suicidal feelings are passive wishes that you will just simply disappear—not wake up in the morning—or that you will be the victim of a crime or fatal accident. Hopefully things stop here, but sometimes they evolve into active thoughts about how you might take your life. Finally, you may even begin making preparations—hoarding pills, buying a gun, preparing a will, or writing a suicide note. At the extreme, you may make an attempt on your life. Some people are so terrified by the suicidal thoughts that they finally seek treatment. Others are comforted by the idea that suicide provides a last resort "ace in the hole solution" to their seemingly intractable despair. Suicidal thoughts result from the powerful cognitive distortions caused by depression. You have become convinced that your entire future will be negative, at least as bleak as the present. You lose sight of the fact, or don't believe, that almost everyone with depression will eventually get better

37

and come to see both the past and the future very differently and more realistically.

Paradoxically, you may even be at greater risk to actually kill yourself when you begin to recover from depression than when you are trapped within its depths. At the nadir, you simply don't have the energy or decisiveness to act on your suicidal feelings. As you improve, you may become well enough to kill yourself before you are well enough to realize that it would be a foolish and selfish thing to do. It can be lifesaving to realize that your illness is twisting your thinking and making things seem ever so much worse than they really are or will be. You have no right or reason to make an irrevocable life or death decision based on how you feel on your very worst day.

Also, keep in mind that the aftermath of suicide is a painful legacy that will haunt your loved ones for the rest of their lives. Most suicide attempters imagine that their friends and family will be much better off once they are out of the picture. You feel as if this is the only way you can relieve other people of the enormous burden of caring for you. It does not work out that way. You may be a burden when you are depressed, but your suicide will be anything but a relief. The family members who remain behind almost inevitably feel like killers and are tortured by a lifelong sense of failed responsibility. "He [or she] would be alive today if only I had done [this or that], or cared more, or showed I cared, or tried harder, or wasn't so selfish, or had taken the time," etc., etc., etc. This is doubly traumatic if relatives have to deal with a corpse left on their hands. Your relatives will also have a much greater risk of committing suicide themselves if you place this irrevocable burden on them.

If you are a family member, it is important to realize that depressed people will often not spontaneously share their suicidal thoughts or impulses. Don't worry that asking about suicidal thoughts will make them worse. Asking gives the person a chance to share his painful feelings rather than having to face the calamity all alone. Also remember that people contemplating suicide are often looking for a hint from fate, loved ones, or the environment—should I, or should I not, kill myself? They may misinterpret an everyday statement ("I am tired of your being so sick." "Can't you do something about this mess?" "How can you stand yourself?") as a message that you want them dead. It is no fun, and certainly very frustrating, having to live with someone who is deeply in despair. This is not what you bargained for. But remember that you can easily get irritable with them and say something that may be taken out of context and result in tragedy. Keep your message absolutely and unambivalently clear—you want your loved one alive, no matter how much trouble the illness is causing both of you. Always blame the depression and not the person and stay hopeful because today, given enough time and patience, virtually everyone can be helped to get better.

Subtypes of Major Depression

Everyone with clinical depression has at least five of the symptoms we have just described, but this does not mean that people with this problem look at all alike in the way the illness takes shape. Determining the precise pattern of symptoms that accompany a depression is very important because it helps to determine which particular treatment is most likely to be effective for it. The following are the most important subtypes. If the depression falls neatly into one of these categories, the treatment recommendation should be pretty straightforward.

Depression with Psychotic Features: This is the most severe and dangerous type of depression with the highest rate of suicide, aggression, and need for hospitalization. You lose your grip on reality and experience either wildly distorted beliefs (delusions) or wildly distorted perceptions (hallucinations). (See Chapter 15, page 310, for a more detailed discussion about psychotic symptoms.) Most typically, the delusions or hallucinations are filled with negative feelings about yourself. For example, you may be convinced that you are personally responsible for the ills of the world; or are the most evil person who ever lived; or have incurable cancer; or that your insides are "rotting out." You may hear voices calling your name, cursing and criticizing you, saying you deserve to die, or rehashing past misdeeds.

People with psychotic depression are especially likely to hurt themselves and other people. They have a potentially deadly combination of lousy self-esteem, poor judgment, delusional thinking, and command hallucinations. A depressed father may be taunted by voices ordering him to cut his wrists so that his family will be relieved of the shame and burden of his failures. A mother may try to smother her newborn infant because she is convinced it lives under a curse and has been fathered by the devil.

Safety must always be the first consideration. The watchful eye of family members or hospital staff may be needed to ensure that you do not act on your distorted beliefs or perceptions. The initial goal of treatment is to eliminate the psychotic symptoms as quickly as possible. This usually involves taking the combination of an antipsychotic medication and an antidepressant medication—together they have a 60 to 70 percent chance of promoting recovery. If this doesn't work, electroconvulsive therapy has a 95 percent recovery rate (see "Treatment Options" for more details). These depressions are so severe and so dangerous that it makes sense to stay on medication for a long time to avoid possible recurrences.

Depression with Melancholic Features: This is another especially severe form of depression in which you withdraw into a dense cocoon of misery that nothing can penetrate. You could win the Olympics, the lottery, an Academy Award, and the Nobel Prize all in one day and still not feel very happy about it. Your grandchild's sunny smile sheds no warmth and is no longer infectious. You are frigid and have lost the capacity to experience pleasure. The mood is hard to describe, but it definitely feels completely different and worse than any of the other bad feelings you have ever experienced in your life, even the death of a beloved. Other symptoms include the disappearance of your appetite, severe weight loss, and a terrible problem getting any sleep. Your body seems almost as broken as your mind.

The daily course of the depression takes on a characteristic ebb and flow. You wake up at 3 A.M. feeling absolutely rotten, desperate, and agitated. You turn on TV but can't watch, pick up a book but can't read, try soothing music but feel irritated by it. You return to bed—but toss, turn, and fret in the endless hours before dawn. As the sun rises, you begin pacing around the apartment but feel no relief or comfort and finally go back to bed. You feel worthless wasting time in bed but you are too washed out to get up. Your mind is filled with self-criticism, ruminations, catastrophization, and worries. As the day progresses, you feel a bit better. By late afternoon you are relieved enough to eat a light meal and get dressed. The evening is not fun, but it is not an agitated torture. By 3 A.M. the next morning, however, you are back in the lowest circle of hell.

Some people become so impaired that they are unwilling or unable to dress, may stop washing or feeding themselves, may stop eating, and may wind up spending the entire day alone lying in bed ruminating in a frantic and agitated state. This can lead to a medical emergency with dehydration, malnutrition, exhaustion, and suicide risk. Psychotherapy by itself is totally ineffective in treating this type of severe depression and can even make it worse because you experience it as yet another added burden. The person needs to know he is sick, that he will get better, and that relief is at hand. Antidepressant medication is usually the treatment of choice but electroconvulsive therapy may be necessary if rapid results are needed or if the medicine has not worked very well.

Depression with Atypical Features: This is a totally misnamed type of depression that is not a bit "atypical" in terms of frequency of occurrence. Many of you will experience this type of depression and should know about it because it has a very different implication about treatment than the types described above. The characteristic pattern of symptoms is just the exact opposite of what we described for the melancholic type. You are exquisitely responsive to negative or positive external events and will feel deeply depressed or somewhat hopeful depending on the latest twist of fate or interpersonal vicissitude. Your mood will brighten considerably when dining out with friends or enjoying a good movie, only to slip back into the dark depths when you are once again home alone at the end of the evening.

The depression usually follows an interpersonal rejection by a lover, boss, or close friend. This is in direct contrast to people with melancholia, who usually don't react much either way to positive or negative events. Atypical depression tends to cause overeating and oversleeping, whereas melancholia brings on weight loss and insomnia. If you are disappointed in someone or feel abandoned, you are likely to head straight for the refrigerator or the candy dish, and to feel a leaden paralysis that makes it hard to get out of bed. Chocolate is particularly important as a comfort food, perhaps because it contains a specific chemical that may have antidepressant properties. Recognition of atypical depression provides a good clue about which family of antidepressants will work best (serotonin reuptake inhibitors like Prozac, Paxil, Zoloft, or Luvox or monamine oxidase inhibitors like Nardil or Parnate), and which to avoid (tricyclic antidepressants, like imipramine, desipramine, and nortriptyline). Psychotherapy is also more likely to be helpful here—particularly to make you more resilient in response to losses and perhaps to improve your selection of less disappointing partners.

Seasonal Depression: Here the specific timing of episodes is occasioned by the tilt of the earth in its annual rotation around the sun. The depressions almost always begin and end around the same time of the year because they are triggered and turned off by shifts in the length of the day/night cycle. Most likely, you are especially sensitive to the diminishing hours of daylight in the late fall or early winter and go into a kind of depressive hibernation. The episodes usually begin in November or December, are at their worst in December and January, and usually improve with the lengthening of daylight in the spring. For obvious reasons, seasonal depression is more common at the higher latitudes that enjoy fewer hours of winter light (like Canada or Scandinavia) and is much less likely in more southerly locations like sunny Florida and Southern California. Most of us feel some slumping of mood as the days become shorter but this is not to be considered seasonal depression unless the symptoms are severe enough to meet the criteria for a Major Depressive Disorder listed above. Daily exposure to artificial bright light therapy may be helpful in avoiding this problem—the lights can fool the brain into thinking it is summertime even during the winter months. Seasonal depressions are particularly common in people who have Bipolar Disorder, so if you have winter depression you should check out the next chapter to see if your mood also has a tendency to upswings.

Postpartum Depression: "Postpartum blues" is a very frequent and completely normal consequence of childbirth. This mild letdown disappears quickly as the hormonal and psychological systems get back on track and the mother gets wrapped up in her child. Unfortunately, some few women develop a much more severe depression that begins in the weeks following delivery and can impair their ability to mother the child and fall in love with it. Being detached then makes her feel even more depressed and inadequate about not being a good mother. What was meant to be a joyful time has turned into a nightmare. At the extreme, the postpartum depression may be accompanied by dangerous delusions (worst of all, thinking the baby is in some way deformed or cursed) or hallucinations (that may command violent acts). This can occasionally culminate in a tragic episode of suicide and/or infanticide, or both. A mother killing a child in these circumstances usually does it as part of her own suicide—the child is not seen as fully separate from her and she could not bear to leave it behind and helpless. It is important to be alert to the possibility of a severe depression after delivery—especially in women who have had one after previous pregnancies, those who are prone to bipolar depression, and anyone who has gone off antidepressant medication during pregnancy to protect the fetus from possible harmful effects.

Dysthymic Disorder

This is a chronic form of depression that starts at an early age, remains a relatively constant fixture in your life, and places a constant and dark cloud over your head, day in and day out. You are pessimistic about your future, regretful about your past, and blind to the opportunities of your present. The depression is an integral part of your way of life and represents the entirety of how you see yourself and your world. It can be especially tough to spot Dysthymic Disorder because you have been this way as long as you can remember and have no baseline of brighter outlook against which to compare the gloom that you feel and bring to each new situation and relationship. Although the symptoms of Dysthymic Disorder are less severe cross sectionally than those of Major Depressive Disorder, the cumulative effect of decades of even a relatively mild depressed mood are often devastating and just as bad as having episodes of severe depression that punctuate otherwise normal functioning. In fact, people with Dysthymic Disorder often have as much total functional impairment and risk of suicide as those with Major Depressive Disorder. Dysthymic Disorder is relatively common, occurring in approximately 4 percent of the general population.

According to the diagnostic manual, you have Dysthymic Disorder if:
- You have had depressed mood most days for at least two years, but the symptoms are less severe than the episodes described in Major Depressive Disorder, above.
- At least two of the following:
  (1) Your appetite is poor or you are overeating.
  (2) You sleep too little or too much.
  (3) You are tired or your energy level is low.
  (4) You feel down about yourself.
  (5) Your concentration is poor or you have difficulty making decisions.
  (6) You feel hopeless about the future.

DESCRIPTION

This condition is usually incompatible with anything close to normal self-esteem or self-confidence. You constantly feel inadequate, that you don't measure up, that you are boring to others, lacking in skills, and that you will never succeed at anything. You are a downer among your friends and family because you expect the worst from each new situation and relationship. This usually also leads to social withdrawal and a very restricted life. You are a brooder and a worrier. It is your constant preoccupation to second-guess the decisions you have made, the things you have done, and the things that you have left undone.

Although Dysthymic Disorder and Major Depressive Disorder differ in severity and duration, you are very likely to have both and they really represent no more than two variations on the same depressive theme. Whereas Dysthymic Disorder is chronic, milder, and usually has an early onset, Major Depressive Disorder is more episodic, severe, and can begin later in life. If you start having chronic mild depression, you will probably wind up eventually also having superimposed episodes of more severe depression.

The biggest problem with Dysthymic Disorder is that it may be many years, even most of a lifetime, before the depressive illness is identified for what it is. The "I've been this way as long as I can remember" nature of Dysthymic Disorder makes this a stealth disorder. It seems "normal" to be depressed, pessimistic, and down. The chronic feelings of doom and gloom become such a natural state of being that it can be difficult for you to appreciate their pathological nature and all of their negative ramifications. Do you always see the half empty, not the half full? Are you one to grab defeat from the jaws of victory? Do you constantly see what is wrong with everything and miss what is right? Have you adjusted your career aspirations downward to take your depression into account? Have your friendships and love relationships suffered because of your always being a harbinger of doom? It might be helpful to run this issue by other people who know you long and well in order to get a more objective perspective. Effective treatments for Dysthymic Disorder are available (see treatment options) and it is never too late to lift that persistent cloud and turn your life around.

Differential Diagnosis

Many substances have an impact on brain chemistry to cause depression. Some, especially alcohol and many tranquilizers, cause depression during intoxication. Others, especially the stimulants cocaine and speed, cause depression during the crash that follows after the high has worn off. Sometimes it works the other way around—rather than the depression being triggered by drugs, some people drink or take street drugs in order to "self-medicate" their depression. Figuring out the cause-and-effect relationship between mood symptoms and drug use is crucial because the initial focus of the treatment may depend on the underlying cause. When depression is the root of the problem, providing effective antidepressant treatment often solves both the depression and the drinking or drug problem. When depression is a consequence of drug use, abstinence will often eliminate the depression. Of course, achieving abstinence is often easier said than done.

Anyone who has ever gotten an upset stomach after taking an aspirin knows that medications can have very unpleasant physical side effects. Most people are less aware that depression can develop as a behavioral side effect of a medication—even if the medication is taken exactly as prescribed. This is especially important to remember if you are taking more than one medicine at the same time, since they may interact and cause more side effects than would any one medicine taken by itself. Also as you get older, you are likely to clear medicine more slowly from your system and may develop excessively high blood levels on doses that would have been well tolerated when you were younger. The medicines most likely to cause depression include oral contraceptives, steroids, anticancer agents, painkillers, and heart and hypertension drugs. If you are taking one of these medicines and experience symptoms of depression, *do not* just stop taking the medication on your own. Your doctor will help determine whether there is a causal relationship between the medicine and depression or whether the depression is just coincidental. Your doctor can then adjust the doses, or use an alternative medication if necessary.

Another important cause of depression is medical illness. There are so many medical conditions that can cause depression it is impossible to list them all, but just assume that any medical problem you have could be responsible for your feeling bad. A comprehensive medical workup should always be part of a complete evaluation of depression. When depression occurs for the first time late in life, the odds are very high that it may be caused by an underlying medical illness or a dementia that has not yet been diagnosed. This should be checked out with special care.

A medical condition can cause depression in any number of different ways. For example, depression commonly occurs following a stroke. It can be triggered by the psychological stress of having to adjust to the paralysis or the speech impairment caused by the stroke. Or the stroke may have damaged an area of the brain responsible for mood regulation. And don't forget that depression may be a side effect of the antihypertension medicine that many stroke victims are probably also taking.

Depression is especially easy to miss in the medically ill because many of its characteristic symptoms (fatigue, weight loss, and insomnia) may be mistakenly attributed to the physical illness. Also, don't fall into the trap of explaining the depression away as fully understandable given the circumstances ("I'd be depressed, too, if I had cancer"). This can result in unnecessarily prolonged mental suffering on top of the physical discomfort already caused by the medical illness. The identification and successful treatment of depression in the physically ill are also crucial because they reduce the risks of developing medical complications and improve recovery from the illness. Perhaps most dramatically, the risk of dying after a heart attack is much higher if the patient is depressed. Studies are now underway to see if treating the depression can be lifesaving.

Finally, don't forget that depressions can also occur as part of Bipolar Disorder—to be covered in the next chapter. In Bipolar Disorder, the pendulum swings back and forth and includes periods of elevated mood along with periods of depressed mood. If there is *any* possibility that you have had such mood swings (even the mildest and most pleasant of highs), read Chapter 2 very carefully because Bipolar Disorder requires a very different treatment—what would make perfect sense for treating the depressions described in this chapter can make a Bipolar Disorder devastatingly worse.

AM I OKAY?

Freud once said (jokingly we think) that the goal of psychotherapy is to turn neurotic suffering into everyday misery. When bad things happen (as inevitably they do), it is "normal" to feel "depressed" at least for a while. Distinguishing clinical depression from sadness or grief is often a tough call. An occasional black mood is no more than an inevitable, expectable, and even adaptive hue in the emotional palette of life. The severity and duration guidelines that are listed in the DSM-IV criteria sets are meant to help you determine whether your depression has crossed the line from normal to clinical. Are you down in a steady unremitting way, *day after day* for a long time? Are the mood changes accompanied by bodily symptoms like loss of appetite, lost sleep, extreme fatigue, and agitation? Is your mind slowed down or thinking strange thoughts? Furthermore, the depression must have a concrete negative impact on your life. For example, trouble concentrating makes it extremely difficult for you to do your job; lack of interest in doing anything keeps you at home doing little or nothing; feelings of self-loathing make you want to avoid contact with your friends or family. After having spent the night tossing and turning, you are so irritable the next day that you get into arguments with everyone around you. You stop going to classes or doing homework because you no longer have the energy or desire to do so. Even if you do manage to hide your symptoms so that no one is aware of them, you feel terrible inside and even lonelier because you cannot share the misery you are feeling with anyone else. In contrast, lots of people will have bad days or even weeks, particularly when they are under stress or when things are going poorly in their lives. These are transient and self-limited, and will disappear with time or when the troubles are surmounted.

One situation that deserves special mention is the relationship between grief and clinical depression. As we keep emphasizing, it is "normal" to feel down in response to bad things happening, and generally the more severe the loss, the more severe the reaction. It follows that after experiencing the ultimate loss, the death of a loved one, people often have a severe and relatively prolonged grief response that may include many of the symptoms that we have just been discussing—sadness, decreased ability to experience pleasure, trouble sleeping, loss of appetite, difficulty concentrating, and fatigue. These experiences may be completely compatible with a normal grief reaction occurring after a devastating loss.

Distinguishing between a necessary grief versus clinical depression is difficult but important because the two have radically different treatment implications. If the diagnosis is uncomplicated grief, your feelings are a normal and unavoidable part of the human condition and will heal with time (as best such wounds ever heal completely). If the diagnosis is clinical depression triggered by grief, the recommendation would be treatment with psychotherapy or medication or both.

There are two clues in making this distinction. Certain symptoms arise so rarely following the death of a loved one that their presence points to the start of a major depressive episode. Special red flags include thoughts of suicide or suicidal behavior, persistent feelings of worthlessness, being so slowed down that you operate in slow motion, being out of touch with reality, or having a complete breakdown in functioning. Another indicator that a grief reaction has evolved into a clinical depression is an abnormally long duration of intense symptoms. If you are still severely depressed two months after experiencing the loss, it is likely that you will remain depressed a year later unless you begin treatment in the meantime. Active intervention now can prevent months or even years of unnecessary suffering and detrimental effects on your health. Although grieving is a necessary process, depression is not. Prompt treatment will limit your suffering and impairment. Grief is painful enough on its own.

Dysthymic Disorder is, by definition, less severe than Major Depressive Disorder. Establishing its boundary with "normal" sadness or a pessimistic personality is even more difficult. The key factors are whether the sadness and other symptoms are significantly distressing and whether they are persistently unremitting day in and day out for long periods of time. Unless you successfully treat them, dysthymic symptoms will weigh you down and haunt your entire life. We have treated many people who have had years of unsuccessful psychotherapy, which failed precisely because it did not identify or address their chronic depression. Once the depression responds (to medicine or psychotherapy or both) it is as if the stormy weather disappears and the sun comes out. "I didn't think life could ever be like this" is a common reaction. In doubtful cases, a brief trial of medication makes sense—it is not that hard to do and can make such a big difference if it works.

TREATMENT OPTIONS

Unipolar depression is one of the most treatable of the mental disorders. Fortunately there is an extensive menu of effective treatments from which to choose so that everyone's needs and preferences can be accommodated. Given enough time and patience, it is usually possible to customize the treatment, get the right match, and achieve a good outcome.

The first step in mastering depression is education. You and your family need to learn everything possible about its causes, symptoms, complications, treatments, and support groups. Some of this will be a very general education, some of it will be entirely specific to you. What are the particular environmental triggers that get depression started? What is your risk of suicide and how can this be reduced? What treatments work best for your kind of depression? Which are your earliest symptoms and how can you identify them rather than be influenced by them? When you start feeling worthless, can you say, "I am depressed again" or will it be, "I don't deserve to live"? The more you understand, in a practical not a textbook way, the better armed you will be to master the illness rather than to be mastered by it.

The tools for treating depression can be divided into the somatic and the psychological. Somatic treatments include antidepressant medications, electroconvulsive therapy, and light therapy. Psychotherapies for depression include cognitive therapy, behavioral therapy, interpersonal therapy, and insight-oriented therapy. Sometimes the particular form of depression dictates which treatment is most likely to be successful (refer to the above discussion of subtypes of depression). Often, several alternative treatment options are likely to be equally effective so that the choice is based more on your preference than on anything else—and sometimes combinations work better than one treatment given alone.

For those suffering from Major Depressive Disorder, antidepressant medications are very effective—the overall odds that an antidepressant treatment will work eventually are probably at least 90 percent. But you have to be patient and forbearing along the way. It usually takes at least several weeks for the medication to begin working, and a couple of months before it has reached its maximum effect. It might also take time and effort to find the most effective medication for you and to determine its proper dose. Some people must endure several trials of different antidepressants until they find the one that is a winner for them. To give you some perspective, two thirds of depressed patients will have a good response to the first medicine that is tried. For those who do not respond initially, the odds of a second antidepressant working are about fifty-fifty—this gets us to about 80 percent total response rate. If you have still not yet responded after two tries, a third or a fourth or even a fifth try may be necessary to find the medicine or combination of medicines that will eventually work. The good news is that there are close to thirty available antidepressants on the market and new ones are being developed all the time. Hopefully sooner, but almost certainly eventually, one of these or some combination will work for you.

The use of antidepressant medication has risen dramatically over the past several years, but many people who might benefit have misconceptions that make them reluctant to give one a try. One common concern is that the changes resulting from antidepressant use are artificial and, by implication, somehow illegitimate. Others worry that they will become physically dependent on antidepressants in the same way that a heroin addict cannot function without his daily fix. Yet others feel that having to rely on antidepressant medication to maintain one's mood (and productivity) represents a weakness in moral fiber—that you should be able to get rid of the depression by sheer will power alone.

None of these makes a great deal of sense. Depression is really no different than hypertension. Medicines that treat high blood pressure are taken to reestablish the body's ability to maintain a normal blood pressure. Antidepressants work in the same way—restoring brain neurochemistry to its original natural state. In contrast to drugs like heroin and cocaine, which make virtually everyone feel euphoric, an antidepressant does nothing for a person without depression except produce unpleasant side effects. There is no street market for antidepressants and they are not addictive. Finally, in the same way that it would be ludicrous to think that someone can simply will their elevated blood pressure down to normal, true grit is not by itself sufficient to cure clinical depression.

So how does a psychiatrist decide which antidepressant to use? As is true with most things in life, the past predicts the future. If you have responded well to a particular antidepressant in the past, you are likely to respond well again this time around. Another guide is a family history—if a particular medication has been helpful to a family member, it is likely to be helpful to you. Lacking such information, the choice of antidepressant generally depends on tailoring the side effect profile to your symptoms, lifestyle, and personal preferences. One person's side effect is another person's godsend. For example, some antidepressants are particularly sedating. This side effect is a plus for someone who has insomnia, but may be terrible for someone who drives a truck for a living or has to get up early for work. In general, the older antidepressants are more likely to cause side effects that are poorly tolerated.

Reading this, you might conclude that we think medication is necessary for everyone with depression. On the contrary, antidepressant medications are probably overused. Three of the top ten best-selling medications in the United States are antidepressants: Prozac, Zoloft, and Paxil. Interestingly, most of the prescribing is done by primary care physicians and *not* by psychiatrists. While antidepressants have been used more and more widely, they have probably been used less and less wisely, often for individuals who do not really need them. It has long been recognized that only part of the healing power of antidepressants can be attributed to the medication itself. The passage of time, positive expectations, and the supportive role of the person administering the medication all play a critical role in treatment response. For this reason, treatment studies of depression almost always include a so-called "placebo group"—people who are given a dummy pill instead of active medication. In a typical drug study, around 60 to 70 percent of those who receive the tested antidepressant have a significant improvement, as compared to about 30 to 40 percent of those on the placebo. Although these results establish a significant superiority of medication over placebo, about half of the medication "responders" would have done just as well without medication!

The catch in trying to apply this information in clinical practice is that there is no way to know in advance *which* half of the group will get better if given only active medication. Moreover, since it is unethical to deceive patients about what they are being prescribed, there is no practical way to "try out" a placebo. Being forthcoming as to the true nature of the pill would likely compromise its effectiveness since the belief that one is taking an active medication is probably an important element.

We find two lessons in this. First, while antidepressants are clearly necessary for many people with depression, they are not always needed—other options are equally viable for mild and brief down periods. Second, patients who have experienced only one depression can usually have their medicine gradually reduced, and eventually eliminated, after six months to a year in order to see if they really need it. In contrast, those who have had many episodes of depression will require antidepressant medication on a very long-term and even a lifelong basis.

The vast majority of patients who are being started on an antidepressant for the first time are now receiving one of the newer medications (Prozac, Zoloft, Paxil, or Luvox) in preference to the more traditional tricyclic medications that have been the mainstay of treatment for more than thirty years. This is not because they are any more effective—if anything the traditionals may have the efficacy edge, especially in treating more severe depressions. The appeal of the newer drugs has been that people much prefer taking them and are more likely to stick with treatment. They do not cause the troubling side effects of weight gain, blurred vision, dry mouth, constipation, palpitations, or dizziness that made the traditionals so unpopular. But the newer drugs do have a special side effect problem of their own—up to half the people taking them experience lessened sexual interest or difficulties in performance. It is fascinating that given the choice of suffering blurred vision and constipation versus a reduction in sexual life, most people are voting with their feet (as it were) and picking the newer drugs.

Electroconvulsive therapy (ECT), sometimes referred to as "shock therapy," labors under the undeserved curse of a terrible name and a terrible reputation. Don't let this fool you. ECT is a terrifically effective treatment that is also relatively safe considering the great benefits that can often be gained. ECT is especially useful for psychotic mood disorders, people who need a really fast response, medication nonresponders, and for those who cannot tolerate antidepressant medication. Electroconvulsive therapy has a higher response rate (80 to 90 percent versus the 65 to 70 percent achieved by medication combinations) and also works more rapidly. However, it has the disadvantage of providing fewer clues as to what type of medication is likely to work to prevent recurrences in the maintenance phase. Due to misguided fears, ECT has been most typically considered a treatment of last resort when nothing else works. It probably deserves to be used earlier and more often. Unfortunately, few can forget the horrifying scene in the film *One Flew Over the Cuckoo's Nest* when the Jack Nicholson character, R. P. McMurphy, is administered ECT without anesthesia, seemingly more as a punishment than as therapy. *Cuckoo's Nest* was a great movie but a terribly unrealistic depiction of mental illness and of ECT.

Bright light therapy seems like an appealing treatment option because it is so "natural." Sitting in front of a bright light for an hour in the early morning extends the perceived length of your day and convinces the brain that it is summertime even during the winter months. Unfortunately, bright lights are helpful only for the seasonal-type patients whose depression consistently develops in the fall or early winter and gets better in the spring.

The latest rage in treating depression is an extract from the plant St.-John's-wort that can be purchased in any health food store. There has been very little systematic study of St.-John's-wort and it is not yet clear whether it is effective, for what indications, and with what side effects. A few small studies performed in Germany suggest it may be useful for milder depressions and a large study now underway at ten sites in the United States should provide more definitive answers. There is usually no free lunch. St.-John's-wort is probably a weak antidepressant but with fewer side effects. It certainly does not make sense to go off a winning medicine with effects you know for the uncertainties of St.-John's-wort, particularly since it is possible that the antidepressant may not work as well the second time around.

This brings up the question of other health store or homeopathic treatments for depression. Be cautious. It does make intuitive sense that there may be any number of "organic" and "natural" antidepressants. Nature is a much smarter and more comprehensive chemist than the combined efforts of the research departments of all the pharmaceutical companies and it has had lots of time to invent millions of possibly medicinal compounds. Some of our most effective medicines have been brewed by nature and it is no accident that botany and medicine grew up together. The early medical schools all had botanical gardens. Linnaeus, the great classifier of the plant kingdom, had his day job as a physician and studied plants as a sideline. Undoubtedly, many future drugs of great value will come directly from nature's already created bounty. On the other hand, finding them is something of a needle in the haystack proposition and folk wisdom about medicinal benefits is much more often based on anecdote than on fact. St.-John's-wort shows some promise, but it is usually a mistake jumping on bandwagons before you know the direction they are taking.

Among the many different types of psychotherapy that are effective in treating depression, by far the most studied is cognitive therapy. Cognitive therapy concentrates on correcting the distortions in thinking and perception that underlie and reinforce depressed mood. People with depression spend most of their waking hours preoccupied with dismal thoughts about themselves, the world around them, and their future. They are flooded with so-called "automatic negative thoughts" of being worthless, reprehensible, despicable, burdensome, and doomed. Under the influence of depression, thinking becomes negatively distorted so that every event, comment, or feeling is experienced as damning evidence of inadequacies. For example, if something bad happens, it is automatically your fault, a sign of personal inadequacy, and proof that nothing will ever work out right for you. On the other hand, if something positive happens, your immediate assumption is that it is just dumb luck that is limited to this one specific situation and that it is unlikely ever to occur again.

The goal in cognitive therapy is for you to take a large mental step back to gain better perspective. Identify your automatic negative thoughts for what they are: distortions that are the by-products of your depression. Once such "bad thinking" is identified, the next step is to challenge it with more rational alternatives. Let's say you are preoccupied with the thought that you are a complete failure as a husband and father because you are unable to get out of bed. The therapist would encourage you to label this unreasonably harsh self-evaluation as a "symptom" of depression and suggest you counteract it with a more realistic alternative explanation ("my inability to get out of bed is no more than a temporary result of my being clinically depressed and is not at all a reflection of my overall value as a person").

The behavioral treatment for depression aims at reversing vicious cycles caused by loss of pleasure and inactivity. Because of your depression, you have less ability to experience pleasure and are doing fewer things. This in turn fosters your sense of isolation, hopelessness, and depression, which further intensifies your unwillingness to venture out of your cocoon. Behavior therapy breaks the cycle of despair by prescribing that you engage in pleasurable activities despite your conviction that it "won't do any good." Once you get started, you will often be surprised to learn that it is still possible to feel some pleasure, even if temporarily and in a limited way. It is wise not to expect too much in the beginning, but a virtuous cycle can begin with very small steps—eat some ice cream, watch a favorite television show, take a bath, or sit in the sun—whatever it is you like doing, spend more time doing it. Gradually, you come to realize that doing pleasurable things is still rewarding. This leads to more activity, a greater sense of control, hopefulness for recovery, and ultimately an improvement in mood.

The basic premise of insight-oriented psychotherapy (also known as psychodynamic psychotherapy) is that you are experiencing depression because of unconscious psychological conflicts. Increasing your understanding of the underlying themes, thoughts, and behavioral patterns can result in improved mood both in the short and the long term. These psychodynamic themes fall into three categories. The most common trigger of depression is the loss of an important relationship. While the therapy can't undo the pain of the loss, it helps by encouraging appropriate grieving and promoting a fuller understanding of the psychological significance of the loss. The second most frequent trigger of depression is a loss of self-esteem, often a result of the failure to be appreciated by others or to achieve your self-expectations. Therapy can help you lick your wounds by providing an empathic setting for dealing with the disappointment and developing more realistic expectations. Finally, depression can result from your having an overly punishing "superego" or conscience that can be devastating in three ways. When the wrath of your harsh conscience is directed inward it leads to inappropriate guilt; when it is directed outward it results in your being overly critical of others; and when it is projected outward onto others, you experience them as being overly critical of you. Therapy can help by uncovering the unconscious conflicts, exposing them to the light of day, and bringing them under your conscious control.

Interpersonal psychotherapy focuses on the fact that depression is often triggered by difficulties with family, friends, peer groups, co-workers, or colleagues. This type of psychotherapy helps you to identify the connections between interpersonal conflicts and depression, and then to work toward modifying your relationships to make them less stressful and more supportive. The most common targets include unresolved grief, conflict-laden relationships with partners or other family members, difficulty with a social role transition ("empty nest" issues, for example), and a lack of social skills that may have a chronically negative impact on relationships.

When choosing among psychotherapists, it is important to be an informed consumer. Be sure to ask about educational background and experience in treating depression. Many providers of psychotherapy (whether they be psychiatrists, psychologists, social workers, counselors, or nurse practitioners) tend to concentrate on one particular form of psychotherapy.

Also ask which types of psychotherapy the therapist is most familiar with and how flexible he or she is. Ask about licensing—in order to be licensed, therapists must have had a certain minimum of supervised psychotherapy hours and have passed a proficiency examination. Finally, go with your gut feeling. A number of studies have found that therapist-patient "chemistry" is by far the most important factor in a successful outcome. If you have a bad feeling about the therapist, trust it and go elsewhere.

As you can see, there is a wide (and perhaps potentially bewildering) array of effective treatments for depression. Which one is best for you? As psychiatrists, we have to tackle this question every time we formulate an initial treatment plan for depression. One general guideline is that the more severe the depression, the more likely it is to require somatic treatment (medication or ECT) and the less likely it is to respond to psychotherapy alone. Milder depressions tend to improve equally well with either medication or psychotherapy—in such cases, we present the relative advantages and disadvantages of each and go along with the patient's personal preference. The major advantage of medication is a faster response, while the major advantages of psychotherapy are the lack of side effects and more likely long-term benefit stemming from your mastering new skills that may be helpful over the long haul. Remember that the melancholic and psychotic subtypes of depression always require either medication or ECT.

A final consideration regarding the treatment of Major Depressive Disorder is whether it will take place in a hospital or in an outpatient setting. Under current stringent managed care cost controls, insurance coverage for inpatient hospitalization is reserved for those who have demonstrated a need for the protective setting of a hospital—because of the risk of suicide or violence, the presence of psychotic symptoms, the need for ECT, or an accompanying medical illness that complicates treatment. Hospital stays for depression are brief, generally seven to fourteen days. The patient is discharged as soon as the immediate danger has passed and well before antidepressant medication can promote an appreciable improvement in the symptoms of depression. It is important to understand that the role of hospitalization today is to provide a temporary safe haven and not to cure the depression.

Up until the last few years, most people with Dysthymic Disorder received psychotherapy, usually without accompanying medication. While this was helpful for some, many others may have gained some insight but were not relieved of their depressive symptoms. There is accumulating evidence showing that antidepressant medication can be very helpful in treating Dysthymic Disorder. Studies generally reveal a response rate to medication of at least 50 percent, compared to a very low placebo response rate of only 10 percent. This extremely low placebo response rate in Dysthymic Disorder is interesting. It probably reflects the fact that people with chronic depression are pretty much immune to any form of hopefulness and positive expectation. Whether psychotherapy or medication is used (or, as is often best, the combination of both), the treatment for Dysthymic Disorder is almost always a long-term proposition. There is a high relapse rate when someone with Dysthymic Disorder goes off medication. Moreover, it is likely to take at least a year of psychotherapy to counteract years of entrenched negative attitudes, beliefs, and problematic interpersonal relationships.

Suggested Additional Readings

Darkness Visible: A Memoir of Madness
   William Styron
   Vintage Books, 1992

Feeling Good: The New Mood Therapy
   David D. Burns
   Avon, 1992

Overcoming Depression
   Paul A. Hauck
   Westminster John Knox Press, 1973

Understanding Depression: A Complete Guide to Its Diagnosis and Treatment
   Donald F. Klein, M.D., and Paul H. Wender, M.D.
   Oxford University Press, 1993

Where to Go for Help
(Self-help, support, for more information)

Postpartum Support International
(education, advocacy for postpartum emotional changes)

927 North Kellogg Avenue
Santa Barbara, CA 93111
(805) 967-7636
FAX: (805) 967-0608
E-mail: thonikman@compuserve.com
Web: http://www.iup.edu/an/postpartum

Depression After Delivery
(support and information for postpartum depression)

P.O. Box 1282
Morrisville, PA 19067
(908) 575-9121
(800) 944-4773

Depressed Anonymous
(twelve-step program for depressives)

P.O. Box 1747
Louisville, KY 40217
(502) 569-1989
E-mail: mailto:depanon@aol.com

Emotions Anonymous
(twelve-step program for people with depression
and other psychiatric symptoms)

P.O. Box 4245
St. Paul, MN 55104
(612) 647-9712
Web: http://www.mtn.org/EA

National Organization for Seasonal Affective Disorder (NOSAD)
(information and education about SAD)

P.O. Box 40190
Washington, D.C. 20016

Depression and Related Affective Disorders Association (DRADA)

Meyer 3-181
600 North Wolfe Street
Baltimore, MD 21287-7381
(410) 955-4647 (Baltimore, MD)
(202) 955-5800 (Washington, D.C.)
E-mail: drada-g@welchlink.welsh.jhu.edu
Web: http://www.med.jhu.edu/drada/

National Depressive and Manic-Depressive Association (NDMDA)
(support and information)

730 North Franklin Street
Suite 501
Chicago, IL 60610
(312) 642-0049
(800) 826-3632
FAX: (312) 642-7243
Web: http://www.ndmda.org/

National Alliance for the Mentally Ill (NAMI)

200 North Glebe Road
Suite 1015
Arlington, VA 22203-3754
(703) 524-7600
(800) 950-NAMI
Web: http://www.nami.org/

National Foundation for Depressive Illness
(information and national referral list)

P.O. Box 2257
New York, NY 10116
(800) 248-4344

National Alliance for Research on Schizophrenia and Depression (NARSAD)

60 Cutter Mill Road
Suite 404
Great Neck, NY 11021
(516) 829-0091
Web: http://www.mhsource.com/narsad.html

National Mental Health Association

1021 Prince Street
Alexandria, VA 22314-2971
(703) 684-7722
Web: http://www.nmha.org/

CHAPTER 2

EUPHORIC
OR IRRITABLE MOOD

The rewards and punishments dished out by evolution have shaped the kinds of creatures we are and how we behave. Even the most primitive of life forms knows how to approach what feels good to it and avoid what feels bad—otherwise it would not have survived. Indeed, primitive creatures have remained primitive precisely because their reward systems were so well adapted from the very start that there was no need to evolve into something more advanced. No matter how complex any living creature has become, its basic survival rests ultimately on the simple ability to do well in reaping rewards and in avoiding punishments.

Mania represents the unrestrained and inappropriate firing of the reward systems that have been built into our brains to make us feel good about the things that are good for us. Our emotions evolved as a form of communication—to ourselves as well as to others. The ability to feel good, bad, fearful, or angry provides us with important information about our environment and how we should respond to it. Usually our emotions are exquisitely well honed and responsive to our current circumstances in the real world. In Bipolar Disorder, the regulation of emotion flies out of whack. Our usually reliable and stable brain produces wildly fluctuating, unpredictable, and extreme mood states that are generated by an instability in nerve transmission, not the real rewards and punishments of the external world.

How does mania feel? Life has its very special moments when we are rewarded with a temporary high—perhaps after receiving an award, or winning a jackpot, or meeting a soul mate, or starting a summer vacation, or watching a favorite team finally win the championship. Imagine feeling high, not just for a few moments or hours, but all day every day for days or months on end, often to the point of complete exhaustion. If this be mania, you might wonder, what is so bad about it? Who would not want to prolong an elevated mood for as long as possible? You wouldn't—for the simple reason that way too much of a good thing can be simply terrible. Certainly we are lucky that nature has equipped our brains with systems to register rewards and make us feel good—but it never meant for these reward systems to be running full blast all the time, for weeks or months on end, with no relation to the survival needs of the real world.

Mania can be just as destructive as depression and can even come to feel at least as uncomfortable. The euphoric feelings quickly lose their charm and spin wildly out of control. What begins as mild overconfidence builds into the conviction that you can communicate with God, control the weather, or unfailingly predict the stock market. You are so unquenchably sociable that you must call every friend you ever had, day and night, until they never want to hear from you again. You feel so energetic that you go with little food or sleep for weeks on end, until you collapse. You become uncharacteristically impulsive and so convinced of your absolute infallibility that you spend or gamble like a sailor, make foolish investments, drive 110 miles per hour, or have unprotected sex with a stranger who may be HIV positive. And then, there is the inevitable crash—no one stays high forever. Very often, the high is followed by a low.

Making a correct diagnosis of mania and initiating immediate treatment is extremely important. The disinhibited behavior instigated by mania can be disastrous, not only for you but also for the family members and friends who have to endure the recklessness and help pick up the pieces. Getting the right treatment early increases the likelihood the medicine will work and reduces the burden of the illness on your career and family life.

Mania also seems to feed on itself by a process called "kindling"—a little spark of mania ignored can grow into a big flame that is much more difficult to put out. The more time your brain spends in a manic state, the more destabilized it becomes and the easier it is for the manic wiring to be activated again and again in the future. For some especially unfortunate people, this can evolve into a "rapid cycling" pattern of alternating manic and depressive episodes, often without any periods of normal mood in between. Having lots of episodes in your twenties and thirties makes you much more vulnerable to having multiple recurrences in your forties, fifties, and beyond—with the episodes becoming more frequent and more difficult to control if the illness has not been treated well and tamed early on.

Although much less common than unipolar depression, Bipolar Disorder is not at all rare. Estimates of its frequency in the general population range from 1 to 3 percent. The lifetime risk of suicide is significant (10 to 15 percent) and aggressive behavior in Bipolar Disorder is at least three times more common than in the general population. Because violent acts are more likely during the first few years of the illness, early recognition and intervention can be lifesaving. You really owe it to yourself (and your loved ones) to take the very well-established steps in treatment and prevention that will help keep to a minimum your total number of lifetime episodes.

Unfortunately, elevated mood is often difficult to diagnose accurately and you may end up seeing many different doctors over a period of years before someone spots it. There are several different ways the diagnosis is missed. Many people equate mania with elation and ignore that it may also cause you to be irritable, tense, driven, and paranoid, and even to have intermittent crying spells and depression. Before the symptoms get really severe, it may be mistakenly assumed that the highs are no more than a normal mood fluctuation. The excited behavior in a person who smells of alcohol may be written off without considering the possibility that there is also an underlying manic-depressive illness. Because it is often confused with Schizophrenia (page 313) or Major Depressive Disorder (page 33), Bipolar Disorder must be considered as a crucial part of their differential diagnosis.

What goes up must always come down. Bipolar Disorder gets its name because of its unpredictable swings in mood—often from spectacular over-driven highs to deep moribund lows, and vice versa. Once you have had even one single clear manic episode, it is pretty certain that you will go on to have many bouts of mania and depression throughout your life. In this chapter, we will cover three different types of Bipolar Disorder—Bipolar I Disorder (severe manias and severe depressions); Bipolar II Disorder (much milder highs coupled with severe depressions); and Cyclothymic Disorder (quickly oscillating mild ups and mild downs).

BIPOLAR I DISORDER ("MANIC DEPRESSION")

In Bipolar I Disorder, both the ups and the downs are extreme and disabling. The illness almost always begins sometime between puberty and age thirty-five and continues for life. Very rarely, the first episode begins in childhood—almost always these early onsets occur in someone who has a strong family history suggesting genetic loading. Usually, the earlier in life Bipolar Disorder appears the more difficult will be its lifetime course unless there is active treatment over many years to minimize the risk of recurrence.

Having a first manic episode after age fifty is so unusual that Bipolar Disorder is unlikely to be the cause. A thorough medical workup is necessary to rule out the possibility of a medical condition (a brain tumor, an infection, an endocrine disturbance) or substance use (including a medication side effect) that might be masquerading as mania.

For men with Bipolar I Disorder, the first episode is more likely to consist of mania, whereas for women it is more likely to be depressive. No one knows why. The average number of mood episodes is four in the first ten years of the illness. Some people have almost equal numbers of manias and depressions, whereas others have almost exclusively manic or exclusively depressive episodes. The most common pattern is for a mania immediately to precede or immediately to follow a depression. One of the challenges in the treatment of both mania and depression is to avoid triggering the switch to the opposite type of episode. Depressions in bipolar disorder are in most ways just like the unipolar depressions we discussed in the last chapter, except that they are more likely to be of the atypical type (with overeating and oversleeping); to occur seasonally in late fall; and to follow childbirth.

An untreated manic episode is likely to last only for a few weeks to months, whereas an untreated depressive episode usually persists for six months or much longer. Most people completely recover between episodes and then go on for months or years without any symptoms—until the next episode. Some people, however, never completely get back to a normal mood and instead endure a chronic low-grade state of being either up or down (or both) between episodes.

The most dreaded course is "rapid cycling," which is like being on a roller coaster, perpetually in some sort of episode going without respite from highs to lows and back again. Rapid cycling is more likely in women, particularly if they have thyroid problems. It is also promoted by exposure to antidepressant medications, especially if you are not also taking a mood stabilizing medicine to cover this risk. Identifying, preventing, and aggressively treating rapid cycling is simply crucial since it is especially difficult to break the rhythm once it has built a head of steam.

According to the diagnostic manual, you have Bipolar I Disorder if:
- You have had one or more *manic episodes* in which you feel abnormally "high," hyper, wired, or unusually irritable. These get you into trouble, make you unable to function at work or at school, or result in your being admitted to the hospital.

- During these manic episodes, at least three of the following symptoms are present:
    (1) You feel overly self-confident or even grandiose.
    (2) You need much less sleep than usual.
    (3) You cannot stop talking.
    (4) Your thoughts are racing.
    (5) You are easily distracted.
    (6) You are much more active sexually or socially, or are much more productive at school or at work than is usual for you, or you feel agitated much of the time.
    (7) You get involved in pleasurable activities without considering the consequences (e.g., buying things you cannot possibly afford or having unprotected sex with a stranger).
- You also have had one or more *depressive episodes* like those described for Major Depressive Disorder on page 34.

DESCRIPTION

Mania comes in two forms—euphoric and dysphoric. In euphoric mania, you have an intense feeling of optimism, creativity, power, and boundless energy. Life seems full of irresistible possibilities limited only by your imagination. Almost as common, but much less pleasant, is dysphoric mania. In addition to being high, you also feel irritable, agitated, wired, impatient, on edge, frustrated, depressed, paranoid, or some combination of these. Sometimes the experiences of euphoria and dysphoria are intermixed. You start out feeling overjoyed and energized, but your mood quickly turns ugly when you run into obstacles. Without having made reservations, you loudly insist on getting the best table in an exclusive restaurant because you are working on a deal with Donald Trump and then take a surprise poke at the maître d' when he refuses to seat you.

Unrealistically elevated self-regard can result in dramatic changes in behavior that often have disastrous consequences. Someone who has previously shown only a marginal interest in writing becomes convinced that he is immensely talented and resigns from his job to begin work on the Great American Novel. A fiscally conservative businessman (using his newly discovered, absolutely foolproof, no-risk investment strategy) suddenly invests his entire life savings in a highly speculative stock. A casually religious nurse suddenly believes she is in direct communication with God and is on a divinely directed mission to save the world's children. A high school science teacher claims to have invented a way to power cars with solar energy and becomes convinced that the major oil companies have bugged her telephone in an attempt to steal the secret. A scrupulously honest accountant hatches a harebrained Ponzi scheme and solicits the investments of his friends, convinced that eventually he will make them all rich.

Monitor your sleep patterns carefully. If you suddenly feel little or no need for sleep, this is the most reliable signal of the impending onset of a manic episode. And the return of normal sleeping is a good sign that a manic episode is coming under control. Keeping your sleep patterns regular is important because sleep deprivation can actually trigger a new episode. A string of sleepless nights is always a very bad sign, however much you enjoy feeling tireless and may welcome the increased productivity. Consult a psychiatrist immediately to head off the development of a full-blown manic episode, or at least to reduce its intensity and duration.

Manic speech is hard to miss and hard to follow. Your flow of words is literally torrential, pouring out of you like water gushing from a fire hydrant. Carrying on a normal give-and-take conversation is usually impossible and your friends complain they can't get a word in edgewise. Speech feels like a bottleneck that prevents you from communicating the full richness and variety of your ideas. You just can't talk fast enough and the rapid, pressured speech mirrors your racing thoughts. These jump rapidly and with flimsy connections from one topic to the next, punctuated by jokes, puns, and verbal playfulness ("Doc, do you have any money? Money? Money? Money makes the world go round—round, round, round we go—we all fall down—merry-go-round, don't fall down, round the mulberry bush—Johnny B. Goode, be good to yourself and others, always. Doc, do you know that you are really one hell of a guy? Doc, does anyone want to buy a duck?")

You are scattered, distractible, and not at all focused on the task at hand. Your conversation is plagued by frequent detours that can be triggered by random background sounds (hearing an engine backfire suggests the merits of hunting to control the deer population), your doctor's name ("Dr. Green, how pretty, green is the color of my true love's hair"), a picture on the wall, a nurse walking by, a newspaper headline, or whatever else might conceivably capture your almost nonexistent attention span.

You are driven to accumulate a dazzling array of short-term pleasures and excitements with little regard for their possibly dangerous long-term implications. Your spending is profligate. Your credit cards become dangerous enablers of your need to buy everything in sight. Five-, or even six-, figure debts can be accumulated in a remarkably short time. You engage in gambling, drug taking, risky or unusual sexual experiences, or reckless driving in a way that would meet your own stern disapproval were you not captured by the manic state.

At the outset of a manic episode you feel, and may actually be, temporarily more productive and creative than usual. The combination of burning self-confidence and ultra-high energy can have a temporary payoff in getting things done—whether it is finally clearing your desk, cleaning the house, calling neglected friends, writing your memoirs, or breaking sales records. People with a history of mania sometimes pine for the advantages of these moments and forget the heavy price. They may reduce or stop their medication hoping to conjure a period of controlled mood elevation with increased productivity. This ignores the risks involved and is the equivalent of an addict taking stimulant drugs to perform better—a strategy that never works in the long run. You are much better off being safe and steady than stellar and sorry.

Mania brews a dangerous combination of poor impulse control, poor judgment, irritability, and grandiosity. Even if you are ordinarily a very law-abiding person with the highest moral values, you may engage in crimes, sins, or indiscretions that are completely at odds with your usual character. Murders, embezzlement, rape, spouse abuse, and adultery have all been committed by extremely nice and virtuous people when they were in a manic state. Juries are completely unsympathetic to the argument that the crime was caused by mania and generally assume that the person probably knew right from wrong at the moment the crime was committed. You will probably be held both legally and fiscally responsible for all actions taken during a manic episode even though you could not control your impulses because of the impact of the illness.

BIPOLAR SPECTRUM DISORDERS

Bipolar I Disorder, with its combination of wild out-of-control highs and soul-crushing lows, has been recognized and categorized for the past several thousand years. Much more recently, it has become evident that the phenomenon of recurrent mood swings occurs on a continuum—many people have a bipolar-like pattern that falls far short of the extreme highs and extreme lows that characterize Bipolar I Disorder. Recognizing these disorders is crucial. People with Bipolar Spectrum Disorders are at higher risk of later developing a full-blown Bipolar I Disorder and they may be made worse by the commonly prescribed antidepressant medicines. Like those with Bipolar I Disorder, people with these Bipolar Spectrum Disorders are more likely to have relatives with Bipolar I Disorder and may need lifelong use of mood stabilizers.

The DSM-IV includes two Bipolar Spectrum Disorders: Bipolar II Disorder and Cyclothymic Disorder. They resemble Bipolar I Disorder in that the person's mood is unstable, swinging back and forth between days of elevated mood to days of depressed mood. They differ in terms of the intensity of the mood swings. The top of the figure below illustrates the typical pattern seen in Bipolar I Disorder: very high and very low. In Bipolar II Disorder (middle drawing) the pattern consists of mild highs (called hypomanic episodes, see below) and severe episodes of depression. In Cyclothymic Disorder (lower drawing), mild highs continuously alternate with mild lows.

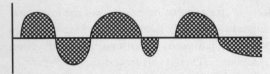

Typical Pattern in Bipolar I Disorder

Typical Pattern in Bipolar II Disorder

Typical Pattern in Cyclothymic Disorder

Bipolar II Disorder

Bipolar II Disorder is on the border between Bipolar I Disorder and unipolar depression. As in unipolar depression, there are recurrent severe downs but in addition there are also occasional small highs (that are called hypomania). It is like Bipolar I Disorder in the up and down nature of the mood changes and in having a similar treatment, course, and family history. Don't be fooled into thinking that Bipolar II Disorder is a benign condition just because its hypomania is less severe than the full-blown mania of Bipolar I Disorder. This condition has an appreciable risk of suicide and the depressions in Bipolar II Disorder can be dreadful.

Everyone who takes antidepressant medication needs to know a great deal about Bipolar II. Each day, many millions of people take an antidepressant medicine often prescribed by a primary care physician who has little training in psychiatry and little time to ask detailed questions about your psychiatric history. Only rarely will the doctor uncover the crucial information of whether you or anyone in your family has a tendency toward Bipolar Disorder. Antidepressant medications have the potential to muck up the life of anyone prone to Bipolar Disorder by switching depressions to mania and by causing rapid cycling. If you have any tendency toward Bipolar Disorder, you don't want to be on antidepressants unless they are managed very carefully and you are also taking a mood stabilizing medication.

Your past history of hypomania is likely to be overlooked unless you pay careful attention to the material in this section. Hypomania can be missed easily because it is much less pronounced than the extreme highs of mania. The stakes are high. One in six people with unipolar depression eventually goes on to develop a Bipolar Disorder. If you have Bipolar II Disorder, there is an even higher risk that you will have a full-blown manic episode in the next five years. You can reduce these odds by determining whether you have had hypomanic episodes so that your doctor can be cautious in the way he or she prescribes antidepressant medication.

According to the diagnostic manual, you have Bipolar II Disorder if:
- You have had one or more *depressive episodes* like those described for Major Depressive Disorder (see page 34).
- You have also had one or more *hypomanic episodes*. These are like the manic episodes described on pages 63–65, but are not nearly as severe or impairing.

DESCRIPTION

Hypomania is like a manic episode with the volume turned way down (the word "hypomania" literally means "below mania"). The DSM-IV boundary between mania and hypomania depends on whether the elevated mood results in serious adverse consequences—like hospitalization, dangerous behavior, being fired from a job, getting arrested, wrecking a marriage, or ruining a close relationship. The most common pattern in Bipolar II Disorder is for the depressive episodes to be immediately preceded by, or to be followed by, a hypomanic episode.

Hypomania would seem to offer many of the positive aspects of an elevated mood (like increased energy, excitement, optimism, sociability, and assertiveness) without the serious negatives of mania. You are uncharacteristically self-confident and self-assured without crossing the line into reckless grandiosity. Speech is speeded up as compared to baseline, but not to the point where two-way conversations become impossible. A greatly increased activity level translates into greater productivity at work, school, or home—rather than the exhaustion or agitation that accompany mania. During hypomanic periods, job performance may suddenly improve and long-neglected projects and tasks are speedily completed. Hypomania usually lasts for days or weeks, sometimes months. You may even come to rely on the flurry of activity that occurs during the frenetic hypomanic times to compensate for your fallow depressive periods.

Hypomania also has its serious downsides and is a clear danger signal that Bipolar I Disorder may lurk down the road. Although you feel just fine, others may find you obnoxious because you are so wired or they may be troubled by the totally unpredictable swings in your behavior from supercharged to low key. Your judgment may be impaired—what seemed like a fantastic business deal or a very creative short story turns out to be a bust or a waste of time or much worse. Hypomanic episodes often include hair-trigger irritability, with runs of days in which you are consistently impatient and get into arguments over every little frustration. You may even get into fistfights. This is usually accompanied by sleeplessness and hyperactivity.

Worst of all are the inevitable lows. People tend to crash from hypomania in a fashion that resembles a hangover after a stimulant high and may sometimes progress to a full-blown depression. Perhaps most troubling is that some people come to crave the hypomanic episodes and may even stop taking mood stabilizing medication in order to encourage them to emerge. This can lead to an extremely rocky and unstable course. People who stop and start mood stabilizing medicine run the risk of ruining its effectiveness—for unknown reasons, a medication that worked well in the past may lose its punch if it is used intermittently in this way.

Bipolar II is much harder to diagnose correctly than is Bipolar I Disorder. Full-blown manic episodes are so dramatic that you and your doctor don't easily forget them. If you have Bipolar II Disorder, you almost always seek help only when you are depressed. This makes it easy for the doctor to overlook the possibility that you may have had hypomanic episodes in the past. Hypomania is likely to be missed unless you pay really careful attention even to the very mild highs that you enjoyed and never thought were a signal of trouble. Be sure to bring up any even brief period of feeling unusually good, irritable, energetic, active, or sleepless that was different from your normal self. This one step alone can save a tremendous amount of lifetime heartache.

Cyclothymic Disorder

For some people, constantly recurring but mild mood swings are the rule rather than the exception. Cyclothymic Disorder describes a chronic pattern of up and down "stable instability" in both mood and behavior that is never severe enough at either end to constitute full-blown mania or full-blown depression. This condition generally starts in adolescence or early adulthood and lasts throughout life unless it is successfully treated. Cyclothymic Disorder is easily overlooked if your mood swings have become so much a part of your personality ("just the way I am") that you are resigned to experience life on a seesaw. This is unfortunate because treatment can stabilize mood, reduce unpredictability, calm relationships, and help you to become more consistently productive at school or work. It is also important to recognize and deal with Cyclothymic Disorder because it puts you at an increased risk for eventually developing Bipolar I Disorder (estimated to be anywhere from 15 to 50 percent). Taking the necessary steps in prevention may spare you from ever developing the much more severe illness.

According to the diagnostic manual, you have Cyclothymic Disorder if:
- Your mood bounces unpredictably up and down—with "ups" that are less severe than manic episodes and "downs" that are less severe than major depressive episodes.

• Although the ups and downs each by themselves do not cause significant problems, the instability of your mood makes you unreliable and reduces your productivity.

DESCRIPTION

By definition, Cyclothymic Disorder is the least severe of the Bipolar Disorders in the intensity of its mood swings. All of the up periods are the less severe hypomanic variety (rather than full-blown manic episodes) or else the diagnosis would be Bipolar I Disorder. All of the periods of depression are less severe than major depressive episodes or else the diagnosis would be Bipolar II Disorder. This does not necessarily mean that Cyclothymic Disorder is necessarily a "mild" condition. You have such frequent and unpredictable mood shifts that you and your family cannot count on any kind of consistency—the only thing that is predictable is the unpredictability of your mood. This is terribly disconcerting for you and for everyone around you and ruins planning because you never can know what your mood, energy level, or productivity will be on any given day.

Given its early onset and chronic course, Cyclothymic Disorder is often confused with Borderline Personality Disorder, which also has rapidly changing moods and unstable behavior. Indeed, many experts believe that the distinction between Cyclothymic Disorder and Borderline Personality Disorder is a meaningless artifact of the diagnostic system and that these are no more than two different ways of looking at the same thing. You may want to read about Borderline Personality Disorder (page 224) to see if any of the issues described there also apply to you.

DIFFERENTIAL DIAGNOSIS

Having periods of abnormally elevated mood does not necessarily mean that you have Bipolar Disorder. Indeed, given the treatment implications of a diagnosis of Bipolar Disorder (a lifelong need for medication to maintain mood stability), it is important to make sure that the other possible explanations have been ruled out.

Substance use is the most common cause of an abnormally elevated, euphoric, or irritable mood. Many substances ("uppers," cocaine, speed, crystal meth, diet pills) produce a high that is indistinguishable from a manic episode except for the fact that the elevated mood diminishes as the acute effects of the drug wear off. Wild fluctuations in mood can also be a side effect of some prescription medications, particularly steroids.

The differential diagnosis can be particularly difficult in an adolescent who presents with hyperactivity, distractibility, sleeplessness, and impulsive behavior. Before concluding that the problem is Bipolar Disorder, it is important first to consider substance use and Attention-Deficit/Hyperactivity Disorder (page 387). The distinction between Bipolar Disorder and Attention-Deficit/Hyperactivity Disorder is based on the difference in age of onset (ADHD has to show itself before age seven, whereas Bipolar Disorder usually has its onset after puberty) and typical course (Bipolar Disorder is more clearly episodic).

Even the most experienced clinicians have difficulty distinguishing Bipolar Disorder from Schizoaffective Disorder (page 317), so we wouldn't expect you to be able to do it. These two disorders are hard to tell apart because they have overlapping symptoms (delusions, hallucinations, agitation, grandiosity, sleeplessness) and a comparable age of first onset (puberty to ages thirty-five to forty). The key is whether the psychotic symptoms are part and parcel of the mood episode or whether the psychotic symptoms have a life of their own. Bipolar Disorder is the diagnosis if the psychotic symptoms occur exclusively during episodes of mania or depression (the person hears voices only when he is manic or depressed; never otherwise). Schizoaffective Disorder is the diagnosis if the person has extended periods of psychotic symptoms that persist even after the mood symptoms get better (the person's depression or mania completely resolves but he still hears persistent voices). There is evidence that Schizophrenia and Schizoaffective Disorder are overdiagnosed in everyday practice because many clinicians miss the diagnosis of Bipolar Disorder.

Some people develop episodes of elevated mood only while being treated for depression with antidepressant medication, electroconvulsive therapy, or light therapy. The verdict is still out as to whether they have a true form of Bipolar Disorder or whether they are simply overreactive to the antidepressant treatment. Many have family histories of Bipolar Disorder and eventually go on to have spontaneous manic episodes. Others never develop manic episodes when off antidepressant treatment. If you have been flipped into a high by antidepressant treatments, be cautious about them, especially if you are not also taking a mood stabilizer.

More rarely, an episode of elevated mood may be a symptom of a medical condition—dementia, stroke, head trauma, brain tumor, hyperthyroidism, or Cushing's disease. Consider one of these as the most likely culprit wherever there is a late onset of first mania (after ages forty to fifty) since Bipolar Disorder almost always starts earlier in life. Other clues suggesting a medical cause of mania are the presence of neurologic "soft" signs (mild abnormalities on neurological examination); cognitive impairment (problems with orientation or memory); or physical symptoms (weight loss, intolerance to heat).

AM I OKAY?

The amplitude of mood elevations is on a continuum that goes gradually upward from normal good spirits to hypomania to mania to absolute mayhem. If you ever have had a full-blown manic episode, you almost definitely know about it and will never be able to forget it or its consequences. Although it has its enjoyable moments, especially very early on, a manic episode is usually a devastating event for you and for your loved ones. Individuals in a manic state lose money, jobs, and friends, and often wind up in the hospital. At the crest of an episode, you are likely to be clueless that anything is wrong and will probably even believe that your social, intellectual, and creative skills have been greatly enhanced. In actual fact, you are more likely to be scattered, intrusive, abrasive, demanding, impatient, irritable, and argumentative. The very projects that seem to be going well usually wind up being disasters. And you will likely crash from the mania into a full or partial depression.

Distinguishing hypomania from "normal" good mood is crucially important because the distinction defines the boundary between recurrent unipolar depression and Bipolar II Disorder—leading to very different treatment recommendations. Unfortunately, it is especially difficult to draw a clear line between hypomania and just plain feeling good. In this one instance, we cannot rely on the oft-quoted DSM-IV requirement that the behavioral or psychological symptoms are causing you significant impairment or distress. This is because the very essence of hypomania is that the elevated mood does not necessarily have a significant negative impact on your functioning (or else it would be considered mania). Hypomania occurring by itself (in the absence of any recurrent depressions) is not considered a mental disorder—and your energy and high spirits may even make you the temporary envy of your friends and co-workers.

So how does one tell the difference between hypomania and normal good mood? Perhaps the most important thing is that the elevated mood in hypomania is clearly and objectively different from your usual nondepressed mood. There must be more than just a subjective change in how you feel—the hypomania should transform you enough that other people notice it and can confirm the difference. For example, it is probably hypomania when a reticent, reserved, and deliberate person who requires eight hours of sleep suddenly becomes uncharacteristically gregarious and spontaneous in social and business interactions and goes for weeks on end needing only three hours of sleep. Duration is another factor—it is not hypomania if you feel on top of the world for a couple of days after getting a high score on an admissions test. Feeling revved up all day, every day, for a week or month is a different story.

Figuring out what is normal mood and what is hypomania is especially difficult if you have experienced years of chronic depression. It may not be that easy to decide what is your "usual" nondepressed mood. Any good day may feel like a "high" to you if you are accustomed to feeling depressed and lousy most days for months at a time. To be considered hypomania, the good days should be more than neutral—they should be positively radiant. Your energy level should be more than you can ever remember having. You will probably be sleeping for much less than eight hours a night. We usually require many fairly convincing hypomanic episodes before feeling confident in making a diagnosis of Bipolar II Disorder—having just a single period of elevated mood has little diagnostic significance, especially if it is brief. Having a family history of Bipolar Disorder greatly increases the odds that your periods of hyperactivity are truly hypomania.

Much has been written about the apparent connection between creativity and "madness." The number of artists, writers, and composers who have suffered from mood disturbances seems to be disproportionately high and includes as prominent examples Vincent van Gogh, Franz Schubert, and Eugene O'Neill. A number of theories have been cited to account for this association. Perhaps the interior pain, turmoil, and the "turning inward" that are characteristic of depression provide a person with greater access to inner thoughts and feelings, or perhaps mania unfetters creative expression by disinhibiting socially learned tendencies toward conventionality. Perhaps artistic creativity and a predisposition to mood instability are traits that are biologically co-inherited. Romanticized notions about mood disturbance are unfortunate because they may lead people who worry about a loss of creativity to go off medication for the sake of their art, often with disastrous results to their health. In our experience, most people with Bipolar Disorder are much more solidly productive and creative when their mood is normal. The common concern that treatment of the mood disorder will dampen or even eradicate creative outflow is usually unwarranted and fails to take into account that the fantastic creativity of a bipolar episode is often more subjective than objective. In the cold light of recovery, the brilliantly creative work often turns out to have been fool's gold.

Treatment Options

Perhaps the toughest thing to accept about having Bipolar Disorder is that the treatment is going to be a lifetime affair. Almost everyone who has had one manic episode is destined to have additional manic and depressive episodes and prevention of future episodes is at least as important as the active treatment of the current episode. The biggest mistake you can make is to go off your medication once you start feeling better. Relapses are bad not only because of the direct trouble they cause but because the more episodes you have, the harder it is to treat each new episode and the easier it is to have a future episode and to develop rapid cycling.

Between one half and two thirds of patients with Bipolar Disorder abuse drugs—usually depressants like alcohol or stimulants like cocaine or amphetamines. The depressants are used to help the person calm down. The stimulants are used in one of four contexts—to pull the person out of a depression; as part of the reckless pleasure-seeking that is characteristic of a manic episode; to counteract drug side effects; or to mimic the missed endogenous highs previously caused by the episodes. Any treatment effort to prevent episodes of Bipolar Disorder must pay close attention to these substance use tendencies and make every effort to deal with them.

Having Bipolar Disorder means that your brain is already set on too tight a trip wire. Taking any substance that further reduces the calm and stability of the brain's cell membranes and receptor systems will likely wreck the calm and stability of your mood and your life. This can occur in two ways—through the direct effect of the drug itself on the brain or as a secondary effect if the drug reduces the regularity of your sleep pattern. Bipolar Disorder is a cyclical condition that is closely related to basic body rhythms. Your sleep changes when you have a manic episode, but changes in sleep can also cause an episode. Although caffeine may not have the direct effect of causing manic episodes, it can cause them indirectly by promoting sleep deprivation.

Taking mood stabilizers on a daily basis for many years is essential to keep recurrences to a minimum and to increase the chances of a good long-term course. Some people with Bipolar Disorder have three to four episodes in an entire lifetime. Others will have literally hundreds of episodes and may require dozens of hospitalizations. The difference probably has something to do with the natural course of the illness, but it is even more influenced by how gracefully you adjust to it. Like diabetes and hypertension, if you control Bipolar Disorder well, it is an unpleasant but very manageable inconvenience in your life. If you can't respect the needs of the treatment regimen, the illness can ruin your life or end it. Responding well to Bipolar Disorder requires some combination of finding just the right medication and making lifestyle changes that will reduce the risk of relapse.

Unfortunately, staying on the medication is easier said than done. Many people experience annoying side effects (e.g., tremor, weight gain, hair loss, memory problems, or clouded thinking), or miss the "highs" of the manic episodes, or begin to question the need for daily medication to prevent something that is "old history." Even though we strongly advise all our bipolar patients to remain on maintenance medication for the long haul, we recognize that some will need to experience the cause-and-effect relationship between discontinuing medication and relapse before they get the point. Find a doctor you can trust and work with her to see what management strategy works best for you. This can take time—it is like finding just the right fit for a tailor-made piece of clothing and the fit may change as you do over time.

The treatment of an acute manic episode often involves hospitalization because of psychosis, suicidal risk, or aggressive behavior, or to avoid the consequences of impulsivity and poor judgment. You are living in a speeded-up world and are unlikely to take the therapist or the treatment very seriously. It feels as if you are a fast-moving hummingbird surrounded by slow-moving turtles. Rather than show up for the next appointment, you may well be jetting off to another city. Many patients in an acute manic episode become so impulsive, disorganized, or unaware of the severity of their symptoms that outpatient management is unlikely to be successful. The hospital becomes a safe environment to weather the worst of the manic episode until the danger has passed. Hospitalization is never suggested unless it is absolutely necessary to ensure your safety or to guarantee that you have access to treatment on a daily basis.

Patients in an acute manic episode always need medication to calm down. Mood stabilizers (lithium, Depakote, Tegretol) are essential, both to control the acute episode and to prevent future recurrences. The discovery that lithium salts control mood swings revolutionized the treatment of Bipolar Disorder. Lithium is related to sodium in the periodic table of elements and does a remarkable job of controlling both manic and depressive episodes. Unfortunately, more than most medications, lithium is tricky to use because its "therapeutic window" is so narrow—the difference between the blood level needed for it to be effective (between .8 and 1.2) and the blood level that indicates possible toxicity (over 1.5 to 2.0) is uncomfortably tight. For this reason, people taking lithium need to have their lithium blood levels checked regularly, both to ensure that it is high enough to be in the therapeutic range and to safeguard against it being dangerously high. Less frequent but periodic monitoring is essential even for people on the same dose of lithium for years since a number of factors can affect blood levels over time. The warning signs that your lithium level might be too high are hand tremor, nausea, diarrhea, sedation, or neurological problems. Sometimes lithium toxicity causes agitation that can be confused with the onset (or worsening) of a manic episode. This can lead to doing exactly the opposite of what is right (raising rather than lowering the dose)—unless blood levels are checked to shed light on the problem.

The other medications prescribed as mood stabilizers are usually used as anticonvulsants to control seizures. Depakote (sodium valproate), Tegretol (carbamazepine), Lamictal (lamotrigine), and Klonopin (clonazepam) have been prescribed to treat Bipolar Disorder. Depakote is especially well tolerated and is most indicated especially for mixed mania and rapid cycling. Because mood stabilizers often take several weeks to reach their maximum effect, many patients also need other medicines to reduce acute insomnia, agitation, or psychotic symptoms. Antipsychotics (such as haloperidol) or sedatives (such as Ativan) may be helpful.

Patients with Bipolar I Disorder often need acute treatment for the severe depressive episodes that are an integral part of the condition. The treatment of depression is the same in Bipolar Disorder as it is for Major Depressive Disorder (see page 48) except for two issues. First, mood stabilizers must *always* accompany the use of antidepressant medication to reduce the risk of the person switching from depression into a manic episode or developing rapid cycling. Everyone on antidepressants should be asking, "Do I have a bipolar problem?" and "Is my antidepressant making me worse?" To avoid rapid cycling, antidepressants should be used more sparingly and tapered more rapidly than they are in the treatment of Major Depressive Disorder. Since antidepressant medication is essential for the treatment of the severe depressive episodes in Bipolar Disorder, clinicians must walk a fine line between giving enough of them to treat the depression while avoiding unnecessary exposure that may make Bipolar Disorder worse.

Psychotherapy and lifestyle changes are also essential to the successful long-term management of Bipolar Disorder. Accept that this is a tough illness, but one you can live with and control. Work with the doctor to find the right medicines that balance effectiveness with minimal side effects. Don't use drugs or alcohol. It is simply not worth the risks. Sleep regularly—no all-nighters, no frequent jet lagging, and keep caffeine to a minimum. Don't take on too much stress or load your plate with too many activities. Keep your family involved, get them educated about the disorder, and make them allies, not adversaries in learning to manage it. When you are well, work with them to develop advance directives for what should be done if you become sick again. Planning for the future is best done when you have full insight and good judgment. And join a support group. Bipolar Disorder is tough to live with, but very manageable—if you take it seriously.

Suggested Additional Readings

An Unquiet Mind
>Kay Redfield Jamison
>Knopf, 1995

A Brilliant Madness: Living with Manic-Depressive Illness
>Patty Duke
>Bantam Books, 1996

We Heard the Angels of Madness: A Family Guide to Coping with Manic Depression
>Diane Berger and Lisa Berger
>Quill, 1992

Where to Go for Help
(Self-help, support, for more information)

Lithium Information Center

Dean Foundation for Health Research and Education

2711 Allen Boulevard
Middleton, WI 53562
(608) 827-2390
Web: http://www.deancare.com/info/info11.htm

Depression and Related Affective Disorders Association (DRADA)

Meyer 3-181
600 North Wolfe Street
Baltimore, MD 21287-7381
(410) 955-4647 (Baltimore, MD)
(202) 955-5800 (Washington, D.C.)
E-mail: drada-g@welchlink.welsh.jhu.edu
Web: http://www.med.jhu.edu/drada/

National Depressive and Manic-Depressive Association (NDMDA)
(support and information)

730 North Franklin Street
Suite 501
Chicago, IL 60610
(312) 642-0049
(800) 826-3632
FAX: (312) 642-7243
Web: http://www.ndmda.org/

National Alliance for the Mentally Ill (NAMI)

200 North Glebe Road
Suite 1015
Arlington, VA 22203-3754
(703) 524-7600
(800) 950-NAMI
Web: http://www.nami.org/

National Alliance for Research on Schizophrenia and Depression (NARSAD)

60 Cutter Mill Road
Suite 404
Great Neck, NY 11021
(516) 829-0091
Web: http://www.mhsource.com/narsad.html

National Mental Health Association

1021 Prince Street
Alexandria, VA 22314-2971
(703) 684-7722
Web: http://www.nmha.org/

CHAPTER 3

ANXIETY, FEAR, AND AVOIDANCE

N atural selection has favored those creatures that were blessed with the capacity to experience fear. Responding to danger well is probably the most basic of all survival skills. We humans have evolved as a fairly fearful species for the very simple reason that this has kept us alive in a pretty dangerous world. Any completely fearless individual does not make it for long in the hazardous environments our species must negotiate, whether jungle trail or corporate boardroom. The anxiety disorders represent the price we pay for the gift of fear. People with anxiety disorders have fears that occur for no reason at all or the fears occur out of all proportion to any realistic danger, as if the fear mechanism is poorly calibrated or has too quick a trigger.

The anxiety disorders are classified based on the nature of the symptoms and whether there is something particular that triggers them. The most important distinction separates anxiety that occurs in almost explosive attacks (called "panic attacks") from anxiety that occurs only upon exposure to a specific object or situation (called phobias) and from diffuse anxiety that is present most of the time (called generalized anxiety). We will discuss each of these separately even though they often overlap in the same person.

PANIC DISORDER

Anyone who has ever had an unexpected panic attack will almost certainly never forget the sudden and terrifying burst of symptoms, both physical and psychological. It feels as if you were in a small cage with a large hungry tiger—only there is no objective danger. Imagine yourself sitting at home comfortably watching TV. All of a sudden, you get a horrible sensation of dread, your heart begins to race, and you don't know why. You think that you are having a heart attack. Before you know it, you are sweating, have trouble catching your breath, feel dizzy, and are frightened to death. You feel as if you need air, as if you need to move around, as if you need to do something/anything to stop these terrible feelings. You try to calm yourself, but it doesn't work. You are rushed to the hospital but, by the time you get to the emergency room, your symptoms have disappeared and you feel silly about getting everyone so worked up. You have a thorough examination and blood check and the doctor says he cannot find anything wrong with your heart. It was "just" an anxiety attack. Just an anxiety attack? You felt as though you were going to die! Now you feel you are going crazy.

There is a close connection between your mental state and how you feel physically. Heart rate, skin temperature, blood pressure, and respiration are all strongly influenced by mental input. When we get nervous, we feel it physically—the "butterflies" in our stomach before a final exam or asking someone out on a date. The first step in the treatment of Panic Disorder is to recognize that all the scary feelings and physical symptoms are part of the well-recognized and very treatable Anxiety Disorder that is defined below.

According to the diagnostic manual, you have Panic Disorder if:
- You have had two or more panic attacks that came on out of the blue and for no apparent reason.
- A panic attack is a discrete episode of extreme fear and anxiety. The symptoms come on suddenly and reach a crescendo within ten minutes. The attack ends within a few hours.
- During a typical panic attack you developed four (or more) of the following symptoms:
  (1) Your heart raced, pounded, or skipped beats.
  (2) You were sweating profusely.
  (3) You were trembling or shaking.
  (4) You had trouble catching your breath.
  (5) You felt as if you were choking.
  (6) You had chest pain.
  (7) You felt sick to your stomach.
  (8) You felt dizzy, light-headed, or as if you were about to faint.
  (9) You felt as though everything about you was unreal or as though you were detached from your body.

(10) You felt as though you were losing control or going crazy.

(11) You felt as if you were going to die.

(12) You felt numbness or tingling sensations around your mouth or in your fingers.

(13) You felt chills or hot flushes.

- These panic attacks had a significant impact on you, in that you either:

   (1) worried a lot about having more attacks

   (2) worried a lot about whether the attacks meant you were sick or "going crazy"

   (3) made changes in your normal routine because of the attacks, like avoiding places or situations because you were afraid they would trigger the trouble

---

DESCRIPTION

Panic attacks probably represent a vestige of our inborn "fight or flight" survival mechanism. When faced with danger, our body produces a burst of adrenaline that temporarily gives us the strength, speed, and stamina either to confront the danger head-on, or else flee for our lives. You are standing in front of an automatic teller and suddenly are confronted by a man with a knife, demanding that you withdraw two hundred dollars. Immediately your heart starts racing, you gasp in quick, shallow breaths; you perspire uncontrollably; you feel sick to your stomach; and you are about to faint. Under the circumstances, this is a totally expectable reaction to a realistic danger.

Certain organ systems are revved up in the "fight or flight" response (the increased heart rate, breathing, sweating) and other organ systems are temporarily "turned off" (feeling sick to your stomach because blood is diverted away from your digestive tract). Some of the symptoms (lightheadedness, numbness, shortness of breath) are the result of hyperventilation. Your heart rate and breathing increase to satisfy the body's possibly increased need for oxygen. Sweating dissipates the heat that results from momentarily cranking up metabolic functions. Your pupils dilate in order to sharpen visual acuity. You are ready for "fight or flight." In Panic Disorder, this same drastic response occurs with no realistic triggering danger.

There are two different, but complementary, theories to explain what is going on. Many researchers believe that panic attacks are caused mostly by biology—the neurochemical threshold for triggering the normal "fight or flight" response has been set so low for some people that it goes off unpredictably without environmental or psychological provocation. Other researchers believe that panic attacks are more caused by psychology—some people are hypervigilant about any unusual bodily sensations and quick to assume a catastrophe whenever their heart jumps a beat or their breathing becomes even a bit labored. Their misinterpretation of innocuous physical sensations creates a vicious cycle that increases their anxiety and then further intensifies the physical symptoms that started it all. Soon, even more terrifying "fight or flight" and hyperventilation symptoms chime in (sweating, uncontrollable trembling, blacking out, or choking), throwing more fuel on the fire. This positive feedback loop quickly snowballs into a full-blown panic attack.

Both of these theories help to explain panic attacks. Biological and cognitive factors each play an important role and treatments can be used to target them separately or together. Hyperventilation is a frequent trigger for panic attacks that neatly ties together the underlying biology and psychology and provides a wonderful target for treatment. Some people breathe too fast when they are nervous. Rapid chest breathing blows off carbon dioxide at a greater than usual rate which changes the ratio of carbon dioxide to oxygen in the bloodstream. This sets off reflexes that cause dizziness, palpitations, a pins and needles feeling, and spasms in your fingers and toes. Unless you have been taught to understand the simple cause of these physical symptoms, your natural assumption is that something terrible is happening. This catastrophic thinking—you are having a heart attack or going crazy—leads to even more hyperventilation, more physical symptoms, more terror, and finally a full-blown panic attack.

The frequency and intensity of the panic attacks vary widely from person to person and across the lifetime of the illness in any one person. You may have one or two panic attacks a week on a regular basis for months or years or you may have shorter periods of much more frequent attacks, perhaps as many as ten or twenty a day. Some people have only a few lifetime panic attacks but become preoccupied with worries about having additional attacks and take elaborate steps to avoid them. In a desperate attempt to figure out a cause-and-effect relationship between the surroundings and the attacks, you start avoiding any situations or places that might be causing the trouble. The avoidance tends to spread and before long you may become housebound or travel only with great difficulty—a condition called "agoraphobia," described in the next section.

Here is how panic attacks lead to agoraphobia. Let's say you have your first panic attack while standing in the cashier's line of a crowded department store. Understandably, you assume that the panic attack was somehow caused by being in a stuffy crowd. The next time you go shopping, it is with an undercurrent of anxious anticipation about having to be in a crowded place. You worry about the embarrassment of having an attack in front of other people and of the impossibility of making a fast and graceful getaway. The anxiety builds and leads to another attack. The danger zone spreads and the dread generalizes. You develop an aversion to being in any situation that might predispose you to having attacks. Before long, your entire life revolves around trying to establish and stay within a safe haven protected from future attacks. At its most extreme, you are a housebound prisoner—having drawn the miserable conclusion that every step out of the house may trigger a panic attack. And even being at home is not a complete solution because attacks can occur there as well. Especially if you are alone.

Differential Diagnosis

Panic attacks can occur in a number of conditions other than Panic Disorder. A number of substances cause panic attacks—sometimes by their direct effects, sometimes upon withdrawal. Panic attacks may be provoked by any type of stimulant, including diet pills, decongestants, amphetamines, cocaine, and caffeine (which turns up in unlikely places—including many soft drinks other than colas, over-the-counter stimulants, and cold preparations). Panic attacks may disappear altogether or become much less severe once the stimulant is stopped. Substances taken to reduce anxiety—alcohol, sleeping pills, minor tranquilizers—can cause withdrawal panic attacks when their use is cut down or stopped suddenly.

Panic attacks are also sometimes caused by a medical condition—most likely overactivity of the thyroid or adrenal gland, asthma, or a heart arrhythmia. This differential diagnosis works both ways. Some people going to a psychiatrist with a suspected diagnosis of Panic Disorder wind up having a medical cause for it. Lots of people going to cardiologists or emergency rooms with a suspicion of heart problems wind up instead with a diagnosis of Panic Disorder.

Panic attacks can occur as part of a number of the other anxiety disorders but these differ from Panic Disorder in that the attacks are always caused by a specific trigger. For example, someone with a snake phobia may have a panic attack if a garden snake turns up in the backyard or he or she even suspects one might be lurking there. Someone afraid of public speaking might panic on the speaker's platform. If you have an Obsessive-Compulsive Disorder preoccupation with contamination (page 101) you may have a panic attack when caught off-guard in front of a sloppy sink. If you have Posttraumatic Stress Disorder (page 110) after being in combat, you might have a panic attack the next time a car backfires. Panic Disorder is diagnosed only when at least some of the panic attacks come on completely out of the blue and without a clear trigger.

AM I OKAY?

Having an isolated panic attack does not mean that you have Panic Disorder. Surveys show that about 25 percent of the general population have a single panic attack at some point in their lives, but very few ever go on to have full-blown Panic Disorder. Different people react differently to having a panic attack. Some are so rattled that they cannot stop thinking about it or worrying about when it will happen again. Most just shrug off the experience and move on without giving it much thought. The diagnosis of Panic Disorder applies when the attacks are frequent, terribly upsetting, and/or have a significant impact on your life.

TREATMENT OPTIONS

You can beat Panic Disorder. There are many treatments that work and almost everyone will eventually get better. Virtually every need and preference can be accommodated. Medications and psychotherapy, either alone or in combination, are very effective and fortunately there are lots of different medications and different psychotherapies.

Most of the antidepressant medications also block unexpected panic attacks, usually in the same doses that work for depression and after a period of three to six weeks. Anxiety and agitation can be side effects of antidepressant medications especially in Panic Disorder patients who are very sensitive to these feelings. It is good to begin lower (and go slower in dosing) than would be the case in depression.

Antianxiety drugs like Xanax, Ativan, and Klonopin also reduce panic symptoms and have a much quicker effect—usually within days. Unfortunately, these medications also have a serious disadvantage that drastically limits their long-term usefulness. They are all potentially addictive at the relatively high doses required to reliably block panic attacks. Once you start, it is very difficult ever to stop using these medications because their withdrawal symptoms perfectly mimic what it is like to have a panic attack. One useful strategy that attempts to combine the best of both worlds is to begin treatment with very low (and nonaddicting) doses of an antianxiety medication in combination with an antidepressant or psychotherapy. This provides some immediate relief until the antidepressant or psychotherapy has taken effect. The antianxiety medication can then be discontinued (usually in three to six weeks) without provoking withdrawal symptoms.

Cognitive/behavioral psychotherapy teaches you how to prevent the escalation of uncomfortable physical sensations into full-blown panic attacks. You are probably hypervigilant and prone to catastrophize the significance of uncomfortable bodily sensations. Through therapy, you learn that it is normal to experience a wide variety of bodily sensations—a short run of palpitations does not mean there is anything necessarily wrong with your heart. Your therapist may even give you homework like having you run up and down several flights of stairs so that you can get used to having a fast heartbeat without freaking out.

You are also likely to be hyperventilating, but may not be aware of it. It takes only a few minutes of rapid, shallow chest breathing to blow off enough carbon dioxide to set off reflexes that make you dizzy. Being dizzy makes you anxious. This increases your hyperventilation, which further amplifies your unsettling body sensations, leading to even more anxiety, which in turn cranks up the volume of the physical sensations even further. Therapy can break this cycle. Breathing retraining makes you aware of when you are hyperventilating and teaches you to counteract this by breathing slowly and with your diaphragm.

Medication and psychotherapy each have advantages and disadvantages. Medication works faster and requires less time, effort, and courage on your part—but it may also have troublesome side effects. Furthermore, once started on a medication, you often need to stay on it indefinitely in order to keep from having future panic attacks. Psychotherapy takes longer to work initially and is more labor-intensive. However, the techniques learned in therapy can be applied indefinitely so that remission is often maintained long after the therapy has ended. Some people may also feel more in control if they can avoid the need for medication. One sensible approach is to start medication and psychotherapy simultaneously and then very gradually taper away the medication once the psychotherapy is taking hold and you are feeling better.

After you gain confidence that you are free of at least the worst of the panic symptoms, the target of treatment shifts to the agoraphobic avoidance that is such a common complication of panic attacks. The first step is educational—explaining the causal relationship between the panic attacks and the situations that are avoided because of them. Unfortunately, knowledge alone is not enough to accomplish behavioral change—a good deal of work is needed as well. You have to reclaim the dangerous territories by entering them and making them safe once again. This cognitive/behavioral therapy for phobias has an excellent track record in breaking the stranglehold of agoraphobia.

PHOBIAS:
AGORAPHOBIA, SOCIAL PHOBIA, AND SPECIFIC PHOBIA

Avoidance occurring at the right time, in the right place, and in the right measure helps to keep us out of harm's way. Having a clinically significant phobia means that your level of fear is way out of proportion to the actual danger of a situation. This results in paralyzing anxiety and unnecessary avoidance. The range of objects and situations that can strike terror seems limited only by the dark recesses of our fruitful imaginations. For example, *Stedman's Medical Dictionary* catalogs over two hundred specifically named phobias, ranging alphabetically to include air ("aerophobia"), bees ("apiphobia"), the cold ("psychrophobia"), dogs ("cynophobia"), flowers ("anthophobia"), ghosts ("phasmophobia"), heights ("acrophobia"), lightning ("astropophobia"), being naked ("gymnophobia"), odors ("osmophobia"), sermons ("homilophobia"), snakes ("ophidiophobia"), the number 13 ("triskaidekaphobia"), and vomiting ("emetophobia"). Believe it or not, there is even a phobia to having phobias ("phobophobia")!

DSM-IV distills this complicated universe of phobias down to just three entities: Agoraphobia (the generalized fear of a large variety of different situations); Social Phobia (fear restricted to social situations); and Specific Phobia (a circumscribed fear of one very specific situation).

Agoraphobia

The term "agoraphobia" was coined in ancient Greece to describe "fear of the marketplace." In current usage, Agoraphobia is more broadly defined as the avoidance of many different places and situations that on the surface seem unrelated. You may be afraid of crowded places like a supermarket, department store, or movie theater; of driving on a bridge or a busy highway; of taking public transportation; of traveling farther than a specified distance from home; of being home alone—or all of these. Different people have different rosters of situations to avoid and these may expand, contract, or shift over time.

The seemingly haphazard pattern of fears makes sense once you understand how agoraphobia typically develops. Agoraphobia is the end result of your desperate attempt to control panic attacks by avoiding the situations that seem to trigger them. Unfortunately, this fails to contain the problem because panic attacks arise more from within than from without and are likely to keep popping up in different situations. For example, if your first panic attack occurs while driving on a crowded interstate highway, you might begin by avoiding rush hour. As more attacks occur, the universe of dreaded situations widens and your life constricts. The next panic attack begins while you are driving on a bridge, so that bridges are added to your inventory of forbidden places. A subsequent panic attack while you are driving to work has you avoid cars altogether. Additional panic attacks occurring on buses, in stores, or while alone, lengthens the list of to-be-avoided-at-all-costs danger zones. The noose tightens.

The level of impairment and suffering caused by Agoraphobia varies widely from person to person. Some people with this problem are among the most disabled of the patients we ever see in psychiatry and can become virtual prisoners in their own homes. Others can move around freely only within the boundaries of a clearly defined "safe zone" (for example, taking walks around the block, or traveling within a one-mile radius from home), but become very anxious when venturing out into the rest of the world. For others, travel is restricted not by distance but by specific feared situations that must be circumvented. For example, someone who must avoid both bridges and busy interstates has to travel twenty circuitous miles in slow-moving traffic on local roads to get to work. In very mild versions, getting around poses no particular problem so long as the person can avoid relatively few feared situations like crowded stores or restaurants.

Some people will venture into feared situations if certain precautions are taken. Ensuring an escape route may allow you to do things that would otherwise be impossible—choosing an aisle seat in a movie theater, or a table near the bathroom in a restaurant, or taking the local as opposed to the express train because it has more frequent stops. Certain situations (plane travel, cruises, business meetings) may be especially difficult because they afford no easy way out. Bringing along a companion—a trusted friend or family member—often works wonders but can also become a crutch that is hard to give up unless you also start venturing forth on your own. Sometimes, the phobic companion can be an inanimate object or a pet.

According to the diagnostic manual, you have Agoraphobia if:
- You are afraid of going places or doing things from which you might not be able to escape if you have a panic attack.
- Because of these fears, you avoid these situations or enter them only with great discomfort or with a trusted companion.

Social Phobia

Human beings are fundamentally social animals. For most of us, social ostracism, rejection, and public humiliation are as much to be feared and avoided as animal bites, falling from high places, or being trapped in a smothering cave. This leads to the paradox that some people are so afraid of being embarrassed in front of others that they avoid the very social situations that are so important to a complete life.

In the most common form of Social Phobia, the social anxiety is circumscribed and confined to a fear about performance in very specific types of interpersonal activities or social situations. The person functions perfectly well so long as these situations can be successfully avoided. Probably the most common fear is of public speaking. The mere prospect of being called on in class or making a presentation at work is enough to cause a cold sweat. You are terrified of the public humiliation that will result from exposure of your flaws, missteps, or inadequacies. You might say something ignorant, foolish, or awkward; or stumble over your words; or show your anxiety by blushing, trembling, or sweating; or become frozen stiff by the paralyzing fear. You are your own worst critic and imagine that everyone else will be watching you and judging you as harshly as you judge yourself. You are extraordinarily self-conscious and monitor yourself much more vigilantly than anyone else would possibly ever care to do.

The negative effects of intense anxiety on performance can lead to a vicious cycle that serves to perpetuate the problem. For example, a salesman loses his train of thought because he is anxious during an important presentation, blows his punch line, and finally has to sit down feeling humiliated and foolish. The next time he is called upon to give a similar presentation, he is preoccupied with worries that he will mess up once more, overprepares and overrehearses, and becomes so tight that he is likely again to lose his concentration and get flustered.

Other common circumscribed performance fears include using a public rest room while others are present, playing a musical instrument in a concert, being observed while working, signing your name in public, or eating in a restaurant. It is the prospect of being under the watchful eyes of others that is paralyzing, not the activity itself. So long as there is no audience, you can comfortably give a speech in front of a mirror or can effortlessly perform a piano piece.

Sometimes, Social Phobia is much more generalized. The fear is triggered not just by one specific performance situation but instead is a more general response to any type of social interaction. You miss school or work because you can't face the people, avoid asking someone out on a date, and will not go to a party unless all of the other guests are people you already know. At the extreme are those who are morbidly fearful of any situation that involves interacting with others. Such globally shy people tend to live alone or with their parents, gravitate to occupations that allow solitary work, shun contact with strangers, and may even become housebound. The reclusive, painfully shy Laura in Tennessee Williams's *The Glass Menagerie* is a poignant depiction of extreme social avoidance.

According to the diagnostic manual, you have Social Phobia if:
- You are afraid of being humiliated in social situations or when performing an act in public.
- You try your best to avoid social or performance situations and are extremely nervous or have a panic attack when you are stuck in them.
- Your avoidance of social situations significantly impairs your life.

Specific Phobia

Specific Phobias are ubiquitous, but usually not bothersome, because most people can conveniently avoid encounters with whatever is the feared object or situation. If you fear heights, you don't become a window washer working on a skyscraper. People with a fear of snakes avoid hiking on mountain trails. If you have mild claustrophobia, you avoid crowded elevators and decline a ride if it requires sitting in the backseat of a compact car. People with bridge phobias carefully choose their driving routes to avoid negotiating any difficult river crossings. In each of these situations, the person has arrived at an equilibrium that is acceptable at least to him. The benefits of the avoidance (reduced anxiety) seem to outweigh its cost (restrictions on daily routine or sphere of travel).

Treatment for Specific Phobias is usually sought after a change in life circumstances topples the balance and makes avoidance untenable or intolerable. A person with a height phobia is relocated from a ground-floor office in a suburban location to a top-floor office in a high-rise. A family with a frisky Irish wolfhound moves in next door to someone with a dog phobia. A person with a fear of injections is diagnosed as having cancer and forced to undergo chemotherapy. Someone with a snake phobia has to move to Arizona.

The response to a phobic stimulus is both predictable and instantaneous when you are unable to avoid exposure to the feared object or situation—intense fear and a desire to escape immediately. You retain a keen awareness that your reaction is way out of proportion to any actual danger—but this insight does not help a whole lot when you are confronted by your nemesis.

The mechanisms underlying Specific Phobia are varied and interesting. For some people, phobias are just an exaggerated version of inborn, ethologically hardwired, adaptive fears. A baby chimpanzee will respond with fear even to a picture of a snake despite having had no previous contact whatsoever with snakes. A baby or a puppy will avoid falling off a height even though they have never had a previous experience of tumbling. Our instincts prepare us to be afraid of those things that were inherently most dangerous to our predecessors in the world of the last million years. This explains why humans are naturally much more afraid of animals, the dark, being alone, suffocation, drowning, heights, and storms than of the more modern (and now considerably more deadly) hazards of fast cars, busy intersections, electric sockets, guns, unsafe sex, and street drugs. It also explains why animals so exquisitely adapted to the dangers of the natural environment are so likely to become roadkill. Our genes have not yet had time to catch up to the fast-changing dangers of the modern world. This type of inborn phobia usually begins in early childhood and continues throughout life. Although it does not have to be learned, the fear can certainly be reinforced by actual negative experiences.

Phobias can also be learned by exposure to the painful consequences of a dangerous object or situation. What probably starts out as an adaptive avoidance meant to prevent subsequent brushes with similar dangers is then taken to an extreme and indiscriminate generalization. Being in a car accident may lead to complete reliance on public transportation; a minor dog nip from a German shepherd pup triggers a fear of all dogs; and being stuck in a crowded elevator provokes a fear of all closed-in spaces.

Some phobias develop through the more vicarious method of learning by example. This is most often seen in the children of parents who were themselves afflicted with severe phobias. One twenty-five-year-old woman was so afraid of dogs that she would avoid living, and even walking, in residential neighborhoods for fear of ever encountering an unleashed dog. Although she had never touched an animal of any sort in her entire life, she came by her fear honestly; her mother was terrified by the prospect even of seeing a dog from across the street. Similarly, many people are terrified of swimming because their parents are so deathly afraid of drowning. Phobias can also spread via the media. Many individuals with a morbid fear of flying have never flown in a plane or had a close relationship with a plane crash survivor. However, the vivid reports of plane crashes that monopolize newspapers and broadcast news are sufficient to reinforce an irrational fear of flying. People without any risk factors may develop an AIDS phobia in response to the repeated well-intentioned warning messages blitzing the airwaves.

Unpleasant exposure to the feared danger is usually only part of the story in causing phobias—not every person who is bitten by a dog develops a dog phobia. Certain people are especially inclined to develop phobias, particularly those born with sensitive triggers and those who are temperamentally shy, inhibited, fearful, and risk-averse.

The diagnostic manual groups the Specific Phobias into four different types. The Animal Type includes phobias to dogs, cats, snakes, spiders, insects, or rodents. The Natural Environment Type includes phobias to storms, heights, or water. These evolutionarily determined phobias usually start in childhood, are most likely to be "hardwired," and often require no special traumatic experience to get them started.

The Blood-Injection-Injury Type includes phobias to seeing blood or having a medical or dental procedure. This is a particularly fascinating phenomenon. The sight of blood, having an injection, or seeing an animal killed on the road can make you light-headed and even faint because of a sudden lowering of pulse and blood pressure. This is just the opposite of the increased heart rate and blood pressure that occur routinely in all of the other kinds of phobias. As always, nature is devilishly clever. All of the other phobias mimic a "fight or flight" activation of the cardiovascular system. Here, we see an exaggeration of an opposite but equally adaptive physiological response—a lowering of blood pressure that would serve to reduce the bleeding from a traumatic injury.

Most Situational Type phobias (fears of driving, being alone, or taking public transportation) start in early adulthood and are more likely to develop as a learned response to an actual traumatic experience, like a car accident or being a crime victim. Additional fairly common phobias include fears of vomiting, choking, or contracting an illness such as AIDS.

According to the diagnostic manual, you have Specific Phobia if:
- You are unreasonably and excessively afraid of a particular object or situation.
- When you are exposed to the situation, you immediately and predictably react with severe anxiety or a panic attack.
- You recognize that you are much more afraid of the object or situation than makes sense.
- You try your best to avoid these situations or else you endure them only with intense dread.
- Your fear or avoidance of the object or situation significantly interferes with your life.

DIFFERENTIAL DIAGNOSIS

Fear and avoidance occur in many other psychiatric disorders. A thirty-one-year-old pregnant woman develops Posttraumatic Stress Disorder (page 110) after losing her husband and fetus in a gruesome car accident. Afterward, she refuses to be a passenger in the front seat of a car because of the terror this trigger invokes in her. A young man with an Obsessive-Compulsive Disorder (page 101) who is preoccupied with becoming contaminated avoids public bathrooms because he is worried that exposure to them will trigger unbearable anxiety. A young child with Separation Anxiety Disorder (page 406) becomes hysterically frightened and tearful whenever his parents go out for the evening. A teenage girl with Anorexia Nervosa (page 157) is mortified when she has to go out with her family to a restaurant because she is afraid that the menu will contain only high-calorie foods. A forty-year-old delusional man (page 303) who is convinced that all his phone calls are being monitored by the CIA avoids using the telephone at all costs. A separate diagnosis of Specific Phobia is not necessary if the fear and avoidance are part of another condition described in this book.

AM I OKAY?

Most of us have at least one situation we fear more than makes sense. A clinical diagnosis of one of the Phobic Disorders is appropriate only if the avoidance exerts a significant negative impact on your life. Suppose you have an irrational fear of flying but don't have to travel for your work. You may never get to see Europe, but you can certainly have a very satisfying life without ever boarding an airplane. In contrast, if you are a sportscaster who has to cover games all across the country, the fear of flying will result in an awful lot of highway mileage, a change in careers, or white-knuckling the flights. A fear of earthquakes is no big deal if you live on the East Coast but may make your life an unrelieved misery if you are stuck in California.

Similarly, some degree of social anxiety is more rule than exception for most people. Very few of us are completely comfortable when giving a speech or having to mingle with strangers at a party. In clinical Social Phobia, however, the anxiety becomes torture and impairs your ability to perform or to put yourself in play at all. Most socially anxious individuals rationalize away their avoidance—you decline the party invitation because you are "busy," avoid the blind date because you are overworked, and refuse the job interview because you don't want extra responsibility. In judging whether social avoidance is causing you trouble, please take into account all the wonderful experiences in life you may be missing. Don't justify your avoidance as being a matter of taste or habit.

TREATMENT OPTIONS

Short-term cognitive/behavioral psychotherapy is the clear winner here. The most effective technique is exposure therapy. This simple and straight-forward approach capitalizes on the fact that we quickly get used to things, however unpleasant. Pool water that feels "freezing" when we first jump in becomes comfortable in just a few minutes. After a while, we no longer notice a bad smell in the air and some people can't fall asleep without what has become the reassuring sound of street traffic.

Similarly, the sting can be taken out of a phobic anxiety if you are repeatedly and systematically exposed to it and face down the things you are afraid of. One strategy is akin to dipping your toe in the water to get your body acclimated in gradual stages. You expose yourself to the feared phobic stimulus one small step at a time, starting with the least upsetting task (imagining a dog) and moving toward the most difficult (petting a friendly golden retriever). Flooding is an exposure strategy that is more like taking a running jump into the pool. This works faster but you have to be willing to endure prolonged exposure to your most feared situations. One of the authors defeated his height phobia by spending several afternoons climbing up and down the narrow steps of a pyramid, forcing himself to look down while fantasizing what it would be like to fall. Exposure therapy works remarkably well whether it is done in "baby steps" or with the "sink or swim" technique. Choose the one that best suits you. A few sessions of clenched fists and sweaty palms may translate into years of freedom from fear. However, most people will prefer the more gradual approach.

Phobia prevention also requires a willingness to immediately reexpose yourself to the feared situation. If a child falls off a swing, he should be put right back on or he may be afraid of swings for life. Similarly, if you have a car accident, try to get back behind the wheel as soon as possible. If you get knocked down by a wave and swallow water, go back in and keep swimming. And if you are mugged in broad daylight near your office, go back to the scene of the crime so that it does not retain a toxic association.

If one person in a family has severe phobias, it is not very long before everyone gets involved as a phobic partner. Phobic partnerships have their strong and weak points. Physically accompanying the phobia sufferer through phobic situations is often the only way of getting the person to venture forth into danger zones, at least at the beginning. However, the phobic partnership can foster excessive dependency and become a difficult-to-give-up crutch, especially if it is also meeting the family member's need to be helpful or to avoid his own phobias. The therapy is usually most effective when it includes the person with the phobia as well as any potential phobic partners, like spouses, siblings, parents, or children. This helps relieve initial anxiety by ensuring a secure phobic companionship initially, but then encourages the patient to give it up gradually as the treatment starts working.

We have already discussed how antidepressants can be effective in reducing or eliminating panic attacks. This is often a necessary prelude to the successful treatment of Agoraphobia. If you are confident that you will no longer have disabling panic attacks, it becomes much easier to brave the feared situations that previously were out of bounds. One by one, danger zones become drained of their ability to trigger anxiety and instead become safe places. Antianxiety medications (like Valium, Xanax, Ativan) are sometimes helpful by temporarily preventing the anxiety that is being triggered by the phobic stimulus. As already mentioned, however, this class of medicines should be used with great caution because they can be both psychologically and physically addicting. They are most useful only in small and occasional doses as a kind of "insurance policy" to help you to confront the phobic situation. Often the knowledge that you have a pill ready at hand to take "just in case" is enough reassurance to spur you onward. You will usually never need the pill.

Two very different types of medication treatment are used in Social Phobia, depending on whether the fears are circumscribed or generalized. Medications called beta blockers can be very helpful for circumscribed performance anxieties because they blunt the body's adrenaline response. This reduces the physical manifestations of anxiety—blushing, sweating, trembling, and racing heart. You may feel anxious inside, but will not show it on the outside. It builds your confidence knowing that whatever anxiety you feel can be kept as your secret and will not be obvious to everyone around you. For the generalized type of Social Phobia, the SSRI's (Prozac, Zoloft, Paxil, Luvox) and the MAO inhibitors (Nardil and Parnate) are often effective in reducing both the discomfort and the social avoidance.

GENERALIZED ANXIETY DISORDER

Some people seem to be nervous, tense, and anxious almost all of the time. Usually this starts early in life and becomes a way of life. You feel like a spring that is wound way too tight. At the slightest provocation, or maybe without any external trigger at all, waves of worry and fear flood your thinking so that it becomes hard to concentrate on anything else. After hearing about a car crash on the radio, you spend the rest of the day wondering about whether your children will get home safely. After reading about a single reported case of meningitis in Florida, you frantically call your elderly parents several times a day for updates on their health. Every down day in the stock market leads to a tension-filled evening of worrying about whether there will be enough money left for your retirement. An off-handed negative remark from your boss results in a night of sleepless worry about being fired.

This chronic state of tension, irritability, and feeling on edge is exhausting and terribly inefficient. So much psychic energy is expended on fruitless worry that little is left for productive pursuits. With apologies to Shakespeare—a brave man dies just once, someone with Generalized Anxiety Disorder dies a thousand deaths.

According to the diagnostic manual, you have Generalized Anxiety Disorder if:

- You are excessively anxious, worry about all kinds of things, and find it difficult to control the worry.
- Along with anxiety and worry, you have at least three of the following six symptoms:
  (1) You feel restless or on edge.
  (2) You get tired easily.
  (3) You have trouble concentrating or your mind goes blank.
  (4) You feel irritable.
  (5) Your muscles are tense.
  (6) You have trouble falling or staying asleep.
- The anxiety is not related to substance or medication use, to having a medical illness, or to having another psychiatric disorder.

DIFFERENTIAL DIAGNOSIS

Anxiety is a common side effect of any substance that can rev up the central nervous system—most especially caffeine, diet pills, cocaine, and speed. For most people the effect is dose-related (the more one takes, the higher the risk for anxiety), but some people are exquisitely sensitive and develop anxiety even at low doses. As with panic attacks, substances that depress the central nervous system (like alcohol, tranquilizers, sleeping pills, narcotics) cause anxiety when they are withdrawn. Prescription medications are also common causes of anxiety, especially those that are used to treat asthma, high blood pressure, and Parkinson's disease. The antidepressant and antipsychotic medications sometimes have anxiety as a potential side effect. If you are taking any medication and are experiencing anxiety, ask your doctor whether there might be a connection. No matter what, though, do *not* go off your medication without first speaking to your doctor—stopping suddenly could make things worse. Medical problems such as cardiovascular disease or oversecretion of thyroid, adrenal, or parathyroid hormone must also be considered as a possible cause of anxiety.

Anxiety is often no more than an associated feature of another psychiatric disorder. A common error made by clinicians and patients alike is to focus attention exclusively on treating whatever anxiety is present without considering whether it signals the presence of an underlying condition. A pharmaceutical company is currently capitalizing on this trend by running magazine advertisements imploring anyone with the symptoms described in the first two criteria to contact their primary care doctor to obtain medication. They conveniently leave out the third criterion, which makes it clear that Generalized Anxiety Disorder is a "diagnosis of exclusion"—to be considered only after other sources for the anxiety have been fully ruled out.

You can distinguish among the various anxiety disorders based on what triggers the anxiety and what form it takes. In Panic Disorder, the anxiety comes on abruptly, often out of the blue, reaches an intense panic peak in just a few minutes, and then disappears within a few hours. The anxiety in phobias is tightly tied to the phobic stimulus and occurs only when you are confronted by your triggering fear and can't get out of harm's way. In contrast, the anxiety in Generalized Anxiety Disorder is long-term and is not yoked to any specific trigger.

AM I OKAY?

Worry has both its upside and its downside. A proper bit of controlled worry is a great motivator to get you to study for tests, submit your taxes on time, and save money for the future. In contrast to "normal" worries that serve to focus attention and motivate behavior, the worries in this disorder are wildly excessive, uncontrolled, misplaced, counterproductive, and interfere with your ability to handle the problem effectively. The worries pervade your thinking, involve a wide range of different situations, and far exceed any rational calculation of the risks being faced. For example, it would clearly be excessive to worry so much about passing a course that you can't study for a final examination or to worry constantly about your child from the moment he walks out the front door in the morning until he comes back from school in the afternoon. On the other hand, worrying enough about a test to study for it or worrying for several days about a child going to camp for the first time would be realistic and well within the bounds of normal.

Treatment Options

Cognitive/behavioral psychotherapy focuses on reducing the tendency toward catastrophization that underlies much of the worrying in Generalized Anxiety Disorder. You are taught to identify the exaggerations and distortions that feed your worries and to substitute more rational and realistic alternatives. The first step is to identify your "end of the world," "the sky is falling," "Chicken Little" kind of thinking. "Just because my husband is ten minutes late from work does not mean he has been killed in a car accident—it is just my tendency to make a mountain out of a molehill working overtime." Many individuals worry excessively because they experience themselves as passively helpless creatures in a hostile world where everything that possibly can go wrong will go wrong. Assertiveness training can help to build a sense of self-confidence, mastery, and control. "Certainly some things will always go wrong, that is to be expected, but it is no big deal and I'll handle it when it happens."

Effexor and Buspar are the only medications approved by the FDA for the treatment of Generalized Anxiety Disorder. They have the virtues of not being addicting, having minimal side effects, and not causing withdrawal symptoms, but some psychiatrists have found their effectiveness to be sometimes disappointing. Other antianxiety medicines like Valium, Xanax, Ativan, or Klonopin are very often effective in the short term, but often lose their effectiveness over the long term.

Psychotherapy and/or Buspar are much safer bets given the persistent nature of this condition and the fact that medication may be needed for the long haul. Many people who appear to have Generalized Anxiety Disorder also suffer from depression. For many of these people, antidepressant medication will treat not just the depression but the anxiety symptoms as well. Therefore, if you have any symptoms of depression, even if it seems as though you are depressed because of your anxiety problems, it may make sense for your doctor to prescribe an antidepressant medication for you first.

Suggested Additional Readings

Triumph over Fear: A Book of Help and Hope for People
with Anxiety, Panic Attacks, and Phobias
Jerilyn Ross and Rosalynn Carter
Bantam, 1995

Don't Panic: Taking Control of Anxiety Attacks
R. Reid Wilson, Ph.D.
HarperCollins, 1996

Anxiety Disorders and Phobias: A Cognitive Perspective
Aaron T. Beck, Gary Emery, and Ruth L. Greenberg
Basic Books, 1990

Beyond Shyness: How to Conquer Social Anxieties
Jonathan Berent and Amy Lemley
Fireside, 1994

The Hidden Face of Shyness: Understanding & Overcoming Social Anxiety
Franklin Schneier, M.D., and Lawrence Welkowitz, Ph.D.
Avon Books, 1996

Where to Go for Help
(Self-help, support, for more information)

Anxiety Disorders Association of America

11900 Parklawn Drive
Suite 100
Rockville, MD 20852-2624
(301) 231-9350
FAX: (301) 231-7392
Web: http://www.adaa.org/

Agoraphobics in Motion (A.I.M.)
(self-help group)

1729 Crooks
Royal Oak, MI 48067-1306
(248) 547-0400

Phobics Anonymous
(twelve-step group)

P.O. Box 1180
Palm Springs, CA 92263
(619) 322-COPE

ABIL, Inc.
(support group for Agoraphobia, anxiety or panic disorders)

3805 Cutshaw Avenue
Suite 415
Richmond, VA 23230
(804) 353-3964
FAX: (804) 353-3687
E-mail: abil1996@aol.com

TERRAP (TERRitorial APprehensiveness)
(national network of treatment clinics for Agoraphobia)

932 Evelyn Street
Menlo Park, CA 94025
(650) 327-1312

CHAPTER 4

OBSESSIONS
OR COMPULSIONS

Rituals and superstitions are an essential part of human existence. They give us a sense (sometimes illusory) of exerting control over external events and inner impulses that are usually more out of our control than we would like to admit. For many people, daily life is infused with knocking on wood, not stepping on cracks, or throwing salt over a shoulder. All of us live with, and by, rituals and compulsive acts that have an adaptive component at their core. These can get out of hand, however. Feverishly washing one's hands until the skin is raw in response to obsessive concerns about contamination is a distorted version of a healthy impulse to stay clean. Obsessive-Compulsive Disorder (OCD) is present when the attempts to exert control over your inner and outer world have themselves become uncontrollable.

This disorder used to be encountered only rarely in clinical practice. Most people suffered with OCD in silence either because they were too embarrassed to seek help or too pessimistic about the prospects for successful treatment. This has changed radically now with the availability of very effective and well-publicized treatments. We now know that OCD is a fairly common problem occurring in about 2.5 percent of the general population.

According to the diagnostic manual, you have Obsessive-Compulsive Disorder if:
- You have had either obsessions or compulsions (or most likely both):
  - (1) Obsessions are disturbing thoughts, impulses, or images that you find very distressing but which keep coming back to you even when you try to think about something else.

(2) Compulsions are repetitive ritualized behaviors (or thoughts) that you are driven to do (or think) to relieve the anxiety caused by obsessions.

- The obsessions and compulsions are upsetting to you, take up a lot of your time (more than an hour a day), or interfere with your life in some important way.

DESCRIPTION

The term "obsession" has gained a widespread and broad usage in colloquial speech to mean any worry, preoccupation, or rumination. In psychiatry, the term has a much narrower meaning. Obsessions are extremely upsetting and anxiety-provoking thoughts that are completely alien to your usual sense of yourself and what you should be thinking about. A devoted mother is tortured by the recurring image of stabbing her child; a nun has sacrilegious thoughts that "God" is "dog" spelled backward; or a faithful husband is haunted by pornographic images that disgust him. Obsessions seem to come from nowhere, are outside your control, and are experienced as intrusive, inappropriate, and not making any sense. The most common obsessions involve contamination, doubting, ordering, and aggressive or sexual impulses. Everyday worries about real-life problems like shaky finances, job problems, or difficult personal relationships do not count as obsessions.

The word "compulsion" has also acquired a misleadingly broad popular usage. In everyday speech, it is used to describe any repetitive (and usually pleasurable) action that is hard to resist (e.g., "compulsive" eating, drugs, sex, gambling, or shopping). In psychiatry, the term "compulsion" has a much narrower meaning that entails a different and very specific motivation. It refers only to those repetitive and ritualized behaviors that are performed in order to neutralize the anxiety that accompanies an obsession. For example, nonstop hand-washing is an attempt to alleviate the anxiety triggered by the obsession that one is contaminated. Even though hand-washing gives you a temporary sense of relief, it is not an inherently pleasurable activity.

Perhaps the most poignant aspect of OCD is your inability to control the ritualistic behavior despite the realization that it is maladaptive and self-destructive. You want to resist the compulsion but any attempt to do so inevitably leads to an increase in anxiety. At the extreme, you may become a total slave to the compulsion and spend every waking hour devoted to performing futile rituals. This disorder inflicts a cruel paradox on its sufferers. Although you are preoccupied with the need to be in control of things, you instead come to experience your life as being more and more controlled by the intrusive and unwanted obsessions and compulsions.

Obsessions and compulsions go hand in hand—people who have one almost always also have the other. One of the most common obsessive/compulsive combinations involves contamination. You cannot get over the horrifying thought of being filthy or covered with "germs" particularly after contact—shaking hands, touching money, reading a newspaper, or going to the bathroom. The consequent cleaning compulsions may involve extraordinarily vigorous, meticulous, and constant hand-washing, body cleansing, clothes cleaning, dish washing, furniture dusting, or floor scrubbing in a futile attempt to eradicate every germ.

Another common OCD pairing links obsessive doubting with compulsive checking. An exceedingly careful driver cannot get over the thought of having possibly run over a small dog while backing out of the driveway. The person returns to the driveway over and over and over and over again to the exact same spot in order to check and recheck and recheck for signs of blood. Or you check the oven ten times to be sure that it is off but still have to go back that eleventh time to be absolutely sure . . . and before long a twelfth time, a thirteenth, and so on. Front doors can be a special problem. Some people are always late for work because they must repeatedly check that their house is locked. Others spend many hours every day going back and forth from the kitchen to the front door before they finally feel that the house is safely locked. Others spend hours before sleep shuttling back and forth from bed to front hallway.

Ordering compulsions are associated with obsessions about disarray or asymmetry. A person may spend many hours ensuring that every wall hanging in the house is perfectly straight or that each piece of furniture is perfectly aligned. A Ph.D. candidate who is obsessed with the prospect of making an error in the doctoral dissertation ritualistically orders and reorders the references. You may have to check that every item in the house is precisely in its assigned place before you can go to sleep.

Some compulsions are meant to neutralize the anxiety associated with sexual, sacrilegious, or violent obsessions. A devout woman struggles to banish intrusive thoughts of having sex with Christ by constant prayer and counting rituals. The mother who cannot eradicate the recurrent mental image of plunging a knife through her child's heart is compelled to check his chest methodically to ensure that there is no wound, must ensure that all of the knife drawers are padlocked, and spends hours a day praying for the child's safety.

While OCD sometimes starts in childhood (especially in males), the onset is usually in adolescence or early adulthood. Without treatment, most people with this disorder have a waxing and waning course, with worsenings often related to stress. The severity varies greatly from one person to another. In milder cases, you experience considerable distress as a result of the obsessions or compulsions but can function normally. At the other extreme are those unfortunate people who spend virtually all of their waking hours engaged in rituals.

DIFFERENTIAL DIAGNOSIS

Repetitive intrusive "obsessive" thoughts and driven "compulsive" behaviors are characteristic of a wide variety of other psychiatric disorders. What distinguishes true obsessions from other repetitive thoughts is the weird and ego-alien nature of their content. It makes no sense to you that you are having the thought or feel forced to do the ritual, but you still can't help it from happening. For example, in Generalized Anxiety Disorder (page 95), the repetitive difficult-to-control worries, although excessive, are realistic (for example, about one's finances or the health of one's loved ones). This is in contrast to the repetitive unrealistic obsession that your house is on fire, or that your daughter has been raped, or that you may stab someone with your steak knife. Ruminations that you are evil or worthless as part of a Major Depressive Disorder (page 33) make sense in the context of your illness insofar as they fit in with the typical depressive theme of being down on yourself. Repetitive intrusive worries about one's health or bodily appearance are better diagnosed as part of Hypochondriasis (page 254) or Body Dysmorphic Disorder (page 256). Repetitive thoughts that represent a break from reality are best diagnosed as part of a Psychotic Disorder (page 303).

The compulsions in Obsessive-Compulsive Disorder are not pleasurable except insofar as they result in a reduction of the rising anxiety that is caused by the obsession. This is in contrast to the loosely named "compulsive" behaviors that characterize other psychiatric conditions that differ from true compulsions because they have their own built-in rewards. These include ritualized eating behaviors that are a part of an Eating Disorder (page 155); the "driven" sexual behaviors in Paraphilias (page 179); "compulsive" substance use (page 120) and compulsive gambling (page 272); and the uncontrolled hair pulling that is a part of Trichotillomania (page 277). These behaviors are all probably better considered impulsive rather than compulsive.

Later in this book we discuss a condition called Obsessive-Compulsive Personality Disorder (page 212). Despite the misleadingly similar names, these disorders are actually quite different. To get a diagnosis of OCD, you must have true obsessions or compulsions. People with Obsessive-Compulsive Personality Disorder (OCPD) have an excessively inflexible and perfectionistic style of dealing with other people, their jobs, or schoolwork, and even tasks around the house. People with OCPD may have a slightly increased risk of also having OCD but most people with OCPD do not have OCD and most people with OCD do not have OCPD.

Am I Okay?

Certainly, most people who are concerned about cleanliness, order, and checking do not have OCD—within broad limits, being well organized is generally a key to success rather than a liability. Similarly, this diagnosis does not apply to every off-the-wall thought or every superstitious ritual that all of us occasionally succumb to. The core requirement for a diagnosis of Obsessive-Compulsive Disorder is that these thoughts and behaviors cause severe distress, lead to impairment in functioning, or are so time-consuming that they interfere with daily life. Methodically checking that all of the lights, appliances, and faucets are turned off, the heat is down, and all the doors and windows are locked may be prudent—especially if one is going to be away over the weekend—but doing it over and over and over again so that you are regularly two hours late to work is not okay. Systematically cleaning your files, updating your Rolodex, checking your appointment book, and sorting the papers on your desk are all good work habits, but repeating the same activity in a redundant and ritualistic way so that it occupies most of the workday suggests Obsessive-Compulsive Disorder. Occasionally avoiding "cracks" so that you don't "break your mother's back" is no more than a harmless superstition unless your avoidance of cracks becomes so extreme that you have to avoid going out on a date—as was portrayed brilliantly by Jack Nicholson in the movie *As Good As It Gets*.

Treatment Options

Medication and psychotherapy are both very effective treatments for OCD. It is of special interest that the medications (Luvox, Prozac, Zoloft, Paxil, Anafranil, Celexa) that are most effective for OCD all have strong effects on the serotonin neurotransmitter system in the brain. In all of psychiatry, Obsessive-Compulsive Disorder has the most specific relationship to a single neurotransmitter system. This suggests that we may soon find out what are the specific brain mechanisms causing OCD which in turn may lead to even more effective treatments.

The most effective form of psychotherapy for OCD is exposure and response prevention. For example, someone who is afraid of contamination is asked to play with dirt from a flower pot and is not permitted to wash his hands for an hour afterward. At first, exposure causes you considerable anxiety and a feeling of urgency to carry out the ritual. However, with repeated and systematic exposure to anxiety, you gradually feel less need to perform the compulsion and develop a greater sense of self-control. The major work of this treatment occurs not in the therapy session itself but in between the sessions with a full court press of homework assignments. Many individuals benefit most from a combined treatment including both psychotherapy and medication. For younger patients and for the milder forms of OCD, psychotherapy is the first treatment used, with medication added after a month or so if there has been no response or if the person has had trouble performing the exposure exercises without it. For the more severe forms of OCD, particularly in older adolescents and adults, medication and psychotherapy in combination are more likely to produce a satisfactory response.

OCD is tough on family members. It is painful to watch a loved one waste his or her life uncontrollably performing useless rituals. Moreover, the patient may force family members to participate in the rituals—helping to check that doors are locked and that there is no blood in the driveway. The treatment will often include the entire family in an effort to gradually extricate everyone from the rituals. There is also a very effective organization, the Obsessive Compulsive Foundation, that provides support both for patients and their families.

Suggested Additional Readings

*The Boy Who Couldn't Stop Washing: The Experience and Treatment
    of Obsessive Compulsive Disorder*
    Judith L. Rapoport
    New American Library, 1997

Stop Obsessing! How to Overcome Your Obsessions and Compulsions
    Edna B. Foa and Reid Wilson
    Bantam, 1991

Getting Control: Overcoming Your Obsessions and Compulsions
    Lee Baer
    Plume, 1992

Where to Go for Help
(Self-help, support, for more information)

Obsessive Compulsive Foundation, Inc.

P.O. Box 70
Milford, CT 06460
(203) 878-5669
(203) 874-3843 (recorded message)
FAX: (203) 874-2826
E-mail: phs28a@prodigy.com
Web: http://www.pages.prodigy.com/alwillen/ocf.html

Obsessive-Compulsive Anonymous
(twelve-step group)

P.O. Box 215
New Hyde Park, NY 11040
(516) 741-4901

Obsessive-Compulsive Information Center
Dean Foundation for Health Research and Education

2711 Allen Boulevard
Middleton, WI 53562
(608) 827-2390
Web: http://www.deancare.com/info/info11.htm

CHAPTER 5

Exposure
to Traumatic Events

L ife has never been a piece of cake for the human race. Each and every day, our ancestors faced an extreme survival test with danger lurking behind every tree and across every ravine. Beyond the ordinary struggles of making a living, there would be the inevitable life-threatening catastrophes. Weather can be terrifyingly fickle and has always challenged us with hurricanes, lightning, floods, tornadoes, blizzards, droughts, and fires. Although we were excellent predators, we were also excellent prey for the odd hungry tiger, lion, bear, or crocodile. Broken bones or infected wounds were often fatal in a nomadic world where everyone who could not keep up had to be left behind. Being separated from the group for any reason meant a certain and possibly violent death. Childbirth wiped out many of the women, tribal warfare many of the men. Violent crime and rape are certainly not modern inventions. Life was certainly short (if not always nasty or brutish) with very few people ever living to see the age of forty.

We evolved a stereotyped and very effective way of responding to horrible experiences. If our life is threatened, we replay the image of the catastrophic event over and over in our minds awake and asleep as if we can't purge it from our system. We jump out of our skin if confronted with anything that even remotely resembles the threat. And we steer far clear from that type of danger or anything that reminds us of it. This is nature's way of teaching us a painful but important lesson.

POSTTRAUMATIC STRESS DISORDER

When these reactions get out of hand we call it Posttraumatic Stress Disorder (PTSD). PTSD is a much exaggerated and chronic form of what had originally been a perfectly adaptive response that helped remind us how to avoid danger. The images of the event no longer are a useful jog to memory, but now instead take on a life of their own that can dominate your life. PTSD is a great equalizer. It causes the very same pattern of symptoms and behaviors regardless of different cultural background and previous personality style. It is remarkable how people who were so different before the exposure to the terrible event are stamped by it to look and feel so much more alike. This represents the extreme case of how a powerful environment can shape human behavior. Sometimes, an experience that lasted only a few minutes can leave an imprint for a lifetime.

The reported rates of PTSD vary greatly, both in the general population (1 to 14 percent) and in those who are at high risk for developing it—like combat veterans, crime victims, and survivors of natural disasters (3 to 58 percent). This is not surprising. Community rates of PTSD are understandably likely to be higher in Sarajevo or in South Central Los Angeles than in Paris or in Beverly Hills. People in a community who have emigrated to escape from war, famine, or oppression are at especially high risk.

Not everyone who is exposed to a terrible event goes on to develop PTSD. The likelihood depends on the nature of the individual and the nature of the event. Some people, particularly those with preexisting emotional or personality problems, are naturally more susceptible to being scarred by a traumatic event. Some stressors are also much more likely to cause PTSD than others—particularly horrible experiences that are prolonged, intense, ugly, and inflicted by other people (e.g., physical abuse, rape, and torture). The risk of PTSD increases with proximity—the degree to which the stressor is right there in your face (e.g., whether you are close enough to a fire so that you are burned versus watching someone else being burned at some distance). It is likely, though, that each of us has a limit and we would all develop PTSD sooner or later if confronted long enough with something that is really terrible.

Most of the time, PTSD develops shortly after the exposure to the traumatic event. Sometimes, however, it may be delayed months or even years and is then triggered by something that is reminiscent of the original stressor. For example, someone who shrugs off a severe car accident as no big deal has the onset of PTSD symptoms five years later after his spouse has a minor fender bender.

The duration of symptoms can be quite variable. After a life-threatening experience most people have only a transient response that does not last the one month necessary to qualify for a diagnosis of PTSD (such brief episodes are called Acute Stress Disorder in DSM-IV). About half the patients who develop PTSD recover within the first three months. Unfortunately, a minority develop a more chronic course and continue to have symptoms for many years. Posttraumatic Stress Disorder can start at any age, including childhood, and sometimes persists throughout life.

According to the diagnostic manual, you have Posttraumatic Stress Disorder if:
- You have been exposed to a horribly traumatic event that made you feel extremely fearful, helpless, or terrified.
- You keep reexperiencing the event in different ways, such as upsetting memories or nightmares; flashbacks that it is happening again; or having a severe reaction whenever you are exposed to anything that reminds you of it.
- You avoid things that are associated with the traumatic event; cannot remember the details of what happened; feel detached from everyday life; or feel like you will never have a normal life again.
- You are jumpy and hypervigilant, have trouble sleeping, have angry outbursts, or have trouble concentrating.
- These symptoms persist for at least a month and cause either severe distress or problems with school, work, or other people.

DESCRIPTION

The diagnosis of Posttraumatic Stress Disorder was born originally on the battlefield and was known by a number of names such as "shell shock," "combat fatigue," or "war neurosis." PTSD has always occasioned great interest in the military because psychological casualties are usually more common than physical casualties as a reason for giving up the fight. Horrifying experiences are by no means restricted to warfare. Community surveys show that the majority of us have been exposed at some point in our lives to an event that involved actual or threatened death or serious injury.

Some of the dangers are new, some are old: car accidents, industrial cata-strophes, natural disasters (earthquakes, tornadoes, hurricanes, volcanoes, floods, fires, mud slides), torture, concentration camps, rape, other crimes, and sexual or physical abuse. You may have been the victim yourself, you may have witnessed something terrible that happened to someone else, or you may have been confronted with the news of some horrible thing that happened to someone you love. The stressor in PTSD must be at a life- or limb-threatening extreme level of severity. There are many painful events that cause considerable suffering but do not qualify as a cause for PTSD because they are a more expectable part of everyday life—things like the death of an elderly parent, the loss of a job, fights with a boss, flunking out of school, or the breakup of a serious love relationship.

The misfortune of the moment is greatly compounded by your inability to clear it from your mind. The event haunts you both by day and by night. Vivid memories, flashbacks, and nightmares provide a recurrent and intrusive reexperiencing of the traumatic event. Anything that at all resem-bles the circumstances of the trauma triggers a flood of feelings, fears, and pho-bias. The world seems out of joint and nothing is safe after having been through the terrifying experience. PTSD shakes us out of any complacency that this world is a comfortable place to live or that we are masters of our fate.

After being raped and sodomized in an elevator, a woman replays the event over and over again in her mind, has nightmares about it, relives it whenever she tries to have sex with her husband, and becomes terrified when she sees any short white man who resembles the rapist. She breaks out into a cold sweat every time she walks by an elevator. She feels detached from her husband, takes no pleasure in her job or hobbies, and feels guilty that she did not do more to prevent the rape. She is resigned to never being happy again and never being able to bear children.

A native Californian whose house partially collapsed during an earth-quake moves to New Jersey but still panics every time a truck rumbles by. A driver who survives a car accident that kills his wife is haunted by visions of her bloodied and mangled body, jumps out of his skin every time he hears the screech of brakes, and refuses ever again to drive a car. A Vietnam infantryman who killed and body-counted thirty of the enemy during one night of the Tet Offensive has constant "flashbacks" to the killing ground, can't get over how young "Charlie" was, has a hair-trigger temper resulting in frequent brawls, becomes startled and breaks into a sweat every time he hears a loud sound, is never able to readjust to civilian life, and is surprised that he has lived into his forties. A six-year-old child who witnessed a gang shooting has constant nightmares of being shot, refuses to go outdoors, develops numerous physical complaints, becomes obsessed with toy guns, and is convinced he will never grow up to be an adult. An elderly concentration camp victim who has emigrated to the United States was never able to leave the camp behind. Fifty years after Auschwitz, she remains isolated, withdrawn, detached, and fatalistic. She has disgusting flashbacks whenever she encounters a uniformed policeman, a Hitler documentary, a conversation in German, a barbed-wire fence, or a snowy day.

Am I Okay?

Most people experience considerable distress and avoidance after being exposed to a severely traumatic experience. This is completely normal and even adaptive. To have no reaction whatever to a disaster would not be human. Indeed, the reliving in thoughts, images, and dreams may be essential to the healing process and provides a way of achieving mastery over the event. It is reassuring to know that "this too shall pass," that your reaction to the event was normal, that you did your best in coping with it, that the symptoms you are having are a necessary and universal human reaction and are not in any way a sign of weakness or illness. Assume that you will get better and usually you will. It doesn't count as PTSD unless the symptoms continue beyond a month after the traumatic event.

If you have had a traumatic experience, there are a number of things you can do to help avoid the development of PTSD. The general rule is that an ounce of prevention is worth a pound of cure. Your natural tendency is to try to blot out the terrifying memories and avoid anything connected with the event. You probably feel alone and isolated and reluctant to discuss the experience with anyone else. This is probably the worst thing to do. Instead of having the experiences haunt you intrusively and outside your control, it is preferable to face what happened on your own terms.

Share the story with others who care about you in a way that allows you to reexperience the full range of painful feelings associated with it. If you cry or tremble, so much the better. Rather than avoiding situations that remind you of the event, seek them out in order to "desensitize" yourself. For example, if you've been in a car accident, resist your impulse to avoid getting into a car and instead start driving as soon as you can. This may need to be done in gradual steps—first sitting in a stationary car, then being a passenger, then driving accompanied by someone you trust, and finally going solo. Keep yourself in constant touch with reminders of the event so that you can come to terms with it and get it out of your system.

Treatment Options

If your own preventive efforts are ineffective, and you develop PTSD, the good news is that the symptoms will respond to a variety of different psychotherapeutic techniques or medications, or to both together in combination. The choice of treatment will depend on your preferences, level of courage, and which symptoms are currently most pressing. Since the target symptoms of PTSD often vary with time, treatment goals and treatment methods must be periodically reevaluated.

A thorough familiarity with the nature of the symptoms and the ways to cope with them is the first step toward getting better. The central aspect of psychotherapy is catharsis—a technical way of saying that it is crucial for you to reconnect with the emotional state experienced during the trauma, however frightening and painful this may be. This goes against the common sense inclination to put the terrible memories as far out of your mind as possible. However, to the degree that you fail to face the memories and accompanying feelings head-on, they tend to come back unbidden in the form of nightmares and haunting waking images. You felt helpless during the event, now you have to take control of it.

Exposure therapy takes you from the memories to an actual confrontation with the triggers that recall the traumatic event (returning to the scene of the crime, the site of the fire, the field of combat). This can be combined with methods of anxiety management such as deep muscle relaxation, biofeedback, distraction, breathing control, and assertiveness training. The idea is to put you in the driver's seat. If you can face down your fears, they will hold less power over you.

There was a vivid recent illustration of this. A man who randomly shot twenty-two people (killing six) on the Long Island Rail Road insisted on being his own defense attorney. The survivors of the shooting were the main witnesses against him. This led to a dramatic courtroom confrontation that was played out on national TV. The victims were now witnesses who had a chance to respond to their attacker's lawyerly cross-examination with clear and unmistakable testimony that indeed he was their assailant. They were also able to totally discredit the far-fetched excuses he was trying to offer. Their testimony ensured that he received the maximum sentence.

The need to testify exposed the victims to the memory of the shooting, but also gave them the satisfaction of righting the wrong and mastering their attacker. They were all absolutely delighted by the chance to do this. One said afterward, "As witnesses in the trial, it was our opportunity to shoot back." The turning of passive victimhood into active control reduces PTSD symptoms and reverses secondary demoralization. It is not always possible to reproduce confrontations with original danger in such a dramatic way, but you can usually find ways to expose yourself to reminders of the traumatic triggers, come to terms with them, and move on.

Medications can play an important role in the treatment of PTSD. The most commonly used are the antidepressants and these are often effective even if the PTSD symptoms are not accompanied by depression. The mood stabilizing medications (lithium, Depakote, carbamazepine) may also be helpful, particularly when your problems include aggression, hostility, and flashbacks. The increased arousal and insomnia that often occur in PTSD may respond best to sedatives and antianxiety agents but these medications should be used with caution (if at all) in individuals prone to drug or alcohol abuse.

It is also necessary to say a word about the two most frequent complications of PTSD—substance use and depression. These are so common that they must be considered whenever PTSD symptoms are present and will often require independent attention if the treatment for PTSD is to be at all successful. Detoxification is often a necessary first step, but must be done very slowly and cautiously because the substance withdrawal will likely trigger an exacerbation of the PTSD symptoms and make it more difficult for the patient to participate in the treatment.

Suggested Additional Readings

Coping with Trauma: A Guide to Self-Understanding
    Jon G. Allen
    American Psychiatric Press, 1995

The Scared Child: Helping Kids Overcome Traumatic Events
    Barbara Brooks and Paula M. Siegel
    John Wiley, 1996

Straight Talk About Post-Traumatic Stress Disorder: Coping
    with the Aftermath of Trauma
    Kay Marie Porterfield
    Facts on File, 1996

Trauma and Recovery
    Judith Lewis Herman, M.D.
    Basic Books, 1997

Where to Go for Help
(Self-help, support, for more information)

National Organization for Victim Assistance
(support and advocacy for victims of violent crimes and disasters)

1757 Park Road, N.W.
Washington, D.C. 20010
(202) 232-6682
FAX: (202) 462-2255
E-mail: nova@access.digex.net

National Victim Center
(information and resources for crime victims)

2111 Wilson Boulevard
Suite 300
Arlington, VA 22201
(800) 394-2255
(703) 276-2880
FAX: (703) 276-2889
E-mail: nvc@mail.nvc.org
Web: http://www.nvc.org/

Trauma Survivors Anonymous
(twelve-step program)

2022 Fifteenth Avenue
Columbus, GA 31901
(706) 649-6500

CHAPTER 6

ALCOHOL OR SUBSTANCE
USE PROBLEMS

E ven before they had gotten around to writing history and inventing the wheel, our ancestors had already discovered a whole assortment of ingenious methods for producing alcohol and a number of other mind-altering drugs. The spiritual value of these substances was so highly prized that they became central to the religious and cultural rituals of civilizations throughout the world. Substance use also created "folk" medicine—offering an escape from psychic or physical pain; recreation, relaxation, and solace; and a way to enhance performance and sociability. In the United States, it is a rare person who never partakes of caffeine, nicotine, alcohol, or of a prescription or street psychoactive drug. The significant impact of substances on our brains is perhaps best illustrated by the routine failure of all official attempts to prohibit them.

Most people can occasionally enjoy the pleasurable effects of a substance without becoming hooked or suffering significant negative consequences. An important minority, however, cannot maintain anything resembling a casual relationship with alcohol or drugs. Once addicted, virtually their every waking moment is devoted to procuring the substance, using it, looking forward to the next time, and feeling bad about the last time. They are likely to develop severe psychological symptoms or harmful physical consequences. These negative effects extend for beyond the individual drug user. Substance abuse is also ripping our society apart through its contribution to car and work accidents, divorce, crime, violence, lost productivity, and a general lowering of social cohesion and respect for laws.

If you have a substance problem, you will probably be the last to know it and the first to deny it even when confronted with the most compelling evidence. Long before your liver fails, alcohol will cause blackouts and gastritis;

long before you lose your job, you will be late with your work or have frequent sick days; long before your wife divorces you, she will have complained bitterly about your drinking; and long before you are in jail you will have been driving while drinking. As they say in AA, "DeNile is not just a river in Egypt."

Your life is full of painful contradictions and you have become good at lying—especially to yourself. You love your family but neglect your obligations to them. You wish you had someone to depend on, but can't bring yourself to ask for help. You are taking substances to relieve depression, anxiety, and emotional pain only to make the depression and pain worse when the temporary numbness of intoxication wears off. You may be a workaholic who is not getting the job done, alienating your boss and colleagues. You would be horrified at the thought of going to prison, but ignore the fact that it takes only one episode of driving under the influence resulting in a fatality to lead to a manslaughter conviction. You regularly exercise and take megavitamins while at the same time you are ruining your physical health and killing yourself drink by drink or fix by fix. You are dependent on a substance to lift your self-esteem and sense of mastery only to have the substance lead you into a new and much more binding form of slavery. You try to get out of the trap over and over again, only to be dragged back.

Your denial has many causes—your desperate craving for the substance, the false sense of infallibility that accompanies intoxication, an unwillingness to admit loss of control, a desire to avoid embarrassment, and a lack of full awareness of all the harmful effects. You have probably developed a remarkably short-term take on life with all your attention focused on the urgent need to get high now in order to avoid withdrawal symptoms. The longer-term potential disasters that will likely follow seem too remote to worry about now.

We should avoid the tendency to be moralistic about the short-term decision-making of substance abusers. Most of us are surprisingly short-term in our behaviors and maintain our own denial about one or another pet addictive behavior. Natural selection has favored shortsightedness. Primitive peoples were unlikely to live very long even under the best of circumstances. They, therefore, had little reason to worry about the remote future. One of the authors, for example, has a stubborn inability to resist the short-term pleasures derived from chocolate bars, despite a strong conscious desire to do so for the sake of his arteries. The fact that alcohol or cocaine pack a much stronger wallop on the brain than do chocolate bars makes them especially hard for anyone to renounce. The author is suitably humble about his own limited powers of impulse control.

Most drugs mimic the effects of the naturally occurring brain substances that produce our feelings of well-being, relaxation, pleasure, or excitement. For example, heroin operates on the same receptors that are stimulated by the brain chemicals that modulate pain. Amphetamines and cocaine cause the release of dopamine—the brain chemical that produces pleasure and stimulus seeking. But nature never made available to the brain the extremely powerful and highly concentrated substances that can now be purchased on any street corner. When laboratory animals can electrically self-stimulate brain pleasure centers, they do so in preference to acquiring food and water—and may ultimately die of thirst and starvation. Human beings were not meant to bathe their brain receptor sites with such unnaturally high doses of amazingly potent drugs. It is easy to see why denial is so rampant, why "just saying no" is much easier said than done, and why substance abuse is such an enduring problem for our society.

Substance Dependence usually runs in families, transmitted both by genes and by environments (but more by genes). For example, Alcohol Dependence is four times more likely to occur if you have a close relative with the problem. Identical twins have much higher rates of Alcohol Dependence in both siblings than do fraternal twins. The biological children of alcohol-dependent parents are likely to have an alcohol problem even when adopted at birth and brought up by nonaddicted adoptive parents. Genes, however, explain only part of the risk of Alcohol Dependence. An inborn vulnerability interacts with environmental factors like availability, price, and family and cultural attitudes toward substance use.

Of course, simply reading this chapter is not going to cure you (or a loved one) of a substance use problem. Nonetheless, confronting denial with information and admitting that one has a substance use problem has long been recognized as the necessary first step on the long (and usually rocky) road to recovery.

Literally hundreds of substances cross the blood-brain barrier to influence behavior. Reflecting those substances that are the most widely used and that cause the most significant problems to those taking the drugs (and to society at large as well), DSM-IV has divided the universe of substances into eleven specific drug classes: alcohol; amphetamines; caffeine; cannabis; cocaine; hallucinogens; inhalants; nicotine; opioids; phencyclidine; sedatives; and one "other" grab-bag category that includes less commonly abused substances; prescribed and over-the-counter medications; and toxin exposure. For each of these drug classes, DSM-IV classifies drug-related problems depending on whether they result from an overall maladaptive pattern of drug use (Substance Dependence or Substance Abuse) or whether the problems are a direct manifestation of the effect of the drug on the person's neurochemistry (Substance-Induced Mental Disorder). Of course, drug users typically have both kinds of problems—they have ruined their lives because their cocaine use is out of control (Cocaine Dependence) and also may develop paranoid delusions because they have taken too much at one time (Cocaine-Induced Psychotic Disorder).

We will begin by describing each of these problems and then go on to discuss the special characteristics of each of the eleven drug classes.

SUBSTANCE DEPENDENCE

There are two ways that you can become addicted to a substance: physically and psychologically. Most substances (like alcohol, cocaine, amphetamines, or opium) can cause both physical and psychological dependence. Some (like cannabis, LSD, and PCP) can cause psychological dependence even though they are not physically addicting.

Physical addiction occurs because the human brain is so wonderfully gifted at adapting to any new environment. Nerve cells exposed to an external substance adjust to its effects by gradually modifying the number, configuration, or sensitivity of their receptors for that substance. A small dose of heroin initially has an intense effect on brain cells, but this attenuates as they become accustomed to it. This phenomenon—known as "tolerance"—is really a protective mechanism that allows the nervous system to acclimate to a drug. Because of tolerance, the addict must use higher and higher doses to achieve the same effect—eventually exposing the brain (and body) to what is a terribly toxic brew. For example, the average person has one drink per day, but an alcoholic is likely to drink a bottle of vodka or a case of beer. For an alcoholic "one drink is too many and a thousand are never enough."

Ironically, our brain cells can become so exquisitely adjusted to the constant presence of the substance that they can no longer function at all normally in its absence. This causes the "withdrawal" that arises whenever use of the substance is reduced or stopped altogether. The intense discomfort of withdrawal is what makes it hard for someone to give up the substance unless there is a slow process of detoxification to allow the brain to readapt back to its original, substance-free state.

Up until about twenty years ago, Substance Dependence was considered synonymous with physical addiction—a model that worked best in describing the heroin addict craving his next fix or the alcoholic with with-drawal shakes. This definition did not account for substances that can cause psychological addiction even without physical dependence. Marijuana, the hallucinogens, and the inhalants (glue or paint thinner) often cause little or no physical tolerance or withdrawal, but can still exert an iron grip by cre-ating a pattern of compulsive use. Drug-induced pleasurable or relaxed feelings come to dwarf other sources of satisfaction and the person's entire life may center on getting and using the drug.

The risk of dependence varies among different drugs depending on their characteristics, purity, preferred route of administration, and the social context in which they are taken. For example, the quicker a drug delivers the high, the more likely it is to cause dependence—thus injectable heroin is much more addictive than oral codeine tablets. Only a small minority of individuals who try alcohol end up becoming addicted, but most people who give tobacco a serious try will wind up being addicted to nicotine. Cocaine and heroin are in between. Given the same exposure to a drug, people have very variable genetic risks for developing dependence, but cul-tures that allow wider exposure to substances will uncover a larger propor-tion of those at genetic risk.

According to the diagnostic manual, you have Substance Depen-dence if:

- You have developed a pattern of tolerance, withdrawal, and/or problems controlling substance use, as manifested by three or more of the following:

Tolerance

   (1) You need much more of the substance to get high than you did when you first started using it.

Withdrawal

   (2) You get sick when you cut down or stop using the substance.

Evidence of Psychological Dependence

   (3) You often drink more or use more drugs than you intended.
   (4) You want to cut down your substance use but you can't.
   (5) You spend a great deal of time making sure you have the sub-stance, using it, or getting over its effects.

(6) You have given up many important social, occupational, or recreational activities because of substance use.

(7) You continue to use the substance despite the fact that it has caused you physical or psychological problems (e.g., continuing to drink despite having liver problems).

DESCRIPTION

Tolerance means that using the same dose over time, the high eventually falls flat. A person who originally could get drunk after two shots eventually needs six shots to get the same buzz. Although many drugs cause tolerance when taken often and regularly enough, some are especially likely to require huge doses to maintain the same high—particularly alcohol, amphetamines, cocaine, nicotine, opioids, and antianxiety medications. A veteran heroin addict can safely ingest enormous quantities of narcotics that would result in instant respiratory arrest in a nonaddict or in that same individual after detoxification. This accounts for the common scenario of accidental overdoses occurring in drug addicts after detoxification. What happens is that once back on the street, they fail to take into account the fact that the amount of drug they can safely tolerate drops after detoxification, making their "usual" dose suddenly deadly.

One way to detect the extent of Substance Dependence in people who are denying it is to observe whether they can consume large quantities while showing only mild signs of intoxication. People have vastly different inborn capacities to withstand the effects of alcohol and other drugs. The fact that you can easily handle three or four drinks without getting blasted may mean that you are already physiologically dependent or that you have a high inborn tolerance. Such natural tolerance runs in families and is a genetic marker that you may be at high risk for becoming dependent. One way or the other, be forewarned that you should start controlling substance use before it is too late.

The development of withdrawal symptoms is another sure sign of physiological dependence and a major reason why people stay hooked. What started as fun and experimentation winds up becoming a form of enslavement. When you abruptly stop taking a substance, you develop withdrawal symptoms that are usually the opposite of the desired drug effects. Sedative drugs produce arousal on withdrawal while stimulant drugs produce depression and sluggishness. Perhaps the best-known withdrawal is from opioids (drugs like heroin or morphine, and prescribed medications like codeine)—images of the shaky, agitated, achy, teary-eyed, sweating, nauseated addict scrambling to inject his next "fix" have been prominently featured in film (*The Panic in Needle Park* and *Drugstore Cowboy*). Withdrawal from heavy use of alcohol or sedatives is more dangerous, with symptoms ranging in severity from shaking hands, racing pulse, vomiting, and agitation, to hallucinations, seizures, and even death. Withdrawal from stimulants such as cocaine and amphetamines is much less dramatic, but can still sometimes be deadly. Some heavy cocaine users experience such profound depressions after stopping the drug that they are at serious risk for suicide. The fact that the DSM-IV does not include specific withdrawal syndromes for certain classes of drugs (marijuana, inhalants, hallucinogens, and PCP) does not necessarily mean that these drugs never cause withdrawal symptoms. Although heavy users have reported symptoms such as restlessness, irritability, nausea, and depression, they are so vague and variable that no specific pattern has been consistently observed.

The essence of psychological dependence is losing control over drug use. You try to impose limits but can't stick to them. You go to a bar with an absolutely firm resolve to stay for only one half hour and have no more than two drinks, but wind up eight drinks and four hours later driving home drunk and cursing your lack of self-control. You may fully recognize the negative effects on health, work, and family and vow to quit using, but you are repeatedly drawn back and seemingly have no power to resist. Before long, most of your waking hours are devoted to thinking about drugs, procuring them, using them, getting intoxicated, feeling sick, all the while thinking about how you are going to get your next fix—nothing else matters all that much.

Substance Dependence usually lasts for many years with recurring relapses and remissions. Don't feel hopeless about overcoming the habit. Sobriety is a very realistic and attainable goal. Remember that many others have succeeded. It all starts with honestly admitting to a problem and then reaching out, not for drugs, but to people. You will be amazed at how much better everything looks once you put your heart into beating substance use. Many people wise up young. Even for those who don't, the driving need for substances often becomes less powerful as they enter their forties. People who have failed in many previous efforts to overcome addiction are likely to be much more successful once they are out of the high-risk young adult years. You have probably become far too pessimistic about your long-term chances because of your previous short-term failures.

The up and down course of Substance Dependence is not really different than the course of most other chronic illnesses. In diabetes or hypertension, there are also alternating episodes of greater and lesser control and an occasional relapse now and then. We should not be too surprised or too disappointed when someone with Substance Dependence has a relapse—and it does not help matters at all to treat every fall off the wagon as a moral collapse. People get and stay dependent on substances because of a genetic predisposition and the remarkable power of the substances to alter brain functioning—not because they have a weak character.

The risk of relapse, like the risk of the original dependence, is much higher for some drugs (nicotine, cocaine, opioids) than for others (PCP or inhalants). The longer the person is off the substance, the less the risk of relapse. The one-year anniversary celebrated by Alcoholics Anonymous coincides well with an important predictive marker—having achieved one year of abstinence is a good sign that you may achieve a long-term remission. After five years of sobriety, the risk of having a relapse is about the same as the risk for someone in the general population getting the addiction in the first place—but remember that you still cannot ever feel safe picking up that first drink or joint.

Once you admit you are dependent on a substance, the next step is the tough decision to forgo its use completely and for life. Although there is still some lingering controversy about whether controlled use of a substance is ever possible, perhaps only 1 percent of the addicted population can achieve this for a sustained period of time. You probably wish and would like to believe you are included in the 1 percent, but this is such a terrible bet that it is reckless to try controlled substance use. Usually the attempt represents no more than the early (and rationalized) stage of renewed dependence.

The best motivators driving people to go on the wagon are fear (substance use has caused a car accident or medical problem); guilt (substance use has caused spouse abuse, job loss, or divorce); desperation (a person has hit bottom and has no other options left); spiritual awakening (a person realizes that there is a higher meaning in life); support (an individual finds a home in AA); or hope (healthier substitutions that can lead to a better life). In the United States you are most likely to come to treatment because of a job problem. There are approximately ten thousand employee assistance programs and many people self-refer for help. However, it may be pressure from spouse, family, friends, the law, a spiritual counselor, or self-awareness that leads you to decide to get help. Becoming aware of the problem and seeking help are half the battle. After that, simply showing up on a regular basis is likely to lead to success in treatment. Learn to stick to treatment rather than having a drug addiction stick to you.

SUBSTANCE ABUSE

This describes a binge pattern of using a substance that is not sustained enough to cause either physical or psychological dependence, but nonetheless has harmful and even potentially fatal consequences. Substance Abuse is also the royal road to Substance Dependence. Binge use is the common initial pattern in younger, inexperienced users. In general, about one third of teenage substance bingers or "chippers" eventually become dependent; about one third will not have a long-term problem with the substance; and about one third remain recurrent substance abusers. The actual odds vary depending on the drug (cocaine is much more likely than alcohol to cause this evolution from abuse to dependence); the route of administration (intravenous injection and smoking promote dependence much more than does oral use); and individual vulnerability (people with a genetic tendency are especially likely to become dependent once they abuse a substance). It is important to nip Substance Abuse in the bud. Abuse is dangerous in itself and is often a prelude to a physical and psychological dependence that will be much more difficult to break.

According to the diagnostic manual, you have Substance Abuse if:
- You have developed a pattern of substance use that is less severe than dependence but still causes adverse consequences, as manifested by one (or more) of the following:
  (1) You use the substance when it is physically hazardous to do so (e.g., driving while intoxicated).
  (2) Your substance use has gotten you into trouble with the law.
  (3) You are unable to function adequately at work, school, or home because of your substance use (e.g., missing days at work; getting kicked out of school; neglecting your children).
  (4) You keep using the substance despite its causing serious problems with other people (e.g., having verbal arguments or physical fights).

DESCRIPTION

Typically, the person has no problem with the substance most of the time and may even be totally abstinent for weeks or months. Then he has a chaotic weekend (or weekday) that is characterized by alcohol- or drug-induced mayhem. The most common and lethal form of substance abuse is driving while intoxicated. You don't have to be dependent on a drug or alcohol to kill yourself or someone else in a car accident that occurs when you are intoxicated. There are other commonly encountered consequences of substance abuse—many a child or a spouse has been beaten, many a job has been lost, and many a bar fight has been started by someone who is letting off steam with a "good drunk" that quickly escalates from fun to disaster.

To be considered a substance abuser, a person must have a pattern of problematic binge use rather than being involved in just one single, isolated substance-related incident, no matter how severe its consequences. Moreover, not all "recreational" substance use is substance abuse. There must be adverse consequences that seriously impact on the person's life. Of course, the definition of adverse consequences varies considerably with personal and cultural context. What would be considered substance abuse in a fundamentalist Islamic culture may not have the same legal or moral implications in a more permissive cultural setting.

SUBSTANCE-INDUCED DISORDER

Hippocrates wrote, "People drink to alleviate fear and terror." Unfortunately, the very same people who have used substances to feel better often wind up with psychiatric symptoms that make them feel much worse. It is fascinating that the behavioral effects caused by drugs so closely mimic the psychiatric symptoms we see every day in patients who are not using drugs. The brain has only a few different ways of going haywire (like depression, mania, anxiety, delusions, hallucinations). These same symptoms can be produced either by internal problems in brain functioning or by intoxication or withdrawal from an external substance that triggers the same mechanism. A severe depression following long-term cocaine use resembles Major Depressive Disorder; PCP can cause delusions, hallucinations, and agitation resembling Schizophrenia; amphetamines can mimic mania; and withdrawal from Xanax can look exactly like Panic Disorder. The term "Substance-Induced Disorder" is used to describe the psychological and behavioral problems that are caused by the direct effect of the substance on your brain chemistry.

_____

According to the diagnostic manual, you have a Substance-Induced Disorder if:
- You have psychiatric symptoms that begin during intoxication or withdrawal from a substance. These may include psychotic symptoms (delusions, hallucinations), mood symptoms (depression, irritability, euphoria), anxiety symptoms (panic attacks, generalized anxiety, obsessions, compulsions, phobias), sexual problems (inability to become aroused or have an orgasm), or sleep problems (trouble sleeping or sleeping too much).
- The symptoms are not better explained by a preexisting mental disorder (like Major Depressive Disorder [page 33], Schizophrenia [page 313], Delirium due to liver failure [page 337]).
- The symptoms disappear completely or almost completely within one month or so of stopping the substance use.

_____

You must always be alert to the possibility that drug use may be causing your psychiatric symptoms. Whenever a psychiatric problem occurs only during intoxication or within one month of stopping the drug it is probably due to the effects of the drug. The following table will help you track this by indicating the types of psychiatric symptoms typically caused by each of the drug classes.

	Mood Disorder	Anxiety Disorder	Sexual Dysfunction	Sleep Disorder	Psychotic Disorder	Delirium	Dementia	Amnestic Disorder
Alcohol /Sedatives	X	X	X	X	X	X	X	X
Cocaine/Speed	X	X	X	X	X	X		
Caffeine		X		X				
Cannabis		X			X	X		
Hallucinogens	X	X			X	X		
Phencyclidine	X	X			X	X		
Opioids	X		X	X	X	X		
Inhalants	X	X			X	X	X	

THE SPECIFIC SUBSTANCES

Next we will describe some special features of each of the different classes of substances that most commonly cause problems.

Alcohol

Across the world and across time, alcohol is and has been by far the most commonly abused of all substances. In the United States, most adults have used alcohol at some time in their lives. A substantial proportion (60 percent of men and 30 percent of women) have suffered at least one negative event caused by it (such as driving while intoxicated or absenteeism from work or school). Most people learn, usually quickly and from unpleasant experience, to keep alcohol intake at a moderate social level, or to give it up altogether. Unfortunately, perhaps 5 to 10 percent of drinkers eventually become controlled by alcohol and this results in the astounding number of at least two hundred thousand deaths per year in the United States.

Alcohol is toxic to many of our organ systems, causing cirrhosis of the liver, dementia, gastrointestinal bleeding, pancreatitis, cardiomyopathy (damage to the heart muscle), hypertension, dementia, and fetal alcohol syndrome. More than one half of murderers, and also their victims, are intoxicated at the time of death. In 50 percent of all car fatalities, at least one of the parties is under the influence. Disinhibition due to alcohol is often the critical factor that allows a suicidal thought to materialize into a dangerous suicidal act.

Alcohol intoxication creates well-known and seductive changes in thoughts, feelings, and behavior. As the alcohol levels rise early in a drinking episode, you become extroverted, talkative, and content. Unfortunately, however, the alcoholic doesn't know when enough is enough. With each additional drink, good judgment quickly evaporates and the disinhibition of aggressive and sexual impulses leads to behavior that one is sure to regret—assuming you can remember it the morning after. High enough alcohol levels can lead to death, a fact rediscovered on a yearly basis during college fraternity drinking parties.

Regular daily drinking can be a setup for the development of alcohol withdrawal. Withdrawal begins as blood levels decrease, usually within seventy-two hours after consumption has been sharply reduced or discontinued. Most of the withdrawal symptoms go away after about five days, although some symptoms of anxiety and sleeplessness may persist for as long as six months. Typical withdrawal symptoms include heavy sweating, nausea, vomiting, hand tremors, rapid pulse, insomnia, severe anxiety, and hallucinations. A minority of those withdrawing from alcohol develop *delirium tremens* (or "D.T.'s"), with severe agitation, delusions, perceptual distortions, hallucinations, and a 5 percent risk of death. Visual hallucinations and the creepy feeling of animals crawling on the body may create terror and lead to impulsive dangerous acts. Alcohol withdrawal always requires close medical supervision.

Antianxiety and Sleep Medicines

This chemically diverse group of medications includes both prescription and illicitly obtained antianxiety medications, tranquilizers, and sleeping pills that, like alcohol, are central nervous system depressants. By far, the most commonly used class are the benzodiazepines. There are fifteen different benzodiazepines available in the United States; they include medications such as Xanax, Halcion, Valium, Librium, Dalmane, Klonopin, Restoril, and Ativan. (Rohypnol or "rophies," a street tranquilizer that has recently become increasingly popular among adolescent drug users, is a particularly potent benzodiazepine not marketed in the United States.) Barbiturates (including Amytal, Fiorinal, Nembutal, and Seconal), common drugs of abuse in the 1960s and 1970s, have fortunately declined in popularity. They were particularly dangerous as drugs of abuse because of their potential to kill when taken in overdose. Methaqualone (Quaalude) was so prone to abuse that it was withdrawn from the market in 1984 and is currently available only on the street. Other sedative/hypnotic medications that have varying potentials for abuse include chloral hydrate, Placidyl, and Miltown.

Not long ago, this family of medicines achieved great popularity among physicians and patients in the United States. A scene from the movie *Starting Over* shows Burt Reynolds having a panic attack in Bloomingdale's. When his brother, played by Charles Durning, asks if any of twenty random shoppers has a Valium, about half the spectators reach into their pockets or pocketbooks and throw over their bottles. Because the antianxiety medicines have to a large degree been replaced as a physician and patient favorite by the newer antidepressants (like Prozac), they are now much less often a culprit in causing addiction problems. However, it is wise always to be cautious in using these medicines, particularly if they will be taken regularly for a long period of time. They do have an important role for people who really need them and who have no addiction problems, but should never be used as casually as they once were.

These central nervous system depressants are probably so popular because they constitute a kind of pill form of alcohol, causing similar behavioral and psychological changes (a sense of well-being, impaired judgment, slurred speech, disinhibition, incoordination, and inattention). Not surprisingly, they have cross tolerance with alcohol—if you are addicted to alcohol you probably can handle large doses of antianxiety agents and vice versa. Also as with alcohol, memory impairment and blackouts can occur during intoxication with high doses. The withdrawal from these drugs is like alcohol withdrawal—including increased heart rate, sweating, tremors, insomnia, anxiety, and nausea. Taking these substances can alleviate alcohol withdrawal and vice versa, so that many people become addicted to alcohol and sedatives at the same time, interchanging them depending on availability or taking both together. The longer these medications have been taken and the higher the dosages, the more severe will be the withdrawal symptoms, sometimes including visual and/or auditory hallucinations and grand mal seizures.

As with alcohol, some withdrawal symptoms, such as anxiety and insomnia, may persist for months. This leads to an unfortunate paradox. The symptoms of sedative withdrawal can be exactly the same as those for which you initially began taking the drug. This makes it difficult ever to stop using the medicine because whenever you try the symptoms come back and you naturally assume that you are having a recurrence of the original anxiety or insomnia. For this reason, when antianxiety medicines are necessary, it is a good idea for your doctor to prescribe low doses for only a short period of time.

There are two patterns of dependence with this class of medicines. Women are at higher risk for becoming dependent on medicines that have been prescribed originally by a doctor to treat anxiety or insomnia. A woman finds she has to use a progressively increasing frequency and higher dosage of medicine to get the same antianxiety effect and eventually gets hooked. Tolerance sometimes develops in as few as two to three weeks and dependence can occur with doses that are not much higher than what was prescribed by the physician.

The more common pattern of abuse involves younger people, usually males in their teens or twenties, looking for a recreational high. The progression is from initial occasional usage (often in combination with alcohol or other drugs) escalating over time to daily use, with eventual physical dependence and tolerance. Sometimes people become dependent on these substances after initially using them to counteract the undesired agitating effects of the other substances they are abusing (especially cocaine, heroin, or amphetamines), or to boost the sedating effects of other drugs (especially opioids or alcohol). It is extremely dangerous to use these medicines with alcohol. The combined sedative effects can cause coma or death and the combined withdrawal effects can be devastating. Accidental overdoses and suicides involving the combination with alcohol are not uncommon. Furthermore, these drugs can cause or worsen severe depression.

If you haven't gotten the message so far, let's be even more explicit. Antianxiety and sleep medications do have a definite but quite limited role in medicine and psychiatry. The risks of addiction and complications are appreciable. These medications must be prescribed and used with considerable caution—only for people who have a clear-cut indication and no personal or family history of addiction.

Cocaine and Amphetamines

Cocaine and amphetamines are powerful central nervous system stimulants that cause euphoria, impaired judgment, talkativeness, anxiety, grandiosity, hypervigilance, and a rapid heart rate. Both substances can be smoked or taken orally, intravenously, or nasally. The smoking and intravenous routes of administration are particularly likely to result in a quick progression from recreational use to dependence.

Because cocaine has a short half-life, the addict requires frequent dosing to maintain the "high"—this can lead quickly to a life devoted to doing whatever it takes to procure supplies. Crack is a particularly dangerous form of cocaine that is smoked to produce an instant wallop to the central nervous system. Crack is a devastating public health problem because it is relatively inexpensive, highly addictive, widely available, and is associated with serious medical problems such as strokes, heart attacks, seizures, and comas. The ups and downs of our national crime statistics seem to correlate surprisingly closely with the degree of cocaine use at any given time.

The amphetamine counterpart to crack cocaine is a pure form of methamphetamine known as "ice." Aggressive and violent behaviors are often associated with amphetamine abuse, especially when high doses are smoked in this form. The effects of amphetamines tend to be longer-lasting than those produced by cocaine, regardless of the form of administering the substance. Individuals abusing amphetamines sometimes develop enormous tolerance to the substance, needing ever higher and more frequent doses to achieve the same effects. This requires large sums of money to maintain the habit and encourages a lifestyle of illegal behavior, including stealing, prostitution, or selling drugs. Heavy and prolonged use of either cocaine or amphetamines can result in paranoid delusions and auditory hallucinations that mimic paranoid schizophrenia.

There are two different patterns of cocaine and amphetamine use— episodic and chronic. An episodic pattern of abuse consists of "binges" or "runs" occurring over a period of days and ending when the drug supply has been exhausted. Intense depression and listlessness, known as "crashing," often follows a "run" and requires several days of recovery after the binge. In chronic daily use, the substance is taken almost constantly all day long, usually with increasing doses required over time. Withdrawal symptoms from cocaine and amphetamines may begin within hours and include depression (often with suicidal thoughts), fatigue, vivid and disturbing nightmares, hypersomnia, agitation, increased appetite, and lack of energy.

Caffeine

Caffeine is by far the most frequently used psychoactive substance in the entire world. It is readily available from numerous sources, the most popular of which are coffee, tea, soda, over-the-counter cold remedies, appetite suppressants, analgesics, and chocolate. The average person in the United States consumes approximately 200 mg of caffeine each day. The caffeine dosage varies with source—the most potent and common is coffee at 50 to 125 mg per six-ounce cup; followed by cola sodas (45 mg per twelve-ounce serving); tea (40 mg per six-ounce serving); cold remedies (25 to 50 mg per tablet); weight loss drugs (75 to 200 mg per tablet); and chocolate candy (5 mg per bar). For some especially sensitive people, symptoms of caffeine intoxication may sometimes be observed after as little as 100 mg of caffeine per day. These include insomnia, restlessness, flushed face, diuresis, gastrointestinal disturbance, and increased heart rate.

There was an interesting debate whether caffeine dependence and caffeine withdrawal should be included among the substance-related disorders in the DSM-IV. Certainly, millions of the people who regularly ingest large amounts of caffeine show unmistakable and daily signs that they are physically and psychologically dependent upon it. Deprived of caffeine, they have decidedly unpleasant withdrawal symptoms of fatigue, irritability, headaches, gastrointestinal disturbance, and generally feeling lousy. There are a few people (particularly those with heart problems or Panic Disorder) who get into serious trouble if they are unable to forgo caffeine. Nonetheless, the labeling of caffeine dependence as a mental disorder would have trivialized the concept. The term "mental disorder" has connotations of severity and impairment that don't apply very well to most caffeine users who have developed a stable and reasonably comfortable relationship to their dependency. A desperate need for a caffeine fix has become so ubiquitous that it is now almost normative. There is a section on Caffeine Intoxication included in DSM-IV because this is a problem for some people and is important to consider in differential diagnosis. Caffeine consumption or withdrawal should always be considered as a possible cause of anxiety, sleep, or mood problems, especially in women who, during the premenstrual period, may have very high levels in their bloodstream due to the effect of hormonal changes on caffeine metabolism.

Cannabis (Marijuana)

Cannabis is the most widely used illegal substance in the world (with an estimated 200 to 300 million regular users) and has a long history of use for recreational as well as medicinal and religious purposes. The cut and dried leaves, flowering tops, and stems of the Indian hemp plant (*Cannabis sativa*) are referred to as marijuana, whereas the dried resin from the plant is known as hashish. The main active ingredient in these forms of cannabis is delta-9-tetrahydrocannabinol, or "THC."

Marijuana was introduced in the United States in the 1920s and 1930s. Its use was relegated mostly to fringe segments of the population until the 1960s when it was incorporated into the youth counterculture. Marijuana use peaked in 1978 (when up to 10 percent of surveyed high school students reported using it daily) and then went on the decline until 1992 (where 1.9 percent reported daily use). However, since 1993, surveys suggest that marijuana use is again on the rise.

Patterns of marijuana use vary widely, ranging from people who have tried it once or twice (with or without inhaling), to intermittent users who may smoke one or two joints weekly or monthly, to heavy daily users who have severe problems with dependence or abuse. Like alcohol, the proportion who progress from use of marijuana to dependence on it is relatively low. However, most users of so-called hard drugs (like cocaine, speed, and heroin) start first with marijuana and some people have their lives totally ruined by marijuana dependence.

Marijuana and hashish are usually smoked to produce a high that begins in approximately 10 to 30 minutes and lasts for a few hours. When consumed orally, the intoxication takes several hours to begin, lasts considerably longer, and often results in more intense psychoactive effects. Cannabis intoxication is characterized by a euphoric "high" feeling, grandiosity, inappropriate laughter, heightened introspection, and sedation. Perceptual changes are common—there may be a subjective sense that time has slowed down and that colors or sounds are more intense and vivid. At high doses, there may be intense feelings of being unreal or that the external world is unreal, panic attacks, paranoid delusions, or even frank hallucinations. Physiological signs of cannabis intoxication include rapid pulse, dry mouth, increased appetite, and reddening of the eyes. Tolerance to the effects of marijuana is very variable—some users have to increase their frequency of use, but most do not. A well-defined withdrawal syndrome has not been clearly established, but some heavy users develop symptoms of restlessness, irritability, insomnia, nausea, diarrhea, and chills following abrupt discontinuation.

Cannabis intoxication markedly impairs recall, inhibits ability to store memory, reduces attention span, makes it more difficult to verbalize thoughts, and inhibits one's ability to perform goal-directed tasks that require multiple steps. Marijuana use at school, work, or while performing complicated tasks (such as driving) can have disastrous consequences. There is no convincing evidence of cognitive impairment once the acute effects of the THC wear off.

The long-term effects of marijuana on behavior are controversial. There is little question that some particularly heavy marijuana users have a so-called "amotivational syndrome" characterized by apathy, social withdrawal, and poor concentration. The problem here is establishing cause-and-effect. Do these symptoms result from chronic heavy use or are the people who are characterologically unmotivated predisposed to fill their otherwise empty lives with a marijuana high? The most likely explanation is some combination of both. Laboratory studies have raised concerns about possible long-term health effects of heavy use (for example, cannabis suppresses immune function and interferes with reproductive functioning in animals). There is little question that marijuana smoke causes lung diseases, including bronchitis and asthma. Joints contain much more tar than tobacco smoke and in animals are much more carcinogenic.

Hallucinogens

The psychedelic drugs comprise a diverse group that includes LSD, mescaline, MDMA ("Ecstasy"), psilocybin, peyote, morning glory seeds, and certain types of mushrooms. They have been used throughout history by numerous cultures, often as an integral part of religious practices. The primary feature of hallucinogen intoxication is perceptual distortion. The type, content, and intensity of the experience varies with the drug; with the user's personality, expectations, and prior exposure; and with the cultural expectations.

The perceptual changes may include altered sensations (e.g., colors are more vibrant); illusions (e.g., misperceiving the petals of a flower as blazing flames); visual hallucinations; and a curious blending of sensory experiences that is known as synesthesia (e.g., sounds are not only heard but also seen as colors or felt as touch). Sound or touch hallucinations may also occur, but more rarely. Feelings of euphoria often alternate with anxiety and paranoia, known as a "bad trip." It is also not unusual for the person to experience depersonalization and derealization—a strange and uneasy sense of being unreal and trapped in a dream that will never end. The physical symptoms of hallucinogen intoxication include rapid pulse, sweating, pupil dilation, heart palpitations, blurred vision, and nausea.

Fortunately, reality testing usually remains intact—most people intoxicated by hallucinogens are aware that their perceptual distortions are due to the substance and do not respond to them as if they were real. However, the perceptual alterations sometimes evolve into psychosis, especially when high doses are consumed by susceptible individuals. This can be dangerous and even fatal (e.g., someone who jumps off of a roof believing he can fly or who darts across a busy street to avoid imagined assassins). Terrible behavioral reactions to hallucinogens are especially common in people with preexisting mental disorders, who should do everything possible to stay away from them. The combination of impaired judgment and perceptual disturbances makes driving extremely dangerous.

Tolerance to the psychedelic and euphoric effects of hallucinogens can develop quickly with repeated use. While there do not seem to be any specific symptoms associated with withdrawal, many individuals experience a morning-after psychedelic drug "hangover" characterized by fatigue, insomnia, headache, loss of balance, and sore jaws and teeth resulting from clenching during the intoxication.

Hallucinogen users may experience flashbacks, especially when environmental cues recall aspects of previous trips. Hallucinogen flashbacks may also be triggered by other drugs, anxiety, fatigue, or stress or may be self-induced (i.e., sitting in a dark room and making an effort to conjure up the visual images experienced while previously intoxicated). Flashbacks usually subside within a couple of months of drug use but sometimes may persist for years or may reoccur after an interval of years.

Phencyclidine

Phencyclidine was originally manufactured as an anesthetic for animal surgery. It first appeared as an illicit street drug in the 1960s and soon achieved a surprising popularity under a variety of names, such as PCP, angel dust, hog, peace pill, and tranq. It can be administered intravenously, consumed orally, snorted, or smoked. The most common method of ingestion is smoking marijuana cigarettes laced with PCP. Phencyclidine causes symptoms similar to hallucinogen intoxication, but with even more volatile emotional and behavioral responses—intense euphoria, bizarre acts of aggression, agitation, belligerence, and unpredictability. Fighting, violent murders, and suicide are complications of PCP intoxication. The drug takes effect in a few minutes to an hour and lasts from ten to twenty hours, but especially high doses can cause problems that continue for days.

The intoxication symptoms depend on the amount of PCP taken. Lower doses produce slurred speech, nausea, euphoria, talkativeness, disinhibition, impaired judgment, dizziness, muscle movements, unusual eye movements, and poor coordination. Intermediate levels of PCP intoxication cause distortions in sensory perceptions and body image, an attenuated response to pain, confusion, depersonalization, and feelings of unreality. Delirium, seizures, amnesia, and coma can occur at higher doses. There is little or no tolerance to the effects of PCP, nor does there seem to be an associated withdrawal syndrome. Problems associated with chronic use are most apt to stem from the legal and interpersonal difficulties that result from the aggressive behavior and poor judgment that are typical of PCP intoxication.

Opioids

The opioids are useful medications that are prescribed as pain relievers (morphine, Demerol); cough suppressants (codeine); and antidiarrheal preparations. Heroin is the most notorious member of the opioid family and has no medicinal application. Methadone is prescribed for the control of heroin addiction, but it also has its own appeal as a street drug among opioid addicts. As opioids may be obtained by prescription, it is not unheard of for users to fake a painful illness in order to acquire them from a physician. People in occupations where opioids are most accessible (such as physicians, nurses, and pharmacists) are at an increased risk for developing a problem with their use.

Opioid intoxication—especially early in the course—is characterized by a highly reinforcing euphoric "rush," followed by apathy, sadness, agitation, and impaired judgment. Physiological changes associated with opioid use include slurred speech, inattention, constipation, memory lapse, pupillary constriction, and drowsiness (also known as being on the "nod"). High doses can result in respiratory distress, coma, or even death. While opioids can be snorted, eaten, or smoked, the most common mode of administration is by intravenous injection. People who engage in chronic intravenous use of opioids have puncture marks and develop hardened veins known as "tracks" all over their arms and legs. Sometimes this requires their switching to veins in the neck or groin area or injecting directly into the skin ("skin popping"), often with resulting abscesses and lesions.

Tolerance to opioids develops quickly, especially to their euphoric effect. Before long, the person craves the drug not to feel great, but just to feel normal. Once a person's opioid use becomes chronic and escalates to a level of dependence, it usually remains continuous for several years. Opioid withdrawal (going "cold turkey") is characterized by intense anxiety, muscle soreness, restlessness, nausea, fever, irritability, depression, and a persistent and overwhelming craving for more drugs. Acute withdrawal symptoms usually begin within six to twenty-four hours following the last dosage and may persist for several days. Although decidedly unpleasant, opioid withdrawal has been somewhat overdramatized in the movies and is much less dangerous medically than withdrawal from alcohol or sedatives/hypnotics.

Dependent individuals engage in a remarkably compulsive pattern of use devoting virtually all of their time and energy to drug-seeking and drug-taking activities. The high cost often requires that they engage in illegal activity to obtain their "fix." The addict frequently adopts a lifestyle that would have been unthinkable prior to the addiction, living in squalor, neglecting personal hygiene, engaging in unsafe sex, and sharing needles. Rates of HIV infection among inner-city heroin addicts are as high as 60 percent. Heroin addicts also die from overdose, violence associated with obtaining drugs, suicide, accidents, and other medical complications.

Craving can continue for years after recovery. You approach Manhattan from Newark Airport and suddenly have an intense opioid need as soon as you see the needle of the Empire State Building and have an image of your street contacts near the Port Authority Bus Terminal. You get goosebumps, your muscles cramp, and you want a fix.

Although the opioid medications carry a serious risk of potential dependence, they are simply indispensable in managing some painful medical conditions that do not respond well to anything else. Completely irrational concerns about the risk of dependence have led to a national pattern of undermedication, causing much needless suffering especially among terminally ill cancer patients. Common sense and simple humanity dictate that the risk of addiction is meaningless in this situation and that patients should be made as comfortable as they can be.

Inhalants

Because inhalants are cheap and can be purchased off the shelf at any hardware store or drugstore, they constitute a young person's or poor person's easiest route to intoxication. The most commonly used inhalants are glue, gasoline, spray paint, paint thinners, lighter fluid, nail polish remover, and typewriter correction fluid. Aromatic hydrocarbons are the shared active ingredients contained in this seemingly diverse group of products. The most common method of inhalation is to place a cloth soaked with the volatile substance over the mouth and nose. Others prefer to use a bag or to breathe directly from a container or aerosol can. The effects are rapid (usually within minutes) and consist of euphoria, a sense of invincibility, slurred speech, disinhibition, blurred vision, impaired judgment, visual distortion, dizziness, and loss of coordination. Higher doses can result in respiratory distress, stupor, coma, and death.

Most inhalant abusers are teenage boys in economically depressed areas who are also involved in truancy, delinquency, and family conflict. There is some tolerance to the effects of chronic inhalant use, but no withdrawal syndrome. Long-term use of these substances can result in a "glue sniffer's rash" around the nose and mouth and permanent severe damage to the central nervous system, liver, and kidneys. Death can result abruptly due to respiratory arrest or heart attack (known as "sudden sniffing death"). Many who get their first teenage high with inhalants later move on to other, more expensive drugs as they grow up and into the adult drug culture.

Nicotine

The most remarkable thing about nicotine is that it is by far the most addictive of all substances—tobacco company propaganda notwithstanding—despite the fact that it does not produce a very dramatic high. The ratio of users who become dependent is higher for nicotine than for any other substance, including heroin. More than 95 percent of smokers ultimately become hooked on cigarettes, whereas fewer than 10 percent of drinkers become hooked on alcohol. The unpleasant nicotine withdrawal symptoms probably explain the high rates of relapse among those who attempt to quit smoking. These begin within a few hours of nicotine deprivation and include intense cravings, anxiety, difficulty concentrating, agitation, depressed mood, increased appetite, decreased heart rate, and insomnia. Although more than 80 percent of smokers want to kick the habit, only 5 percent are successful on their own. The use of the nicotine patch raises success rates to about 20 percent, a medication called Zyban has even higher rates of success, and the combination of patch and Zyban may help up to 50 percent of smokers to quit—at least in the short run.

Nicotine addiction can develop with any of the tobacco vehicles, including cigarettes, pipes, cigars, chew, and snuff. The greatest danger in cigarette smoking comes not from the nicotine, but from the dreadful health impact of the tars and gaseous waste products. The patch and nicotine chewing gum are also addictive, but much less likely to cause medical complications. The severity of the dependence is related to the rapidity of absorption and the amount of the nicotine, with smoking being more addictive than the oral or transdermal modes of administration. Paradoxically, the attempt to lower nicotine content in cigarettes turns out to be counterproductive since it encourages people to smoke more cigarettes, inhale more deeply, smoke down to the butt, and cover the filter with their fingers, all of which increase the overall exposure to the more harmful tars.

The despicably deceptive marketing promotions of the tobacco industry are by now legendary. Campaigns have been targeted at teenagers, women who want to be slim, and minority groups. Fewer than half of all people who have ever smoked will eventually stop smoking. Certain smoker characteristics are predictors of success in beating the habit. Those who have smoked many packs a day for many years experience more problems in stopping. People who smoke immediately after waking up in the morning, who smoke more in the earlier part of the day, and those who cannot stop for even one day are particularly hard cases. Unfortunately, most people become addicted in their early teens and smoking often becomes a lifelong and very ingrained habit. Six months after quitting smoking, half the people still report having a desire to smoke within the prior twenty-four hours. This shows the remarkably powerful and enduringly addictive effects of nicotine.

Nicotine addiction is the most preventable of all the causes of serious public health problems. Smoking increases the risk of lung and mouth cancers, other lung diseases, heart disease, strokes, and ulcers. Smoking in pregnant women increases the risk of low birth weight and other fetal complications. Fortunately, widespread education about nicotine has been a great public health success story and the number of smokers in the United States has declined to about 25 percent of the adult population. Many of these remaining smokers have problems discussed elsewhere in the rest of this book, particularly Substance Dependence, Anxiety Disorders (Chapters 3, 4, and 5), mood problems (Chapters 1 and 2), and Schizophrenia (page 313). Treating these problems and using the new methods of treating nicotine addiction that are now available may help reduce this proportion further. Reduced advertising and stricter controls on teenage use may also further prevention efforts. This is no time for complacency. Tobacco use is responsible for four hundred thousand deaths a year—or the equivalent of four jumbo jets going down every day.

MEDICATIONS

Everyone is familiar with the fact that medications have physical side effects like rashes, dizziness, nausea, diarrhea, dry mouth, blurred vision, and headaches. Less well appreciated is that many medications can also cause behavioral side effects like anxiety, agitation, insomnia, depression, delusions, hallucinations, memory loss, and sexual dysfunction. Before assuming that you have a primary psychiatric disorder, find out more about the possible behavioral side effects of any medicines you may be taking. Be mindful that over-the-counter medications (Dexatrim, decongestants, sleeping pills), herbal medicines, nutritional supplements (melatonin), and other holistic preparations may not be completely innocuous. Steroids are particularly likely to cause problems and are often taken inappropriately by athletes and bodybuilders. Also remember that the drugs prescribed by psychiatrists to help anxiety, depression, and psychosis also may have unintended behavioral side effects that can be misinterpreted as a worsening of the illness they were meant to treat.

TOXINS

The behavioral consequences of toxin exposure have been very much in the news these days because of the controversy surrounding Gulf War Syndrome and claims about psychiatric symptoms arising from defoliant exposure, lead poisoning, industrial exposures and accidents, and the "sick building syndrome." There is no doubt that significant toxin exposure can lead to serious behavioral consequences resembling the mental disorders described in the rest of this book. It is, therefore, important to evaluate any possible role that toxin exposure may play in relation to the development of any psychiatric illness. However, in particular incidents, it is difficult (and sometimes inherently impossible) to determine whether toxin exposure has played a causal role—especially when the toxin exposure is questionable or at a low level and when the symptoms are mild, nonspecific, and of the kind that commonly occur in the general population.

For example, it has become clear that some soldiers were exposed to toxins in both the Gulf and Vietnam wars and that many veterans of these wars currently have a variety of nonspecific psychological and physical symptoms that they attribute to the exposure. At least for some of these veterans, this attribution could be an accurate assessment of the possible negative effects of toxin exposure on the central nervous system. On the other hand, since time immemorial soldiers have reported nonspecific emotional and physical symptoms that persist after combat experiences in which there was no apparent toxin exposure. Most likely, these symptoms can be understood as a psychological response to the life-threatening events endured in combat. Moreover, vague psychiatric symptoms are not at all uncommon in the general population and thus may be completely independent of any possible toxin exposure or the combat experience. The lingering controversy surrounding Gulf War Syndrome shows how difficult it is to resolve the question scientifically or clinically or politically.

There is a similar problem in establishing a causal connection for toxin exposures occurring in civilian life. Following either an industrial accident or persistent low toxin levels in the workplace, there may be lawsuits claiming psychiatric damages based on toxin exposure. In the absence of controlled studies, comparison groups, and baseline data concerning the possible presence of preexisting psychiatric symptoms, it is often impossible to know which psychiatric symptoms are due to toxin exposure and which are not. Three questions, each with often nonobvious answers, need to be addressed in order to establish a direct cause-and-effect relationship: 1) Was there potentially dangerous toxin exposure? 2) Are the psychiatric symptoms significant and unfeigned? and finally, 3) Is the toxin exposure directly responsible for the psychiatric symptoms? Evaluating these questions becomes even more complicated when the atmosphere is charged by the legal necessity to determine liability and eligibility for compensation and disability.

AM I OKAY?

A lot of people use drugs and alcohol with no (or very few) negative consequences. They do not develop physiological dependence (tolerance and withdrawal), have no pattern of compulsive use (suggesting psychological dependence), and do not get into the legal, work, or interpersonal problems characteristic of Substance Abuse. Such alcohol or drug use is part of a social, cultural, or religious ritual shared with many others in a way that limits the possible harm the substance can cause. It is of interest that the Air Force recently approved the use of peyote in the religious rituals conducted by its Native American personnel.

The problem is that a lot of people think (or at least say) they are okay in their substance use when really they are not. You started using substances for fun; but after a while, it is not fun anymore, it is something you have to do to feel comfortable. If you stop using the substance, you start to feel dreadful. But denial is tough to overcome and you do not own up to the problem. One simple test of whether you might have an alcohol or a drug problem is the CAGE questionnaire. "Yes" replies to three out of the four questions strongly suggest that you have an alcohol or a drug problem. Even one or two yes answers should get you thinking.

C Has anyone ever recommended that you *Cut back* or stop your drinking or drug use?

A Have you ever gotten annoyed or *Angry* if someone comments on your drinking or drug use?

G Have there ever been times when you felt *Guilty* or regretful for something that occurred because you were drinking or drug use?

E Have you ever used alcohol or other drugs (an *Eye opener*) to get started in the morning or to steady your nerves?

Be especially alert about your risk of dependency if you have a strong family history of substance problems, have a high natural tolerance, or if you have already gotten into trouble as a result of your substance use. Driving under the influence may seem harmless enough, but one accident can be deadly to you or to the person you wind up hitting with your car. If you are driving intoxicated even occasionally, this by itself means you have a serious substance problem that needs immediate attention.

Once you have been dependent on a substance, it is highly unlikely that you will ever be able to use it (or probably any other addicting substance) without an unacceptably high risk of relapse. It is almost always kidding yourself to say that you will have just this one drink, this one joint, or this one snort. Sooner or later, this one drink will almost certainly return you to the roller coaster of relapse and remission that is so characteristic of people fighting a lifelong battle against substances.

The daily pot smoker is often determined to justify regular substance use as a lifestyle issue, rather than as a matter of Substance Dependence—equating pot use with cigarettes, coffee, or having cocktails. Even discounting legal or moral objections to pot smoking as a way of life, it is important to consider the impairments in motivation, concentration, and energy that frequently accompany chronic marijuana use.

By its definition, Substance Dependence must go beyond physical addiction to include at least some elements of psychological addiction. A Frenchman who develops alcohol tolerance and withdrawal as a result of culturally sanctioned heavy wine drinking would not get a diagnosis of Alcohol Dependence unless there is also evidence of a loss of control over his drinking. However, his not having an official diagnosis of Substance Dependence does not protect him one bit from the risks of developing alcohol-induced cirrhosis, dementia, or pancreatitis.

If you have any doubts whether your substance use is okay, get help with it. Accept that you are probably underestimating your problem and downplaying its risks. The most dangerous lies in life are the ones you tell yourself. Remember that substance use is the single best predictor for car accidents, homicides, suicide, being killed by someone else, HIV exposure, and a whole host of medical and psychiatric conditions. It is far better to be safe than sorry. If you have gotten into substance-related trouble (even though it may appear that you are a victim of circumstances, bad timing, or bad luck), take a hard look at yourself in the mirror and don't shrug off what you see. When in doubt, go to an AA meeting and give it a fair hearing. You have nothing to lose, and a great deal to learn.

TREATMENT OPTIONS

The treatment of substance-related problems depends on the type of substance, the specific problems it is causing, the stage of the illness, your insight and motivation, and whether the environment is more likely to support efforts at change or to provide temptations to stay hooked. Before there is even a chance that treatment can be effective, you must recognize that you have a serious substance problem and be motivated to change your behavior and stop using alcohol or drugs. Often the person with the problem is the last to know and will consider treatment only after others confront the denial in the most unmistakable terms.

Unfortunately, our society is also in denial and is not providing anything approaching adequate resources for the treatment of substance problems. Every year there is a disproportionate expenditure of vast sums of public funding in a futile attempt to seal our borders and "interdict" the smuggling of illegal substances. Similar fortunes are spent on the correctional system in an equally futile attempt to seal away those whose crimes are the direct or indirect result of substance use. Despite the best efforts to make drugs unavailable, they remain remarkably cheap and easily purchased on many street corners across the entire country. A new smuggler, a new pusher, and a new addict are all ready to spring up whenever their predecessors are incarcerated. Serious efforts to develop adequate treatment resources have been sacrificed in the mindless (and politically motivated) charade of border patrols and explosive prison building. The entry into substance abuse treatment by managed care companies promises to make this bad situation even worse. These companies enhance their short-term profitability by reducing treatment resources for substance-related problems and are strongly motivated on financial grounds to deny care or restrict its access.

What has been almost completely lost in the shuffle is that treatment for substance-related problems is very cost-effective—especially considering the long-term direct and indirect costs both to the individual and to society of not providing treatment. Untreated substance use leads eventually to expensive medical illness, psychiatric illness, lost productivity, family disruption, policing, judicial proceedings, and prisons. Unfortunately, the allocation of treatment resources for addictions is remarkably shortsighted and system-specific. There is constant penny-pinching, pound-foolishness that fails to account for the indirect cost savings that adequate treatment might promote across the medical, psychiatric, and correctional systems.

For example, the criteria for admission for inpatient detoxification have been set so high that most people who want to beat their addiction are not eligible unless they also have a serious medical or psychiatric problem. This extraordinary stringency in inpatient admission criteria has been justified based on the theoretical possibility that outpatient detoxification will be adequate and the fact that many people revert to their substance use anyway shortly after an inpatient detoxification. Unfortunately, the vast majority of addicts referred for outpatient detoxification never wind up receiving it—either because they don't show up or because the programs are so overwhelmed that they are put on a long waiting list. Left to their own devices on the street, these people are likely to contribute to crime, AIDS, and the spread of drug addiction. Given the long-term indirect costs of not providing help, inpatient detoxification is a relatively inexpensive and worthwhile treatment, even if only a small fraction of the people who receive it are able to make the substantial next step toward rehabilitation.

This is a situation that cries out for staunch patient, family, clinician, and political advocacy—and has so far received almost no such support and lobbying. There are as yet no "addictions" equivalents to the National Alliance for the Mentally Ill (which advocates so successfully for Schizophrenia) or the National Depressive and Manic Depressive Association, or the Obsessive Compulsive Foundation, and so forth. AA is a highly successful organization that provides extremely effective treatment, support, and information but it does not define a political role for itself. This means that there is no counterbalance to the know-nothing good politics (but failed policy) of interdiction, incarceration, and "just say no." We should not abandon hope, however. Ten years ago, Schizophrenia was the lost stepchild of medicine—now it has achieved parity in medical benefit plans, an enthusiastic advocacy that includes many senior politicians, increased funding for research, and a promise of more powerful treatments. We may be on the verge of similar advances in public support and research contributions to the treatment of Substance Dependence.

Detoxification is the crucial, absolutely necessary, and difficult first step in the treatment of all addictions. Some drugs like marijuana, phencyclidine, amphetamines, and cocaine can be discontinued without much problem. Abruptly stopping depressant drugs like alcohol and sedatives can trigger a potentially life-threatening withdrawal. Detoxification of alcohol, barbiturates, and sleeping pills requires substituting with equivalent doses of a sedative (like Librium or Ativan), which is then tapered in a controlled way to avoid withdrawal. Although the withdrawal symptoms that arise during detoxification of opioids are not life-threatening, they are uncomfortable. Medications like clonidine (an anti-high blood pressure medicine) are helpful in softening the intensity of the symptoms.

Patients often fail at this stage because it is so tough to overcome craving and unpleasant withdrawal symptoms. There is also a paradox in physicians' attitudes that may account for the problems many addicts have with withdrawal. Physicians are taught to be very careful and deliberate in tapering any of the psychiatric medications on the assumption that too abrupt a removal may lead to withdrawal symptoms or a recurrence of the illness the medications were meant to treat. In contrast, when it comes to the powerful substances that cause addictions, clinicians usually recommend detoxification regimens that are remarkably abrupt, tapering from extremely high doses to nothing in five days. It is no wonder that such rapid detoxification often fails. Even for those substances that cause no physical tolerance or withdrawal, a more prolonged detoxification period is often necessary to reduce craving and the physical and psychological triggers to relapse.

Our advice to society would be to expend more resources on detoxification so that it becomes universally and easily available. Our advice to the individual clinician and patient is to stay focused on detoxification as a potential turning point in life. Don't be discouraged if there have been many failed efforts at detoxification. Circumstances and people change. Almost everyone who successfully goes on to beat a habit has had a large number of failed previous tries at detoxification. Most addicts appear to be much sicker psychiatrically than they really are because of the noxious effects of the drugs. It is difficult to evaluate someone's psychiatric status if he is forever either intoxicated or withdrawing from a substance. There will often be a substantial improvement in emotional status once the person is successfully detoxified.

During the detoxification period, it is also important to evaluate for any concurrent medical or psychiatric illnesses that have previously been ignored or undertreated. The patients who develop the most serious withdrawal problems are usually those who also have medical problems like cirrhosis, malnutrition, vitamin deficiency, or undetected infections.

Each day that a person succeeds in maintaining abstinence greatly improves the odds of a successful rehabilitation. This led to the development of so called "twenty-eight-day" inpatient rehabilitation programs. While sometimes wonderfully successful and occasionally absolutely necessary, such programs have fallen out of favor because of high costs and high recidivism rates. Twenty-eight-day programs have become a luxury—available only for the rare few who can afford them. A good substitute is an intensive outpatient program or a halfway house that is provided right after, or instead of, a short-term inpatient detoxification. The patient is seen many times a week to continue the detoxification and the medical and psychiatric stabilization, to begin group and family counseling, and to be introduced to social and vocational rehabilitation.

Alcoholics Anonymous (and its offshoots) is the great success story in the treatment of addictions. On any given day, more people go to AA groups around the world than attend any other form of therapy. The message of AA is compelling and translates very well across different drugs, social classes, and cultures. AA groups are so numerous and so varied that almost anyone can find a congenial one that is readily available, conveniently located, and probably meeting that night. AA provides hope, a philosophy of life, a spiritual reawakening, an emotional experience, concrete support, a sounding board, great advice, and help for family members. It is all the more remarkable that it does all this with virtually no bureaucracy or budget.

The goal of treatment must be complete abstinence from the substance, probably for life. Almost always, people with substance problems resist this goal, hoping instead to return to a state of "controlled" substance use. Although there is an occasional person with Substance Dependence who can eventually go back to social use, this goal is totally unrealistic for the vast majority of users. Becoming dependent seems to reflect a fundamental inability—mediated at the brain level—to just have a little bit, without needing more. You may have periods in which you control your drug intake by setting up stern self-imposed limits ("I'm only going to have one joint tonight." "As long as I don't drink alone, it's okay." "No drugs after 10 P.M."). Invariably, and before very long, there are seemingly endless and irresistible reasons to bend a rule slightly ("I'm under a tremendous amount of stress." "I'm celebrating a promotion." "All work and no play make Jack a dull boy."

"This is a special party." "I am cured of my depression and can now control my use." "Therapy helped me understand why I lost control." "Getting sober was easy—I can always do it again."). Soon there is an escalation to the previous pattern of dependency. After another crisis, there may be a new and totally sincere resolve to reassert control, set new limits, and the cycle begins anew. The only way to avoid being trapped by substances is to avoid using them altogether—and this means probably for your entire life.

Maintaining abstinence is hard work. You may have spent much of your adult life intoxicated or preparing to become intoxicated. It is not just a matter of giving up an old life, it is equally a challenge to create a new one. The good news is that most people feel much better once they stop using drugs. However much fun the substance intoxication was at the start of the game, ingesting a daily quotient of a toxic brain poison takes its toll. The side effects accumulate with time, the highs diminish. By the time people get around to quitting, their substance use is geared to just getting back to neutral, not to feeling good.

Withdrawal is a tough hurdle—and can sometimes last for weeks or months in mild form—but once cleared you will feel better than you have in years. Substance use is a classic case of behavioral conditioning. You become hooked in the first place because the substance reinforced pleasures, you stay hooked because of the punishments of withdrawal, and it is hard to stay abstinent because reminders of the highs provoke powerful craving. The smell of marijuana smoke, the sight of a certain park bench, being around old friends, the sound of certain music—all of these can trigger memories that induce drug craving and "conditioned" withdrawal symptoms. It will feel as if your brain receptors are crying out to be fed. Identify and systematically avoid such situations to the extent you possibly can because they are a lure that can drag you down. If going to parties or bars gets you drinking, avoid them—or go late and leave early. Stick to food rather than drink. Stay away from friends who get you started. Don't book hotel rooms with mini-bars.

If you can't avoid your triggers, at least formulate a plan to deal with the craving once it begins. Immediately contact a trusted friend from your AA group. Exercise, leave the party, read a magazine, eat a meal—whatever it takes for you to nip the need in the bud. Even if you have a "slip" from time to time, don't be too hard on yourself. Recognize that such slips are common (if not inevitable) and do not necessarily signify a total descent back to dependence. Most illnesses have a relapse from time to time. Pick yourself up and start over again.

Family or marital therapy is often helpful, and is sometimes necessary. Family members have often been placed in the role of "enabler" by the person with Substance Dependence. The negative effects of a person's dependence invariably create enormous strains in relationships, both inter-personally and financially. Recasting family members from victims to active participants in the treatment is crucial for success. Self-help groups for family members of substance users (Al-Anon, for example) provide wonderful support. A total family "intervention" may be necessary to confront the person's denial about the extent and harmful effects of the substance use.

Although AA (or an equivalent) is the best long-term treatment for most addicts, and is a useful adjunct for almost all, there are some individuals who are turned off by the twelve-step approach and prefer a more medical or psychiatric model of treatment. This is sometimes combined with the use of medications. The very idea of treating a drug problem with drugs has become a counterintuitive anathema to many people in recovery. This is understandable but reflects more an ideology than a practical approach that is based on doing what is most likely to work best. Some substances are terrible for the brain and promote addiction, but medicines can be good for the brain and promote cure and health. This is not a question of ideology or good moral fiber—getting over Substance Dependence is hard enough without tying at least one hand behind your back. Get whatever help you can. Many AA groups are tolerant or even supportive of medication use.

Antabuse is an underutilized treatment. It is a pill that is taken every day to make you sick when it is combined with alcohol. Since Antabuse stays in the body for several days, once you take your daily dose you are unable to drink impulsively without paying a price. Instead of being tempted to drink throughout the day, the decision to drink or not to drink is made just once when you take the pill. This provides a kind of insurance policy against drinking that can be reinforced further if the pill is dispensed by a family member. Naltrexone is another medicine that is useful in treating both Opioid and Alcohol Dependence. Antidepressant medications are also sometimes helpful when depressive symptoms are present and to ease withdrawal particularly from the amphetamines and cocaine. Although the antianxiety agents often play a role in treatment, especially in detoxification, they can create their own addiction problems and must be used cautiously over the long haul.

A medication strategy unique to the treatment of Opioid Dependence is to replace the illegally abused drug (usually heroin) with the safer pre-scribed doses of the alternative medication, methadone. While purists cringe at the idea of actively supporting long-term Opioid Dependence rather than shooting for abstinence, thirty years of experience with methadone prove that it is often the only thing that works for many people.

The treatment of substance problems has been made all the more urgent by the HIV epidemic. Infection rates among IV users in many cities approach 60 to 70 percent. This is not only a terrible public health problem for them but also represents a virus reservoir available for spread to the rest of the population. In addition to altruistic concerns, everyone has a self-interest in supporting adequate resources for treating substance problems as a way of containing illness and reducing crime.

Suggested Additional Readings

The Addiction Workbook: A Step-by-Step Guide to Quitting Alcohol and Drugs
Patrick Fanning and John T. O'Neill
New Harbinger, 1996

Educating Yourself About Alcohol and Drugs: A People's Primer
Marc Alan Schuckit
Plenum Press, 1995

I'll Quit Tomorrow: A Practical Guide to Alcoholism Treatment
Vernon E. Johnson
Harper San Francisco, 1990

Another Chance: Hope and Health for the Alcoholic Family
Sharon Wegscheider Cruse
Science & Behavior Books, 1989

Prescription Drug Abuse: The Hidden Epidemic: A Guide to Coping and Understanding
Rod Colvin
Addicus Books, 1995

Concerned Intervention: When Your Loved One Won't Quit Alcohol or Drugs
John O'Neill and Pat O'Neill
New Harbinger, 1993

A Bridge to Recovery: An Introduction to 12-Step Programs
Robert L. DuPont and John P. McGovern
American Psychiatric Press, 1995

Where to Go for Help
(Self-help, support, for more information)

Alcoholics Anonymous, Inc.
(self-help support group for those
with Alcohol Dependence)

P.O. Box 459
Grand Central Station
New York, NY 10164
(212) 870-3400
Web: http://www.alcoholics-anonymous.org/

Cocaine Anonymous World Services
(self-help support group for those
with Cocaine Dependence)

3740 Overland Avenue
Suite C
Los Angeles, CA 90034-6337
(800) 347-8998
(310) 559-5833
E-mail: cawso@ca.org
Web: http://www.ca.org/

Marijuana Anonymous
(self-help support group for those
with cannabis dependence)

P.O. Box 2912
Van Nuys, CA 91404
(800) 766-6779 (recorded information)
E-mail: info@marijuana-anonymous.org
Web: http://www.marijuana-anonymous.org/

Methadone Anonymous
(self-help support group for methadone
maintenance patients)

c/o Man Alive Research, Inc.
2100 North Charles Street
Baltimore, MD 21218
(410) 837-4292

Narcotics Anonymous
(self-help support group for those with opioid
or other Substance Dependence)

P.O. Box 9999
Van Nuys, CA 91409
(818) 773-9999
E-mail: info@wsoinc.com
Web: http://na.org/

Rational Recovery Systems
(self-help groups)

P.O. Box 800
Lotus, CA 95651
(916) 621-4374
(800) 303-2873
FAX: (916) 621-2667
E-mail: rrsn@rational.com
Web: http://www.rational.org/recovery/

S.M.A.R.T. Recovery Self-Help Network
(Self-Management and Recovery Training)
(self-help groups for individuals with "addictive behaviors"
—alcohol, drugs, gambling, eating disorders)

24000 Mercantile Road
Suite 33
Beachwood, OH 44122
(216) 292-0220
FAX: (216) 831- 3776
E-mail: srmail1@aol.com

Chemically Dependent Anonymous
(information, phone support, and referrals)

P.O. Box 423
Severna Park, MD 21146
(410) 647-7060
E-mail: williee@atlantech.net

Women for Sobriety, Inc.
(self-help support group for women
with Alcohol Dependence)

P.O. Box 618
Quakertown, PA 18951
(215) 536-8026 voice and fax
(800) 333-1606
E-mail: wfsobriety@aol.com
Web: http://www.mediapulse.com/wfs

Al-Anon, Alateen, and Adult Children of Alcoholics/
Al-Anon Family Group Headquarters, Inc.
(support group for families and friends of alcoholics)

1600 Corporate Landing Parkway
Virginia Beach, VA 23454-5617
(800) 344-2666
Web: http://www.al-anon.alateen.org/

Co-Anon's World Service Office
(support group for families of those
with Cocaine Dependence)

P.O. Box 64742-66
Los Angeles, CA 90064
(818) 377-4317
Web: http://www.co-anon.org/

Nar-Anon World Service Organization
(self-help support group for families of those
with Opioid Dependence)

P.O. Box 2562
Palos Verdes, CA 90274-0119
(310) 547-5800

Co-Dependents Anonymous (CoDA)
(self-help support group for spouses or partners
of those with Substance Dependence)

E-mail: info@ourcoda.org
Web: http://www.ourcoda.org/

Families Anonymous—World Service Office
(self-help support group for families of those
with Substance Dependence)

Box 3475
Culver City, CA 90231-3475
(800) 736-9805
E-mail: famanon@earthlink.net
Web: http://home.earthlink.net/~famanon/index.html

Prevention Online: SAMHSA
(sponsored site for alcohol and drug information)

P.O. Box 2345
Rockville, MD 20847-2345
(301) 468-2600
(800) 729-6686
Web: http://www.health.org/

National Drug and Alcohol Abuse Information
and Treatment Referral Hotline/National Institute
on Drug Abuse Helpline

12280 Wilkins Avenue
Rockville, MD 20852
(800) 662-HELP

PRIDE (Parent's Resource Institute for Drug Education)
3610 DeKalb Technology Parkway
Suite 105
Atlanta, GA 30340
(404) 577-4500
E-mail: prideprc@mindspring.com
Web: http://www.prideusa.org/

CHAPTER 7

ABNORMAL EATING

Because our ancestors were the survivors in a world where calories were hard to come by, natural selection made us efficient in converting calories into fat whenever there was a feast—in order to protect against the inevitable famines.

Unfortunately, natural selection did not have the prescience to foresee the development of the plentiful and relatively stable food supply that came with the agricultural revolution. Clearly, our bodies and our minds are not prepared for the temptations posed by refrigerators or for a world that no longer requires vigorous exercise as a condition for survival. It will take many thousands of years for our genes and our psychology to adjust to a situation in which the next bite of chocolate cake is much more likely to harm us than prevent starvation.

There are a number of inevitable consequences in societies where food is overabundant and all too enticing. Certainly, a greater percentage of the population is overweight than has ever been the case. Moreover, standards of beauty also change. In a world of starvation, fat is beautiful. Despite (or perhaps because of) the increasing heft of the average person, thinness and fitness have become more valued and idealized than ever before. We are caught in a thicket of mixed messages: paper-thin models adorn the covers of magazines that overflow with luscious food advertisements.

Dieting is endemic but usually futile. We eat more and more fat-free food and consume sugar-free beverages, but the average weight of the population continues its upward creep. People make heroic efforts at weight loss only to rebound and even exceed their original weight. The human body is programmed to make it difficult to lose weight and keep it off. As we lose weight, our body reacts as if it were facing starvation—it hoards calories by making energy utilization more efficient and by lowering the metabolic rate.

Obesity, the most frequent eating problem, is not included as a psychiatric disorder in DSM-IV. Instead, it has been regarded more as a medical problem than a psychiatric or a psychological one. Of course, this is a false dichotomy that does not do full justice to the complex interactions among genes, learned behavior, and food as self-medication that contribute to obesity. However, it is certainly true that little is known about the psychiatry of obesity and we will not spend much time discussing it here.

Eating and weight problems are, however, very much a concern to psychiatrists in a number of other ways. Overeating and weight gain are common side effects of many medications used to treat psychiatric disorders (lithium, older antidepressants, antipsychotics) and are not uncommonly the reason that patients stop taking them. Weight loss or weight gain can be a prominent symptom of a number of the psychiatric conditions covered elsewhere in the book, especially Major Depressive Disorder (page 33), Bipolar I Disorder (page 61), Cocaine Dependence (page 131), Anxiety Disorders (Chapters 3, 4, and 5), and Schizophrenia (page 313). Furthermore, one of the chapters in DSM-IV is devoted exclusively to two important and very interesting conditions which we will be discussing in considerable detail in this chapter: Anorexia Nervosa and Bulimia Nervosa.

A person with Anorexia Nervosa has a very low body weight caused by self-imposed starvation. In women this also results in a cessation of menstrual periods. People with Bulimia Nervosa engage in a pattern of binge-eating episodes followed by inappropriate and harmful compensatory behaviors such as self-induced vomiting, excessive exercise, and abuse of laxatives and/or diuretics. They are usually of normal or slightly above average weight. The underlying link between Anorexia Nervosa and Bulimia Nervosa is that both conditions are characterized by an overriding preoccupation with body size and shape.

As with almost all mental disorders, the cultural context plays a significant role. Individuals living in industrialized societies are bombarded with messages from the media promoting the idea that, particularly for women, being thin is not only essential to physical beauty but is also a key to romantic and financial success as well. The post-Twiggy idealization of thinness may be a contributing factor to the apparent increase in the frequency of eating disorders over the past three decades, and helps to explain why 90 percent of individuals with eating disorders are female. Ironically, but not surprisingly, it appears that these eating disorders are not encountered in countries where food is scarce or where stereotypic images of beauty do not center on thinness. A basic conflict exists between, on the one hand, the wide availability of food and the emphasis on enjoyment through eating and, on the other, an often unattainable idealized body shape.

Racial background also appears to have a significant influence on body image. For instance, there are major differences in the way white women and African-American women view their bodies. A recent study found that 90 percent of white high school girls were dissatisfied with their weight and a large proportion were obsessed with dieting. Among their African-American counterparts, 70 percent were very satisfied with their body size and 64 percent said that in general it was better to be overweight than underweight. It is, therefore, not surprising that the incidence of eating disorders is significantly higher for white women than for African-American women in the United States.

Perhaps the most amazing thing about eating is that so many people can regulate it well without even trying very hard. Imagine how easy it would be to eat just one extra candy bar every day for a year—and reflect on the fact that this would put on dozens of pounds. Why doesn't this happen? Most people are able to maintain a more or less stable and reasonable body weight without constant conscious monitoring, because this is what appetite tells them to do. The problem is that our appetite for food is much less tightly regulated than the drives that govern breathing or drinking. If we don't breathe appropriately, we die in minutes; if we don't drink fluids appropriately, we die in days, whereas starvation takes weeks to be lethal. This greater forgivingness results in our having a much looser control over eating behaviors that at their extreme can result in Anorexia Nervosa, Bulimia Nervosa, and obesity. There are no parallel mental disorders related to the regulation of breathing or drinking fluids precisely because these bodily functions are so crucial to our immediate survival that no margin of error is allowed.

ANOREXIA NERVOSA

Many clinicians like to believe that they can make a psychiatric diagnosis just by looking at a person, a hazardous endeavor given how appearances can be so deceiving. One exception is Anorexia Nervosa—few clinicians can forget the unnerving sight of a young woman who, despite resembling a concentration camp victim, refuses to eat because she is afraid of turning into a "blob." Public awareness of the existence and grave danger of Anorexia Nervosa has increased over the past years with the revelation of some tragic celebrity cases such as Karen Carpenter and a number of gymnasts and ballet dancers. Unfortunately, this condition is not rare and rates have been steadily increasing over the past few decades. In a sense, Anorexia Nervosa is the most extreme manifestation of the clash between our culture's obsession with thinness and the ready availability of food. For those with Anorexia Nervosa, the goal of maintaining a thin body becomes the very centerpiece of existence, a value that takes precedence over everything else, including health, survival, sex, and even being beautiful.

It is critical to recognize the signs and symptoms of Anorexia early in the game, because terrible outcomes are much more easily prevented with prompt intervention. Unfortunately, awareness of the problem by friends and family members is only half the battle. Many people with this condition are either unable or unwilling to acknowledge that their bodies are disappearing, despite the alarm expressed by everyone around them and the unmistakable tale of the tape and scale. If you are reading this section because other people are on your case about your low weight, please keep an open mind about the possibility that you may be on the road to starving yourself to death. Also remember that a characteristic hallmark of this condition is denial and an unfortunate inability to see the dangers before it is too late to respond to them.

According to the diagnostic manual, you have Anorexia Nervosa if:
- Your intense fear of becoming fat results in your weight being much lower than it should be.
- Your experience of your body is distorted in one of the following ways: You still feel fat despite being clearly underweight; you ignore the serious health consequences of your low weight; or your sense of self-worth depends almost completely on your body weight or shape.
- You have stopped having menstrual cycles.

DESCRIPTION

When it comes to understanding Anorexia Nervosa, you can be thrown off track immediately by the fact that it has been misnamed. The term "anorexia" literally means loss of appetite—but this could not be more misleading. People with Anorexia do not lose their appetite. On the contrary, you are often voraciously hungry but unable to allow yourself to eat without feeling very guilty or having to do something (like vomiting, using laxatives, or exercising like crazy) to compensate for the calories consumed. You see every morsel of food only in terms of its potential to cause weight gain, losing sight of the basic fact that one needs to eat to stay alive and healthy. This abstinence from eating fattening food often takes on moral or spiritual overtones. Eating food is equated with gluttony and weakness, while denying yourself becomes equivalent to a sublime state of purity and self-control.

Anorexia Nervosa typically starts out innocently enough as "normal" dieting, but evolves into scrupulously strict caloric restriction and vigorous and prolonged physical activity. The food restrictions and exercise take on a compulsive quality. Calories are counted to the point of absurdity, with food being meticulously weighed before eating. Some eliminate whole categories of foodstuffs, restricting their diets to a limited number of "safe" low-calorie foods. The exercise regimen becomes longer and more involved, taking up hours every day and frequently leading to injuries. Ultimately, the activities associated with maintaining a low-caloric intake and a high energy output become the dominant force of your life.

Many of the psychological and physical manifestations of Anorexia Nervosa stem from the starvation it causes. The main psychological symptoms—single-minded food obsessions and eating rituals—also occur in people who are starving because of famine, natural catastrophes, and prison camp experiences. You may deny yourself food while at the same time you collect recipes, make elaborate dinners for others, hoard food you never eat, and engage in rituals of eating only a few specific foods in a particular order and at the same time every day. Many of the physiological manifestations of Anorexia Nervosa are the same as those seen in involuntary starvation: loss of menstrual periods, abdominal pain, dry skin, jaundice, intolerance to cold, and constipation. Some people with the disorder may even grow a fine hair on their body called lanugo.

You have a remarkably distorted image of your body weight and appearance and see yourself as fat even though you are a walking skeleton. You are obsessed with weighing yourself and checking out body parts that still feel fat no matter how much weight you lose—those stubborn skin folds on the arms, thighs, buttocks, and cheeks that continue to be "flabby" even when you weigh seventy-five pounds. Almost uniformly, body image becomes the total yardstick by which the person measures herself.

One of the more important aspects of Anorexia Nervosa is the interruption in the menstrual cycles in women. Some women become very concerned about not having periods because they worry about its impact on their childbearing potential. For others, especially teenage girls, not having periods may feel like a reprieve. The relationship between menstrual cycles and starvation in Anorexia Nervosa has an interesting parallel with the effects of starvation on animals in the wild. The fertility of female animals drops radically in response to starvation, undoubtedly because natural selection favors those animals who ration their reproductive abilities to times when they are most able to nurture offspring. It makes no sense to give birth to more children if you cannot feed yourself or the ones you already have.

People with Anorexia Nervosa are among our most reluctant patients. Most are notoriously in denial about the grave risks posed by starvation and rarely seek help on their own. They often perceive their only problem to be that they are not yet thin enough. Moreover, their body image is so distorted that they do not acknowledge the serious medical consequences of their emaciated state. Most often, family members and/or friends must intervene to obtain treatment for their loved one.

As with most DSM-IV disorders, there is a tremendous variability in the presentations of patients with Anorexia Nervosa. However, this heterogeneity falls pretty much into one of two types: a Restricting type and a Binge-Eating/Purging type. Both subtypes are characterized by severe weight loss and body image problems, but the people are very different in their eating habits and personality features. The restrictors become emaciated through some combination of extreme dieting and overzealous exercise. Their personality characteristics often include stubbornness, inflexibility, and compulsive need for structure. The Binge-Eating/Purgers have frequent breakdowns of their restrictor discipline resulting in binges with enormous caloric intake, which are then frantically compensated for by self-induced vomiting or laxative abuse. Also in contrast to the restrictors, the bingers tend to be impulsive rather than compulsive and also are more likely to abuse alcohol or drugs.

Other psychiatric symptoms often accompany Anorexia Nervosa and may become so severe that they take on a life of their own. Probably the most common associated problem is depression and it may be a good idea for you to review Chapter 1. Another serious problem is social withdrawal. It's difficult to maintain relationships with people if you are always embarrassed about eating (or not eating) in front of them. Other frequent symptoms to look for include insomnia, irritable mood, and a decreased libido.

DIFFERENTIAL DIAGNOSIS

Abnormal weight loss is a nonspecific symptom that is certainly not unique to Anorexia Nervosa. Many medical illnesses, such as cancer and AIDS, can lead to severe weight loss and emaciation. Drug abuse can also cause weight loss, either due to the direct effect of the drug on appetite (like amphetamines or cocaine) or indirectly due to the person's life becoming preoccupied with drug use to the exclusion of meeting other needs—including adequate nutrition. Furthermore, decreased appetite and weight loss related to diminished interest in pleasurable activities (or just no longer caring about life) is often part of Major Depressive Disorder (page 33). Anorexia Nervosa is the likely diagnosis when no other cause seems more compelling and when there is a body image problem with extreme fear of fatness accompanying the low body weight.

AM I OKAY?

Especially in our culture, which so overvalues thinness, the line between beauty and eating disorder is sometimes hard to draw. This is particularly problematic among those girls and young women who participate in activities that demand extreme thinness such as modeling, gymnastics, and ballet dancing.

In order to warrant a diagnosis of Anorexia Nervosa, three symptoms must be present at a level of severity that is concerning: a very low body weight, loss of menstrual period, and a distorted body image. Of course, each of these occurs on a continuum and you can have elements of all three at a mild level and that does not require a diagnosis. A guideline provided by DSM-IV for abnormally low weight is that it be less than 85 percent of what is expected given the person's height and age. This definition depends on what standard is used for determining "expected" weight—a problem not just for the definition of Anorexia Nervosa but also for physicians, diet centers, and insurance companies in trying to determine recommendations regarding optimal weight.

Traditionally, "normal" weight guidelines have come from tables that are based primarily on a statistical distribution of weight given a particular height for a random sample of individuals living in the United States. Interestingly, these "standards" have been creeping upward, reflecting the steadily increasing girth of the American population. In the past several years, life charts have been replaced by a mathematically determined value, called the Body Mass Index (BMI). This is calculated by dividing one's weight (in kilograms) by one's height (in meters) squared. If the BMI is less than 17.5 kg/m^2, one's weight is in the below-85 percent range and concerns should be raised about whether Anorexia Nervosa is present. Of course, it is important to remember that these are only guidelines that will vary with body build and that having a BMI of greater than 17.5 kg/m^2 does not necessarily give one a clean bill of health (at least with regard to a diagnosis of Anorexia Nervosa).

Many women, especially during adolescence, have occasional irregular or even missed periods. Not every thin girl or woman with a skipped period has Anorexia Nervosa. Most often the amenorrhea in Anorexia Nervosa goes on for many months or even years and DSM-IV suggests that at least three consecutive missed periods must occur before the diagnosis is confirmed.

Treatment Options

In its most severe form, Anorexia Nervosa constitutes what may be a dire medical emergency. Death, when it occurs, results most often from multiple organ failure and/or severe electrolyte imbalance caused by starvation. After medical stabilization, the absolute first priority is to end the starvation, which is a prerequisite for treating the psychological and medical complications of the condition. Because of the patient's characteristic intense denial and terror of calories, the reversal of starvation is almost invariably met with stiff resistance. It is critical to take a firm stance that continued starvation may be incompatible with survival and therefore cannot be accepted. Initially, the refeeding process usually entails the use of liquid nutritional supplements. In some cases, particularly when the person is unable (or unwilling) to eat, a nasogastric tube (or the threat of one) is necessary.

The temporary use of a liquid diet has several advantages. Liquid calories often meet with less patient resistance because they sidestep the avoidance rituals associated with solid food. You are also likely to get more calories per swallow and complain less of being bloated. Because liquids are absorbed more rapidly, there is less opportunity for self-induced vomiting. Finally, using a liquid diet allows for a more careful calibration and measurement of total daily calorie intake.

The next steps involve psychoeducation, behavior modification, and cognitive therapy, all directed toward establishing healthier eating habits and body image. A large part of the treatment of Anorexia Nervosa is psychoeducation—challenging the person's cherished tenets about food and body weight and providing a healthy undistorted alternative. The treatment of Anorexia Nervosa is quite difficult—it entails having you do the *exact* thing you have been deathly afraid of—gaining weight. Therefore, the initial step in treatment is to convince you of the necessity of weight gain and the downsides of your food deprivation. Clarifying the causal connection between your low weight and the symptoms of Anorexia—low energy, difficulty concentrating, mood swings, food obsessions—is often eye-opening and is critical in helping you weather the inevitable struggles ahead.

Behavioral therapy begins with a weight gain contract expecting that a pound or two will be put on each week. Positive and negative behavioral reinforcements are established to help provide motivation—things like TV privileges, going out with friends, or telephone time. A nutritionist can help normalize eating patterns and establish healthy meal plans. A crucial time is the switch from liquid to solid diet. Phobic desensitization techniques can be helpful if you experience intense anxiety when eating even reasonably caloric foods. You make a list of foods, ordered from least feared (lettuce) to most feared (chocolate cheesecake). With the therapist's support, each type of food is confronted and conquered. Another behavioral strategy involves figuring out which environmental cues or situations trigger food restriction and excessive exercise. For example, you may be weighing yourself many times a day, and starving because your weight is too high. You should be barred from weighing yourself more than once a week.

Cognitive therapy aims to identify and challenge your distorted thinking about food and body shape. Catastrophization is common—you are sure that eating a few cookies will result in gaining a pound. You are taught to identify such gross distortions and to counter them with realistic alternatives (it takes more than one hundred low-calorie cookies to equal a pound of fat). Similarly, you must accept that you have lost the ability to objectively assess your weight and body shape. Just as a color-blind person cannot trust his ability to match clothing, you must learn to consider yourself weight-assessment-impaired.

Medication treatment for Anorexia Nervosa has not been particularly successful. Although a wide array of medicines have been tried, none has been shown convincingly to promote weight gain. Antidepressant medication can be effective when significant depressive symptoms accompany Anorexia Nervosa.

BULIMIA NERVOSA

People with this problem can't control their eating any more than an alcoholic can control his drinking. Binge-eating episodes alternate with frantic efforts to off-load calories—paying for the binges by vomiting, using laxatives, fasting, or constant exercising. The dilemma arises from the contradiction that you can't control your caloric intake, but want to control your weight. If you didn't care about your body shape, your unrestrained binge eating would lead to obesity. But you do care very much and are engaged in a desperate attempt to neutralize the effect of the binges in order to avoid gaining weight. This leads to its own vicious cycle.

Bulimia Nervosa is an all too common problem, especially for young women between puberty and the early twenties. It often starts with dieting efforts to get off the baby fat. Dedicated fasting triggers breakthrough pig-outs, which in turn increase the motivation for even more fasting. Before long you discover vomiting or laxatives, or both, as another compensation and punishment for the binge episodes. The cycles of bingeing and "antibingeing" come to completely dominate your life.

You are remarkably ashamed both of the binges and of the things you do to counteract them. You are filled with disgust when you think about sneaking into the bathroom, making yourself vomit, flushing the toilet, and having to do everything possible to hide the smell. You try to keep this a secret from everyone, even the people who love you, and will admit to the problem only if questioned directly. New relationships are avoided for fear your dirty secret will be discovered.

According to the diagnostic manual, you have Bulimia Nervosa if:
- You have episodes of binge eating during which your eating is out of control and you consume an amount of food that is definitely larger than what most people would eat in a similar period of time and under similar circumstances.
- To offset the caloric intake and to keep from gaining weight, you do inappropriate things such as making yourself vomit; abusing laxa-

tives, diuretics, or enemas; fasting for extended periods; or exercising excessively.
- You frequently engage in the bingeing and compensatory behaviors (e.g., on average, at least twice a week for three months).
- As in Anorexia, your feelings about yourself are excessively influenced by your body shape and weight.

DESCRIPTION

An episode of binge eating is like a feeding frenzy. You lose control and eat until it hurts and you can't eat any more. Then you may vomit and start all over again. The food goes down so fast you can barely taste it. You will eat anything in sight but prefer soft, sweet, gooey high-caloric junk foods like ice cream, doughnuts, cake, and cookies. When you are done, you feel lousy, loathsome, and disgusted. Binges are almost always done solo because they are so embarrassing.

It is no accident that the word "binge" works equally well to describe both the excessive consumption of food and the excessive consumption of alcohol. Many people use food in just the same way an alcoholic uses a cocktail—to soothe, relax, pass the time, and counter boredom. Just as with drinking, this can get out of control. Repeated binge eating is the equivalent of repeatedly getting drunk, but is even more difficult to control because it is impossible completely to abstain from food in the way an alcoholic can go on the wagon. This is why bulimics focus on the compensatory behaviors. It is easier to vomit up or defecate out the calories than to stop eating altogether or to eat in a controlled way. Fasting in bulimia is like going cold turkey in substance dependence, but it can't last forever because eventually you have to eat to live. The fast is usually broken with another binge, not a normal controlled meal.

Self-induced vomiting is by far the most commonly used compensatory behavior. As in most things, practice makes perfect—people become increasingly adept at making themselves vomit. After learning to stimulate the gag reflex using a finger or utensil, they may progress to inducing vomiting at will. Others may prefer the use of enemas and laxatives and a few add diuretics. These compensatory behaviors serve both to alleviate the fear of gaining weight and to restore a desperately needed feeling of control.

Sometimes the act of purging becomes an end unto itself and relieves anxiety or actually becomes pleasurable in its own right.

There are two subtypes of Bulimia Nervosa, depending on the compensatory method used to counteract the impact of the binges. The Purging Type involves the use of self-induced vomiting or the abuse of laxatives, diuretics, or enemas. The Nonpurging Type is for those who use fasting and excessive exercise to counteract the weight-gaining effects of a binge. People with the Purging Type of Bulimia are more apt to show signs of depression and are even more preoccupied with their body image than those who do not purge.

Bingeing and purging can be bad for your health. Wild and reckless eating can result in food being inhaled into the windpipe with the potential for sudden death or pneumonia. Self-induced vomiting and laxative or diuretic abuse can result in a number of serious and sometimes life-threatening problems. Frequent exposure of the teeth, mouth, and upper gastrointestinal tract to acidic stomach contents can lead to permanent tooth erosion, painful inflammation of the salivary glands, and ulcers of the esophagus. The loss of fluids through vomiting, laxatives, diuretics, or enemas can cause dehydration and electrolyte imbalance with occasional serious heart rhythm disturbances. Overuse of laxatives or enemas can lead to dependence on these methods to stimulate bowel functioning.

Differential Diagnosis

There is a continuum of weight accumulation among binge eaters—from the markedly underweight Anorexia Nervosa; to the normal or slightly overweight Bulimia Nervosa; to the vastly overweight people with obesity. The various outcomes obviously depend on the extent of the binge eating and degree to which it is balanced by compensatory purging, fasting, or exercise. Sometimes a single individual goes from one to another category as the balance shifts between the bingeing and the antibingeing behaviors. Binge eating can sometimes be a symptom of Major Depressive Disorder (page 33) or Dysthymic Disorder (page 42) or can be part of a general pattern of overly impulsive behavior (as in Borderline Personality Disorder—page 224).

AM I OKAY?

Most people have occasional times when they gorge themselves to the point of being more than comfortably full. This is a ubiquitous part of Thanksgiving, office Christmas parties, Caribbean cruise packages, catered affairs, and all-you-can-eat buffets. And don't be too hard on yourself if you lose control occasionally when given free access to favorite foods like chocolate or potato chips. It happens to everyone. The capacity to binge was probably very useful to our ancestors, who could literally never be completely sure where their next meal was coming from. Such temporary and occasional overindulgences would not indicate a diagnosis of Bulimia Nervosa, which requires frequent and recurrent episodes of out-of-control bingeing. Also, by "abnormal," we are not talking about five cookies; we are talking about some combination of an entire cake, a full gallon of ice cream, a complete bag of snack food, and a whole large pizza. The binges must occur regularly over several months before a diagnosis of Bulimia Nervosa should be considered.

The diagnosis also requires that there be extraordinary compensatory punishments to avoid the weight-gaining effects of eating so much food. In our weight-conscious society, it is standard operating procedure for people to be more watchful of their caloric intake or to increase activity level in response to brief periods of overindulgence (hence the upswing in post-holiday enrollments in diet plans and health clubs). Again, the diagnosis is warranted only for extreme measures such as relentless purging, extended fasting, or constant overexercising (to the point of inducing injury or taking up an excessive amount of the day).

TREATMENT OPTIONS

There is a great deal more known about the treatment of Bulimia Nervosa than about Anorexia Nervosa. A variety of different medications and psychotherapeutic techniques are helpful. The antidepressant medications work well even in people who are not depressed. Although they were initially discovered (and subsequently marketed) for their efficacy in treating depression, it turns out that most antidepressants are also effective for a wide variety of other mental disorders including Panic Disorder, Social Phobia, Obsessive-Compulsive Disorder, Generalized Anxiety Disorder, and even Cocaine Dependence. In the treatment of Bulimia, they help reduce the frequency of both binge eating and purging episodes, improve mood, and diminish the intensity of the disturbed attitudes regarding body shape and weight.

Psychotherapy is also very helpful on its own or when combined with medication. It is important for you to appreciate that binge eating is a "normal" response to starvation. Any attempt to sustain an unrealistically low weight by extreme dieting is a setup for breakout binge eating. You have to shoot to maintain a healthy weight range as determined by your height, build, long-term weight history, and family history. Looking like a model is not healthy and often is not even beautiful. Normalize your eating pattern by making it more regular, moderate, and predictable. You probably deprive yourself of food during the day, and then have an evening of grazing and evacuating. Instead, eat three healthy average-sized meals a day to break this pattern and reduce the urge to binge. It is a good idea to monitor the frequency of your binges and purges and to record in excruciating detail the amount and type of food you have consumed. Self-monitoring by itself may be enough to significantly reduce binge frequency and will likely limit how much you ingest each time.

Behavioral interventions rely on the fact that binges are usually preceded by triggers. The cue may be situational—like being alone in the kitchen at night, or watching TV, or walking by a fast-food restaurant—or maybe emotional—like feeling loneliness, self-loathing, or boredom. Behavioral modification can work by altering the cues or the responses to them, or both. To bypass the triggers, reduce physical hunger by eating frequent small snacks, avoid problematic situations (no eating ever in front of TV), and learn other ways to deal with tension and painful emotions. Substitute other behaviors—call a friend, go for a walk, listen to a relaxation tape—to break the cycle of binges. Finally, prolonged exposure to your triggering cues without permitting yourself to respond to them in your usual way will gradually cut the connection between the cue and the response.

Cognitive interventions involve having you note your internal thoughts and feeling states immediately preceding, during, and subsequent to the binges or purges. Cognitive distortions ("If I binge today, that means I am a despicable person who doesn't deserve to live" or "If I have this one cookie, I will blow up like a balloon") are examined, dissected, and replaced with more rational alternatives ("Gaining one pound does not mean that I am fat and that all my friends will not want to have anything to do with me"). Similarly, the inevitable relentless dissatisfactions with one's body shape and weight are labeled for what they are: pathological distortions in body image.

Suggested Additional Readings

The Deadly Diet: Recovering from Anorexia and Bulimia
    Terence J. Sandbeck, Ph.D.
    New Harbinger, 1993

Dying to Be Thin: Understanding and Defeating Anorexia and Bulimia
    Marc Zimmer and Ira M. Sacker
    Warner Books, 1995

Bulimia Nervosa and Binge-Eating: A Guide to Recovery
    Peter J. Cooper
    New York University Press, 1995

Where to Go for Help
(Self-help, support, for more information)

American Anorexia/Bulimia Association, Inc.
(self-help group that provides information and referrals)
165 West Forty-sixth Street
Suite 1108
New York, NY 10036
FAX: (212) 278-0698
E-mail: AmAnBu@aol.com
Web: http://members.aol.com/AmAnBu

Overeaters Anonymous
6075 Zenith Court N.E.
Rio Rancho, NM 87124
(505) 891-2664
FAX: (505) 891-4320
Web: http://www.overeatersanonymous.org/

National Eating Disorders Organization
(treatment resources in the United States and internationally;
information about eating disorders)
6655 South Yale Avenue
Tulsa, OK 74136
(918) 481-4044
E-mail: lpchnedo@ionet.net
Web: http://www.laureate.com/

National Association of Anorexia Nervosa and Associated Disorders (ANAD)
(information on self-help groups, therapy, and referrals to professionals)
Box 7
Highland Park, IL 60035
(847) 831-3438

S.M.A.R.T. Recovery Self-Help Network
(Self-Management and Recovery Training)
(self-help groups for individuals with "addictive behaviors"
—alcohol, drugs, gambling, eating disorders)
24000 Mercantile Road
Suite 33
Beachwood, OH 44122
(216) 292-0220
FAX: (216) 831-3776
E-mail: srmail1@aol.com

CHAPTER 8

SEXUAL
OR GENDER PROBLEMS

We expect this chapter to be among the most avidly read in this book. This interest would not stem from any epidemic of sexual dysfunction that is running rampant in the population. Rather, it would reflect the widespread preoccupation with sexual functioning that pervades our culture—combined with misinformation. The topic of sex arouses both intense curiosity and intense anxiety. How do I measure up? What am I missing out on? What can I do to make it better? Am I normal? We are bombarded by pop opinions conveyed by tabloids, self-help books, talk shows, folk wisdom, and even pornography, all of which unfortunately far outweigh the availability of authoritative information.

What we do know is that "optimal" sexual functioning is in the eye of the beholder. What one person may consider to be healthy sexual activity, another may find insufficient, disturbed, or deviant. Even such a straightforward issue as the usual frequency of sexual activity is almost entirely subjective. A classic split-screen scene from the Woody Allen film *Annie Hall* illustrates how two partners in a relationship can view the same scenario in opposite ways: Man (on right) complaining to his therapist: "We hardly ever have sex—maybe three times a week!" Woman (on left) to her therapist: "We're constantly having sex— I'd say three times a week!" To further complicate matters, what is considered "normal" sexual activity is not only influenced by age, culture, and religious background but often changes over time.

The disorders of human sexuality are traditionally divided into three different categories, each of which is presented separately in this chapter. Problems with one's ability to function sexually, known as Sexual Dysfunction, are among our patients' most frequent concerns. The other two categories of sexual problems are much less common. "Paraphilia" is the technical term for sexual perversion and describes people whose sexual lives, in fantasy or in action, are centered on deviant sexual stimuli or preferences (for example, sadism, fetishism, having sexual relations with children). Gender Identity Disorder describes people who feel that their sexual anatomy is at odds with their internalized sense of gender and are very distressed by this mismatch.

SEXUAL DYSFUNCTION

To understand better how things can go wrong sexually, it may be helpful to examine the four phases of the "normal" sexual response cycle. The first phase is sexual desire, which includes thoughts and fantasies about sexual activity. The second phase is sexual excitement, which consists of the physical changes that occur when one is sexually aroused. For men, this involves erection of the penis and for women vaginal lubrication and swelling of the genitalia. The next phase is orgasm, the culmination in a pleasurable release of the sexual tension that has built up from the first two phases. Orgasm in men is reached with an ejaculation of semen, and in women with vaginal contractions. The last phase of the sexual response cycle is resolution, which consists of a feeling of both physical and mental relaxation. During this phase, men have a refractory period lasting a variable amount of time during which they are not able to respond physically, either by erection or orgasm, to further stimulation. Women, on the other hand, do not have this refractory period and may become aroused again during the resolution phase.

According to the diagnostic manual, you have Sexual Dysfunction if:
- You have one (or more) of the following problems with sexual functioning: low sexual desire, aversion to sexual contact, difficulty becoming aroused, difficulty in achieving orgasm, premature ejaculation, or pain during intercourse.
- The problem is *not* caused by a medical condition, a side effect of a medication you are taking, or drug or alcohol use.
- You are distressed by this problem or it is causing significant problems in your relationships with other people.

DESCRIPTION

Sexual Dysfunctions can occur in any of the first three phases of the sexual response cycle. However, because the various phases build upon one another, problems in one phase often result in problems in another phase. For example, a profound lack of desire usually results in problems in arousal and in achieving orgasm. Going the other way, a man who has a problem with premature ejaculation may anticipate failure to perform well and develop a secondary problem with arousal or desire.

There are two kinds of Sexual Dysfunction that relate to the sexual desire phase—Hypoactive Sexual Desire Disorder and Sexual Aversion Disorder. Hypoactive Sexual Desire Disorder applies when someone has extremely low desire for sexual activity and rarely engages in sexual fantasy. Such people may participate in sex but often do so reluctantly only at the urging of a partner. There may be little desire for any sexual activity at all or desire only for quite restricted types of sexual expression. For example, the person may masturbate but has no interest in sexual intercourse. Interestingly, the DSM-IV does not include abnormally high levels of sexual desire as a specific separate sexual disorder.

It is unusual for someone to seek treatment for low sexual desire. Usually the person is dragged in by a dissatisfied sexual partner, who may complain specifically about the lack of sexual desire or instead may initially focus on other aspects of the relationship that are easier to talk about. The wide variability in "normal" sexual appetite makes it unclear whether one person wants it too much, the other too little, or more likely whether it is just a mismatch between their sexual needs.

A much more extreme problem with sexual desire is Sexual Aversion Disorder—people who try to avoid sexual contact altogether and become extremely agitated or repulsed when faced with any sexual situation. They are likely to focus on a particular aspect of sex or sexual intercourse that is particularly disgusting to them, for instance, penetration or contact with semen or with vaginal secretions. Some carry the aversion toward sexual interaction so far as to avoid any kissing and hugging, or other bodily contact.

The problems in sexual excitement include difficulties in getting aroused at all or in keeping the arousal going long enough to culminate the sexual encounter. Even though the desire is there, the genitals feel dead and unable to pitch in and cooperate. A man has problems becoming erect or maintaining an erection during sexual activity. A woman does not experience adequate expansion, vaginal lubrication, or genital swelling. In some cases, intercourse may not be possible at all or may be painful at best.

Even if the sexual response cycle is working well in terms of desire and excitement, things can still fall apart at the orgasm phase. For women, the problem at its most severe is a lifelong inability to have orgasms. Milder forms would be having infrequent orgasms that occur only after unusually prolonged intercourse or oral sex, or only during masturbation. When deciding whether a woman who is having trouble reaching climax has a true Sexual Dysfunction, it is important to keep in mind that women vary greatly in the ease with which they reach orgasm, as well as in the degree and preferred type of sexual stimulation. It appears that many women have orgasms more easily as they grow older and become more experienced sexually.

In men, orgasm problems occur in both directions—too fast and too slow. In premature ejaculation, orgasm occurs quickly and with minimal stimulation, much sooner than the person (or the partner) wants. The problem is usually worse with a new sex partner, when there are performance worries, or if a long time has elapsed since the last climax. Often the man can control ejaculation while masturbating, but not during sexual activity with a partner. Premature ejaculation is an almost ubiquitous concern of younger men who have limited sexual experience. In contrast, much less commonly a man may suffer delayed orgasms with ejaculation occurring only after intense, prolonged, and almost painful sexual activity. For some men, the problem is situational—they may be able to climax after a reasonable time in response to oral sex or masturbation, but not during intercourse.

There are two other disorders of sexual functioning that are not related to any one particular phase in the sexual response cycle. Dyspareunia describes the experience of significant pain or discomfort during sexual intercourse. Although more common in women, this can also sometimes occur in men. Vaginismus describes vaginal muscle spasms that make sexual intercourse painful and frustrating for both parties involved. Some women also experience spasms during gynecological exams. Women who suffer from vaginismus usually are not aware that they are having involuntary spasms—they may experience only a physical discomfort during intercourse or exams.

In assessing any problem with sexual functioning, it is important to consider the context in which the difficulty is experienced—whether the problem is generalized or situational. The dysfunction is considered to be generalized if it occurs in most or all sexual situations, regardless of the specific partner or the type of sexual stimulation. For example, a man has trouble achieving orgasms no matter how hard he tries through masturbation, intercourse, or oral sex. In contrast, situational Sexual Dysfunction happens only with certain partners and/or during a specific type of sexual experience. For example, a man who has no trouble becoming erect during masturbation or oral sex may be unable to attain an erection during intercourse. Distinguishing situational from generalized Sexual Dysfunction is helpful in determining the underlying cause and in deciding what type of treatment is most likely to work.

DIFFERENTIAL DIAGNOSIS

Identifying one single cause of Sexual Dysfunction is often impossible because so many different interacting factors are involved. The most common causes of sexual dysfunction include psychological issues in one or both individuals; nonsexual problems in the couple's relationship; side effects of prescribed medications; alcohol or other drug abuse; medical conditions; other mental disorders; or any combination of two or more of these. Understanding the cause(s) is essential to choosing the appropriate treatment.

The first clue to the cause is whether the person's sexual problems are generalized or situational. Obviously, situational Sexual Dysfunctions are much less likely to be caused by a medical problem, medication side effect, or drug use than are generalized Sexual Dysfunctions. If a man has spontaneous erections upon awakening or a woman can have orgasms during masturbation, the most likely cause of sexual problems in other situations will be something to do with psychology or with the relationship. On the other hand, if your sexual functioning is compromised in every situation, it is important to take a careful look at the medicines you are taking, drug and alcohol use, and get a thorough medical evaluation.

A surprisingly wide range of prescribed and illicitly obtained drugs have sexual side effects. The most common culprits are the medications used to treat depression, seizures, and hypertension. One of the major problems with the new and otherwise very popular SSRI antidepressants (Prozac, Zoloft, Paxil, Luvox) is their significant rate of delayed or inhibited orgasm, decreased desire, and problems with arousal. Similarly, it is quite common for abusers of various substances, such as alcohol, amphetamines, cocaine, sedatives, and steroids, to experience a variety of different Sexual Dysfunctions.

Many different medical conditions can interfere with sexual functioning—in fact, the sexual problem may sometimes be what brings the person to see a doctor even before the underlying illness has been diagnosed. The most common medical illnesses to think about are diabetes, multiple sclerosis or other neurological diseases, circulatory problems, post-surgical complications after prostate operations, or spinal injuries. As always, things get complicated. Let's say a patient with the common combination of diabetes and hypertension has a problem maintaining erections. The cause(s) could be any combination of the following: nerve damage or circulatory problems from diabetes; a side effect of the drugs used to treat the hypertension; performance anxiety related to past difficulties; and/or a reduction of desire from marital strain. It is often impossible to establish to what degree each specific cause contributes to the overall problem. However, things often do sort out over time as you evaluate the effects of the different treatment strategies targeted to the different causes (better control of diabetes, reducing or changing the antihypertensive, psychotherapy, couples treatment).

Most of the psychiatric problems described elsewhere in this book can also interfere with sexual performance. For example, sexual desire is one of the first things to disappear during depression. And keep in mind that the medicines used to treat these problems have frequent sexual side effects.

There is one last and very tough diagnostic call that comes to the forefront after all the above causes of Sexual Dysfunction have been ruled out. This is to tease apart the separate contributions of, or interaction between, psychological problems and relational problems. Is the sexual problem a result of psychological conflicts you would bring to each and every new relationship or is it more a sign of trouble in this particular relationship? You can see why this question is so important to people and so difficult to evaluate. The most common psychological problems relate to fears of failure, intimacy, injury, or to feelings of embarrassment, inhibition, shame, or guilt. The relational problems that cause sexual dysfunction sort into two types. In the first, conflicts about nonsexual matters (e.g., over finances, child rearing, control) get played out in the bedroom. In the second, there is a sexual mismatch between the partners (e.g., different preferences for frequency or type of sexual activity, a lack of passionate attraction, or different standards of dress or hygiene).

Even if a couple walks into the office screaming at each other, the cause-and-effect relationship between their interpersonal conflict and their sexual problem is often more complicated than meets the eye. Low sexual desire or arousal can certainly result from a deep-seated hostility between the partners in a long-troubled and rancorous relationship. On the other hand, relational problems can easily develop under the strain of a Sexual Dysfunction in one member of the couple or a lack of passion between them. It is often difficult to determine which comes first in the chicken-and-egg cycle between the relationship problem and the Sexual Dysfunction—they often overlap and exacerbate one another. The underlying causes may become clear only after a trial of treatment.

Am I Okay?

Implied in the question Am I okay? is the concern whether one's sexual functioning falls within the standard for "normal." This is a question that is much too often on the minds of people whose sexual functioning is perfectly fine, while it is too often downplayed by people who do have sexual problems. In fact, persistent concerns about not being sexually normal can be the ultimate self-fulfilling prophecy—performance fears beget performance failure. In our sex-obsessed society, many individuals subject their sexual behavior to a degree of scrutiny and self-evaluation that it should not have to bear—taking the fun out of the act and even having a detrimental effect on performance. Judgments about the optimal sexual frequency and the appropriate repertoire of sexual behaviors depend on a complex combination of cultural expectations, prior personal experiences, and normal individual variability in sexual appetite. There is surprisingly little hard data regarding normal sexual practices and attitudes. Occasional problems with sexual performance are an everyday part of the human experience and no big deal. The routine pressures of life, the availability of a partner one finds attractive, or marital troubles are bound to create an ebb and flow in sexual desire. Worrying less about being okay is a good idea for most people. Have sex for fun and intimacy—not as a performance sport, rite of passage, or contest.

Treatment Options

First and foremost, effective treatment of Sexual Dysfunction depends on an accurate diagnosis of what is causing the problem. You can't expect to successfully treat a cocaine-induced arousal problem with behavioral techniques alone. If a drug, medication, or medical condition is identified as at least part of the cause, the treatment will inevitably require that these issues be addressed first. Similarly, if the Sexual Dysfunction is a symptom of another psychiatric disorder, then the treatment must also center on that disorder. For example, it is not uncommon for people with Major Depressive Disorder to lose interest in sex. Usually after successful treatment of the Major Depressive Disorder, sexual desire and functioning return to normal. Finally, if the sexual problem is a direct outgrowth of a conflicted relationship, couples therapy that addresses these issues usually must precede or at least accompany any other interventions.

Cognitive/behavioral sex therapy is the most commonly used approach for those whose sexual problems result from inexperience, inhibition, or psychological conflict. The specifics of the treatment will depend upon which phase of the sexual response cycle is affected. For arousal and orgasm problems, the first step is to reduce the emphasis on performance and instead to emphasize the obtaining and giving of pleasure. "Sensate focus" is a fancy term that simply means retraining the individual or couple to enjoy the full erotic potential of the entire body by expanding attention well beyond the genitals. Couples may at first even be enjoined from touching the genitals at all in order to reduce their emphasis on performance and orgasm. Individuals or couples with inhibitions are instructed to explore each other's bodies and become versed in each other's preferences and dislikes. The less you think about sexual performance, the more fun you have and the better your sexual performance will therefore be.

For Male Erectile Disorder, the treatment has been revolutionized by the introduction of Viagra, an oral medication that increases penile blood flow during periods of sexual arousal. Whether it proves to be similarly helpful for Female Sexual Arousal Disorder remains to be seen.

For premature ejaculation, the easily learned "squeeze technique" has become the standard and very effective treatment. This involves bringing the man right to the point of orgasm and then providing a gentle squeeze just below the glans of the penis in order to prevent ejaculation. Doing this repeatedly for a brief period of time will give the man much greater control over his ejaculations. Self-confidence and reduced anxiety are more than half the battle.

Problems with sexual desire are often the hardest to treat. Psychotherapy is usually necessary if these result from intrapsychic conflicts in one or both partners. Other techniques that work with varying success include reintroducing romance to the relationship, improving appearance and grooming, suggesting fresh techniques or settings to expand a couple's previously stale repertoire, and exposure to sexually arousing materials and fantasies. Dealing with problems in the relationship can also be very helpful.

PARAPHILIAS

The previous section covered problems in sexual performance. This section describes aberrant sexual fantasies, urges, and behaviors that cause distress and sometimes lead to criminal behavior. Paraphilia is the clinical term for a sexual deviation or sexual perversion—a repertoire of sexual turn-ons that deviates markedly from some hard-to-determine standard of "normal." What is abnormal is clear at the extremes: Someone who obligatorily and regularly engages in sexual behavior that victimizes others (sadism, pedophilia, exhibitionism) definitely has a Paraphilia. At the milder reaches when no harm is done, what constitutes normal sexual behavior is much less clear and varies dramatically, depending on cultural and religious values. Also, what may be "normal" enough if restricted to sexual fantasy may be markedly deviant or even criminal if acted out.

DSM-IV lists eight separate Paraphilias, based on the nature of the deviant turn-on. These include sexual sadism, sexual masochism, exhibitionism, voyeurism, fetishism, transvestic fetishism, frotteurism, and pedophilia, based on the particular trigger for the deviant sexual fantasies, urges, or behaviors. Since these are probably variations on the same theme, we will consider them as one.

Interestingly, almost all instances of Paraphilia occur in men, with the exception of sexual masochism. No one is really sure why this is the case. Freud attributed the lopsided gender ratio in perversion to male castration anxiety—that some men used perversions as a way of coping with the (to them) bewildering and unpleasant fact that a woman does not have a penis. A more commonplace explanation focuses on what are probably inherent differences in male versus female sexuality—men tend to be more indiscriminately aroused, dependent on visual stimuli, and orgasm-driven; for women, sexual arousal is more likely to depend on a loving relationship.

According to the diagnostic manual, you have Paraphilia if:
- In order to get turned on, you require a sexual stimulus that deviates significantly from "normal." These include using fetishes, cross-dressing, masochism, sadism, exposing yourself, being a "Peeping Tom," rubbing against a nonconsenting person, or sexual activity with children.
- Having this deviant arousal pattern harms other people, interferes with your relationships, or is upsetting to you.

DESCRIPTION

The kind of Paraphilia that involves the use of inanimate objects during sexual activity is known as fetishism. The actual object or fetish is commonly lingerie, high-heeled shoes, or leather boots. The fetishist usually becomes sexually aroused only when seeing, feeling, and/or smelling the fetish object. He may insist that a partner wear the object or it may be used during masturbation. Often the passion for the fetish is so strong that the individual fails to become aroused unless it is in some way involved in the sexual activity. In transvestic fetishism, he becomes sexually excited by dressing up in women's clothing and masturbating while fantasizing himself to be both the male and female participants in the sexual encounter.

Paraphilias may also involve degrading oneself or inflicting suffering on one's sexual partner. Individuals who have sexual masochism are aroused when being humiliated, tied up, spanked, gagged, blindfolded, or made to feel pain or humiliation in other ways by a partner during sexual activity. Masochists may also get aroused by inflicting pain on themselves by piercing their bodies with sharp objects, giving themselves electric shock, and various other types of self-mutilation. In sexual sadism, the person is sexually aroused by causing psychological or physical pain in another person. The sadist may become sexually excited by hurting or humiliating a consenting partner (who is often a masochist) or may derive pleasure by torturing a nonconsenting victim.

Exhibitionism involves a man being turned on by exposing his genitals, usually to a female, without her consent. Often the exhibitionist will masturbate while exposing himself and fantasize that the observer is also sexually excited by this behavior. In Voyeurism, he is aroused by watching usually unsuspecting, but sometimes consenting, individuals who are either naked or engaging in various sexual activities. The "Peeping Tom" will usually masturbate while engaging in voyeuristic activity or shortly thereafter. Frotteurism involves groping at body parts of an unconsenting victim or rubbing genitals against her body. This usually occurs in a crowded public place, such as the subway, where close casual contact is easy to come by and an easy getaway is available.

By far the most dangerous type of Paraphilia is Pedophilia, involving any kind of sexual behavior with a child. Pedophiles often rationalize their behavior by saying that they have the best interests of the child in mind. They may claim to be providing a form of "sex education" or insist that the relationship is mutual and consenting. There are no ifs, ands, or buts about this issue. Sex with children is always criminal, exploitative, and takes unfair and selfish advantage of the child's inherent powerlessness. Some pedophiles are physically and psychologically aroused exclusively by children, while others may occasionally be attracted to adults. Girls are a bit more common as targets than boys.

The list of eight specific Paraphilias included in DSM-IV is by no means exhaustive. The range of other potential objects or situations that may become the source of sexual arousal is remarkably wide and also includes necrophilia (being turned on by corpses), zoophilia (by animals), telephone scatologia (by making obscene phone calls to unwilling recipients), coprophilia (by feces or defecation), and urophilia (by urine).

A diagnosis of a Paraphilia requires that the sexual deviation be significantly problematic. However, it must be stated clearly that you can't accept at face value the viewpoint of the paraphiliac about whether the impulses are causing trouble. Like Personality Disorders, most people with Paraphilias experience them as being a fundamental and necessary part of their makeup. It is very hard to give up a passion, however aberrant. For this reason, they rarely seek treatment of their own accord and are instead referred for help by their sexual partner or by the authorities as a consequence of criminal activity. From the perspective of the person with the Paraphilia, often the only "problem" is the restriction imposed by legal strictures, lack of available cooperative partners, or societal prohibitions on their ability to express their unusual sexual desires.

Because of the criminal nature of some paraphilic behavior (having sex with children, sexual sadism acted out on an unwilling participant), concerns have been raised that their inclusion in the official manual of mental disorders might serve as the basis for reduced legal responsibility or an insanity defense. An egregious, and fortunately unsuccessful, attempt in this direction was the assertion by Jeffrey Dahmer's expert witnesses that he was not responsible for his cannibalism because it was motivated by uncontrollable sexual impulses. Let's be perfectly clear—when an individual's sexual behavior results in criminal harm to others, or sex with a child, there should be no excuse or diminution of criminal responsibility just because these problems are discussed in a diagnostic manual used by mental health clinicians.

AM I OKAY?

There is no absolute standard about what constitutes the "normal" triggers for sexual arousal. In fact, Freud suggested that the "perversions" were residues of early infantile sexuality and fixations and exaggerations of what occurs during normal foreplay. It can sometimes be difficult to draw the line between exotic turn-ons and Paraphilias. The playing out of harmless voyeuristic, exhibitionistic, fetishistic, sadistic, and masochistic fantasies between consenting individuals may be a source of mutual sexual satisfaction—so long as both parties really like it and no harm is done. People with deviant sexual interests sometimes find complementary sexual partners who are willing (or even eager) to indulge or share in their fantasies. Problems typically set in when the paraphilic focus so dominates a relationship that the partner becomes dissatisfied or resentful. What turns on one person may be totally repulsive to someone else. Some people with Paraphilias are distressed by the guilt the playing out of the Paraphilia engenders. Others may present with an apparent Sexual Dysfunction that, on closer examination, is due to being in a relationship with a partner who is not "into" (or is repulsed by) the behavior. All this open-mindedness aside, there is no excuse—legal or psychiatric—for paraphilic behavior with children or nonconsenting adults. This is bad behavior, not mad behavior.

Treatment Options

We don't have any treatments that can guarantee the cure of severe and criminal Paraphilia. Unfortunately, recidivism rates are high. Paraphilias tend to be chronic and recurrent behaviors that are difficult to control even in those who are remorseful afterward and eager to change. Moreover, evaluating the success of treatment requires a very long-term perspective. Some individuals with Paraphilias may for prolonged periods keep their urges confined to fantasy and masturbation (and may therefore appear to be "cured") but then later revert to criminal action when a special opportunity arises (like an attractive child moving in next door). For this reason, the provision of psychiatric treatment should not be seen as a protection against future criminal activity.

The therapies that have been tried for the severe Paraphilias include behavioral conditioning, cognitive and emotional reframing, and castration. The behavioral therapy has two faces—an aversive pairing of unpleasant stimuli with paraphilic fantasies combined with the pairing of pleasurable experiences with desired healthy sexual alternatives. An additional behavioral technique is to teach the person to reduce the acting out of sexual impulses by substituting fantasy and masturbation. Reframing techniques challenge rationalizations that the criminal behavior is harmless or that the victims were willing partners. There is also an attempt to promote empathy for the victims' experience, especially drawing on the fact that many perpetrators were themselves childhood victims of paraphilic behavior. The most controversial treatment is castration, which can be achieved either through surgery or chemical means (which is, for better or worse, reversible). Aside from the civil liberties issue, the major concern about castration is that it may provide a false sense of security since recidivism, although reduced, can sometimes occur even after it has been performed.

The treatment is much more successful for milder Paraphilias in individuals who are strongly motivated to change. If there is a partner involved, couples treatment is usually preferable. The goal is to broaden the person's repertoire of sexual arousal beyond the narrow paraphilic focus on a particular fantasy or fetish. It may be useful to encourage the person to learn how to be satisfied with keeping things in fantasy or using pornographic material rather than going all the way, that is, indulging in actions (e.g., peeping, exhibiting, or masochism) that might lead to trouble.

GENDER IDENTITY DISORDER

The third type of disorder included in this chapter concerns yet a different aspect of sexuality—namely the fundamental gender sense of whether you are male or female. Gender identification is the end result of a complex biological and psychosocial developmental process. We acquire our sense of maleness or femaleness through some interaction between our inborn constitution and the gender role expectations of our caretakers. For most people, the end result is a clear-cut sense, "I am male" or "I am female," that fortunately is in sync with one's anatomical makeup. However, for some people, the process results in a gender identity that is at odds with anatomy. Such people feel that they are the victim of some cosmic mistake. They simultaneously have a strong desire to turn into the opposite gender and feel a compelling and distressing discomfort with their own sex. At the extreme, they are so repulsed by their own genitals that they want to surgically modify their anatomy to correct nature's error.

According to the diagnostic manual, you have Gender Identity Disorder if:
- You have a pronounced and long-standing identification with, and desire to become, the opposite gender.
- You also have been persistently uncomfortable (often to the point of repulsion) with the anatomical and gender role aspects of your sex.

DESCRIPTION

It is not uncommon for disturbances in gender identification to become apparent as early as two or three years of age. Girls with Gender Identity Disorder often rebel against wearing any kind of feminine clothing, preferring instead to wear masculine attire and short hair. They may request to be called by a boy's name and insist that they are boys. They usually play exclusively with boys, prefer sports and roughhousing, and show little interest in playing with dolls, "playing house," or engaging in other traditionally feminine role play activities. Girls with this condition may also express negative feelings toward the female anatomy. They may claim that they want to grow a penis and not have breasts, and insist on urinating while standing up like a boy.

Boys with Gender Identity Disorder usually dress up in their mother's or sister's clothing. They are often interested in traditionally feminine activities such as playing with dolls or playing house. They prefer girls as playmates and avoid traditionally masculine activities such as contact sports, or playing with toy guns and cars. They may pretend that they do not have a penis by hiding it between their legs and may insist on urinating sitting down like a girl.

The expression of cross-gender desires and behaviors by boys and girls often subjects them to harsh ridicule by their peers. The difficulty they experience in conforming to the stereotypes associated with their assigned gender makes them extremely inviting targets for schoolyard cruelty. Consequently, these individuals often have trouble developing same-sex friendships, which may compound feelings of rejection and isolation. Fortunately, only a small percentage of children with Gender Identity Disorder will continue as adults to have major distress regarding their gender identity. About 75 percent of boys with a childhood history of Gender Identity Disorder go on to develop either a homosexual or bisexual sexual orientation but usually without distressing gender identity problems. Most of the rest grow out of their gender identity problem with a heterosexual orientation. The corresponding statistics for girls are not known.

Adults with Gender Identity Disorder have an intense desire to function in society as a member of the opposite sex. They are often obsessed with altering their appearance to look like the other sex. Many individuals (known as transsexuals) spend large amounts of time and money cross-dressing and undergoing electrolysis, hormone treatments, or even surgery in an attempt to pass as a member of the opposite sex in public. They are extremely uncomfortable functioning within their biologically designated gender. Their sex lives are also quite complicated and they commonly do not allow partners to have any contact with their genitals. Not all adults with gender identity problems have an onset in childhood. Those who develop gender identity issues after adolescence usually get their start after learning that they can become sexually aroused by cross-dressing.

It is important to distinguish problems associated with a person's sense of self as male or female from issues regarding a person's sexual orientation. Being sexually attracted to people of the same sex (homosexuality) or desiring people of the opposite sex (heterosexuality) is a matter of sexual preference, not gender identification. Gender Identity Disorder describes a feeling of being trapped in the wrong body. Which sex one is attracted to is a separate question.

AM I OKAY?

In assessing problems relating to gender identity, one must keep in mind that masculine and feminine stereotypes, and the distress about not conforming to them, are culturally influenced and vary according to the developmental stage. The diagnosis of Gender Identity Disorder should be made cautiously and only when the cross-gender identification is long-standing, pervasive, and results in significant distress or impairment.

Given the lack of absolute standards for gender expression, the diagnosis almost entirely depends upon the level of distress and impairment. This explains why the disorder is diagnosed more often in children than in adults. Children are more likely to be distressed by the disapproval of their parents and by not fitting in with their peers. As they grow up, most children who have received this diagnosis no longer qualify for it more because of a reduction in distress about their gender feelings, rather than any change in their internal gender identification. They usually have found a peer support group that helps them to become less sensitive to both parental and societal disapproval.

The cogent argument has been made that Gender Identity Disorder is not so much a problem in the individual but rather a manifestation of cultural intolerance toward differences in gender self-expression. It is important for everyone (and perhaps particularly parents) to avoid overdiagnosing gender problems just because someone does not meet some narrowly drawn stereotype of what is appropriate masculinity or femininity. It appears that our culture is much more tolerant of cross-gender behavior in girls than in boys as evidenced by the fact that five times as many boys are referred to treatment as girls and that "sissy" has a much more pejorative connotation than "tomboy."

Nonconformity to male or female cultural stereotypes is not enough to warrant a diagnosis of Gender Identity Disorder. It must be part of a larger picture of profound and consuming disturbance and distress about the disparity between one's biologically assigned gender and how one feels about it. It is certainly perfectly normal for a girl to be a tomboy and for a boy to prefer playing with dolls and learning ballet—unless the child is miserable about the situation.

Treatment Options

The treatment of Gender Identity Disorder in children focuses on alleviating the child's current (and future) unhappiness that stems either from inner dissatisfaction or from parental disappointment or the cruelty other kids will often display toward someone who is different. As discussed above, only a small minority of children with Gender Identity Disorder will go on to transsexualism in adulthood, and there is some evidence that early therapeutic intervention may diminish the risk of its later development. In psychotherapy with the child, a goal is to insert a middle ground into the child's polarized view of gender roles. For example, boys who avoid playing male-stereotyped rough-and-tumble games can be encouraged to play board games with other boys. Girls who see athletics as an activity to be done only with boys can be encouraged to play with other athletic girls or on mixed teams. Family therapy can focus on strengthening the child's relationship with the same-sex parent. Fathers who may feel alienated from their sons because of a lack of interest in athletic play should be encouraged to find other mutually enjoyable activities (for example, camping, model building) that can serve as a foundation for building a renewed relationship. Peer stigmatization is a potent source of distress for the child that can lead to chronic low self-esteem. Behavioral techniques (parental explanations, reward systems) can be employed in younger children to discourage the overt display of cross-gender behaviors that lead to teasing. Although such superficial changes in behavior are unlikely to produce substantial internal changes, they do result in greater peer group acceptance and an enhanced self-image. When the child grows older and is mature enough to appreciate the pros and cons of unconventional behavior, then he or she can make a more informed decision.

For adolescents and adults with gender identity concerns, psychotherapy is the primary treatment. The primary goals of therapy are to address the self-blame for being different (often accompanied by a lifelong striving for self-punishment) and to explore the options available for comfortably coping with their gender condition. Options range from learning to integrate both male and female gender awareness into daily life, to living in the preferred gender role (aided by cosmetic aids and hormonal therapy), to sex reassignment surgery. Many people who are convinced that sex change surgery is their only viable option are uninterested in psychotherapy, feeling that it is merely an impediment on their way to a "real" cure. It is important for them to recognize that sex reassignment surgery is not for everyone and is likely to be successful only after the person has been psychologically prepared. For this reason, six to twelve months of psychotherapy is usually a prerequisite to surgery and the person must go through a six-to-twelve-month period of assuming the desired gender role (called "living the true-life test"). Sex change surgery is much less popular nowadays than it once was because the results can be disappointing, especially if selection and preparation are not done very carefully.

Suggested Additional Readings

Love Again, Live Again: New Treatments, New Hope for Today's Couples
    Facing Male Impotence
    Steven Morganstern
    Prentice Hall, 1994

The Kinsey Institute New Report on Sex: What You Must Know
to Be Sexually Literate
June M. Reinisch, Ph.D.
St. Martin's Mass Market Paper, 1994

Becoming Orgasmic: A Sexual and Personal Growth Program for Women
Julia Heiman and Joseph Lopiccolo
Simon & Schuster, 1988

Where to Go for Help
(Self-help, support, for more information)

Impotence Information Center

P.O. Box 9
Minneapolis, MN 55440
(800) 843-4315
Web: http://www.ams-pfizer.com/

American Association of Sex Education
(listings of sex counselors and sex therapists)

P.O. Box 238
Mt. Vernon, IA 52314-0238

Impotents Anonymous (IA) and I-Anon.
(information and support for impotent men
and partners of impotent men)

Impotence Institute of America
10400 Little Patuxent Parkway #485
Columbia, MD 21044-3502
(800) 669-1603
(301) 565-2718

CHAPTER 9

SLEEP-RELATED PROBLEMS

S leep is one of the great mysteries and joys of life—and a bad night's sleep, or a series of them, is one of its great miseries. Sleep is pretty much a universal in the animal kingdom reaching down to very primitive forms. The many variations of the sleep-wake cycle all undoubtedly evolved as different and creative adaptations to the day-night rhythm of our planet.

While all humans must sleep for a substantial fraction of each day, there are wide individual differences in sleep quantity and quality. This is probably no accident and serves its own adaptive purpose. A tribe would benefit from having very different types of sleepers—from early birds to night owls—so that there would be a continuity of lookouts, night watchmen, and fire tenders. The fitfulness of our sleep can be a nuisance but is also useful—humans are easy to rouse because being sluggish could be fatal.

Sleep patterns also undergo considerable change across the life span of any one person. Newborns sleep an average of sixteen hours a day. This decreases to an adult average of about seven to nine hours, with women requiring about one hour more each day than men. Starting in middle age, sleep efficiency progressively declines and there is more difficulty falling asleep, more awakenings during the night, and less really deep sleep. It is a good idea to tailor your sleep expectations to your gender and age. If a man and wife keep the same hours, she is likely to be sleep-deprived. If you expect to sleep as well at seventy-five as you did at twenty-five, you will be frustrated, disappointed, and risk resorting to sleeping pills that will end up making your sleep much worse.

Reasonably adequate sleep is essential for normal physiological and mental functioning. Individuals subjected to sleep deprivation exhibit irritability, inability to concentrate, blurred vision, slurred speech, memory lapses, and poor performance on tests of cognition and coordination. In extreme cases of continuous sleep deprivation, some people develop brief hallucinations and other psychotic symptoms. Poor sleep may be both a trigger and a sign of a number of the other psychiatric disorders described elsewhere in this book. Nonetheless, most people probably get more sleep than they realize and have unrealistic expectations of perfect sleep.

Sleep has a characteristic architecture. There are five different stages each with a characteristic pattern on sleep electroencephalography—four stages of non-rapid eye movement (NREM) sleep and one stage of rapid eye movement (REM). Normal sleep begins with a transition from the state of wakefulness to the lightest form of "falling" asleep. This NREM Stage 1 is the shortest of sleep stages, accounting only for 5 percent of the time spent asleep. NREM Stage 2 Sleep occupies half to about three quarters the sleep time of healthy adults and is when sleep talking occurs. Stages 3 and 4 of NREM Sleep occupy about 20 percent of the total sleep period and represent the deepest levels of sleep with much slower EEG wave-forms. It is during these stages that sleepwalking and night terrors occur.

REM Sleep is among the most fascinating of human experiences. It is during the bursts of eye movements that our dreams occur. If we understand surprisingly little about the function of sleep, we still understand next to nothing about how and why we dream. Typically, episodes of REM Sleep occur about every 90 minutes throughout the sleep cycle, and increase in length as the night progresses. Other phenomena occurring during REM Sleep include erections, sleep paralysis, and blood pressure increases.

There are basically four types of sleep difficulty: sleeping too little (insomnia), sleeping too much (hypersomnia), sleeping at the wrong times (circadian rhythm disturbance), or having unusual events during sleep, like sleepwalking. The Sleep Disorders are also distinguished from one another based upon whether it is possible to identify the underlying cause—substance abuse or a medication taken for a medical illness, a psychiatric condition, or a mismatch between body rhythms and external demands. If no specific cause can be determined, then the diagnosis is Primary Insomnia, Primary Hypersomnia, or one of the Parasomnias (Nightmare Disorder, Sleep Terror Disorder, or Sleepwalking Disorder).

SUBSTANCE-INDUCED SLEEP DISORDER

If you are having trouble sleeping, the first thing to wonder about is whether a substance or medication may be causing your problem. Caffeine and alcohol are the most frequent offenders and probably cause more sleepless nights than all of the other causes combined. The use of caffeine, amphetamines, and cocaine stimulates arousal and delays sleep, whereas withdrawal results in hypersomnia. Alcohol, sedatives, and opioids are initially sedating, but wind up fragmenting and ruining sleep.

Over-the-counter decongestants, diet pills, and sleep aids are frequent unrecognized causes of insomnia, and antihistamines may be responsible for falling asleep at the wheel. Antidepressants frequently have sleep side effects that can go in either direction (insomnia or hypersomnia), depending on the type of medication and individual variability in response. For example, even though the SSRI's (Prozac, Paxil, Zoloft, and Luvox) are usually "activating" and more likely to cause insomnia, some people respond with sedation and hypersomnia. Most of the illegal drugs interfere with normal sleep patterns, often in a major league way.

Sometimes it is hard to tell which came first, the sleep problem or the drug use that accompanies it. A frequent scenario is that you begin taking a medication or a nighttime drink of alcohol to help with insomnia. After a while, however, you become physiologically dependent on the sleeping aid and develop a more severe and persistent insomnia if you miss taking it than you ever had in the first place.

According to the diagnostic manual, you have a Substance-Induced Sleep Disorder if:
- You have problems falling asleep or staying asleep, are sleeping too much, or are feeling sleepy during the day.
- Your sleep problem is due to drinking alcohol, taking too much of a drug (such as caffeine, cocaine, or amphetamine), withdrawing from a drug that you have been taking for a long time (such as sleeping pills), or is a side effect of a medication that you have been taking.
- Your sleep problem is severe enough to interfere with your ability to function on a daily basis.

SLEEP DISORDER DUE TO
A GENERAL MEDICAL CONDITION

Most physical illnesses can cause sleep disturbances—usually as a consequence of the associated symptoms of pain, urinary frequency, coughing, respiratory discomfort, esophageal reflux, or itchiness. Other medical conditions, such as Parkinson's disease and Alzheimer's disease, can disrupt sleep through their direct impact on the brain.

Sleep apnea has alternating periods of extremely loud snoring and gasping, followed by thirty seconds (and sometimes much longer) of silence during which breathing stops. You are probably unaware of the nighttime dramatics unless you have been told about them by your terrified bed partner. Your sleep is unrefreshing and you nod off during the day. Sleep apnea can have a number of different causes, but is most frequently seen in people who are overweight.

Narcolepsy is an inherited neurological condition with disturbed regulation of REM sleep. You have repeated, uncontrollable sleep attacks that can happen in inappropriate and even dangerous situations—while driving a car, attending a class, or even in the middle of a conversation. The sleep interludes usually last approximately fifteen minutes, after which you wake up fully rested and refreshed but the extreme sleepiness may return and lead to another attack within a few hours. Many of the symptoms in narcolepsy represent elements of REM sleep intruding into daily life. Cataplexy is a sudden loss of muscle tone that may be so extreme that it causes you to collapse. This can be understood as an attack of sleep paralysis (which is a normal part of REM sleep) occurring during the day. Cataplexy is usually precipitated by powerful emotions of anger, despair, or shock, or by uncontrollable laughter. Sometimes elements of REM sleep take over as you fall asleep or when you wake up. Even though you are awake, you have dreamlike hallucinations and find yourself unable to speak or move any muscle in your body. Although quite terrifying, such episodes usually resolve after a few minutes. Perhaps this is the source for some zombie legends.

According to the diagnostic manual, you have Sleep Disorder Due to a General Medical Condition if:
- You have problems falling asleep or staying asleep, are sleeping too much, or are feeling sleepy during the day.
- Your sleep problem is due to the direct effects of a medical condition or because of the discomfort it causes.
- Your sleep problem is severe enough to interfere with your ability to function on a daily basis.

SLEEP DISORDER RELATED
TO ANOTHER MENTAL DISORDER

Sleep problems are a common feature of most mental disorders and often are the initial reason for seeking help. For example, people with Major Depressive Disorder (page 33) often have trouble falling asleep, wake up during the night, or have early morning awakening. In Bipolar I Disorder (page 61), there is much less need for sleep during manic episodes and prominent insomnia or hypersomnia during depressive periods. People suffering from Generalized Anxiety Disorder (page 95) often worry themselves out of falling asleep and may also awaken in the middle of the night contemplating the horrors of tomorrow. Nocturnal panic attacks can disrupt sleep. Posttraumatic Stress Disorder (page 110) may cause a dread of falling asleep "perchance to dream" the terrifying details of the traumatic event. Schizophrenia (page 313) sometimes results in a reversal of day/night sleep patterns.

If you have a psychiatric disorder, it is always a good idea to keep track of how well you are sleeping since this can tell you something about how the disorder is doing. A pattern of disrupted sleep is often the first signal of a relapse and a good sign that you need to get help. Sleep deprivation may also trigger episodes of psychiatric illness.

According to the diagnostic manual, you have Sleep Disorder Related to a Psychiatric Disorder if:

- You have problems falling asleep or staying asleep, are sleeping too much, or are feeling sleepy during the day, and these problems have lasted for at least one month.
- Your sleep problem is really a symptom of another psychiatric disorder, like Major Depressive Disorder (page 33), Bipolar I Disorder (page 61), or Generalized Anxiety Disorder (page 95).
- Your sleep problem is severe enough to interfere with your ability to function on a daily basis.

CIRCADIAN RHYTHM SLEEP DISORDER

The trouble here does not arise from any inherent problem in your ability to sleep, but is caused instead by a mismatch between your innate sleep-wake cycle and the demands dictated by your environment. There are four different scenarios.

The first is the "night owl." Your internal circadian rhythm is delayed and has you waking and sleeping several hours behind the rest of your world. Left to your own devices, you fall asleep well past midnight and wake up around noon or even later. You have no problem with this sleep pattern unless you are forced to conform to a "normal" nine to five work schedule. You find it impossible to fall asleep and wake up when everyone else does, gradually become sleep-deprived, have excessive daytime sleepiness, require several alarm clocks to get up, and feel miserable all morning.

The advanced sleep phase pattern, a.k.a. "early birds" or "starlings," describes people with the opposite problem. You fall asleep shortly after dinner and wake up raring to go hours before sunrise. This usually results in less work or school impairment than being a night owl (and may even increase productivity), but starlings can miss out on a lot of nighttime recreation and put quite a damper on family fun.

The third kind of Circadian Rhythm Sleep Disorder is caused by frequent jet lag resulting from repeated travel to and from radically different time zones. There is a strong correlation between the severity of the impairment and the number of zones you traverse. The greatest difficulty results when you travel through more than eight different time zones in less than twenty-four hours. Most people are able to adapt more easily to westward travel and have a really tough time coming east. Starlings do better, however, adjusting to the advancing hours of eastward flight.

The fourth type of Circadian Rhythm Sleep Disorder results from the unsettling schedule demands of shift work. Nearly a quarter of Americans are employed in jobs that are off the typical 8 A.M. to 5 P.M. schedule. Working the night shift, or constantly rotating shifts, results in inadequate hours of sleep, poor sleep continuity, and the disruption of circadian rhythms. People who work rotating shifts tend to suffer the most impairment because they must constantly readjust their sleep-wake cycles. Even those with regular runs of overnight shift work (for example, four overnight shifts followed by three days off) have trouble because of the desire to keep going back to a "normal" schedule on the days off in order to be in sync with family members and store-opening hours. Insomnia is also common because of ambient daytime disturbances (traffic noises, sunlight, ringing telephones, and family and social obligations). Job performance and morale can be jeopardized by on-the-job fatigue resulting from the inability to sleep during off-hours.

According to the diagnostic manual, you have Circadian Rhythm Sleep Disorder if:
- You have a problem falling asleep or excessive sleepiness during the day caused by a mismatch between your body's internal clock and the sleep-wake requirements of your external world.
- The mismatch comes from your being a night owl or an early bird, or having to do shift work, or constantly flying across time zones so that your body can never adjust to the time changes.
- Your sleep problems are severe enough to interfere with your ability to function on a daily basis.

PRIMARY INSOMNIA

Primary Insomnia describes difficulties in falling asleep or maintaining sleep that are not due to one of the specific causes of insomnia we have discussed above. You are not using a substance, have no medical or psychiatric illness, and do not do shift work or international consulting, but you are still having a terrible problem getting a decent night's sleep. You may have trouble falling asleep, or you may wake up intermittently throughout the night once sleep has been achieved, or you may wake up at 4:30 A.M. and can't go back to sleep, or all of these. You may also feel that whatever sleep you do get is not very restful or restorative. As a result, you are sleepy all day and have poor concentration, lethargy, irritability, and decreased motivation. Because of insufficient nighttime sleep, you may unintentionally fall asleep in the daytime, often while performing tedious tasks or attending boring meetings. This can be dangerous if you are driving, operating machinery, or engaging in any other activity that requires you to be on full alert.

Primary Insomnia often starts with faulty sleep habits and bad sleep hygiene. The most likely culprits are irregular sleep patterns, working or studying late into the night, frequent or extended daytime naps, or sleeping in extremely late. Trouble sleeping is likely to increase during periods of social, occupational, medical, or psychological stress. Insomnia tends to feed on itself because of negative conditioning triggered by the tossing and turning that goes on in your bed. You are so worried about not being able to sleep that sleep becomes impossible. The harder you try to sleep, the less able you are to turn your worries off. Your own bed becomes the last place in the world where you can fall asleep. Instead, you doze off in front of the TV or while reading in an easy chair. Then you wake up after midnight to go to bed, but you can't sleep another wink for the rest of the night because you start worrying again about not being able to fall asleep. You sleep better while on the road in hotels or in the guest room of your own house.

According to the diagnostic manual, you have Primary Insomnia if:
- You have trouble falling or staying asleep or you feel the quality of your sleep is poor.
- This leads to daytime fatigue and drowsiness that is severe enough to interfere with your functioning on a daily basis, and has lasted for at least one month.
- All other causes for the sleep problem have been considered and ruled out—the insomnia is not due to a medical condition or substance, is not a side effect of a medication, and is not a symptom of a psychiatric condition, like depression.

PRIMARY HYPERSOMNIA

People with this disorder can't get enough sleep. They are still tired after having slept what for others is more than an adequate number of hours. Although your sleep may be continuous, it is not restful, refreshing, or restorative. You have trouble getting up even after ten to twelve hours of sleep. You need two alarm clocks to rouse yourself out of bed, after which you wander around in a daze, a condition known as "sleep drunkenness." It may take hours before you are even reasonably alert. Your excessive sleepiness persists into the daytime hours, causing frequent naps. Low-stimulation situations (attending a lecture, watching TV) cause you to drift off.

Although sleepiness is certainly common enough in this modern world, cases of Primary Hypersomnia are relatively rare, accounting for less than

10 percent of people seeking treatment for excessive fatigue and need for sleep. Excessive daytime sleepiness can usually be traced to sleep deprivation (often as a result of insomnia or burning the candle at both ends) or to narcolepsy, sleep apnea, or a medication side effect.

According to the diagnostic manual, you have Primary Hypersomnia if:

- You spend too many hours at night sleeping and yet still feel sleepy during the day.
- The daytime fatigue, drowsiness, or excessive sleeping is severe enough to interfere with your functioning on a daily basis and has lasted for at least one month.
- Your sleepiness is not just because you are chronically sleep-deprived.
- All other causes for the sleep problem have been considered and ruled out.

NIGHTMARE DISORDER

Lots of people have the occasional odd nightmare. This is certainly scary and unpleasant, but is not considered a sleep disorder unless the episodes are persistent and cause impairment. You are awakened from your sleep by recurrent frightening dreams filled with impending danger. You are being chased, physically assaulted, or even killed. In less common dream scripts, the danger is more subtle—having to pitch the World Series in your underwear or constantly getting lost on your way to take a test. Or you may have to "relive" a traumatic event that occurred in your life by dreaming the terrifying details of the war zone, or the rape scene, or the hurricane, over and over again. The nightmare ends with your abrupt awakening—fully alert, covered in perspiration, heart racing, but relieved it was just a dream. Often you can't get back to sleep. The scary nightmares may occur with such frequency that you try to avoid sleeping altogether or have great difficulty falling asleep. Nightmares occur solely during the REM phases of the sleep cycle and are therefore more likely to occur, and to be more intense, later in the night. The resulting sleep disruptions can lead to excessive daytime sleepiness, irritability, and lack of concentration.

According to the diagnostic manual, you have Nightmare Disorder if:
- You are repeatedly awakened by detailed and vivid terrible dreams.
- The dreams and sleep interruptions are frequent enough and upsetting enough to interfere with your ability to function on a daily basis.

SLEEP TERROR DISORDER

Sleep terrors are frightening experiences occurring during sleep that, unlike nightmares, are not associated with dreaming. The person is in the midst of a deep Stage 4 sleep but experiences a feeling of terror, often accompanied by screaming, crying, rapid breathing, and sweating. He may actively resist others' attempts to provide comfort by kicking, hitting, and lashing out as if to avoid imaginary harm. Most of the time, he does not fully awaken and instead resumes sleeping with no recollection of the episode the next morning. If he does wake up during the sleep terror episode, he will feel bewildered and disoriented. Sleep terrors are more apt to occur toward the beginning of the night when deep sleep is more prominent. Sleep terrors are most common in children—6 percent of children experience them as compared to less than 1 percent of adults. The problem usually starts between ages four and twelve and resolves spontaneously during adolescence.

According to the diagnostic manual, you have Sleep Terror Disorder if:
- You have frequent episodes in which you suddenly wake up with a scream and with signs of extreme fear (like racing pulse, heavy breathing, and sweating).
- In contrast to nightmares, you have no memory of a bad dream when you awaken and do not remember the incident the next morning.
- You (or your family) are so upset about these episodes that you seek professional help.

SLEEPWALKING DISORDER

The person has recurring periods of walking, sitting, speaking, or eating while asleep—usually lasting from a few minutes to half an hour. The sleepwalker seems unaware of the surroundings, has a blank stare, and does not react to the efforts of others to awaken him. He may get out of bed, walk downstairs, eat, use the bathroom, or even leave the house. Articulation is slurred and difficult to understand. While the behavior in sleepwalking is usually simple, more complex tasks like driving a car or operating machinery are sometimes performed. The episode may include inappropriate actions, such as urinating in the kitchen or climbing into someone else's bed. Occasionally, the sleepwalker may appear to run away, as if fleeing from some pursuing danger.

If awakened (which is extremely difficult to do), he is disoriented for a brief time and then regains a normal level of alertness. He may then return to bed, continue sleeping, and have no recollection of the episode in the morning. This can be unsettling if you awaken in a location different from where you originally went to sleep, having no idea how or why you got there. Sleepwalking usually occurs during Stage 3 or 4 of NREM sleep, usually early in the night. Episodes may be provoked by alcohol or drug use in someone who is vulnerable. Sleepwalking is common in childhood—from 10 to 30 percent of children have had at least one episode of sleepwalking. However, fewer than 5 percent have repeated episodes. It usually begins between ages four and eight and resolves on its own during adolescence. A child who sleepwalks is often unwilling to sleep over at a friend's house or go away to overnight camp because of embarrassment about the problem.

According to the diagnostic manual, you have Sleepwalking Disorder if:
- You repeatedly have episodes of sleepwalking during which you do not respond when others try to communicate with you.
- After you wake up, you have no memory that you were walking around.
- These incidents put you at potential hazard for injury.

AM I OKAY?

From time to time most people are dissatisfied with the quality or refreshingness of their sleep. There is no clear boundary between a clinical Sleep Disorder and the occasional and expectable problem any of us will sometimes have sleeping. Be mindful that there is no standard for "normal" sleep and no one can expect to have perfect sleep. People vary a great deal in the number of hours of sleep they need to feel rested. The fact that sleep efficiency declines with age means that we all eventually must adjust to increasing difficulty falling asleep, nightly wake-ups, and getting up earlier in the morning. Women generally need more sleep than men and should not see this as hypersomnia or laziness. It is also of great interest that many people who complain of insomnia underestimate the actual number of hours they sleep as measured by a sleep laboratory. You may be getting more rest than you think. It is important not to exaggerate the significance of everyday sleep complaints because the treatment is often worse than the problem, or at least likely to make the problem worse. The use of sleeping pills probably creates more insomnia than it improves.

Before assuming that you have a Sleep Disorder, make sure that the problem is persistent (for at least one month) and that it is causing you serious trouble. Mild situational sleep problems don't count. Is your sleep problem happening day after day? Does it cause daytime tiredness that makes it difficult for you to stay awake at your job or keep your car on the road? Are you having problems concentrating? Do you feel miserable, testy, and on edge during the day because you didn't get refreshing sleep the night before?

Also, don't assume you have a Sleep Disorder if you tend to burn the candle at both ends. There is a limit on how much we can evade the dictates of our powerful circadian rhythms without paying a severe price.

Occasional nightmares, sleep terrors, or sleepwalking have no special clinical significance, especially in children. A diagnosis should be made only if the problem is causing trouble on a regular basis.

TREATMENT OPTIONS

Probably the biggest problem in the treatment of sleep problems is that there has been far too much of it—especially too much use of sleep medicines, which usually make matters worse. The first step is to have realistic expectations. Many of us are far too preoccupied with the notion that we must have a perfect night's sleep every night and be ready to perform at peak levels the next morning. This ideal is just not in the cards for everyone every night and is very far from being achieved by most people, most nights.

Part of the problem is that we were evolved in an environment that was much more sleeper-friendly than the modern world. Before candles and electricity, night was dark, quiet, boring, and restful. Before clocks, people slept more to their own schedule following the mysterious beats of their internal body rhythms. They also did not routinely bathe their brains in stimulating substances and did not often have the luxury of a preslumber gorge. The heating, cooling, mattresses, and blankets may not have been as comfortable then but everything else was infinitely more soporific than anything we now experience at bedtime.

The modern world almost makes sleep an endangered species. We have too much light, sound, variety, things to do, fun to have, problems to worry about. We expect our brains to work overtime on full alert and then turn off at the snap of the light switch. It doesn't work that way. A revved-up motor needs a cooling down. Add to this the reduced sleep efficiency that comes with aging, the use of substances, changing time zones, and wake-up calls and it is no great surprise that so many people want help with their sleep.

Do the simple things first. Perhaps most important, get into the habit of easing into sleep, not charging at it in battle formation. Have as regular a bedtime as possible, one that suits your body rhythms rather than constantly fights them. Do things before sleep that slow you down, soothe, and calm you. Whatever relaxes you or bores you is likely good preparation. Put the worries of the day where they belong—on the shelf. There is plenty of time to attend to them tomorrow and nothing ever looks as important in hindsight. A steady plodding regular approach to sleep that goes with your natural flow is the best protection from insomnia.

There are a few other simple things to do that are just part of good sleep hygiene. Don't nap excessively during the day unless that is part of your natural rhythm. Don't do vigorous exercise after sunset—it may get you going. Don't use substances. Pick a room temperature that works best for you. Keep out light and noise or use a noise generator if you like. Don't do a late night pig-out—a light snack will hit the spot.

Many people become behaviorally conditioned by years of insomnia to associate bedtime and their bedroom with tossing, turning, and worrying about falling asleep. Stimulus control therapy attempts to break this negative connection and restore the status quo by reassociating bed with restful sleep. The instructions include going to bed only when you are sleepy, using your bed only for sex and sleep (no reading, TV watching, or eating in bed), and getting out of bed and going into another room if you are unable to fall asleep within twenty minutes, returning only when you are sleepy. Some people find this the perfect time to do the paperwork they have piled up—if you are lucky, having to face it will put you right to sleep. Others find reading a long novel or watching a movie or listening to music most conducive to nodding off. Some do relaxation exercises or meditation to wash out the day and prepare for the night.

Poor sleepers sometimes lengthen their time in bed in order to increase the opportunity for sleep. This is a terrible strategy that results in tossing fretfully and having disrupted sleep. Sleep restriction therapy counteracts this by more closely matching your time in bed with your sleep time. The first step is to stay in bed for only the amount of time you think you are sleeping each night, plus fifteen minutes. For example, if you have been sleeping five hours at night and normally get up at six, you are allowed to get to bed no earlier than 12:45 A.M. Once you are able to successfully remain asleep for around 90 percent of the allotted time, you increase the in-bed time by going to bed fifteen minutes earlier. This process is successively repeated until the desired sleep time is achieved, which usually takes from three to four weeks.

Although sleeping pills may help for a few days to a few weeks, they don't work for the long term. Their best use is for short periods in people who need an immediate relief from insomnia because it is a symptom of mental disorder or medical illness. The sedative/hypnotics, tricyclic antidepressants, and antihistamines all have their advantages and mostly disadvantages. Most of the sedative/hypnotics, the most widely prescribed sleeping pills, come from the same chemical class, the benzodiazepines. Some are specifically marketed as sleeping aids (Dalmane, Restoril, ProSom, Doral, Halcion, and Ambien) and most of the others (like Ativan, Xanax) are sometimes used in this way. Although in the short term, these medicines can induce sleep with minimal hangover effects, they are ineffective for long-term use and can produce physical or psychological addiction. People develop tolerance to the sleep effects and must continually raise the doses to keep having an effect. Abruptly stopping the medicine (because you forgot to take your pills on a trip) results in rebound insomnia that may be worse than the original problem. Amnesia is common, making these impractical for use by people who might have to function unexpectedly in the middle of the night (like a physician-on-call). Finally, the elderly have to be especially careful because these medicines can cause confusion, delirium, or falls (see Chapter16).

Several of the antidepressants have been used to help induce sleep, taking advantage of their sedating side effects. Desyrel, Sinequan, and Elavil are probably used most often. Although they have the advantage of not causing addiction, some people experience significant next-day effects, finding that they feel foggy. Many cold and allergy medications containing antihistamines (such as Benadryl) cause significant drowsiness as a side effect and are used by many to assist sleep. Antihistamines are the most common active ingredient in over-the-counter sleeping pills. Hangovers, unfortunately, are common.

Hypersomnia is even more difficult to treat. Behavioral treatments have not been particularly successful in shortening sleep time or reducing daytime drowsiness. Usually the treatment focuses on counteracting daytime fatigue with stimulant medications, such as Ritalin, Cylert, or Dexedrine.

Circadian Rhythm Sleep Disorder can be treated with maneuvers to reset the body's internal clock so that it more closely matches the demands of the environment. Delayed ("night owl") or advanced ("lark") sleep phase problems can be improved by exposure to bright light at the right time of day—morning for the "owl" and evening for the "lark." Bright light exposure is not particularly effective for shift workers because it can advance the body's clock only gradually, by an hour or two a day, which does not keep up with the rapidly changing requirements of changing shifts. For jet lag, appropriately timed bright light can help to shift your internal clock in the direction of the local time. For example, if you are going from the East to the West Coast, you might try bright light exposure in the mornings before departure in order to shift your clock earlier. Because it usually takes several days to change your internal clock, for short stays it often makes sense not to resynchronize your sleep pattern to the local time but instead to stick with your usual sleep times, if your schedule allows. The health food supplement melatonin appears to have some effect in shifting the internal clock, working in the opposite direction of bright light (that is, a dose of melatonin in the morning moves the clock later rather than earlier).

Because accidents during Sleepwalking Disorder can be life-threatening, safety measures are essential. Sleep on the ground floor, lock doors and windows, and remove potentially dangerous objects from the bedroom. Sleepwalking and sleep terror occur only during deep NREM sleep. If you avoid sleep deprivation, this reduces the time spent in the deeper stages of sleep and reduces the risk of sleepwalking. Fortunately, most children who have these problems outgrow them.

Suggested Additional Readings

Getting to Sleep: Simple, Effective Methods for Falling and Staying Asleep, Getting the Rest You Need, and Awakening Refreshed and Renewed
Ellen Mohr Catalano
New Harbinger, 1990

67 Ways to Good Sleep
Charles B. Inlander and Cynthia K. Moran
Walker, 1995

Coping with Sleep Disorders
Carolyn Simpson
Rosen, 1996

Where to Go for Help
(Self-help, support, for more information)

American Narcolepsy Association
P.O. Box 26230
San Francisco, CA 94126-6230
(800) 222-6085
FAX: (415) 788-4795

American Sleep Disorders Association
1610 Fourteenth Street, N.W., Suite 200
Rochester, MN 55901
E-mail: asda@asda.org
Web: http://www.asda.org/

National Sleep Foundation
729 Fifteenth Street, N.W., Fourth Floor
Washington, D.C. 20005
E-mail: natsleep@erols.com
Web: http://www.sleepfoundation.org/

Shuteye Helpline
(800) SHUTEYE [(800) 748-8393]

Narcolepsy Network
(support and education)

P.O. Box 42460
Cincinnati, OH 45242
(513) 891-3522
FAX: (513) 793-4348

CHAPTER 10

PERSONALITY DISORDERS

Personality is the enduring pattern of our thoughts, feelings, and behaviors. Each of us displays our unique personality fingerprint in the special way we think, love, feel, make decisions, and take action. The extraordinary range of human personality is what lends special color to our lives and is the stuff of tragedy, comedy, and melodrama. Gaining a better understanding of your personality will give you more control over your life and a clearer perspective about why things work out for you and why they don't.

Fortunately, most of us are born already equipped with great intuitive skill in evaluating personality (at least other people's). We humans evolved as a very social species. Our ancestors survived and had offspring to the extent they were skilled in predicting the likely behavior of a potential mate, friend, or foe based on a quick personality read. These same natural skills remain highly rewarded in modern society, perhaps most especially among poker players, politicians, coaches, businessmen, and psychotherapists.

The systematic study of personality had its origins very early in the history of medicine and philosophy. The ancient Greeks guessed correctly that differences in behavior are caused by differences in bodily functioning. Hippocrates, the father of medicine, believed that temperamental differences resulted from an excess or deficit in what he thought were the four essential bodily fluids (blood, yellow bile, black bile, and phlegm). For example, if someone had an excess of blood this would result in an optimistic and extroverted personality (the "sanguine" temperament) and in the extreme could also cause mania. An excess of black bile would produce a pessimistic personality (the "melancholic" temperament) and a tendency to depression. Yellow bile was associated with an angry and irritable outlook on life (the "choleric" temperament) and an abundance of lymph was behind a stoic and apathetic personality (the "phlegmatic" temperament).

Subsequently, there have been many theories attributing personality to physical characteristics other than body fluids. Aristotle believed that differences in personality were related to differences in facial expression. Gall attributed them to the shape and contour of the bones of the skull. Kretschmer and Sheldon described three different body types, each with its own specific personality characteristics and illness tendencies. A slim and fine-boned body build (an "ectomorph") was associated with shyness and introversion and an increased risk for Schizophrenia. A muscular physique (a "mesomorph") was related to activity and assertiveness and an increased risk for Antisocial Personality Disorder. A soft and round body type (an "endomorph") resulted in an extroverted and jovial personality, with a risk for mood disorders.

The modern concept of personality functioning has its roots in the work of Darwin and Freud. Darwin observed that human behavior evolved from animal behavior under the same shaping pressures of natural and sexual selection responsible for the evolution of our physical characteristics. The best way to understand the essence of human nature is to study its relationship to the animal behavior from which it is derived. Darwin once joked (with great seriousness) that we could learn more about philosophy by studying baboons than by reading John Locke. Freud went Darwin one step further. He suggested that differences in personality result from differences in inborn instinctual endowments, which are then shaped in the interaction with early life experiences. Erik Erikson extended the model to cover personality development as a response to the different rites of passage from birth to death.

This "nature interacting with nurture" model of personality has been confirmed most compellingly by studies comparing the temperamental similarities and differences in identical versus fraternal twins. Identical twins have identical genes, while fraternal twins are no more genetically similar than are any set of brothers and sisters. The consistent finding across many comparisons of identical versus fraternal twins is that variations in temperament are strongly influenced by differences in genetic endowment. A wonderful cartoon illustrating this point shows two identical twins carefully hiding from one another their remarkably complex, but absolutely identical, inventions—the caption says, "Separated at birth, the Rosenzweig twins meet for the first time at the Patent Office."

How shy, aggressive, or extroverted you are is about one half determined by your genes and about one half determined by your environment. Your personality functioning is influenced by genes almost as strongly as is your IQ. Most parents come to realize that the temperamental differences among their children can be clearly distinguished within a few months after birth. Studies show that these early indications remain fairly good predictors of later temperamental differences at least throughout childhood, adolescence, and early adulthood.

There is currently a very active research effort aimed at determining the specific mechanisms responsible for personality differences. The basic questions are: Which genes are involved in causing which temperaments? How do these genes cause differences in brain neurotransmitters and neuroreceptors? And, finally, how does this biology influence and get influenced by the person's environment and experience? Hippocrates was absolutely right in guessing that biology influences temperament, but the limitations of his science prevented him from picking the right "fluids." The hunt to find the biology of personality is still on, but now for the first time we have the powerful scientific tools needed to do the job. Within the next three decades, we should have answers to questions about human nature that have teased the best minds for the past three millennia.

Character strongly determines fate. Our destinies are much more written in our personalities than in our stars. Personality functioning exerts enormous influence over how our lives are lived. People with Personality Disorders have more difficulty in every aspect of life. They are less likely to have happy marriages, be successful parents, and function as effective team players at work. They are more likely to have psychiatric and medical disorders, to have a poor response to psychiatric and medical treatment, to get in trouble with the law, and to be generally miserable.

———————

According to the diagnostic manual, you have a Personality Disorder if:
- You have an enduring pattern of inner experience and behavior that puts you at odds with the expectations of the world around you. This shows itself in the following ways:
  (1) How you perceive and understand yourself and others
  (2) How you respond emotionally
  (3) How you interact with people
  (4) How you control your impulses
- You are unbending and inflexible and cannot adjust your behavior to the needs of a particular situation, activity, or relationship.
- Your personality problem started early in life (by adolescence or early adulthood) and has persisted in a pretty stable way over time.

- Your personality is upsetting to you or limits your success at school, at work, or in relationships.
- The behavior is long-standing and is not caused by another chronic or recurrent psychiatric disorder, by a medical condition, or by substance use.

Having a personality disorder means you are not the kind of person who can adapt smoothly to the normal give-and-take of everyday life. Instead, you expect the world and people to change for you rather than being able to adjust to the requirements of different situations and relationships. You behave in a rigid and inflexible way that perpetuates vicious cycles and fulfills your worst prophecies.

Having a closed mind means that you misperceive or filter out new information that does not support your expectations. Then you act in a way that elicits just those responses from others that will make your negative expectations a reality. For example, suppose you are paranoid and believe that everyone is conspiring against you. You will inevitably become suspicious and mistrustful of them in a way that will cause them to become reciprocally mistrustful of you—which in turn confirms your feeling of being conspired against. Similarly, if you are shy because you anticipate rejection and humiliation, you will act in an anxious and socially inept way that ultimately leads others to reject and tease you—which then makes you even more shy and avoidant. Having a Personality Disorder means that you get in the same fix over and over again and can never figure out quite why or how.

DSM-IV describes ten separate Personality Disorders, which may occur singly, or even more often, in combination. Each Personality Disorder is a maladaptive accentuation of personality traits that in milder form would be normal or even desirable. This is very much in the spirit of the ancient Greek concept of health as a golden mean. It is better to have a balance of the various temperaments rather than to express any one of them in the extreme. For example, someone with Paranoid Personality Disorder must always be on guard and at the ready even when there is no external threat. You do not have a Paranoid Personality Disorder if you are just a bit more suspicious than the next fellow of others' motives or if you are living in a realistically dangerous environment that requires you to be on the lookout.

We can take this point one step further. All of the personality characteristics described below are adaptive and even necessary if they occur at the right time, in the right place, and in the right measure. This is precisely why these traits in milder form have survived as part of the human endowment. Although we fear and hate someone with Antisocial Personality Disorder for his ruthlessness and aggression, the same tendencies, if well modulated, characterize the successful corporate raider, trial lawyer, politician, linebacker, or combat hero. This human capacity for assertive self-interest is undoubtedly an inheritance from our past history as the world's most successful predator. Similarly, the obsessive-compulsive striving to be absolutely excellent often becomes the enemy of achieving even the good enough, but a more restrained pursuit of good performance has obvious survival value. The seductive, flamboyant, self-dramatization of the Histrionic Personality Disorder can become an annoying caricature of itself, but probably represents no more than an extreme and maladaptive exaggeration of the normal courtship behavior that is so helpful in attracting a mate. Someone with Avoidant Personality Disorder may be so frightened of getting his feet wet that he winds up missing out on the broad currents of life, but milder and less reflexive forms of avoidance keep people out of trouble. Having a Dependent Personality Disorder reduces your ability to fend for yourself in our very individualistic society—but being able to depend on others when we need to is a terrific trait that makes us most fundamentally mammalian. Finally, the vain arrogance of the Narcissistic Personality Disorder often represents great pride strutting precariously before the fall—however, an appropriate appreciation of self-worth is nice for anyone to have and a smattering of narcissism is probably a necessary attribute in all successful leaders.

The ancient Greeks had two brilliant intuitions about personality functioning—first off, that our characters are to a large degree inborn, influenced by biology, and predestined to determine our fate; and second, that it is safer and healthier (although not nearly so heroic) to strive for the golden mean rather than to go for the extreme. The essence of Greek tragedy is a celebration of, and a mourning for, those few among us who possess both a touch of greatness and a touch of Personality Disorder. The tragic Greek hero is someone driven inexorably by his character to realize his seemingly unavoidable fate by taking an extreme action that temporarily raises him above his fellows, but ultimately leads to his downfall. In a like way, each of the following Personality Disorders contains the seeds of its own failure, because having an excessively strong and inflexible character prevents someone from adapting well to the changing needs of his world. On those rare occasions when Personality Disorder is combined with enormous talent and great luck, a world historical figure or a modern tragic hero emerges—but more often, Personality Disorder creates unfulfilled hopes and stormy relationships.

We now continue with descriptions of the ten Personality Disorders included in DSM-IV. While reading each one, you should keep in mind that not all aspects of the description need apply to you in order for you to have the Personality Disorder. As can be seen in each of the criteria sets that follows the descriptions of the disorders, only a certain minimum number of characteristic traits is required to justify a diagnosis.

OBSESSIVE-COMPULSIVE PERSONALITY DISORDER

People with this disorder seek perfection at all costs and live rigid, tightly structured, strangled lives. They constantly attempt to control the environment and relationships beyond what the situation and the people can bear. So much time and energy is spent planning and scrutinizing every aspect of a project that it never gets done. You are a great one for attending to details and micromanaging—to the point of being hopelessly inefficient. More effort goes into making extensive lists of things to do than it would take to do them. You obsess over the most insignificant decisions and annoy everyone with your constant procrastination. Excessive caution, with constant rechecking for potential mistakes, results in tremendous delays that are more damaging to the project than any minor mistake would be. Someone works diligently on his Ph.D. thesis for ten years but is never able to finish it because he is never completely satisfied with his latest draft.

You are rigid in your moral standards, viewing ethical issues as simply black or white and without any softening shades of gray. Always going "by the book" means that you are guided by the letter, not the spirit, of the law. Rules and procedures should be followed slavishly regardless of the circumstances. This "scrupulosity" is directed both inward and outward and is also projected onto others—you are overly critical of yourself, of others, and expect them to be harshly critical of you.

Being a workaholic pretty much chains you to your job and to constant efforts at self-improvement. There is no time to relax or do things simply for the hell of it. All attention is focused on one or a few projects, leaving the rest of your personal and professional life in complete disarray. On rare vacations, every minute is scheduled and no one in your family is allowed to relax or waste time. You participate in sports or hobbies with your usual dogged and methodical emphasis on perfection and constantly strive to improve your marathon time, golf handicap, or chess openings.

Relationships with colleagues don't go well either. You may defer slavishly to figures of authority or get into power struggles with them. You are stubborn, inflexible, believe that your way is the best (and perhaps only) way, and expect obedience from those who work or live with you. Compromise is difficult and you feel irritated if other people do not follow your detailed instructions to the letter. It is hard to gracefully delegate responsibility because you believe that only you can get the job done right. But you get so bogged down in petty details, the deadline is often missed despite your best intentions.

Your love relationships are fraught with frustration because of your constant monitoring, nagging, meddling, improving, hectoring, and controlling of the people you care about. The level of perfection you expect in others drives them nuts and makes them furious with you. They find you stiff, rigid, and stingy in your expression of emotion and praise. Although you can feel things deeply inside, it doesn't come out easily and you feel uncomfortable around people who are more demonstrative. There is a secret soft, sentimental, and nostalgic part of you—you cry silently at movies, or while reading a book or listening to music—but you retain a stiff upper lip whenever your emotions must meet the light of day. Even in your most intimate relationships, there may be a sense of "holding back." You rarely give compliments and have trouble expressing affection, tenderness, and warmth, even when you feel it.

You are unnecessarily cheap in financial matters, exercising unreasonably strict restraint on what you spend, give to others, and let them spend. This penny pinching may be pound foolish; you know the price of everything but the value of nothing. Money is something to be hoarded beyond any need for the "rainy day" and you are a "pack rat" whose living space is cluttered with piles of coffee cans, old newspapers, rubber bands, pieces of string, and other useless paraphernalia, because one day they might "come in handy."

According to the diagnostic manual you have Obsessive-Compulsive Personality Disorder if:
- You have a pattern of being preoccupied with orderliness, perfectionism, and control—at the expense of flexibility, openness, and getting things done. This pattern is expressed by your having at least four of the following maladaptive traits:
  (1) You are preoccupied with details, rules, lists, order, organization, or schedules so much so that the major point of what you were doing gets lost.

(2) Your perfectionism and overly strict standards interfere with your ability to complete tasks.

(3) You are so excessively devoted to work and being productive that you have little time left for friendships or having fun.

(4) You are overly strict, unbending, and scrupulous, and inflexible when it comes to morality, ethics, or values.

(5) You have trouble throwing out things that are worn out or worthless—even those that have no sentimental value.

(6) You have trouble letting others help you out or do things for you unless they do them exactly the way you would.

(7) You are excessively miserly and have extreme difficulty spending your money.

(8) You are extremely rigid and stubborn.

AM I OKAY?

Most of the time, and in most people, compulsive behavior is not only okay but is wonderful. The effort to achieve organization and control is responsible for the remarkable efficiency and productivity of modern society. Obsessive-Compulsive Personality Disorder represents too much of a good thing. Control has become an end rather than a means and results in reduced, not enhanced, productivity and satisfaction. The question is, can you control your striving for control? Can your driving for perfection be turned on and off as the need arises? Can you take time to smell the roses, walk your child to school, linger in bed hugging your wife, say "What the hell" once in a while? Working compulsively in preparation for a trial is normal behavior for an attorney and does not by itself indicate Obsessive-Compulsive Personality Disorder. However, you begin to wonder if the same person is equally regimented at home, coaches his son's Little League team as if it were always playing in the World Series, schedules every vacation hour from 5 A.M. to 11 P.M., and drives everyone in the family to abject obedience or open rebellion with incredibly demanding rules and standards. Can you buckle down to get the job done when you have to, but loosen up and relax when the opportunity arises?

DEPENDENT PERSONALITY DISORDER

People with this disorder are needy, submissive, helpless, and incapable of functioning unless they receive constant nurturance, approval, reassurance, and emotional support. Others assume responsibility for your life because you have trouble making your own decisions on subjects large and small—who to be with, where to live, what type of job to seek, what clothes to wear, where and what to eat, when and where to vacation, how you will spend your money, and how the children should be raised.

Relying so much on other people prevents you from learning age-appropriate decision-making skills—and this further perpetuates your feelings of childishness, dependency, and inadequacy. It is difficult to motivate yourself to do things on your own and you feel helpless and incompetent when circumstances or people force you to perform. To reduce expectations, you fake ineptitude and constantly try to get others to do what you could do yourself. Because you avoid pursuing jobs that require decision-making skills or responsibility your career choices are limited and you never live up to your potential.

You put all your interpersonal eggs in a small basket, try to avoid isolation at all costs, and get very anxious when you are left alone. Social relationships are limited to those few people upon whom you are most dependent. This makes it even more devastating if the eggs break, ending an important relationship. On the rebound, you may immediately and indiscriminately "latch on" to someone else, as if any port in a storm will do. This can lead to some terrible choices—people who take advantage of your weakness and give grudgingly if at all. You take their criticism at face value because it confirms your own lousy self-image. You are passive, acquiescent, clinging, and hate separations. Losing the guidance of others is so terrifying that you won't express any dissent even when you disagree with their advice or won't feel free to express any anger even when sorely provoked. You go to such extreme lengths to be cared for that you may endure unhealthy and even abusive relationships.

There is often a gender difference in the presentation of this Personality Disorder. Women tend to be submissive as a way of getting people to care for them; men are more often demanding and pushy toward the people they need—but no less dependent.

According to the diagnostic manual, you have Dependent Personality Disorder if:

* You have an excessive need to be taken care of, which leads to your being overly submissive and clinging. This pattern is expressed by your having at least five of the following maladaptive traits:

    (1) You are unable to make everyday decisions without advice and reassurance from others.

    (2) You rely on others to take responsibility for most of the major areas of your life.

    (3) You have difficulty disagreeing with those whose support or approval you need.

    (4) You have difficulty getting started on new projects or tasks or doing things on your own without help from others.

    (5) You go to such lengths to obtain nurturance and support from others that you end up volunteering to do things that are unpleasant or really put you out.

    (6) You feel uncomfortable or helpless when you are by yourself because you are convinced that you cannot take care of yourself.

    (7) Right after a close relationship ends, you desperately seek out another relationship to replace it.

    (8) You spend hours worrying about what will become of you if there is no one to take care of you.

Am I Okay?

The characteristics of passivity, submissiveness, and docility are highly valued in most societies. Dependency does not mean Personality Disorder unless it is getting you into trouble because greater independence is called for. It is also important to distinguish "state" versus "trait" dependency. People are much more than usually dependent whenever they are physically ill, have a psychiatric problem, or are undergoing a stressful period in their lives. This kind of needfulness is temporary and things will almost always get back to normal once the transient issue or illness is resolved. In contrast, Dependent Personality Disorder involves a lifelong pattern of getting others to take over responsibility for you and of avoiding situations that require you to act on your own. You bring this to every situation, not just the especially stressful ones.

AVOIDANT PERSONALITY DISORDER

People with this disorder are extremely self-conscious and fearful of criticism, humiliation, and rejection. Social situations are simply a nightmare to be avoided at all costs. You feel painfully timid, inadequate, and inhibited especially when meeting someone new or having to do something that is unfamiliar. It is terrifying that you might say or do the wrong thing and also that everyone will know just how terrified you are. Whenever you are dragged into a social situation, you are a wallflower and do your best to disappear into the woodwork.

Other people frighten you because you assume that they will always be unreasonably judgmental, demanding, and impossible to please. This is certainly how you are with yourself—always scrutinizing your every move and finding something wrong with it. No one has thinner skin. You are hypersensitive to the slightest hint of rejection and deeply hurt by the most marginally critical remark. The preoccupation with how you are coming across turns every little interpersonal contact into a major challenge. The pressure you put on yourself causes you to fumble interpersonal relationships and act in a way that is awkward and socially inept.

The social isolation makes life lonely and insipid. You want to have friends and get into the swing of life, but your social anxiety scares you off so that you are constantly making excuses to skip the job interview or miss the party. You cancel or refuse dates because of worries you will not wear the right clothes, know what to say, or be appealing enough. School or work is so daunting that you find excuses to miss lots of days and fall behind. This makes it even harder to face the people there and you are always tempted to quit and pull back. You become a chronic underachiever, watching from the sidelines as life passes you by.

Social anxiety is most unbearable when you are forced into contact with strangers. Because it is so difficult to start new relationships, you become especially dependent on the few close and long-standing relationships you already have. This keeps you trapped in a very narrow circle. If you are involved in an intimate relationship, it is probably with family members or with a partner who made the first moves. Self-consciousness usually extends to concerns about your sexual attractiveness and performance. In men, this may cause arousal problems or premature ejaculation; in women difficulty being stimulated; and in both genders a shyness about being naked and an effort to avoid sexual encounters.

Your feelings of social incompetence create the usual self-fulfilling prophecy—the more socially withdrawn you are, the farther you fall behind your peers in developing social skills, and the more awkward and inexperienced you become, until finally they stop trying to engage you in social activity, so that you are indeed rejected and humiliated. It is more natural to be fumbling on a first date at sixteen than at twenty-six, to be sexually inexperienced at twenty-one than at thirty-five, and to wonder how to behave on a job interview at twenty-three than at forty. The longer you avoid expectable developmental steps, the farther behind you feel and the harder it is to catch up.

According to the diagnostic manual, you have Avoidant Personality Disorder if:
- You have a pattern of feeling hypersensitive, inadequate, and inhibited in social situations. This pattern is expressed by your having at least four of the following maladaptive traits:
  (1) You avoid work that involves significant interpersonal contact because you are afraid of being criticized or rejected.
  (2) You are unwilling to get involved with people unless you are sure in advance that they will like you.
  (3) You hold back in intimate relationships to protect yourself from being shamed or ridiculed.
  (4) You are always worrying about being criticized or rejected in social situations.
  (5) You are inhibited when you meet new people because you feel inadequate.
  (6) You believe that you are socially inept, personally unappealing, or inferior to others.
  (7) You are reluctant to stick your neck out or try out new things because they may prove embarrassing.

Am I Okay?

Shyness is normal. Most of us are shy in new situations, especially when these involve having to deal with strangers and with new role expectations. Shyness is particularly common in children as they cross from one developmental phase into another. Don't give yourself this diagnosis unless your avoidance started early in life, goes well beyond normal shyness, and is interfering with your growing up, gaining experience in life, getting close to people, or succeeding professionally. Also consider your cultural background and gender. What may be considered shy and inhibited behavior in one culture may be another culture's socially appropriate modesty, especially in a woman.

But also don't let yourself off the hook too easily by justifying your avoidance as a matter of taste or a busy schedule. If you never venture into new relationships, job opportunities, or hobbies, it may be because you are too scared to take the chance—not that you are satisfied with what you have. If life is not showing you enough, it is probably because you are avoiding and not seeking new experiences. When they sum up their lives, most people feel much more regret for their errors of omission, not their errors of commission. Don't miss out.

HISTRIONIC PERSONALITY DISORDER

People with this disorder are enthusiastic, outgoing, and flirtatious, but nonetheless manage to alienate others because they always need to dominate the spotlight and be the center of attention. They go to great lengths to win everyone over with charming repartee, a confiding manner, elaborate storytelling, subtle or not so subtle seductiveness, and special attention to clothing, makeup, and grooming. Perhaps the most vivid portrayals of this personality are Scarlett O'Hara in *Gone With the Wind* and Blanche DuBois in *A Street Car Named Desire*.

Your emotions tend to run very hot and very cold. A theatricality in the way you do things makes you seem shallow and superficial even when you do really care deeply. It is very disappointing to you when other people are insufficiently involved with you. You feel closer to people than they do to you and tend to become overly and too quickly familiar. You consider even casual acquaintances or business associates to be close friends. You are on a first-name basis with teachers or doctors immediately upon making their acquaintance.

Your seductive behavior is meant to be more social than sexual, but people don't always discern the difference. They sometimes think you are coming on to them when you don't mean it that way and this may lead to embarrassing moments or concerns about sexual harassment. Sometimes, you go overboard and make inappropriately intimate or suggestive remarks to people you barely know. You can be so demonstrative in your emotional and physical display of affection that others sometimes pull back in embarrassment. You bristle in response to any criticism about your appearance and work hard to look much younger than you really are. You are so concerned about looking your absolute best that you must spend hours in front of the mirror before you venture out, even if it's only to go to the store to pick up a quart of milk.

Same-sex friendships usually don't work out well because of your own competitive feelings and the conviction that your gender mates will necessarily be jealous of you. People keep their spouses away from you because of your sexually provocative style. If you seek therapy, it is usually better for it not to be with a therapist of the opposite sex (or same-sex therapist if you are gay) since your efforts to be liked may interfere with the work to be done. You like excitement and variety, fall in love easily, only to become quickly bored and disappointed. Torrid relationships burn out quickly because you fear commitment and have great difficulty becoming emotionally intimate.

Structure, consistency, and organization are not your strong suit. While you may be enthusiastically opinionated, your opinions and feelings shift rapidly and are easily influenced by others. Your behavior and dress fluctuate a great deal, depending on the predominant role you are currently playing—the queen bee, the macho male, the savior, the long-suffering martyr, the helpless child, the dutiful servant, or the selfless benefactor. You are not good at "details," boring drudge work, and repetition and usually don't do your homework or get your ducks in a row. You are also fickle in your career choices, embarking on a new job or project with great enthusiasm, only to lose interest quickly. The continual quest for novelty, excitement, and immediate gratification makes it difficult to make a long-term commitment to any one career. You put in more energy trying to win over colleagues than in getting the job done.

According to the diagnostic manual, you have Histrionic Personality Disorder if:
- You have a pattern of seeking attention and displaying your emotions excessively. This pattern is expressed by your having at least five of the following maladaptive traits:
  (1) You feel uncomfortable when you are in situations in which you are not the center of attention.
  (2) You often act in a sexually seductive or provocative way that is inappropriate to the situation.
  (3) Your emotions appear to others to be rapidly shifting, shallow, and superficial.
  (4) You consistently use your physical appearance to draw attention to yourself.
  (5) You talk in an excessively impressionistic way that is lacking in specific detail.
  (6) You tend to be overly dramatic and theatrical when expressing yourself or telling a story.
  (7) You are overly suggestible and easily influenced by others' opinions.
  (8) You view relationships to be more intimate than they really are.

AM I OKAY?

Influenced by the gender role stereotypes in our society, it seems likely that Histrionic Personality Disorder may be overdiagnosed in women and underdiagnosed in men. Most people are more attuned, for example, to the histrionic flamboyance of Blanche DuBois than to the equally over-the-top macho style of Stanley Kowalski, who has strong histrionic elements as well. What is considered a normal quota of seductiveness, demonstrative behavior, and dramatic emotionality varies greatly with one's age, gender, and culture. "Normal" and adaptive seductiveness can help you attract a partner or charm your way to the top. Being demonstrative can help you bring a vividness and color to all your relationships and activities. A Personality Disorder should be considered only when this need to be the center of things goes over the top and turns people off rather than attracts them.

NARCISSISTIC PERSONALITY DISORDER

People with this disorder are blessed and cursed with an extremely inflated self-image and a strong sense of entitlement that makes them insensitive to the needs and feelings of other people. You have an exaggerated view of your own skills and accomplishments and devalue others except for the chosen few included within your narcissistic bubble. The preoccupation with how others regard you results in a constant need for attention, admiration, and recognition. You are hypersensitive, easily bruised, intolerant of criticism, quick to feel hurt, and to counterattack when you feel the slightest bit unappreciated or humiliated (something that invariably happens in this rough-and-tumble world where other people have their own narcissistic concerns to push forward).

You feel that you have a touch of greatness and should associate only with other individuals or with institutions that share an equally special status (the Harvard complex). Only the best physician, best professor, best car mechanic, best hairstylist, best restaurants and stores, and best brands will do—whether or not you can afford them. Your children are pressured to get into the "best" schools and to mingle with the elite. You assign an idealized value to people you like, but then devalue them harshly when they disappoint you. You envy the achievements and possessions of others and believe that they are equally envious of you. You resent the accomplishments of public figures, colleagues, and sometimes even family members and children. It does not feel fair that other people have success that just seems to fall into their laps.

Feeling entitled allows you to use others almost automatically for your own personal gain. The only people who matter are those who will in some way further your ends, advance your position, or enhance your self-image. Others must cater to you and defer to your needs and priorities. You resent ever having to wait in line because your time is far too valuable and you are condescending with people you rate as not smart or not successful enough. You drive your employees beyond their endurance with complete disregard for the toll it will take on their personal lives.

Interpersonal relationships are one-sided and problematic. Others see you as arrogant, selfish, demanding, cold, and aloof. You have no patience for the everyday civilities or small talk and expect others to be fascinated by your opinions—but become quickly impatient if you have to suffer through hearing theirs. You have little reciprocal interest in other people's feelings and are oblivious to the fact that your offhand comments may be hurtful. A man with this disorder might unwittingly boast about the good health he has recently been enjoying while visiting someone suffering from cancer.

According to the diagnostic manual, you have Narcissistic Personality Disorder if:

- You have a pattern of grandiosity, a need to be admired, and a lack of empathy for others' feelings or needs. This pattern is expressed by your having at least five of the following maladaptive traits:

  (1) You have an overinflated sense of your own importance and exaggerate your achievements and talents.

  (2) You spend hours fantasizing about having unlimited success, power, brilliance, beauty, or the "perfect" romance.

  (3) You are convinced that you are so "special" and unique that you should only associate with other special or high-status people and institutions.

  (4) You require excessive admiration from others.

  (5) You feel entitled to getting special treatment or feel that others should automatically comply with your expectations.

  (6) You exploit others in order to get what you need for yourself.

  (7) You are unable to recognize or empathize with the feelings and needs of others.

  (8) You are constantly envious of other people's achievements or possessions.

  (9) You are arrogant and haughty.

AM I OKAY?

What is being described is not just a reasonable level of confidence and pride in achievement. Narcissistic Personality Disorder is a pervasive pattern of arrogance, grandiosity, and entitlement that drives other people away. Many adolescents transiently display some narcissistic traits (especially a certain degree of self-centeredness and a disregard for the feelings of others), but fortunately most of us grow out of this. Narcissistic behaviors that occur only as part of a manic episode or during substance intoxication also do not count toward this diagnosis. Finally, it is not Narcissistic Personality Disorder if you are the rare lucky person who really is great and knows it, unless you have to go about obnoxiously flaunting it to others.

BORDERLINE PERSONALITY DISORDER

People with this disorder have a lifetime pattern of roller coaster emotions, chaotic relationships, and instability in self-image. Life is extremely intense and tumultuous—you experience some simply wonderful, but many terrible moments—with rapid and dramatic shifts in how you feel about yourself and other people. Sometimes you feel as though your lover is perfect and is the most wonderful person you have ever met and other times you feel as if he is the worst scum of the earth. The shift is usually caused by a disappointment—something that proves your partner does not care enough about you or understand what you need.

Terrified of being abandoned, you will go to great lengths to avoid separations and are hypersensitive to any sign of rejection. You overreact when faced with unavoidable changes in plan and feel despair or lash out in anger when someone cancels a social engagement or arrives a few minutes late. You get far too serious way too early in relationships, disclose very intimate details about yourself, become increasingly dependent and even clinging. This is likely to scare your potential partner off and may cause just the rejection you feared from the outset. You then feel both furious and worthless and may act impulsively and erratically. The pattern of premature intimacy followed by rejection repeats over and over again, resulting in a painful series of "disappointing" loves, often followed by suicide attempts or other self-destructive behavior.

Intermittent periods of intense happiness are no more than isolated islands in a sea of sadness, bitterness, agitation, anger, and resentment. The dramatic shifts in the way you perceive yourself result in fluctuating career goals, values, types of friends. You sabotage your success just as you are on the brink of achieving an important goal. For example, you may drop out of school the semester before you would have graduated or destroy a good relationship just when it seems likely to last. You have tantrums, usually when faced with rejection, but then feel guilty and ashamed. Some of the tantrums may result in harm to you or to the people who disappoint you.

You are impulsive in all sorts of ways that include drug abuse, binge eating, unsafe sex, driving recklessly, gambling, or buying things you cannot afford. You may use physical pain as a distraction from emotional pain—cutting or burning your arms in a frantic attempt to deal with anger, desperation, hopelessness, or a feeling of deadness. You often feel empty and bored, and can't stand your own company.

According to the diagnostic manual, you have Borderline Personality Disorder if:

- You have a pattern of unstable relationships, a constantly changing self-image, mood fluctuations, and trouble controlling your impulses. This pattern is expressed by your having at least five of the following maladaptive traits:
  (1) You make frantic efforts to avoid real or imagined abandonment.
  (2) Your relationships with others are intense and have lots of ups and downs.
  (3) You have a constantly shifting sense of who you are or what you believe in.
  (4) You have trouble keeping self-destructive impulses under control.
  (5) You make suicidal threats or attempts or mutilate your body.
  (6) Your moods shift rapidly, alternating between intense sadness, irritability, or anxiety.
  (7) You feel that deep down inside you there is just emptiness.
  (8) Your anger is often well out of proportion to the circumstances.
  (9) When you are under a lot of stress, you get paranoid or feel detached from yourself, like you are in a dream.

AM I OKAY?

Mental health clinicians tend to overuse the term "borderline personality" in a broad and unfortunately disparaging way to describe anyone who is demanding, obnoxious, and acting self-destructively. If the impulsive and erratic behavior is temporary, it has nothing to do with Borderline Personality Disorder and instead probably arises from substance use, mood disorder, or a difficult life circumstance. Adolescents who are struggling with identity issues may experience short-lived periods of erratic behavior. Being less than completely graceful in making difficult choices about education, career, relationships, and "finding" oneself is often just a part of growing up and does not necessarily indicate a Personality Disorder.

PARANOID PERSONALITY DISORDER

People with this disorder are extremely suspicious of others. They bring a mistrustful way of thinking and behaving to every new situation and relationship and consistently misconstrue other people's intentions in the most negative possible light. Reading between the lines, they find antagonistic underlying meanings hidden behind seemingly benign comments. They are also highly critical, blame others for their own failures, and refuse to accept criticism for their own mistakes.

Often the person may become consumed with doubt about the fidelity and trustworthiness of a spouse, friends, or family. For example, a man becomes concerned that his wife may want to have an affair and cannot get this out of his head despite her heartfelt expressions of love and vehement denials of any errant desires. He badgers her constantly about the most minute and intimate details of each of her past relationships, asks if she doesn't find different acquaintances and movie actors attractive, interrogates her on how she spends her time, wonders who she speaks to on the phone, and checks her pocketbook and clothing for incriminating evidence. Driven by intense jealousy and fears of betrayal, this modern Othello attempts to exert an astoundingly rigid control over his wife's activities and friendships. Ultimately, his wife does rebel in a way that seems perfectly understandable to us, but serves to redeem his worst fears that she has always been disloyal.

There is a great tendency to hold grudges, collect injustices, and feel that people are inflicting serious emotional pain. A woman believes that she did not get a long-expected raise because her co-workers conspired to make her look bad. She thinks that her boss is giving her especially unpromising assignments with a view toward eventually getting her fired. She can't confide in anyone for fear that anything she says will ultimately be used against her. Because she has no way of invalidating her misperceptions, her fears enlarge in the loneliness of increasing isolation. She is combative and quick to counterattack in response to what she perceives to be increasingly humiliating insults and threats of real injury. When not overtly hostile, she is sullen, guarded, unemotional, and stoically resigned to being discriminated against. Not surprisingly, these behaviors elicit fear and hostility from her co-workers, who are increasingly pleased to have nothing whatever to do with her. Their distance confirms her assumptions that nobody likes her and that everybody is working against her.

When asked to describe yourself, you express pride in your ability to identify deceit and malice in your friends and associates. Life is an uphill struggle against adverse circumstances and the hostile intentions of the people around you. You dislike people who are different from you and are attracted to cults or militant groups that subscribe to your beliefs and prejudices.

According to the diagnostic manual, you have Paranoid Personality Disorder if:
- You have a pattern of being pervasively distrustful and suspicious of other people's motives. This pattern is expressed by your having at least four of the following maladaptive traits:
  (1) You suspect, without good reason, that others are exploiting or deceiving you.
  (2) You are preoccupied with unjustified doubts about the loyalty or trustworthiness of your friends, colleagues, classmates, or co-workers.
  (3) You can't confide in others because you are afraid that the information will be used maliciously against you.
  (4) You read hidden, demeaning, or threatening meanings into innocent remarks or events.
  (5) You hold grudges for years and have a hard time forgetting about past insults, injuries, or slights.
  (6) You are quick to retaliate for slights or imagined attacks on your character or reputation.
  (7) You worry constantly that your spouse or sexual partner has been unfaithful to you.

Am I Okay?

An obvious question is whether your "paranoid" feelings are no more than an adaptive response to a realistically hostile or potentially dangerous environment. Being reasonably suspicious toward other people is prudent, especially if they really are out to get you. However, you must also consider that your hostile and suspicious behavior may be triggering the negative reactions from others. If you always act in a distrustful way, people tend to be reciprocally hostile and distrustful, confirming your expectations that they wish you harm. Admit the possibility that you have a paranoid personality if you feel as if you are a minority of one in a world that was created explicitly to annoy you. Check it out with someone you trust—if there is anyone you trust.

ANTISOCIAL PERSONALITY DISORDER

People with this disorder have a lifelong pattern of irresponsible behavior and show little concern for the rights of others, the norms of society, the dictates of conscience, and the law. The problems start early in childhood or adolescence with disruptive troublemaking, disrespect for authority, violation of rules, destruction of property, and maybe even violence toward animals or people. As a youngster, you lied when it suited you and stole when you thought you could get away with it.

As an adult, you have moved on to bigger and better things. You have a tumultuous life with sudden changes in relationships, jobs, and residences and may engage in illegal activities such as theft and drug dealing. When things don't go your way, you get irritated and even aggressive with a short fuse and a low frustration tolerance. You are relatively blasé and reckless about your own safety and the safety of others and take extreme chances with unsafe sex, excessive speeding, heavy substance use, and dangerous criminal activities. There is an appreciable risk that you will die early by homicide, suicide, overdose, or accident. There is a marked gender difference in Antisocial Personality Disorder. It is much more commonly diagnosed in men, probably reflecting the male tendency toward aggressive and impulsive behavior that is almost universal throughout the animal kingdom.

You are self-serving and arrogant, a slick and quick talker who believes that everyone should look out just for "number one." Decisions are impulsive, irresponsible, and spontaneous without consideration for the repercussions. Charm and charisma are used to deceive, manipulate, and con others. You are irresponsible in financial matters, write bad checks, default on debts, and feel callously indifferent to the consequences of your behavior. You expect that others will attempt to attack or exploit you and feel you have to strike preemptively to get there first. Glib rationalizations justify everything you do—you blame your victims for being so stupid or helpless and claim that they had it coming. "If I didn't do it someone else would." It is as if you failed to develop a conscience and have little or no guilt or remorse for the suffering you inflict upon others.

There has been controversy about whether Antisocial Personality Disorder should be considered a mental disorder and be included in DSM-IV. A cogent argument has been made that by labeling outrageous behavior an illness, we may enable irresponsible people to evade responsibility for their actions. Be it known that having a diagnosis of Antisocial Personality Disorder should not and does not confer protection from the law.

According to the diagnostic manual, you have Antisocial Personality Disorder if:
- As a child or teenager, you had a pattern of getting into trouble with your parents, teachers, or the law (see Conduct Disorder, page 377).
- You continue consistently to act in a way that disregards the rights of others and violates the rules of society. This pattern is expressed by your having at least three of the following maladaptive traits:
  (1) You repeatedly do things that could get you arrested.
  (2) You repeatedly lie, use aliases, or con others for profit or because it's fun.
  (3) You are impulsive and fail to plan ahead for the future.
  (4) You repeatedly get into physical fights.
  (5) You have a reckless disregard for your safety and for the safety of others.
  (6) You don't bother to hold a job or to honor your financial obligations.
  (7) You have no remorse about the consequences of your actions. You feel justified or indifferent about having mistreated, stolen from, or hurt other people.

AM I OKAY?

Isolated antisocial acts are never okay, but are not to be confused with the pervasive pattern of deviance in Antisocial Personality Disorder. Sometimes antisocial behavior may be a one-time or temporary survival strategy that is responsive to that specific environment and not necessarily a reflection of the person's long-term personality. Individuals who engage in antisocial behaviors only as part of gang bonding or to protect themselves in a dangerous neighborhood are more likely to outgrow their conduct problems and eventually be capable of much healthier personality functioning. However, if antisocial behavior starts very early in childhood, and includes aggressiveness, it is probably the person and not the environment that accounts for most of the trouble—particularly if there is also a family history of antisocial behavior.

Substance abuse plays a major role in the lives of people with Antisocial Personality Disorder and creates the chicken/egg question—is the drug problem causing the antisocial behavior or is the Antisocial Personality Disorder causing the drug problem? Some people can avoid a pattern of antisocial behavior if they escape the disinhibition of substance intoxication and/or the high cost of obtaining drugs.

This diagnosis would also not apply to a professional criminal who otherwise maintains a stable life as a good husband, father, and pillar of the mafia community.

SCHIZOID PERSONALITY DISORDER

This disorder makes you a stranger in a strange land. You have become an island isolated unto yourself, a loner who is profoundly detached from others. The normal round of interpersonal relationships and social activities has no charm or color. You lack the usual human desire for intimacy, cuddling, sharing, and nurturance and have a sense of puzzlement over what the fuss is all about. As a child, you rarely hung out with other kids, did not participate in school activities, were not chosen to be on teams, and sought isolation within yourself or in the narrowest confines of your family. You have no close friends, have dated little or not at all, avoid sexual activity, and plan not to marry.

The best career is one that allows you to remain solitary—preferably working the night shift and doing something that has you relate to machines or computers rather than people. Your hobbies can be done alone. You may become addicted to woodworking, video games, or computer hacking because you find these much more relaxing than dealing with people.

You freeze and respond inappropriately when interacting with others, coming across as mechanical, socially inept, arrogant, and/or totally self-absorbed. There is little joy in sensuous bodily experiences like having sex, walking on the beach, or watching a sunset. You do not value the companionship or approval of others, nor are you particularly bothered by their rejection or criticism. Rarely do you express emotion or display facial expressions, and you shrug off both positive and unpleasant situations with the same seemingly passive and indifferent manner.

If you do have a best friend, it is likely to be a pet, not a person. If lucky, you may come to learn the meaning of love by getting close to your pet, but this usually does not make it much easier to love people. You feel condemned forever to be set off and feel apart from the other members of your species. You just want to be left alone.

According to the diagnostic manual, you have Schizoid Personality Disorder if:
- You have a pervasive pattern of being socially detached as expressed by your having at least four of the following maladaptive traits:
  (1) You do not desire or enjoy close relationships.
  (2) You almost always choose activities which involve your being alone.
  (3) You care little about having scxual experiences with another person.
  (4) There are very few activities that give you pleasure.
  (5) You have virtually no close friends.
  (6) Other people's praise or criticism is completely unimportant to you.
  (7) You are emotionally cold and detached, as if you have no emotions.

AM I OKAY?

Not all loners have Schizoid Personality Disorder. Many people prefer to live and work in solitary conditions, but do not experience special problems in functioning or in interacting with others when they have to. This diagnosis becomes a possibility if you have never been in love, lack interest in social interactions, and feel exquisitely sensitive and extremely awkward whenever you are forced to be with people.

SCHIZOTYPAL PERSONALITY DISORDER

People with this disorder have all the social isolation just described, but are in addition very noticeably peculiar in the way they say and do things. Their appearance is unusual, with clothing that is likely to be poorly matched, stained, and ill-fitting. Hair may be disheveled and personal hygiene is often below par. Mannerisms, gestures, and facial expressions are odd and put people off. The person is suspicious and mistrustful of others, has problems interacting in social situations, and lacks intimate relationships. Anxiety about being with other people usually does not decrease with increasing contact, but may actually grow worse as you have to spend more time with them. You feel frozen, avoid eye contact, and respond with flat or inappropriate emotional reactions that are often off key.

People find you strange and you may find yourself strange. Repeating nonsensical rituals is annoying to you and to others but you can't stop doing them without becoming very tense. You may believe that you can predict future events, read people's minds, or control their actions by directing their thoughts. You are attracted to mysticism, cults, the occult, fringe religious groups, conspiracy theories, UFO networks, and/or astral travel. You may even develop your own private religious or political system and believe that you have some special mission.

Nothing happens that is not related to you. External events or random remarks have a particular personal meaning or message. Ordinary conversations with strangers are scrutinized for hidden information. People seem to laugh at or talk about you when you walk by. You may experience strange perceptions like feeling the presence of someone who is dead or hearing a voice calling your name. Your speech may be stilted, intellectualized, symbolic, and filled with unusual phrasing that others have difficulty understanding. The world is a remote and unreal place for you and you feel remote even from yourself.

According to the diagnostic manual, you have Schizotypal Personality Disorder if:

- You have a pervasive pattern of eccentric behavior, strange ways of thinking, and feel uncomfortable with close relationships. This pattern is expressed by your having at least four of the following maladaptive traits:

    (1) You feel that the things strangers do or say may in some way refer to you.

    (2) You have beliefs that most other people find unusual or off-the-mark.

    (3) You often have unusual perceptual experiences.

    (4) Other people find your speech hard to follow.

    (5) You are suspicious of other people's motives.

    (6) Your range of emotional expression is restricted.

    (7) Other people find your behavior or appearance to be odd.

    (8) You have virtually no close friends or people you can confide in.

    (9) You are very anxious in social situations because you feel that other people might take advantage of you.

AM I OKAY?

The diagnosis is meant to apply only to people who are severely impaired by their peculiar behavior and unable to relate to others. Not every eccentric has Schizotypal Personality Disorder. Some people are "different" because they are creatively ahead of their time and follow their own drummer. This diagnosis could also be misused politically (and was so used in the old Soviet Union) to label as crazy people who have an alternative lifestyle or legitimate political differences with an authoritarian regime.

DIFFERENTIAL DIAGNOSIS

Before giving yourself a diagnosis of Personality Disorder, consider all the possible alternatives. Most important to remember is that having a psychiatric or medical illness usually brings out the worst in our personalities.

Someone who is usually only mildly dependent, or mildly suspicious, or mildly controlling may transiently become totally helpless, or blatantly mistrustful, or wildly argumentative in the midst of a depression or after suffering a heart attack. It is, therefore, important that you not judge your own personality functioning (or that of your loved one) based on a worst-moment appraisal. Wait until you (or they) have recovered. Personality Disorders always start early in life, persist continuously, and influence every aspect of our functioning. Personality foibles that occur only in the context of a psychiatric or medical illness usually go away promptly when the illness is successfully treated. Be understanding and cut some extra slack for any obnoxious behaviors that occur only in the context of illness. Remember that it is the illness talking, not the person.

The same is true with substance use. People on substances say and do things that otherwise might never be part of their usual personality style. Unless you are off the drug or alcohol for at least a month, it is hard to say whether it is the substance that is making you self-destructive, impulsive, and irresponsible or whether this is the way you really are.

A third issue in differential diagnosis is the distinction between Personality Disorder and role functioning. A Personality Disorder is a pattern of behavior that we carry wherever we go and cannot turn off or tone down even when the needs of the moment would call for a very different and more flexible response. In contrast, certain situations may bring out particular role responses that resemble Personality Disorders, but are really adaptive to and necessary in that situation. It is not really paranoid for one congressional staffer to be suspicious of the motives of rival congressional staffers in the dog-eat-dog world of Washington politics. It is not Narcissistic Personality Disorder when a business leader feels called upon to praise his own accomplishments if he does this mostly to enhance his company's morale. It is also not Personality Disorder when a surgeon is demanding and controlling to ensure the quality of his work in the operating room— so long as he can let his hair down at rounds and can relax with his family.

AM I OKAY?

By definition, a Personality Disorder is present only if your personality traits are so inflexible and maladaptive that they cause you major league problems. Unfortunately, the boundary between average everyday personality traits and Personality Disorder is tough to draw because there is no universal definition of what constitutes a major league problem. Different people will have different takes on the question. Most of us are not the very best observers of our own personality functioning—precisely because our own personality style invitably colors our self-observations. Personality characteristics become so integrally a part of us that we fail to recognize them as unusual or problematic, or even notice they are present. People routinely have trouble assessing and owning up to unpleasant behavior in themselves. Undesirable personality traits (like being self-centered, dependent, or manipulative) are probably outside your awareness altogether or may be hidden from others to make you appear more socially desirable. Ask people you trust to confirm your self-evaluations because very likely you won't always see yourself clearly. Depending on your personality, you may be too easy or too hard on yourself.

Your own personality style will also color how you judge other people's personality functioning. For example, if you have obsessive-compulsive personality traits, you will admire self-restraint in others and look down on people who display even normal demonstrativeness. In contrast, if you have histrionic personality traits, you may prize spontaneity in others and be intolerant of the steady plodding of someone with normal compulsive features. On the other hand, opposites do attract, especially in the dating and mating game. You probably married someone because he or she had personality features that were different and complementary to your own—and then will fight with your spouse for a lifetime because you also have trouble tolerating the very differences that made that person so attractive to you in the first place.

It is also crucial to evaluate Personality Disorders within your own cultural, social, and religious framework. What is considered to be an appropriate thought, feeling, or behavior is relative to context and varies greatly across different societies and subcultures. Behavior that would be excessively showy in a culture that emphasizes emotional and behavioral restraint (the northern European or Japanese) may be considered absolutely "normal" in a culture that values demonstrativeness (the southern European) and vice versa. Behaviors that are pathologically passive and dependent in a culture that values independence might be considered totally "normal" and even desirable in a society that emphasizes group cohesion. Avoid psychological ethnocentrism—that is, judging people from the perspective of your own personality and cultural context, not theirs. Differences in gender expectations also complicate the evaluation of Personality Disorder—to a degree men are indeed more often from Mars and women often do have a personality more shaped by Venus.

TREATMENT OPTIONS

It is a sad, but all too true, fact of life that people do not change their personalities much more readily than leopards change their spots. This should not be surprising considering how deeply engrained and even "fateful" is our personality functioning. We are born with a genetically determined temperament that will continually influence about one half of our behavioral tendencies throughout life. Our constitution meets a nurturing (or sometimes not so nurturing) early environment that quickly crystallizes our inborn tendencies into powerful habit patterns—in ways that are often, and perhaps usually, outside our conscious awareness. Our ability to learn and change is compromised by the fact that we inevitably and constantly edit all of our experiences, filtering them through the distorting lens of our personality attitudes. Indeed, most people are so trapped in the cage of their personality traits that they are completely unaware of them and become surprised and resentful when others—including spouses and therapists—try to point them out. Fortunately, most people do mellow and improve somewhat with age, but in very limited ways.

However difficult, and sometimes even unpleasant, the royal road to wisdom requires that you become more aware of your personality style and functioning. Understanding how your personality affects your life is more than half the battle in living better within its confines. For most people, increased awareness does not lead to radical personality change but rather to a smoothing of the rough edges, a modulation of the most troubling behaviors, and a greater ease in going with their natural flow when this is necessary. Some few of you may have the much more ambitious goal of decisively changing how you deal with your relationships, your work, and yourself. This requires large doses of honesty, hard work, humility, and courage—but the rewards are great both for you and for your loved ones. We don't have space here to go into any great detail, but will touch on some of the high points in managing each of the Personality Disorders. Psychotherapy is often helpful, and sometimes necessary, in helping people identify their personality problems—either to change them or to learn how to work with and around them.

Obsessive-Compulsive Personality Disorder: First off, you will have to own up to the fact that you are more controlling, critical, and perfectionistic than is good for you or for anyone around you. You must accept that your scrupulosity is not really the "virtue" you took pride in, but rather is a "sin" somewhat akin to the sin of pride. Being an absolute perfectionist is inefficient and becomes bad for business and for productivity. Trying to control everything means you control nothing really well. If you try to do less, more will actually get done.

You have a choice between a less ambitious and more ambitious application of your new insights about yourself. The less ambitious route is to accept yourself as you are—that controlling things is as important to you as the air you breathe. You will not succeed in any radical overhaul, particularly if you are in the midst of a crisis. Learn to pick your spots. Control what you can and leave everything else alone. Identify those aspects of your current situation that really do most need your input and that you have some chance of influencing. If the current stressor is an illness, find out all you can from the doctor about its cause and treatment and also read books and articles about it. Ask to be consulted in making those decisions that can most benefit from your preferences (like choosing from among several alternative medication options or finding the right dosage schedule); and make a point of staying away from those choices that are too technical for you to influence (like the specific surgical procedure or post-operative orders). Focus on what counts and find ways to back off on those things that don't really matter all that much in the long run.

The ambitious approach is to challenge your need to control and structure. Take a spontaneous vacation without any (or just a bit of) preplanning—and you will probably have the time of your life. Allow your kids to apply to colleges without your doing the usual exhaustive study of every detail concerning each of the top fifty schools. Hand in work assignments that are good enough and not perfect—but always on time and without the usual procrastination. Make a point of being gentler in your expectations of others and, even more important, gentler in your expectations of yourself.

Dependent Personality Disorder: The first step is to realize that you have a strong need to be cared for and a tendency to be submissive. The less ambitious approach is to improve your skill in choosing the right caretakers and in accepting help in a way that gratifies rather than annoys them. Some potential spouses, teachers, doctors, and mentors love to be generous and will value themselves to the extent that they can be helpful to you. Other potential spouses, teachers, doctors, and mentors are much more self-serving and will make your life at least a little bit miserable for each and every thing you get from them. Learn to pick nurturing types who will respect and respond to your needs and even be grateful for the chance to give to you.

The more ambitious approach is to take gradual steps toward independence. Instead of getting other people to guide your decisions, begin making some of your own calls. Start small with the selection of clothing, or a restaurant, or a movie. Once you get the hang of it, you will realize that errors of omission are usually much worse than errors of commission. You may then move on with surprising ease to much bigger decisions—which courses to take, what job to apply for, whether to call someone for a date. The first steps in becoming more independent are usually the most difficult. Sometimes, a brief course of family treatment is necessary. The people around you may have some trouble readjusting their expectations, as you grow into being more of a separate person.

Avoidant Personality Disorder: This is the personality style that probably lends itself to the most ambitious goals—you can change a great deal if you have the courage to go for it. The exposure and cognitive techniques that have already been described for the anxiety disorders can work very well to reduce your avoidance and desensitize your social discomfort (see page 94). Realize that you are catastrophizing and personalizing the difficulties, pitfalls, and humiliations of social intercourse. Everyone has been through the awkwardness of a first date, a party, a job interview, or a lunch with strangers. All of us have failed numerous times at these tasks and would have loved to disappear into the woodwork to avoid the embarrassment. What separates you from other people is that they stick with it long enough to become less anxious, more experienced, and finally more confident. The longer you put off facing the risk of embarrassment, the further behind you fall developmentally and the more impossible it feels ever to catch up to where you should be. Conjure up your courage. Take hierarchical baby steps, seeking out, rather than avoiding, potential embarrassment. The only thing to fear is fear itself. You will shed your fears with every step. Ask for dates, do lunch, take tennis lessons, play bridge, go to parties, join an Internet chat group, try a job interview—it is much easier than you think once you get started and get the hang of it. The less ambitious approach is simply to back off and take a rest when things feel too overwhelming.

Histrionic Personality Disorder: There are two possible paths once you become aware that you have a powerful, and perhaps excessive, need to be liked. The easier choice is to work at becoming better at picking the right people. Realize that you don't really need to be liked by everyone, only by the people whom you really like or who are important to you. Also learn to individualize your approach. Fine-tune your behavior to the specific opportunities and limits of the situation. Some people will respond better to you if you take a more restrained approach. You can avoid putting them off by learning to tone yourself down a bit when you need to.

The more ambitious goal would have you go more for substance and less for appearance. In a breathless effort to be the center of things, you may be losing your own center. Instead of desperately seeking other people's attention and approval, you may want to pay more attention to yourself and to your own interests. Cultivate the parts of you that you like. A greater inner-directedness evolves in most people naturally as they mature and come to need less external stimulation and playful variety. The process can be speeded up by a deep look at who you are and what really counts in your life. Get more committed to people, a job, and intellectual interests. Go increasingly for depth rather than surface. Get organized and know a few things well rather than a lot of things superficially.

Narcissistic Personality Disorder: We must admit that it is very difficult to make a fundamental change in the core of this Personality Disorder and usually it is not worth trying. More likely your goal will be healing the narcissistic wounds that inevitably occur in life—and doing this as quickly and as gracefully as possible. Learn what are your own particular and personal narcissistic triggers—the school or fraternity you didn't get into, the job offer that never materialized, the woman who got away, the boss who doesn't appreciate you or deserve his position above you, the illness that saps your vitality, or the ravages of aging and death. The more quickly you can identify your narcissistic vulnerabilities, the less likely that a sudden disappointment will jolt you as if it came out of nowhere. Accept that life is filled with slings, arrows, outrageous fate, inevitable losses, and regrets, but also has its moments of undeniable joy, dignity, and triumphs. Keep yourself focused on the things you have achieved and the positive experiences you have had, rather than becoming preoccupied with what you have failed to achieve or what you have lost. Also realize that narcissistic wounds always heal with time, the support of others, new accomplishments, and new opportunities. You can wait out the storm.

Borderline Personality Disorder: The goal is to increase the stability and reduce the roller coaster quality of your life. Realize that you see everything in black and white and begin the systematic search for shades of gray. Accept that you are cursed and blessed with a special gift for experiencing life at its highest intensity. Put things into broader context and look past the excitement or disappointment of the moment. Your next love relationship, however tempting and attractive, will almost certainly not work out—just as past ones have burned and fizzled. Anticipating this may reduce some of the romantic edge, but also makes it easier to relax, have fun, and not be so devastatingly intense that you scare the person off. Recognize that you are impulsive and apt to do things you will later regret. Try to improve controls (both internal and external) on your substance use, spending, speeding, and unsafe sex. When you get outraged, catch the signs early and count to ten or take a walk before you do something dangerous or hurtful to yourself or to someone you care for. Use a flicking rubber band on your wrists or put your hand in a pitcher of ice water when you feel like cutting or burning yourself—these substitutes can do the same job of replacing physical for emotional pain but have the advantage of not leaving scars. Whenever you feel like killing yourself, remember that time heals. Any suicidal impulse you have now will soon be much less intense. The impulsive act of the moment can be irrevocable for a lifetime. Get help instead.

Don't put your emotional eggs all in one basket. Learn to spread your needs across enough people so that none are excessively burdened and no one rejection (real or imagined) is too devastating. Finally and most important, remember that your personality problems will almost certainly get much better with age. You are now experiencing one of the worst times of your life and this makes everything look bleak, both past and future. But with time and reasonable luck, things will improve. You will feel much more content and satisfied with yourself than you would ever have thought possible. We know that this is hard to believe but follow-up studies on thousands of people like you prove it to be true. There is hope.

Paranoid Personality Disorder: Paranoia thrives on ambiguity. It is always possible to imagine the very worst in any scenario when the facts are unclear. Get the story straight and evaluate things as objectively as possible, correcting for your strong tendency to catastrophize. Unfortunately, there is a difficult catch to this recommendation. It requires you to accept that a reasonable degree of uncertainty will always be inevitable—that you can never be completely sure or completely safe. Otherwise, you will torture everyone with your constant questions about their feelings, motives, and behaviors in a way that eventually will turn them against you. Letting down your guard will occasionally get you hurt; but keeping it raised will have you miss out on much that makes life rewarding, comfortable, and fun.

A more ambitious approach would be to try to understand the mechanism of your paranoid thinking. Most often, the things you suspect or hate in others are really a disguised version of your own thoughts and impulses that have been projected out onto them. You are accusing others of thoughts that you can't accept as your own. If you think other people are hostile toward you, it may very well be a projection of your own hostility toward them. If you think others are being very critical of you, it may be because unconsciously you are very critical of yourself. If you think your wife is being sexually unfaithful, it may be because of your own sexual feelings for other people. If you can better understand and accept your own impulses, you won't have the same need to project them onto others. Usually this requires considerable open-mindedness on your part and the help of a therapist whose judgment you will have to come to trust—at least most of the time.

Antisocial Personality Disorder: There is no treatment for this problem. Change, if it happens at all, will come from the passage of time, natural maturation, external structure, getting off drugs, and painful life experiences. Some people wise up early, realize that their exploitive style is not working, and take steps to avoid the jail time or the early death they are probably otherwise headed for. Getting out of the life and away from the gang can sometimes result in a dramatic change in attitude. Getting off drugs can be the turning point. And some find a spiritual rebirth through religion. For the most part, however, antisocial personality tends to be extremely resistant to change until people run out of steam and hormones, usually in their forties or fifties.

Schizoid and Schizotypal Personality Disorders: People with these personality disorders usually don't change much. Instead, the goal will be to help them find the most comfortable solitary niche. Pets, computers, TV, books, magazines, and newspapers can be great companions without the unpredictability that almost always comes from human relationships. Cultivate a job and hobbies that are satisfying and allow you to be on your own. Try to figure out if people find your dress and behavior strange or eccentric and do your best to fit in and not call attention to yourself.

Personality Disorders determine our lives and create our problems because they set in motion vicious cycles of self-fulfilling prophecies. The best way to correct this is to get the ball rolling in the other direction—to start creating virtuous or benign cycles. Do this one step at a time. If you can modify even one small piece of your inflexible behavior, the people you care about will begin to respond differently to you and will treat you better. This should free you up further and enable you to respond even more flexibly to them. Each action gets amplified further by a positive reaction. Small steps eventually can lead to big changes. The key to getting these benign cycles started is self-awareness. As originally proclaimed by the oracle at Delphi: "Know Thyself."

Suggested Additional Readings

The New Personality Self-Portrait: Why You Think, Work, Love and Act the Way You Do
Lois B. Morris and John M. Oldham
Bantam Doubleday Dell, 1995

The Angry Heart: Overcoming Borderline and Addictive Disorders
Joseph Santoro and Ronald Cohen
New Harbinger, 1997

Lost in the Mirror: An Inside Look at Borderline Personality Disorder
Richard A. Moskovitz
Taylor, 1996

I Hate You—Don't Leave Me: Understanding the Borderline Personality
Jerold J. Kreisman, M.D., and Hal Straus
Avon Books, 1991

Where to Go for Help
(Self-help, support, for more information)

Emotions Anonymous
(twelve-step program for people with varied psychiatric symptoms including maladaptive personality traits)
P.O. Box 4245
St. Paul, MN 55104
(612) 647-9712
Web: http:/www.mtn.org/EA

Co-Dependents Anonymous (CoDA)
(self-help support group for spouses or partners of those with Personality Disorders)
E-mail: info@ourcoda.org/
Web: http://www.ourcoda.org/

Workaholics Anonymous World Service Organization
(twelve-step program)

P.O. Box 289
Menlo Park, CA 94026-0289
(510) 273-9253

Fear of Success Anonymous
(twelve-step program)

16161 Ventura Boulevard,
Suite 727
Encino, CA 91436
(818) 907-3953

S.M.A.R.T. Recovery Self-Help Network
(Self-Management and Recovery Training)
(self-help groups for individuals with "addictive behaviors"
—alcohol, drugs, gambling, eating disorders)

24000 Mercantile Road
Suite 33
Beachwood, OH 44122
(216) 292-0220
FAX: (216) 831- 3776
E-mail: srmail1@aol.com

CHAPTER 11

UNEXPLAINED
PHYSICAL COMPLAINTS

People make the assumption that "physical" symptoms (like pain, numbness, nausea, diarrhea, or skin rash) are caused by physical illness and "psychological" symptoms (like depression, mania, or anxiety) are caused by mental illness. That we should think about the causes of symptoms in this dichotomous way is no surprise. It reflects the centuries-old philosophical and commonsense tradition of splitting mind from body, soul from substance, spiritual from corporeal, and mental from physical.

The real state of affairs is by no means so simply black and white. A seemingly "psychological" symptom like depression may be caused by having a brain tumor or dementia and may even precede by months or years the diagnosis of the underlying medical illness. Similarly, people suffering from a psychiatric disorder may present first with physical symptoms. For example, depression frequently causes poor appetite, weight loss, insomnia, fatigue, headaches, and pain. Panic Disorder presents with dizziness, palpitations, numbness, sweating, trembling, shortness of breath, choking, nausea, hot flashes, and chest pain. And people using substances can present with just about any "physical" symptom. Moreover, many people experience and communicate feelings of stress or emotional distress through physical symptoms like headaches, stomach pain, dizziness, or weakness.

As a rough and ready rule of thumb, the reductionistic equations ("physical symptom = medical problem; emotional symptom = psychological problem") are a pretty good first approximation, especially when deciding who to consult initially for a problem. If you have stomach pain, the natural first step is to consult your family doctor under the assumption that an underlying physical problem is responsible. She will typically examine your abdomen and perhaps order blood tests or X-rays, looking for evidence of a physical abnormality. Often enough, nothing turns up during the physical examination and the laboratory tests are negative or "inconclusive"—even though your stomach continues to hurt.

What then are the possibilities? Perhaps there is an underlying physical cause of the stomach pain that has been missed. Given the current cost-cutting climate in medicine, you may be concerned that the doctor did not conduct a thorough enough evaluation of your problem. More likely, the condition is too minor to cause anything that would show—even the very best examinations and laboratory tests have limitations and may not be sensitive enough to pick up the physical abnormality. Finally, for some medical conditions, like multiple sclerosis, there may be no obvious physical evidence in the earliest stages—it is not until later on in the course that the underlying physical cause makes itself known.

Then there is the other possibility we discussed above—the symptoms, although experienced as being "physical," may in fact be a reaction to stress or a manifestation of an underlying emotional disturbance. Because of our predilection to assume physical causes for physical symptoms, this may be a hard pill to swallow—especially given the clumsy way the information is often conveyed: "Mr. Jones, after reviewing all of your tests, I really can't find anything wrong with you. Maybe it's all in your head." Hearing this, you might well draw the obvious and unfortunate implication that your doctor regards your symptom as not real, not legitimate, and not worthy of his precious time and energy.

Indeed many physical symptoms are in fact no more than the transient and expectable aches and pains of everyday life, but when symptoms persist over time it is usually an indication that something is wrong medically or psychiatrically. The challenge is deciphering whether the physical symptom is a clue to the existence of an underlying medical condition, or is instead a manifestation of emotional distress, or reflects some combination of the two.

The conditions in this chapter are alike in that they describe people who have persistent and disabling physical complaints that, despite adequate medical evaluation, cannot be attributed to a clearly defined physical or psychiatric disorder. These conditions differ depending on whether the person is worried about having a physical symptom (as in Somatization Disorder, Conversion Disorder, and Pain Disorder); or a terrible disease (as in Hypochondriasis); or an unusually ugly appearance (as in Body Dysmorphic Disorder).

Because these conditions exist on the cusp between general medical and psychiatric practice, they tend to be diagnosed and treated poorly in both settings. It is important to remember that these are all "diagnoses of exclusion." They are to be entertained seriously only after all medical and other psychiatric causes of the physical symptoms have first been considered and then "excluded."

Herein lies the perplexing rub. It is often much harder to prove conclusively that a medical condition is not present than to find it if it is actually there—especially since some illnesses are slow in declaring themselves clearly. In fact, you can probably never disprove with an absolute certainty the presence of an underlying physical or psychiatric illness. There is always the remote possibility that something was missed or will later become apparent as the disease progresses. As doctors, we reduce this chronic uncertainty to a "reasonable" and "acceptable" level by carrying out medical investigations. After a certain point, however, there are diminishing risk/benefit returns in continued testing as the potential yield of the next diagnostic test becomes less than the cost, pain, and danger in getting it performed.

Especially in a managed-care world, you must be assertive to ensure that you are receiving the medical care you need and deserve. If you feel that the doctor has been dismissive or superficial, by all means be insistent or consider getting a second opinion. However, your initially legitimate health worries can easily cross the line and become dangerous to your health—especially if you go too far in pursuit of a definitive, but impossibly elusive, medical explanation. If no concrete medical or psychiatric explanation has emerged after a methodical evaluation, your health concern may well qualify for one of the diagnoses you will soon be reading about and you may have to resign yourself to living with the uncertainty of negative medical findings.

Here is a common scenario. You start out with a physical symptom or the worry about having a serious illness. After a medical work-up, the doctor attempts to reassure you that you are fine. Instead, you worry either that he has not done a thorough enough job or that he has not taken your concerns seriously. The uncertainty drives you to repeated visits with other doctors—all with a similarly unsatisfying outcome. Along the way, two bad things are likely to occur. Each doctor you see will be under increasing pressure to do something definitive to solve the diagnostic puzzle. Increasingly, more extensive, risky, expensive, and painful procedures are carried out in an effort to further rule out every conceivable diagnostic possibility, no matter how exotic and unlikely. You may also be exposed to trials of various treatments on the odd chance that something will provide relief for your symptom. The tests and treatments all have their risks and side effects and being exposed to enough of them may cause more serious health problems than ever would have been the case had you just been able to let well enough alone.

A more subtle complication of exhaustive "doctor shopping" is that you may develop a reputation as someone who is not to be taken seriously—"the boy who cried wolf" one time too often. As your medical chart gets thicker and thicker, any and all future medical problems are likely to be dismissed out of hand as a figment of your imagination—even if this time there is a definable medical or psychiatric problem that does indeed require testing and treatment.

The trick is to know when to stop—to make sure there has been a complete enough medical evaluation to provide reasonable assurances regarding the absence of a definable and treatable medical or psychiatric cause; but once this is done to accept the remaining medical uncertainty with grace and equanimity.

FOCUS ON PHYSICAL SYMPTOMS: SOMATIZATION DISORDER, CONVERSION DISORDER, AND PAIN DISORDER

All of us have had an occasional unexplained physical symptom. For some people, however, a preoccupation with physical symptoms becomes a primary means of coping with stress, psychological conflict, and emotional discomfort. They are hypervigilant about their body sensations and become focused on their physical status, particularly when things are not going well psychologically. Often the person may have a clearly defined medical illness, but the concern about the physical symptoms exceeds what would be expected for that illness or persists even after the original illness is no longer a causative factor.

Of course, a concentration on physical symptoms can have its advantages, at least in the short term. The distraction that comes from devoting all possible resources to get to the bottom of the physical symptom allows one to avoid having to deal head-on with other underlying problems, emotions, or conflicts. Gaining the sick role and being under the care of a physician provides support and reassurance. Family, friends, and co-workers may become more sympathetic and be less demanding of you. And physical symptoms may directly eliminate a problematic situation, as when someone engaged in a conflict with a boss gets a disability award or reassignment to a different job in another part of the company.

Unfortunately, however, the focus on physical complaints as a coping style is rarely effective in the long term and creates its own specific set of disadvantages. Usually, the underlying problems remain unresolved and are therefore likely to recur. Although the physician, family, and friends may initially be very attentive and empathic about the person's physical complaints, this concern typically erodes quickly and is replaced by impatience and frustration. Finally, repeated visits to physicians will almost always lead to excessive tests and unnecessary treatments, with all the potential complications and cost we have discussed above.

Somatization Disorder

People with Somatization Disorder are plagued with an almost unbelievable number of physical symptoms afflicting virtually every organ system. The essence of this condition is the expression of psychological distress through medical symptoms. The person's life comes to revolve around the persistent medical complaints. Not a year (or month or perhaps even a day) goes by without one or another symptom causing pain or disability that is not explained by medical testing. Usually, the endless and frustrating medical odyssey begins in adolescence and persists pretty continuously throughout adult life. People with Somatization Disorder are seen mostly in medical settings and often are resentful when referred for psychiatric help because this feels to them like a brush-off.

Because it requires an extensive history of multiple unexplained symptoms, Somatization Disorder is relatively rare in the general population (perhaps 1 percent) but is much more frequently encountered in medical settings. Even more common are patients who have some aspect of this condition but fall short of the full-blown picture because their physical complaints are circumscribed and restricted to one (or just a few) organ system(s). For reasons that are not at all clear, Somatization Disorder is much more likely to occur in women than in men.

The physical symptoms wax and wane. They often become worse during times of emotional stress (like a work crisis or the breakup of a relationship); or if the person has a recurring psychiatric disorder (like depression or anxiety); or if a documented medical illness is also causing trouble. When things are more stable, the person may have periods of being completely free of physical symptoms, but usually these are fairly brief. Remember that the diagnosis is made only when the person has a long history of a very large number of distinct and unexplained physical symptoms.

According to the diagnostic manual, you have Somatization Disorder if:

- You have a history of many physical complaints that cannot be fully explained by a known general medical condition or by the direct effect of a substance. The complaints must start by age thirty and occur over many years.
- Your symptoms affect a lot of different parts of your body, and are severe enough to interfere with your functioning, cause you to consult a doctor, or lead to your taking medication. Most typically, the symptoms conform to the following pattern:
  (1) Four (or more) *pain* symptoms (such as head, abdomen, back, joint, extremity, chest, or rectum pain, or pain during menstruation, sexual intercourse, or urination)
  (2) Two (or more) *gastrointestinal* symptoms (such as nausea, bloating, vomiting other than during pregnancy, diarrhea, or intolerance of several different foods)
  (3) One (or more) *sexual* symptom (such as sexual indifference, problems with maintaining erections or ejaculation, irregular periods, excessive menstrual bleeding, vomiting throughout pregnancy)
  (4) One (or more) conversion symptom apparently *involving the nervous system* (such as impaired coordination, paralysis, difficulty swallowing, loss of touch sensation, double vision, blindness, deafness, seizures)

Conversion Disorder

The term "Conversion Disorder" was coined by Freud to describe the presentation of an isolated neurological symptom that is based on psychological rather than physical causes. The most common problems are paralysis, weakness, loss of sensation, numbness, unconsciousness, pseudoseizures, blindness, deafness, or loss of voice. Freud was a neurologist, not a psychiatrist, and much of his early clinical work concentrated on studying and treating patients who had unexplained neurological dysfunction. This was a common enough problem in Vienna in the 1890s to keep a neurological practice quite busy. For reasons that are not completely clear, in the 1990s conversion symptoms are relatively rare in the developed countries, although they continue to occur more frequently in other cultures.

The choice of the word "conversion" reflects Freud's causal theory. He believed that anxiety arising from internal psychological conflicts was unconsciously "converted" into the neurological symptom that provided a symbolic solution to the conflict. Take, for example, the overwhelmed mother of a newborn infant who develops a sudden and medically unexplainable paralysis of her right arm. After some questioning, it turns out that she has been suppressing an impulse to strike her constantly bawling and "impossible to please" baby in order to get him finally to stop crying. Freud's explanation would be that the anxiety stimulated by her unconscious, murderous anger toward the child has been converted into a physical paralysis of her arm, which prevents her from acting out her aggressive impulses and also punishes her for them.

This psychological model, while often plausible and always interesting, is usually not that helpful in treatment. People who "convert" impulses and psychological conflicts into physical symptoms are usually not eagerly receptive to gaining insight into what these impulses and conflicts are and respond better to a physical explanation and treatment plan—e.g., the strong suggestion that the paralysis will soon get better and a prescription for a brief rehabilitation program focused on arm exercises.

It is important to be cautious in diagnosing a Conversion Disorder because of the difficulty in determining with confidence that the "neurologic" symptom does not have an underlying explanation in nervous system pathology. A fair percentage of people who get this diagnosis (perhaps 25 percent) turn out many years later to have had a neurological condition (like multiple sclerosis) that had presented initially in an atypical way that could not initially be picked up by examination or testing. There are several hints that suggest the possibility of Conversion Disorder. Because of the predictability of brain wiring, most neurological symptoms occur in a fairly stereotyped distribution. For example, nerve damage causing loss of sensation affects patches of skin in very specific patterns that the neurologist can trace out quite precisely with a pin. If a patient complains of numbness that defies any known pattern, this suggests that the symptom may be better understood as a manifestation of emotional distress. Another tip is the timing of the symptoms. The sudden onset of the neurological problem in the midst of a crisis may point to a psychological cause. However, someone with a "conversion disorder" can simultaneously have a real neurological problem. For example, many patients who have "pseudoseizures" also have an accompanying real seizure disorder.

According to the diagnostic manual, you have a Conversion Disorder if:

*   You have experienced symptoms that affect movement or sensation (such as loss of coordination, paralysis, difficulty swallowing, loss of touch sensation, double vision, blindness, deafness, or seizures) that, at least from the beginning, appear to be caused by a medical condition.
*   After a thorough medical evaluation, no medical explanation can be found to account for your symptoms.
*   The timing of your symptoms is related to conflicts or stressful situations in your life.
*   Your symptoms interfere with your everyday life or are very upsetting to you.

Pain Disorder

Pain is a common reason for people to seek medical help—it has been estimated that up to three quarters of patients presenting to their primary care doctors are experiencing some significant pain. Our bodies are widely suffused with pain fibers that provide sentinel warning of the risks of illness or injury. Acute pain impels us to withdraw a hand from a hot stove, forces us to stop walking on an injured ankle, and signals that we may have an impacted tooth or an inflamed appendix. However, our experience of pain is not simply the end result of electrical signals being transmitted up to our brain from stimulated pain receptors. Pain is a complex subjective experience that is also modulated by nerve pathways going in the opposite direction—coming down from the higher cortical areas of our brain. We all have had the experience of pain that has been worsened or ameliorated based on our cognitive or emotional state. For example, focusing one's complete attention on a painful stimulus is a sure way to make it worse, whereas immersing oneself in other compelling activities can often lessen its intensity. Personality style, cultural background, and upbringing all have an impact on one's perception and expression of painful stimuli—people raised in cultures that embrace stoicism express pain only when it is of a particularly high intensity.

It is important not to draw the wrong conclusion—that because Pain Disorder is included in the DSM-IV, having pain means you have a mental disorder. Pain that lasts for six months or less is considered to be "acute." This type of pain is almost always clearly indicative of an underlying medical condition that requires direct attention (for example, acute infection, traumatic injury, cancer). For people with acute pain, the likelihood of total remission of the pain with appropriate medical treatment is high.

Once pain has persisted for at least six months, it is considered to be "chronic" and is much less likely to ever completely resolve. Thankfully, only a small minority of people with acute pain go on to have chronic pain. Lingering pain has usually outlived any useful purpose and takes on an unfortunate life of its own. Attempts to precisely tease apart the relative psychological versus physical aspects of chronic pain are usually fruitless. Most often, both physical and emotional factors combine to perpetuate chronic pain. On the physical side, there may be chronic inflammation, injury, or cancer. On the psychological side, the pain and its disabling effects lead to emotional distress that in turn further amplifies the pain and reduces the activities that would provide distraction. The inclusion of Pain Disorder in the DSM-IV reflects the fact that most people suffering from chronic pain can benefit from treatment that addresses both the physical and psychological aspects of the pain. In treating chronic pain, the focus should be not on totally eliminating the pain but rather on how best to cope with it more effectively and to minimize its effects on daily functioning. Although this may feel like an acceptance of defeat, it is important to keep in mind that the perpetual pursuit of the holy grail of complete remission can make things even worse. Continued exposure to increasingly aggressive therapeutic maneuvers usually entails increasingly elevated risks.

Pain management works well to teach people how to live through and around pain. Many people with chronic pain also suffer from depression. Although these people usually feel that the depression is an inevitable consequence of the chronic pain, the actual cause-and-effect relationship between pain and depression is often more complicated. As we discussed in Chapter 1, depression consists of a constellation of symptoms, which may include pain. In fact, some people with depression experience generalized bodily pain as their primary depressive symptom. Furthermore, for those with chronic waxing and waning problems like back pain or arthritis, episodes of depression can lead to a lowering of one's pain threshold. From a purely practical perspective, whether the depression is the cause or effect of the pain is less important since the treatment for both scenarios is the same—counseling and antidepressant medication.

According to the diagnostic manual, you have Pain Disorder if:
- You have experienced pain that has interfered with your everyday life.
- Psychological factors play an important role in how you experience the pain.
- Pain is the main reason for your seeking treatment.

FOCUS ON FEAR OF DISEASE
OR HAVING A PHYSICAL DEFECT: HYPOCHONDRIASIS
AND BODY DYSMORPHIC DISORDER

These are tough problems to live with—both for the patient and for the doctor. Someone with Hypochondriasis is haunted by the unshakable and terrifying feeling that he harbors a serious, but as yet undiagnosed, medical condition that is probably getting worse because he and his doctors cannot get to the bottom of it. Someone with Body Dysmorphic Disorder is consumed by the conviction that at least one of his body parts is unspeakably ugly or defective. In both conditions, there is enormous frustration, anger, depression, and/or hopelessness regarding the medical profession's inability to provide relief or even to take the problem seriously enough.

Hypochondriasis

All of us worry from time to time that our bodies are letting us down and that we might have, or be developing, a serious illness. For those with Hypochondriasis, the concerns about disease persist for years at a time and become the fulcrum of daily existence. The fear or worry becomes so overwhelming as to make it difficult to concentrate on virtually anything else.

Early on, the hypochondriacal concerns may seem understandable and even possibly realistic. Many serious medical conditions start modestly and unfold slowly, heralded at first only by mild or relatively innocuous symptoms—a brain cancer that began with headaches; a heart attack that started with indigestion; a stroke that announces itself with a negligible tingling in the leg; a skin cancer emerging from a small mole; or a leukemia that causes only slight weight loss and fatigue. In Hypochondriasis, the person is hypervigilant about body functioning and immediately embraces as inevitable the worst-case scenario for each and every symptom or bodily sensation. The actual odds are overwhelming that most headaches are not caused by cancer, that most moles are innocuous, and that most indigestion is really no more than indigestion. The comfort that might be offered by these odds of probability is lost on the hypochondriac, who contemplates with near certainty that he is or will be the specially chosen victim of the exceedingly rare catastrophe. He remains virtually impervious to repeated medical reassurances and to the accumulated weight of negative medical examinations and negative laboratory testing.

Here is a typical example. A thirty-year-old marathoner with twenty-five races under his belt reads a magazine article about a famous runner who recently suddenly dropped dead during a routine workout. The cause of death was a heart arrhythmia. Our marathoner starts monitoring his own pulse and becomes totally preoccupied with the idea that the occasional skipped beats mean that he has a damaged heart and may be at high risk for a similar cardiac catastrophe. Soon he is checking his pulse sixty times a day and decides to give up running just to be on the safe side. He sees his highly competent family doctor, who, after a careful physical examination and electrocardiogram, assures him that he is in absolutely superb shape and has the well-conditioned heart of an eighteen-year-old. The doctor suggests that he continue running and forget about the whole thing. Completely unsatisfied, the now ex-marathoner consults a series of cardiologists, each of whom is egged on to perform successively more extensive and invasive testing—but the results are consistently negative and his heart receives universal rave reviews. Instead of helping him to feel better, the good news paradoxically causes him to become even more anxious. It is his contention that the doctors are continuing to miss the problem or that they are withholding bad news. Soon he cannot concentrate on his work because he is so afraid of the undiagnosed illness he is convinced he has. He spends endless hours reading medical texts and journals and browsing the Internet for suggested tests and possible cures. His friends begin to avoid him because he has become so self-absorbed that all conversations center on his health concerns and the failure of his friends and doctors to take them seriously enough.

In Hypochondriasis, the specific choice of feared illness varies depending upon previous personal experience of symptoms or illness, the illnesses experienced by loved ones, the person's general medical awareness, and what is being featured that year in the media. Preoccupation with having AIDS has become increasingly more common, facilitated by the vague nature of early symptoms of HIV infection (fatigue, weight loss), widespread media coverage, likelihood of personal connection to an AIDS victim, and the minuscule but nonetheless inherent fallibility of HIV testing (there is always the possibility, however infinitesimal, of a false negative result).

According to the diagnostic manual, you have Hypochondriasis if:
- You are convinced that you have a serious disease.
- You still believe you are very sick even after going to doctors who have performed comprehensive medical examinations and have told you that there is nothing to worry about.
- The concern is persistent (at least six months) and interferes with your life.

Body Dysmorphic Disorder

It is entirely possible that, ever since the wide availability of mirrors, no human being has been totally content with his or her physical appearance. Certainly, there are many people who seem to make pretty much a life's work out of improving what they look like. Body Dysmorphic Disorder goes far beyond this normal expectable dissatisfaction with body image—so much so that one's appearance becomes an object of both self-loathing and extreme shame. The person develops an unbelievably single-minded and totally self-absorbed preoccupation with the imagined physical failing. Concerns about ugliness interfere with every aspect of functioning.

Perhaps his ears are uneven, too big or too small; or his nose is misshapen; his skin may be too red, too pale, too freckled, or too wrinkled; or some scar, mole, or other facial marking is so repugnant that it cannot be shown in public. Almost any other part of the body can also become the focus of dissatisfaction—the genitals, breasts, buttocks, hips, stomach, arms, legs, hands, feet, or hair may each be the subject of unbelievable attention and self-criticism. To the outside observer, there is usually no obvious defect. The "offending" part really is either reasonably attractive or simply not particularly noteworthy one way or the other. In some cases, there may be some relatively minor imperfection (like slight scarring from acne, a small mole, or a less than totally perfect nose), but the intensity of the person's negative evaluation is far out of proportion to any objective evaluation of the problem.

The worries about appearance become a dominant focus. The person spends so many hours a day fretting about the supposed defect that he is unable to concentrate attention on any other activities. Mirrors may become painful magnets—the person finds himself irresistibly drawn to and captured by any reflective surface, checking and rechecking the appearance of the offending body part and imagining how it looks to others. Or mirrors may be avoided like the plague since it is simply too upsetting to be confronted by the imagined defect. People often assume that strangers are staring at their deformity and talking or laughing about it.

Some make vigorous efforts to cover up by spending endless hours applying makeup or by wearing wigs, bandannas, large sunglasses, elaborate hats, or baggy clothing. Work, school, and other social situations are avoided because of the embarrassment. In extreme situations, the person may become a prisoner in his own house. Unable to face anyone because of the unbearable shame, he goes out in disguise only at night when no one can be a witness. Instant cures are often attempted via the hoped for magic of plastic surgery. However, because the problem is more one of internal perception than external reality, most people remain unsatisfied with the results of surgery or blame it for causing even more unsightliness. Malpractice lawsuits are a common consequence of this disappointment.

According to the diagnostic manual, you have Body Dysmorphic Disorder if:
- You are convinced that there is something seriously wrong with some specific aspect of your physical appearance.
- You continue to believe this even after everyone tells you that your concern is tremendously exaggerated.
- You are preoccupied with this concern and it seriously interferes with your life.

Differential Diagnosis

The most crucial task in the differential diagnosis of all of the conditions in this chapter is to determine whether a medical or psychiatric illness is causing the physical symptoms or disease concern. This is complicated by the fact that some people have the combination of both unexplainable physical symptoms and a definable physical or psychiatric problem. This leads commonly to a Scylla and Charybdis dilemma. On the one hand, it is necessary to be sufficiently systematic and thorough in medical and psychiatric evaluations to determine whether there is a clear-cut cause for the physical symptoms. On the other hand, it is important not to overdo the testing, especially if a person has had a fairly recent negative medical work-up and if the presentation of symptoms is not typical of a clearly defined medical or psychiatric illness but instead conforms more closely to one of the conditions described in this chapter.

Remember that the first symptom of many of the psychiatric disorders described elsewhere in this book may be a physical complaint. Depression, anxiety, and substance use may be missed because the focus is on the physical symptoms caused by them. This underdiagnosis of psychiatric problems is especially likely to occur in the primary care medical settings that are usually the first recourse for patients with physical symptoms. It should be a universal rule of thumb for someone who has unexplained or atypical physical symptoms that a thorough evaluation be performed to rule out the presence of depression, anxiety disorders, or problems caused by substance use. For example, anyone presenting with unexplained shortness of breath, dizziness, palpitations, and numbness in the fingers should be checked out for other symptoms of a panic attack (pages 79–83).

There are several increasingly popular conditions (such as chronic fatigue syndrome, fibromyalgia, irritable bowel syndrome, and hypoglycemia) that remain medically controversial and have thus far eluded attempts to find hard evidence demonstrating a definitive physical cause. Many doctors believe that these seemingly "medical" conditions are really no more than a masked presentation of a psychiatric problem. This is supported by the fact that they are often accompanied by depression and anxiety and sometimes respond to antidepressant medication. On the other hand, proponents of these conditions as specific medical illnesses attribute the lack of physical evidence pinning down their medical cause to current limitations in knowledge. They insist that a physical basis for these conditions—at least in some patients—will ultimately be discovered. They also point out that the accompanying depression is an understandable reaction to the chronic suffering (rather than its cause) and that the efficacy of antidepressant medications is not informative regarding etiology since they are effective for so many complaints, including the relief of neural pain. In our view, the jury is still out (pending more research) concerning the true nature of these conditions. Practically speaking, whether they are physical or psychological (or both) is less important than achieving symptom relief. A trial of antidepressants may make sense after more conservative measures have been tried (like lifestyle changes, more exercise and sleep, avoiding certain foods).

AM I OKAY?

If you let yourself concentrate intensely on your body sensations, you will soon discover that you have many more of them than you had ever previously imagined and it is not too long a stretch before you begin worrying about their possible significance. Our susceptibility to suggestion about physical symptoms is clearly demonstrated by the relatively high rates of side effects that are regularly experienced by people who are given placebo (dummy pills) in double-blind clinical trials of new medicines. It is not difficult for our minds to experience physical "symptoms" in the absence of any specific physical cause.

From time to time, almost everyone has had one or another physical symptom for which there was no ready medical explanation and has perhaps wondered at least momentarily whether a headache might mean a brain tumor, a cough might presage lung cancer, or fatigue might indicate HIV infection. Medical students routinely imagine that they are afflicted with whatever disease they are studying in pathology or have seen in teaching rounds. For many people, reasonable concerns about physical health and fears of possibly having an undetected disease are useful motivating factors for regular physical examinations and laboratory tests (like mammograms, Pap smears, dental X-rays) and for maintaining a healthy lifestyle.

Whether unexplained physical symptoms or excessive concerns about health constitute evidence for one of the disorders in this section or are instead just part of life depends on how severe, persistent, and pervasive they are and how much trouble and impairment they are causing. For example, having mild and occasional stress-induced headaches or episodes of diarrhea is certainly no fun, but would be considered to fall well within the realm of normality if the symptoms do not have a significant impact on functioning. On the other hand, when a person has multiple bouts of severe pains in various parts of the body, chronic nausea and diarrhea, severe menstrual irregularity, and unexplained episodes of paralysis—none of which can be explained even after extensive diagnostic work-ups—and these symptoms have resulted in chronic work absenteeism and social isolation, this strongly points to a diagnosis of Somatization Disorder. By the same token, worrying for a couple of weeks about a slight cough is one thing, but mulling about it for years and going from doctor to doctor to get confirmation of one's worst fears of lung cancer crosses the line into Hypochondriasis. And, in our beauty-obsessed society, it is no wonder that dissatisfaction with appearance is probably more the rule than the exception. Thus, a diagnosis of Body Dysmorphic Disorder is given only when the dissatisfaction becomes so extreme that the person is both preoccupied and tormented by it.

TREATMENT OPTIONS

The first principle guiding the approach to the problems described in this chapter is that it is essential to obtain a thorough medical evaluation and appropriate treatment, but you must avoid going overboard and creating more problems than you started with. This requires a careful review of the lifelong course of previous diagnostic efforts so as not to keep repeating mindlessly what has been done already or to go on to ever more exotic tests or treatments that are likely to have a low yield and to add new risk with little potential benefit. The Hippocratic Oath's most emphatic injunction to physicians is to "first do no harm."

Once the diagnosis of one of the disorders described in the chapter is made, what is the treatment? This is a crucial issue not just for the individual patient but also for the entire health care system. Most studies show that a small minority (about 10 to 15 percent) of patients in any given health plan wind up using about 80 percent of all the health resources. Some of this high utilization is accounted for by those people who have chronic, severe, and expensive illnesses; some of it arises from the problems described in this chapter—the overreaction to physical symptoms and health concerns that leads to constant medical attention.

Not surprisingly, managed care has taken a great interest in reducing costs by promoting lower utilization of services among "frequent flyer" consumers of what may be unnecessary medical testing and treatment. The managed-care approach—known as "demand management"—attempts to substitute a lower-cost for a higher-cost service. For example, a nurse available by telephone may help reassure the patient so that an emergency room visit becomes unnecessary. Or the provision of a support group specifically geared to teach methods of coping with physical concerns may reduce the need for frequent outpatient visits.

Perhaps most important, a program of psychoeducation and psychotherapy may help modify the person's approach to physical symptoms and health worries. These begin with the premise that the physical symptoms or health concerns are not likely to simply disappear. The patient (and family) learn that unexplained physical symptoms are a common part of everyday life for many people and usually do not have dire pathological significance. The goal cannot be to remove totally the patient's discomfort and anxiety about illness, but rather to help promote a better way of dealing with these concerns. The patient is shown that his previous reactions to the symptoms—fear, doctor shopping, multiple testing, forgoing other important life activities—have now become much more dangerous to well-being than the symptom itself.

The patient needs to learn how to gain a sense of control over the symptoms and fears rather than being controlled by them. A regular schedule of gradually increasing physical, mental, and interpersonal activity helps to get the person back in the world and reduces the tendency to be overly self-absorbed with bodily sensations. In some instances, this may require a formal rehabilitation program—in others it can be achieved by self-directed homework assignments. The anxiety related to physical symptoms is not just to be avoided. Rather, the patient may benefit from the same kind of desensitizing cognitive/behavior exposure therapy that has been described for the anxiety disorders on page 94. This includes accepting the remote possibility that any given physical complaint could conceivably be related to serious illness, but to counter this with the knowledge that the odds are overwhelmingly against the previous catastrophic interpretation. The person learns to bear the risk and go on living, realizing that insatiable worry about health is not particularly healthy and is likely to ruin what otherwise might be a reasonably happy life.

Antidepressant medications are often helpful and particularly so if the patient has co-occurring psychiatric symptoms like depression or anxiety. Antianxiety medications are to be used with considerable caution, particularly if the patient has a previous history of Substance Dependence or Abuse.

Suggested Additional Readings

Phantom Illness: Recognizing, Understanding, and Overcoming Hypochondria
    Carla Cantor and Brian Fallon, M.D.
    Houghton Mifflin (Paper), 1997

The Broken Mirror: Understanding and Treating Body Dysmorphic Disorder
    Katherine A. Phillips
    Oxford University Press, 1996

The Body Speaks: Therapeutic Dialogues for Mind-Body Problems
    James L. Griffith and Melissa Elliott Griffith
    Basic Books, 1994

Where to Go for Help
(Self-help, support, for more information)

American Chronic Pain Association

P.O. Box 850
Rocklin, CA 95677
(916) 632-0922
FAX: (916) 632-3208
E-mail: ACPA@pacbell.net
Web: http://members.tripod.com/~Widdy/ACPA.html

National Chronic Pain Outreach Association (NCPOA)

7979 Old Georgetown Road, Suite 100
Bethesda, MD 20814-2429
(301) 652-4948
FAX: (301) 907-0745
E-mail: ncpoa1@aol.com
Web: //neurosurgery.mgh.harvard.edu/ncpainoa.htm

CHAPTER 12

OTHER IMPULSE-CONTROL
PROBLEMS

At our most basic, we human beings, like all the other animals, are driven by aggressive, sexual, and pleasure-seeking impulses. These inborn drives have their evolutionary roots in what were (and usually still are) very adaptive territorial, reproductive, and exploratory instincts. The quality that distinguishes us humans from the rest of the animal kingdom—but, unfortunately, just by a little bit—is our greater capacity for putting off the immediate gratification of instincts in favor of longer-term and culturally taught responsibilities and moral values. The reckless and immediate expression of impulses is not compatible either with longevity or with harmonious functioning in society. Individual differences in the ability to tolerate frustration and to delay gratification arise from the interaction of inborn temperament with early life (and, to a lesser degree, also with later life) experiences. Measures of impulsivity taken even among very young children are fairly good predictors of later impulsivity in adolescence and adulthood, although most people gain increasing control of themselves with age.

Impulse control problems can occur as a consequence of many different medical and mental disorders. Good judgment slips away when the brain is under siege, whatever the cause. Almost anyone who has gotten high at a party can attest to the powerful disinhibiting effects of alcohol and drugs (see Chapter 6). Barroom brawls and spur-of-the-moment sexual encounters are but two of the many harmful examples of substance-induced breakdowns in impulse control. People who suffer brain damage from a stroke, head trauma, or dementia can do things that previously would have been beyond their imagining and beneath their contempt (see Chapter 16). A usually placid woman bites when a nurse tries to bathe her or a usually puritanical man begins to exhibit himself or masturbate in public.

A breakdown in impulse control may also result from a severe mood or psychotic disturbance. A manic salesman overcharges his credit cards purchasing plane tickets for fifty friends to have a weekend reunion in Europe (page 59); a depressed mother impulsively kills herself and her child (page 33); or a homeless man suffering from Schizophrenia sets fires after being commanded by the devil to create hell on earth (page 313). A general pattern of reckless, antisocial, or self-destructive behavior that starts early and is expressed in every aspect of the person's life is best explained by Antisocial or Borderline Personality Disorder (page 228 and page 224).

In all these situations, we assign a diagnosis from elsewhere in this book and offer whatever treatment is appropriate for the underlying condition (for example, abstinence for the person abusing alcohol; a mood stabilizer for the person with mania; an antipsychotic medication for the man with Schizophrenia). The impulse problem may be a very important part of the presentation, but it is not usually the central or most specific aspect of the diagnosis or target of the treatment.

This chapter focuses on five conditions characterized by a repeated breakdown in the ability to resist one or another quite specific type of dangerous impulse. The impulses include violent aggression (Intermittent Explosive Disorder), stealing (Kleptomania), fire setting (Pyromania), gambling (Pathological Gambling), and the persistent need to pull out body hair (Trichotillomania). Although quite different in their surface manifestations, all of these have a common motivation that plays itself out in the same stereotyped way. You feel a strong impulse to commit whatever is your particular releasing act (violence, stealing, setting fires, gambling, or hair pulling); the tension to do the act builds steadily and feels increasingly irresistible; you try to ward off the impulse, sometimes for no more than seconds, sometimes for months or even longer; the tension continues to build and build; you succumb to it and perform the act with an accompanying feeling of pleasure and/or release; and, finally, you feel embarrassed and guilty about having given in again to the impulse—until the need inevitably recurs and the cycle repeats itself the next time—and again and again and again.

INTERMITTENT EXPLOSIVE DISORDER

People with Intermittent Explosive Disorder have episodic, unwanted, and unwarranted outbursts of temper. What seems to be the slightest of provocations provokes an outrageously over-the-top response: a husband beats his wife because she misplaced an overdue bill; a woman cuts her boyfriend's entire wardrobe into thousands of pieces after he criticizes her weight gain; a post office worker hits his supervisor on the head with a mail tray when his productivity is questioned; or a chef throws a butcher knife at a waiter who got an order wrong. Often, there is a Jekyll-and-Hyde quality. A normally timid and quiet person unexpectedly explodes into uncontrollable outbursts that are experienced almost as a "spell" or "rage attack." These storms come on suddenly and without warning and end just as quickly. Once the anger has passed, you feel like an idiot or monster and are genuinely horrified, ashamed, embarrassed, and remorseful about the loss of control, especially if someone has been hurt. In the majority of cases, the inappropriate anger is directed toward a family member, friend, or co-worker.

According to the diagnostic manual, you have Intermittent Explosive Disorder if:
- You have repeatedly lost of control of your anger, leading to serious verbal threats, physical violence, or property damage.
- The intensity of your anger was way out of proportion to the provocation.
- There is no other explanation for these outbursts of temper, like being intoxicated with alcohol or drugs or having a medical or psychiatric condition which causes a loss of control of anger.

DIFFERENTIAL DIAGNOSIS

There are two important considerations in the differential diagnosis of Intermittent Explosive Disorder. First off, it must be distinguished from everyday human violence that should not be explained away or excused as a psychiatric disorder. Then it is important to consider all of the more specific psychiatric and medical disorders that can cause violence.

Most violence has nothing whatever to do with psychiatry. We are, after all, the descendants of the world's most successful predators and the capacity for violence is all too inherent in human nature. Most episodes of aggression and violence are a means to a specific end—to achieve monetary gain, to exact vengeance, for self-defense, to exert social or sexual dominance, to participate in warfare, to make a political statement, or to share in gang culture. In contrast, the aggression in Intermittent Explosive Disorder is far removed from the person's usual standards, is unpremeditated, and serves no useful or directed purpose.

Disinhibition of aggressive impulses can occur as part of a number of more specific psychiatric and neurologic conditions. For example, an episode of violence in the previous year is about ten times more likely in substance abusers (20 percent) than for the general population (2 percent) and is three times more likely for people with severe mood or schizophrenic disorders (6 percent). It is, therefore, always important to make sure that the violence has not really been caused by substance intoxication, head injury, dementia, seizures, other neurological conditions (especially those affecting the frontal lobe of the brain), mania, depression, Schizophrenia, or Personality Disorder.

Am I Okay?

An inborn aggressive instinct is a prime motivator of human behavior, especially in males. One explanation for our keen interest in contact sports is that they allow us to express aggressive impulses vicariously in a relatively safe and socially acceptable form. We all struggle, with varying degrees of success, to control our tendency toward aggression. This diagnosis is certainly not meant to describe every occasion in which someone harmlessly blows off steam. An occasional angry outburst that occurs when you are irritable or frustrated is an inevitable cost of doing human business and has no pathological significance—although it may sometimes get you into trouble. Intermittent Explosive Disorder should be considered only when the outbursts are especially severe; recurrent; out of proportion; out of control; out of character; hurt others; and lead to separation, divorce, job loss, or arrest.

Treatment Options

Necessary to the treatment is your accepting responsibility for the violent behavior and feeling a really strong motivation to change it. Psychotherapy can be helpful in reducing the intensity and frequency of rage attacks by raising your awareness of what are your own special triggers for anger. If you learn to spot the early signs that an attack is brewing, it becomes much more possible to avoid it altogether or at least to reduce the severity. Verbalization of anger in the early stages may deflate pressure before it builds to an irresistible head. Distraction, "time out," getting away from the triggering person, counting to ten before acting, are all simple but remarkably helpful ways of acquiring self-control. They require lots of practice and determination. A number of medications have also been tried to help control aggressive behavior, with variable results. Antipsychotics, beta blockers, antiseizure medications, antidepressants, and mood stabilizers have all shown limited effects but there is no one medicine that is clearly effective in reducing tendencies toward violence.

KLEPTOMANIA

Stealing is a fairly universal activity among most animal species and is all too common among us humans, even after we are presumably civilized. The usual motivation for stealing is the obvious goal of gaining some valuable booty. This is what drives most shoplifters, Wall Street manipulators, tax evaders, professional burglars, embezzlers, con artists, muggers, and those who steal to support a drug habit. As Willie Sutton wisely noted, people rob banks because that is where the money is. On rare occasions, stealing is performed for a far more personal and less practical purpose—as an act of vengeance, to satisfy a dare, or as a kind of "rite of passage" in joining a gang.

None of these reasons for stealing has anything to do with psychiatry in general or with Kleptomania specifically. Kleptomania is the least frequent and most puzzling of the reasons for stealing. You take objects not for their inherent value or because you need them, but rather because the very act of stealing gives you a thrill or, at the least, a relief from tension. In fact, the stolen object may be completely worthless to you—a tin of canned ham taken in the supermarket, despite the fact that you find canned ham detestable. Once the act of stealing is completed and your feeling of tension has abated, you will probably ignore, discard, or even return the object to the store. Ultimately, you get caught committing an embarrassing, seemingly ridiculous theft—taking at great risk something of small value for which you have no need. Once apprehended, you don't want to talk about the impulses that led to the stealing and focus instead on your shame, embarrassment, and guilt.

For many people with Kleptomania, the urge to steal is "triggered" by specific settings (supermarkets in general or a particular corner drugstore) or by types of objects (books, dresses, or penknives). The intensity of the urge to steal may also vary at different times of the day or year and often increases in response to stress or boredom. The thefts are usually committed alone, in secret, impulsively, and without much professional polish. People with Kleptomania rarely come for help spontaneously and are usually referred after being busted. If the act of theft makes sense to the judge, the disposition is usually to the criminal justice system.

According to the diagnostic manual, you have Kleptomania if:

- You have a pattern of failing to resist an impulse to steal objects that you do not need either for their monetary value or for your own personal use.
- Immediately before committing the theft, you experience an increasing sense of tension. Once you have committed the theft, you feel pleasure, gratification, or relief.
- You do not steal as a way of expressing anger or vengeance or for monetary gain.

DIFFERENTIAL DIAGNOSIS

As emphasized already, most stealing represents a criminal, not a psychiatric, problem. Stealing that is for gain, revenge, or bonding has nothing to do with Kleptomania. The vast majority of shoplifters do not suffer from Kleptomania—they are after the goods, not the cheap thrill of stealing them.

There are also a number of other psychiatric conditions besides Kleptomania that may predispose a person to steal. Patients with mania (page 59) sometimes steal as a result of their grandiosity, impulsivity, thrill seeking, and entitlement. Patients with Major Depressive Disorder (page 33) sometimes steal in order to counter a depressed mood and/or to seek punishment. Patients with Schizophrenia (page 313) sometimes steal, usually in a disorganized way and to meet an immediate need. Patients with Antisocial Personality Disorder (page 228) and/or Substance Dependence (page 120) are the most likely to steal repetitively and for gain.

The characteristic feature that separates Kleptomania from the criminal and other psychiatric causes of stealing is that it is stealing purely for stealing's sake—a seemingly irresistible impulse to steal for the thrill of it or to reduce the tension that builds up if the impulse to steal is resisted. One final differential diagnosis for Kleptomania is malingering. Some people who are caught in the criminal act will claim that their stealing is caused by an irresistible impulse in order to mitigate punishment or to evade criminal responsibility. Fortunately, this defense usually fails to sway the court.

AM I OKAY?

W. C. Fields's deliciously cynical movie *You Can't Cheat an Honest Man* is based on the unfortunately safe premise that a little bit of larceny is hardwired into all (or at least most) of us. It is a rare person (someone either superbly moral, or very frightened, or somewhat lacking in imagination, or all three) who has never ever stolen, or even wanted to steal, a single thing in an entire lifetime. An occasional urge to pilfer, especially if it is resisted, is a far cry from Kleptomania. In Kleptomania, the thrill of stealing starts early in life, becomes all-consuming, and follows a chronic course, resulting in multiple embarrassing incidents and arrests.

TREATMENT OPTIONS

This is not a common condition and there is little research on how best to treat it. The major goal is to control the behavior before the person gets into serious trouble. Usually, this means achieving complete abstinence. It is probably just as hard to stop at one theft as it is to stop at one drink. It may be a good idea for the person to avoid the stores or other triggers that stimulate the urge to steal (just as an alcoholic avoids bars). Behavioral techniques include aversive conditioning (having the person picture a repulsive image whenever he feels the urge to steal), systematic desensitization (to control the mounting anxiety and tension preceding the impulse to steal), and distraction (holding one's breath whenever there is an urge to steal). Antidepressants are usually tried, but with only mixed results.

PYROMANIA

Most people start fires for reasons that have nothing whatever to do with Pyromania. Fires are set for profit (collecting insurance after arson); to hide a crime;

to exact revenge; as a particularly destructive form of vandalism; as a political or terrorist act; or to gain attention. Occasionally, fires are set by psychiatric patients in response to delusions (being on a mission from the devil to signal impending Armageddon) or command hallucinations (hearing an incessant voice instructing the person to torch a building). The distinguishing characteristic of Pyromania is that the fires are started exclusively for the love of fire. You have a repetitive and seemingly irresistible urge that can be relieved only by setting a fire. There is no particular gain involved except the excitement of making something burn and watching the consequences.

The person usually has a long history of being a "fire bug," often from childhood. You love fires, firefighters, fire stations, and fire fighting equipment, and monitor police radio to find the locations of fires so that you can be one of the first to get there. When you are not starting actual fires, you set off false alarms so that you can enjoy watching the fire personnel and equipment in action. You have a real taste for it—there is a strong sense of urgency before and then a thrill in seeing the flames roar. Afterward, you feel remorse, particularly if a person or an animal has been caught in the fire. Because the problem is recurrent and persistent, one individual may wind up setting literally hundreds of fires. These can cause devastating property damage and result in inadvertent murder.

According to the diagnostic manual, you have Pyromania if:
- You have a pattern of deliberate and purposeful fire setting.
- Immediately before the act, you feel tension or aroused emotions. After setting the fire, you experience pleasure, gratification, or relief.
- You are fascinated by, curious about, or attracted to fires and fire-related paraphernalia.
- You do not set fires for monetary gain, to further your political ideology, to conceal criminal activity, to express anger or vengeance, or to improve your living circumstances.

DIFFERENTIAL DIAGNOSIS

Before making the diagnosis of Pyromania, it is important to establish that the motivation is pleasure and tension release rather than gain, anger, vengeance, or politics. The next step is to rule out a psychiatric diagnosis that might account for the fire setting. Fire setting is sometimes a problem among hospitalized psychiatric patients (about one quarter of whom have a previous history either of setting fires or threatening to do so), but true Pyromania as defined here is very rarely encountered in psychiatric settings. Most people who set fires wind up in jail, not in psychiatric treatment, and this is probably as it should be.

AM I OKAY?

Many parents have wondered whether their child is a young pyromaniac in the making or is no more than a curious youngster with an average, expectable awe regarding the mysteries associated with matches, lighters, fireworks, chemistry sets, and rocket launchers. A commonsense approach is not to get overly alarmed if your child expresses some interest in fire but not to encourage that interest, however cute it might seem or however determined the child is to pursue it. An ounce of prevention is worth a pound of cure and children who play with fire do indeed get burnt. On the adult side, an interest in (or even something of a fascination with) fire is okay if it is not extreme and does not get you into trouble. Fire starting is never normal, but it is just fine to join a volunteer fire department, to love fireplaces, to have recurrent barbecues, or to enjoy movies that feature gigantic conflagrations.

TREATMENT OPTIONS

Although the track record for treatment of Pyromania has been spotty, it is certainly worth a try because the potential consequences of the behavior are so devastating both for the person and for his potential victims. This is not to say, of course, that receiving treatment should relieve the individual of criminal responsibility for his acts—especially since it is so unclear whether any treatment will lessen future recidivism. The therapist will work with you to determine the events, environmental triggers, feelings, and behaviors that are associated with your urges to set fires. The goal is to help you identify when your impulse to set fires is building up early enough to do something about it and to learn alternative ways for discharging the tension.

PATHOLOGICAL GAMBLING

Gambling is a fairly ubiquitous pastime that is found in one form or another in almost all cultures. It has fostered, and has been furthered by, the development of a really remarkably inventive array of gaming options appealing to every conceivable taste and pocketbook. As many as 80 percent of the adult population in the United States gamble at some time or other. Social gambling and professional gambling must be distinguished from each other and also from the very much less common Pathological Gambling, which is our focus here. Social gambling is a culturally accepted recreation that is not at all preoccupying and does not cause any serious negative consequences. Professional gambling is a full- or part-time job engaged in by sharps who are wise in the ways of practical statistics and commonsense psychology and are highly disciplined in their techniques of play.

In contrast, Pathological Gambling comes to control the person's life. It is estimated that at least two million people in the United States are already unable to gamble without getting into serious trouble and that this number is likely to increase with the further spread of legalized gambling opportunities. The states that have the most open gambling also have the highest prevalence of Pathological Gambling. The choice of preferred gaming activity depends upon individual preference, local availability, and cultural norms. The favorites in the United States are sports betting, lotteries, various types of casino games, horse racing, and the stock market.

Pathological Gambling is so much like substance addiction that it is defined by many of the same concepts (see page 120) and it is no coincidence that Gamblers Anonymous is modeled so closely after AA. The need to gamble at ever-increasing stakes to achieve the same "action" resembles drug tolerance (in which you need increasingly higher doses to get the same buzz). When not in play, gamblers get irritable and depressed—a clear analogy to substance withdrawal. You become psychologically dependent on gambling and are preoccupied with handicapping, reliving past gambling experiences, and getting money to underwrite the next gambling opportunity. After losing, you quickly return in a futile effort to win it all back on the next hand, game, race, or roll of the dice (a process known as "chasing" one's losses). Pathological gamblers frequently try to quit, but are usually unsuccessful in doing so without help.

The course of Pathological Gambling is fairly characteristic. You have a strong family history of gambling and/or of other addictive behavior. You began gambling at a young age and for large stakes and came to feel that you were especially good at it. The initial successes made you a big shot and gave you the feeling of being specially blessed. There may have been years of acceptable social gambling that switched to Pathological Gambling because of increased access (a casino opened nearby), or stress (breakup of an important relationship, being fired from a job), or the onset of a psychiatric disorder (particularly mania).

Unfortunately, almost everyone (except for the professional gambler and the very low-stakes player) loses at gambling—particularly if the bets are placed where there is a prohibitively high house take. The random fluctuations of fortune that are part and parcel of gambling are guaranteed to provide an endless supply of exhilarating highs and demoralizing lows. For the pathological gambler, a string of bad luck and/or bad bets precipitates chasing. Previously more disciplined gambling strategies are discarded in an attempt to win back everything at once in high-stake, all-or-nothing plunges. As the losses build, there is an increased sense of urgency; the bets become heavier and riskier; and the losses build even further. Debts pile up, with only the most immediate and essential of them being paid off. You go through all available resources, overspend credit cards, borrow from friends and relatives, seek bank loans, take out second mortgages, and may resort to the usurious rates demanded by loan sharks and pawnbrokers. You face the loss of a job and love relationships, legal action by creditors, and may even be threatened physically by bookies and loan sharks.

Eventually, you must finally come clean and confess the problem to family or friends. This usually results in a bailout, with debts paid off in exchange for your solemn promise to stop or curtail gambling. Unfortunately, the bailout often sends the wrong message and gives you the feeling that you really can beat the odds and will always land on your feet. Before very long, the same gambling cycle usually resumes and spirals downward. You may resort to behaviors that previously would have been inconceivable: writing bad checks, forging signatures, and the outright theft or embezzlement from family members or employers. This is rationalized as a short-term strategy necessary to get enough money to make the killing that will win back all the losses and right all the problems. Things may slide further downhill. You become irritable, depressed, and ultimately hopeless about ever getting back in control again. You may throw all caution to the winds, gambling just for the short-term exhilaration and relief of tension. At this point, jail, suicide, or a gangland murder may seem the only options open to you.

Female gamblers differ to some degree from their male counterparts. Women are more likely to live alone, play alone, be more depressed, and gamble as an escape from their depressive feelings, whereas the motivation in men is more likely to be the excitement and craving for action.

According to the diagnostic manual, you suffer from Pathological Gambling if:

- You have a persistent pattern of gambling that is out of control and leads to severe negative consequences, as indicated by at least five of the following:

   (1) You are preoccupied with gambling (e.g., you relive past gambling experiences, constantly determine the betting odds for everything, or think of ways to get money with which to gamble).

   (2) You need to increase your bets in order to achieve the same level of excitement.

   (3) You are repeatedly unsuccessful in controlling, cutting back, or stopping.

   (4) You feel restless or irritable when you try to cut down or stop gambling.

   (5) You gamble as a way of escaping from problems or from feelings of helplessness, guilt, anxiety, or depression.

   (6) You chase your losses (e.g., you double your bets in order to "win it all back").

   (7) You lie to family members, therapists, or others in order to cover up the extent of your gambling.

   (8) You have committed crimes (e.g., forgery, fraud, theft, embezzlement) to finance your gambling.

   (9) You have jeopardized or lost significant relationships, jobs, or educational or career opportunities because of your gambling.

   (10) You get others to bail you out of the desperate financial situations caused by your gambling.

Differential Diagnosis

Some people with Pathological Gambling may claim to be (and indeed view themselves as) social or professional gamblers, but their compulsive play, unplanned extensive losses, and inability to resist the temptation to chase losses are the clearly distinguishing features.

Social gambling is pursued for fun and conviviality with friends or colleagues. It is a scheduled activity that lasts for a specified time (for example, one evening a week for just a few hours). The potential losses are limited by predetermined betting limits and are affordable for all the people involved. Professional gamblers are experts at the closely disciplined evaluation of probabilities and controlled risk taking; they are especially competent in knowing how to cut their losses and limit their risks. Pathological gamblers are especially lousy gamblers because they are too hooked on the activity to make rational and disciplined bets. You bet too often, too promiscuously, and at too great an advantage to the house ever to turn the odds in your favor for any extended period of time.

It is sometimes hard to distinguish Pathological Gambling from mania (page 59). The judgment has to be made whether the gambling is an associated feature of a manic episode or whether the manic-like symptoms are an associated feature of Pathological Gambling. Increased, impulsive, and foolish gambling can be one sign of the driven and disinhibited pleasure-seeking that occurs in a manic episode. On the other hand, some people engaged in a gambling binge may transiently appear to be "manic" with rapid speech, reduced need for sleep, and increased activity. In Pathological Gambling, however, the manic-like symptoms disappear when the gambling binge ends.

AM I OKAY?

The odds are stacked so heavily in favor of the house that if you gamble (in other than social settings) long enough and with enough money you will lose significant amounts of it no matter how well played and disciplined are each of your individual bets. Those who keep within their financial limits and view gambling as an occasional entertainment (and the losses as an entertainment cost) may not be fiscally wise but they do not have Pathological Gambling.

The problem in defining an okay level of gambling is that the threshold will vary greatly across people and cultures. Moreover, the person involved may not be the best judge since Pathological Gambling is usually shrouded with the same kind of enormous denial that is also associated with substance use. Pathological Gambling is particularly hard to diagnose in yourself because it is so "ego-syntonic" (i.e., it feels like an integral part of you). Early on at least, you are preoccupied by the action—the intoxication of winning big or the single-minded doggedness to win losses back. The negative consequences of gambling become apparent only when you step back and take a hard look at the effects of gambling on your life—the lost dollars, time, relationships, jobs, and self-respect. Do you lie to family members, co-workers, or therapists to conceal the extent of your gambling? Are you forced to commit illegal activities to finance the gambling (theft, forgery, fraud)? Do you have to depend on others to bail you out of the desperate financial situations that stem from your gambling losses?

It is usually the spouse or significant other who first realizes the need for treatment. If you are a concerned family member, friend, colleague, or lover of a person with a potentially serious gambling problem, you have to confront him honestly about your concerns. It is a safe bet that most people with a gambling problem are lying to others and probably to themselves about its seriousness and the extent of the losses. The spouse often has to borrow money to cover the gambler's debts and is harassed constantly by bill collectors and landlords. Studies show that the spouse of a pathological gambler is at increased risk for suicide, violence, or being a victim of violence. Remember that enabling the compulsive gambler just prolongs the problem and invariably ends up with everyone getting hurt.

TREATMENT OPTIONS

Left untreated, the prognosis for Pathological Gambling is poor—with increasing depletion of financial reserves, disruption in family relationships, inability to function at work, involvement in criminal activity, arrest, incarceration, and sometimes even suicide or becoming a victim of violence. The goal of treatment is abstinence from gambling, rehabilitation of wrecked relationships, restoration of work functioning, and prevention of relapse. Treatment includes joining Gamblers Anonymous, individual and family therapy, and sometimes medication. For some, GA is enough. This is a twelve-step self-help program that is closely modeled after AA. The presence of peers who have struggled with the same impulses provides a ready means to confront denial and to offer empathic support and sponsorship. Individual therapy focuses on discovering why and when you gamble; confronts the false premise that you gamble to win rather than to play; and identifies and promotes the avoidance of known triggers. Family sessions are usually essential to find a common ground between the person struggling for recovery and the justifiably exasperated and suspicious family members. There are few data on the use of medication. Conceivably, because of the high incidence of mood disorder, antidepressants or mood stabilizers may be helpful.

TRICHOTILLOMANIA

This is a complicated name to describe a disturbing pattern of irresistible hair pulling. In the most common scenario, you feel an impulse to pull out your hair, you resist it, the tension builds, and is relieved only when you actually succumb and yank it out. Or you may find yourself absentmindedly pulling out hairs and then experience anxiety and tension when you try to stop. Your episodes of hair pulling may be triggered by stress (work pressure, family problems) or may happen at times when you are feeling relatively relaxed or bored, such as while watching TV or talking on the telephone. Although the eyebrows, eyelashes, and scalp are the most typical sites, virtually any accessible location can be a target. As a result, you may have developed small regions that are locally bald or else have more widespread areas of generally thinned hair. The hair pulling may occur in brief short bursts scattered throughout the day or may go on continuously for many hours at a time.

Hairs are usually pulled out one at a time, either rapidly and indiscriminately or after a careful and probing search for a particularly coarse or prominent specimen. Some people find sensual pleasure in the hair pulling and may even compare it to sexual gratification. Others experience no more than an "itchlike" feeling that has to be relieved. You may make a special effort to capture the hair root and experience a triumphant feeling when you succeed in pulling out the complete shaft. If you also feel compelled to eat the hair you pull, this is called trichophagia and can result in the severe medical complication of bowel obstruction.

You probably feel greatly embarrassed by the hair pulling and/or its effect on your appearance. You do your best to keep the problem a closely guarded secret and try to avoid pulling in front of others, except perhaps for your immediate family members. You take great care to cover up the evidence, hiding bald spots and hair thinning with toupees, wigs, scarves, eyeliner, and false eyelashes. You avoid situations that might reveal the problem, like sexually intimate relationships or activities that require public exposure (swimming, locker rooms). Even career choices can be affected.

Trichotillomania was once thought to be rare, probably because most people who have the problem were too ashamed to seek help. Now that effective treatments are available, people are overcoming their reluctance to come forward and Trichotillomania appears to be not that uncommon after all.

According to the diagnostic manual, you have Trichotillomania if:
- You have a recurrent pattern of pulling out your hair and this has resulted in noticeable hair loss.
- Immediately before pulling out the hair, you have an increasing sense of tension. When pulling out the hair, you experience pleasure, gratification, or relief.

AM I OKAY?

Many people twist and pull on their hair, pick at parts of their bodies, and may even pull out individual hairs when bored or under stress. When it comes to hair pulling, the line between okay and Trichotillomania is a "how much" and how out of control judgment: *How often* does it happen? *How bald* are you becoming? And *how upset* does it make you feel? Minor occasional hair pulling is no big deal, whereas severe baldness that results in social isolation is clearly interfering with your life. Hair pulling in kids under age twelve is generally considered a phase of normal childhood, like thumb sucking and nail biting. This usually occurs between ages five and eight, lasts just weeks to months, and often responds to interventions as simple as pointing out to the child that the behavior is undesirable. For a small minority of children, however, the hair pulling becomes an ongoing problem that may require treatment.

TREATMENT OPTIONS

A brief course of problem-solving psychotherapy may help if your hair pulling is triggered exclusively by stressful situations. This aims at teaching you other stress-management techniques to substitute in place of the hair pulling (like progressive muscle relaxation or self-hypnosis). For those whose hair pulling is less situation-dependent, treatment options include behavioral therapy, hypnosis, and medication. Behavioral therapy involves a technique called "habit reversal" in which you are taught to substitute an opposite behavior in place of the one you are attempting to extinguish. For example, if an episode of uncontrolled eyebrow plucking begins by raising the hand and lifting the eyebrows, the person instead lowers his hand and closes his eyes.

Medications with a serotonin-specific action (like Prozac, Paxil, Zoloft, Luvox, and Anafranil) are the most effective in treating Trichotillomania. Improvement starts with an increased awareness of the urge to pull the hair and a heightened ability to resist the pulling. In time, the urge to pull diminishes and often disappears altogether. Interestingly, these same medications also work best for the treatment of Obsessive-Compulsive Disorder (page 101). This observation, coupled with the fact that both of these conditions involve repetitive behaviors that the person feels driven to perform, may indicate that they are variants of the same underlying condition.

Suggested Additional Readings

Teenagers and Compulsive Gambling
    Edward F. Dolan
    Franklin Watts, 1994

The Psychology of Gambling (International Series in Social Psychology)
    Michael B. Walker
    Butterworth Architecture, 1996

Where to Go for Help
(Self-help, support, for more information)

Gamblers Anonymous
(twelve-step support group)

P.O. Box 17173
Los Angeles, CA 90017
(213) 386-8789
FAX: (213) 386-0300
E-mail: isomain@gamblersanonymous.org
Web: http://www.gamblersanonymous.org/

Gam-Anon International Service Office, Inc.
(self-help group for families of gamblers)

P.O. Box 157
Whitestone, NY 11357
(718) 352-1671
Web: http://www.gamblersanonymous.org/gamanon.html

National Council for Compulsive Gambling, Inc.

445 West Fifty-ninth Street
New York, NY 10019
(800) 522-4700 (helpline)

Trichotillomania Learning Center

1215 Mission Street
Suite 2
Santa Cruz, CA 95060
(408) 457-1004
FAX: (408) 426-4383
E-mail: trikster@cruzio.com
Web: http://www.trich.org/

S.M.A.R.T. Recovery Self-Help Network
(Self-Management and Recovery Training)
(self-help groups for individuals with "addictive behaviors"
—alcohol, drugs, gambling, eating disorders)

24000 Mercantile Road
Suite 33
Beachwood, OH 44122
(216) 292-0220
FAX: (216) 831-3776
E-mail: srmail1@aol.com

CHAPTER 13

DISSOCIATIVE EXPERIENCES

Most of us go through life almost as blissfully unaware of the inner workings of our mind as is a centipede unconscious of what each of its one hundred legs should do in taking a next step. When all is going well, we experience our mental functions (such as memory, perception, our sense of identity, and our awareness of the world) as an automatic, coherent, and seamlessly integrated whole. So much so that we take for granted the comfortable assumption that "I am me—an integrated self who is functioning smoothly in a real world."

Mental functions can become "dissociated" in a number of different ways. Traumatic memories are split off and cannot be recovered. Or a person looks in the mirror and suddenly feels that the face he is seeing belongs to a stranger. Or someone becomes so detached from himself that it feels as if he is watching himself going through the motions like a character in a movie. Or he looks at the people around him and gets the uncanny feeling that they are unreal puppets populating an unreal world. The most extreme cases of dissociation can result in the fragmentation of the self into multiple, seemingly autonomous personalities. Dissociation most often occurs when someone is under severe psychological stress, is medicated or intoxicated, has had a head injury, or suffers from a neurologic or psychiatric problem.

Dissociation most typically represents a breakdown of mental functioning occurring under the stress of a psychological or a physical problem, but it can also be a coping style for dealing with painful experiences. It seems likely that the capacity for dissociation exists in us because it provides adaptive advantages that were favored by natural selection. Our ancient ancestors lived in a remarkably dangerous and painful world. Developing the capacity to tune out the most unpleasant parts of their lives helped to keep them going. Certainly, it can be no accident that dissociation is so universally and readily available to human beings or that so many people seek it out through meditation or drug use.

Under normal circumstances, our everyday experiences are woven into a continuously created fabric, allowing us now to act and feel based on the sum total of what we have previously learned and felt. It may sometimes, however, be more adaptive to isolate the most extreme experiences of physical, sexual, or emotional trauma in order to contain their unbalancing effects. By splitting off a memory, an emotional reaction, or (on very rare occasions) a whole part of one's personality, the remaining parts can continue to function unscathed. Of course, this way of protecting against destabilizing stress can be purchased only at the high cost of having memory gaps, feelings of estrangement, emotional numbing, or even a fragmentation of the self.

DSM-IV groups together the Dissociative Disorders into the categories of Dissociative Amnesia, Dissociative Identity Disorder (formerly called Multiple Personality Disorder), and Depersonalization Disorder. How commonly encountered are these conditions is a matter of heatedly contested debate. There are some who claim that Dissociative Disorders occur frequently, but are often missed because most people and most therapists pay insufficient attention to them. They argue that many more cases would be uncovered were every patient methodically examined for dissociation. This view has recently gained (probably a temporary) currency leading to a veritable "epidemic" of Dissociative Disorders—especially Multiple Personality Disorder. Others believe that this "epidemic" represents no more than a diagnostic fad and that dissociation has become an overplayed diagnosis du jour. This is an important controversy that we will address in more detail as we discuss Dissociative Amnesia and Dissociative Identity Disorder (Multiple Personality Disorder).

DISSOCIATIVE AMNESIA

One way of coping with a severe psychological trauma or an especially embarrassing event is to isolate the upsetting memories of it. People sometimes forget episodes of sexual or physical abuse, a serious automobile accident, a life-threatening war experience, a suicide attempt, a violent outburst, or an act of self-mutilation. The walled-off memory may, nonetheless, continue to exert a profound effect on emotions and behavior. For example, a woman who was raped violently in an elevator has no recollection whatever of the actual rape but still finds herself inexplicably terrified every time she enters an elevator.

The amnesia usually comes in stages. You may have a full memory of what happened immediately after the stressful event but then gradually lose it in the next days to weeks in a process that resembles the gradual fading of a dream in the minutes after awakening. You may be unaware that the terrible memory has been lost unless there is disconcerting evidence of it, such as discovering that your car has been in an accident, finding cut marks on your arms, finding unfamiliar clothes in the closet, or being told that an untoward event has occurred.

Although much less common, the memory loss can sometimes be more generalized and cover an entire period of a person's past. For example, a woman who was sexually abused for years by her father may lose all memories that relate to him or to that period. In the extreme, a person might completely lose all orienting memories. A woman was brought to the emergency room by the police after she had been found wandering the streets of Manhattan without any identification and with no idea of her name or address or phone number. As memories reemerged in the next several days, she discovered that her loss of memory began immediately after she was told that her child had been run over and killed by a car.

According to the diagnostic manual, you have Dissociative Amnesia if:

- You have been unable to recall important personal information, usually of a traumatic or stressful nature.
- All other causes (particularly substance use, medication side effects, head trauma, and other medical conditions) have been considered and ruled out.

DIFFERENTIAL DIAGNOSIS

Amnesia is fairly commonly encountered in medical practice, but in the vast majority of cases it is not due to dissociation. Blows to the head and seizures both can cause blackouts for events prior to, and immediately after, the injury or seizure. Other medical problems (like Alzheimer's disease) affect the parts of the brain responsible for the learning of new information and the recall of recent events. A number of medications and substances cause blackouts by interfering with the conversion of short-term to long-term memory. Doctors take advantage of the amnestic effects of Valium by using it during surgical procedures in which the person is awake in order to block memory of the procedure.

In Dissociative Amnesia, there is no physical basis for the memory loss. This psychological cause for the forgetting is relatively rare and should be considered only after ruling out the other, more common physical causes of memory loss, especially since these may require emergency medical treatment. For example, memory loss after a car accident is much more likely to be due to the head trauma or to concurrent substance use than to a psychological reaction to the event itself. Unlike the medical and medication causes for amnesia in which the memories are not laid down, in Dissociative Amnesia the memories are encoded in the brain but are not readily accessible. They may be brought out by hypnosis or through associative discussions of the situations surrounding the event.

Another possibility to consider before diagnosing Dissociative Amnesia is that the person is consciously feigning the loss of memory. When a defendant says, "I am sorry but I just can't remember committing that murder"—it is possible that the horrible event has been removed from memory through an automatic dissociative process, but it is also possible that the person is faking the memory loss in an attempt to beat the rap or to mitigate punishment.

Recently, there has been a major public controversy concerning how common (depending on your viewpoint) are either "repressed" or "false" memories. Is it possible to reconstruct whether an adult with no conscious memory of early sexual abuse has repressed the painful memories that are now causing psychiatric or behavioral problems? It is also debated whether bringing these lost "memories" into the open has a therapeutic benefit. Certainly, there is increased awareness of the extent of childhood sexual and physical abuse and its possible role in causing later problems. There is also a fairly wide consensus that children who are sexually or physically abused are particularly likely to experience Dissociative Amnesia for the events. However, there is a strong possibility that the recovery of early memories is being wildly overdone by naive therapists in a potentially harmful way. There have been a number of notorious cases in which perfectly responsible parents (or child caretakers) have been accused falsely of ludicrous charges of sexual abuse that were based on memories "recovered" under pressure or under the influence of hypnosis. The witch hunt atmosphere surrounding the most egregious cases has turned a number of towns into ugly modern-day renditions of colonial Salem and has made more difficult the identification of real cases of abuse.

There is no easy answer to this controversy because there is some truth to both positions. Children are particularly prone to dissociate and repress painful experiences and this may have a detrimental effect on them, at the time of the abuse or later. However, it is equally important to remember that memory can be extremely fallible, hard to distinguish from fantasy, and remarkably subject to suggestion and confabulation. Common sense dictates being cautious in accepting the veracity of very early memories especially when these are recalled only after a considerable passage of time, under the influence of hypnosis or suggestion, or when the recovery of memory may promote a secondary gain or a settling of scores.

AM I OKAY?

Imperfect memory is common. Most of us have had the experience of arriving at a destination after a long trip not able to remember anything about the drive that got us there. Partly this is because experienced drivers can steer a car without involving the entire cerebral cortex—using instead only those parts of the brain that take over when we perform behaviors that have become automatic and habitual. Another reason is conservation of resources—we selectively remember more important events and do not bother to preserve the relatively insignificant aspects of everyday life. In Dissociative Amnesia, the opposite situation occurs—the memories lost are so potentially devastating that the person copes by walling them off.

TREATMENT OPTIONS

Most cases of Dissociative Amnesia either cause no problem at all or remit spontaneously with the passage of time. As the person gains some distance from the traumatic event, the memories of it tend to come back on their own or by discussing what happened just before or just after what has become the blank. If the loss of memory is not causing problems, it is a good idea to let well enough alone and not try to resurrect the painful experiences.

There are times, however, when the memory loss persists and causes enough trouble to require treatment. Most people who develop Dissociative Amnesia are easily hypnotizable and some may be helped by it. Under hypnosis, the therapist encourages the person to recover lost memories while maintaining a safe distance by revisiting the scenes as if watching them on a movie screen. The patient can be directed to counteract feelings of distress by imagining that he is in a safe and comfortable situation, like lying on a beach or floating in space. This reduces the need to keep lost memories segregated from consciousness and allows the person to confront them in a supportive therapy environment. Hypnosis can be a two-edged sword, however, especially in inexperienced hands. When under hypnosis, most people are in a state of heightened suggestibility. With the therapist's urging, people can "remember" events that never really happened and feel more traumatized after treatment and more alienated from their families than they were before it. It is, therefore, fortunate that most people with Dissociative Amnesia do quite well without treatment.

DISSOCIATIVE IDENTITY DISORDER
(MULTIPLE PERSONALITY DISORDER)

No doubt about it, Dissociative Identity Disorder (or Multiple Personality Disorder, as it was formerly called) is a fascinating condition. Perhaps too much so. The idea that people can have distinct, autonomous, and rapidly alternating personalities has captured the imagination of the general public, of some therapists, and of hordes of patients. As a result, especially in the United States, there has been a marked increase in the diagnosis of Dissociative Identity Disorder. Much of the excitement followed the appearance of books and movies (like *Sybil* and *The Three Faces of Eve*) and the exploitation of the diagnosis by enthusiastic TV talk show hosts and their guests. Some therapists applaud the increased public and therapist awareness because they believe that Dissociative Identity Disorder was previously missed or misdiagnosed.

There is another side to this story, however. Many therapists feel that the popularity of Dissociative Identity Disorder represents a kind of social contagion. It is not so much that there are suddenly lots of people with lots of personalities as there are lots of people and lots of therapists who are very suggestible and willing to climb onto the bandwagon of this new fad diagnosis. As the idea of multiple personality pervades our popular culture, suggestible people coping with a chaotic current life and a severely traumatic past express discomfort and avoid responsibility by uncovering "hidden personalities" and giving each of them a voice. This is especially likely when there is a zealous therapist who finds multiple personality a fascinating topic of discussion and exploration.

We do not deny altogether the existence of Dissociative Identity Disorder and together have seen what we believe to be three genuine cases in forty-five collective years of practice. However, we are worried that the current overdiagnosis of multiple personality is an illusory fad that leads to misdiagnosis and mistreatment and does a disservice to the vast majority of patients who fall under its sway.

According to the diagnostic manual, you have Dissociative Identity Disorder if:

- You feel that you have two or more distinct identities or personality states that recurrently take control of your behavior.
- You are unable to recall important personal information that is too extensive to be explained by ordinary forgetfulness.

DESCRIPTION

Most of those suffering from true Dissociative Identity Disorder have been exposed in childhood to extremely traumatic events, most commonly chronic physical or sexual abuse, torture, or severe neglect. Each personality fragment (usually referred to as an "alter") develops its own characteristics and its own memories. Often the personalities are based on an identification with individuals from the person's past. For example, there may be an aggressive, abusive, or self-punitive alter, based on an identification with the perpetrator of abuse, and an alter who is the timid, frightened child victim. The symptoms of Dissociative Identity Disorder may be more evident to the outside observer than to the person suffering from the condition. Often the person is not consciously aware of shifting from one personality fragment to the other and the evidence of multiple personality comes only when someone actually sees the change occur or from the frequent gaps in memory that result from different personality fragments being active at different times. Typically, Dissociative Identity Disorder emerges in adolescence or early adulthood and there is often a delay between the initial onset of symptoms and their recognition.

DIFFERENTIAL DIAGNOSIS

This is where the controversy gets especially heated. Fervent believers in Dissociative Identity Disorder are convinced that its diagnosis has been missed by the clinicians who have previously treated the patient. They assert that many patients who receive the diagnosis of Bipolar Disorder, Schizophrenia, or a Personality Disorder are really suffering from Dissociative Identity Disorder in disguise.

More conservative clinicians worry the other way around. They believe that most people who are currently getting the diagnosis of Dissociative Identity Disorder are more likely to have a mood, psychotic, or Personality Disorder. The issue is really important because the patients described are usually quite ill and the treatments recommended would be radically different depending on the diagnosis. Our own tendency is to be cautious in making the diagnosis of Dissociative Identity Disorder and always to make sure that other, more easily treatable conditions have not been missed. A good rule of thumb is that any condition that has become a favorite with Hollywood, Oprah, and checkout-counter newspapers and magazines stands a great chance of being wildly overdiagnosed.

AM I OKAY?

Everyone's personality is complex and multifaceted and our sense of having a coherent identity is subject to ups and downs with life's vicissitudes. We all act and feel somewhat differently in different situations depending upon with whom we are interacting and the role we are expected to assume. How you come across and function in the workplace is likely to be different than the way you behave with family and friends or on a first date. Even though we all necessarily project a somewhat different persona in different settings, we continue to maintain a more or less continuous internal sense of self as a coherent entity.

Dissociative Identity Disorder is not meant to describe these situational changes in one's sense of self or any ambivalence we feel about certain people or activities. Instead there must be really distinct personalities who assume control and have such independent lives that at least some of what occurs in the experience of the different alters is outside the person's consciousness and lost to his memories. This is pretty rare and those few patients who do indeed have Dissociative Identity Disorder usually have very poor insight about it. If you are wondering whether you qualify for this diagnosis it is a very good bet that you almost surely do not.

TREATMENT OPTIONS

Long-term psychotherapy is usually recommended for the treatment of Dissociative Identity Disorder. The notion is that the fragmentation of memory and identity represents a severely maladaptive coping mechanism for dealing with past and current traumatic experiences. The goal of psychotherapy is to allow the person to reexperience the horrible memories and to bring out the different alters in the safe environment of a trusted therapist's office or in the hospital. Past traumatic events are reviewed and are put into perspective. Emotions that have been bottled up are expressed, vented, and shared across all personality fragments—on the assumption that allowing intense feelings to be tolerated in consciousness reduces the need for fragmentation of the self. The alters come to know about each other's existence, become reacquainted, "talk" to one another, and are ultimately rejoined in one integrated personality.

The problem with this form of treatment for Dissociative Identity Disorder is that it may make some people get worse rather than better. If the therapist works hard at bringing out additional alters, the suggestible patient is likely to accommodate. The presumption behind treatment is that making the alters available to consciousness will assist in their integration. The sad result in practice, however, is that therapists are ever so much better at bringing out new alters than in helping the patient to integrate them once they have been released (or created). As the therapy proceeds, more and more alters are born and they never seem to join forces. The current average is twenty-one alters per patient and we have seen one patient who claimed to have sixty-four distinct and named alters (she previously had sixty-five but one had recently killed herself). The label "multiple personality disorder" is also stigmatizing and infantilizing. People so named often feel less responsible for, and less in control of, their behavior. Finally, although the uncovering of traumatic past events can sometimes be helpful in promoting acceptance and integration, it is also often unnecessarily painful and may do more harm than good.

All in all, the world might have been a better place if the diagnosis of Dissociative Identity Disorder had never become so popular and if the uncovering treatment for it were reserved for the very few people who truly have the disorder and can benefit from an ambitious and potentially risky approach to bringing the alters out into the open. For any of you who suspect you have Dissociative Identity Disorder, or are now in treatment for it, our suggestion is to focus your energies on the here-and-now problems in your everyday life. We would recommend avoiding any treatment that seeks to discover new personalities or to uncover past traumas. We believe that the best treatment is probably going to be the one that helps you cope with your current problems and improve your current relationships. It is also crucial to reduce substance use (since this can further worsen one's already diminished sense of a coherent identity) and to identify any other psychiatric problems that may require treatment. There is no evidence that medications are helpful in treating Dissociative Identity Disorder but they may be needed for the other symptoms that commonly occur, like depression and anxiety.

DEPERSONALIZATION DISORDER

The experience of depersonalization is hard to describe if you have not ever felt it. Depersonalization is an uncanny, uncomfortable, disconcerting, and sometimes frightening sense that you are unreal, cut off, removed, estranged, and detached from your self, your body, and from the world around you. You feel like an automaton, floating in a dreamlike state, going through the motions of life without really living it, watching your actions as if you were seeing yourself on a movie screen. This may be connected to thoughts about the meaning (or meaninglessness) of life, the immensity of the universe, and the fragility of time. Tastes, smells, touch, pain—all feel muted, like cardboard, and drained of authenticity. Some people get the feeling that their arms and legs are changing in size or are disconnected from the rest of their body. Depersonalization often goes hand in hand with feelings of derealization. Here, you experience people and the rest of the world as eerily unfamiliar, strange, or unreal.

Most typically, these experiences are transient and brief, lasting only seconds or minutes. For some, however, depersonalization may persist for months or even years and become an uncomfortable way of life. While episodes of depersonalization often occur during panic attacks and in stressful contexts, they may be triggered by more routine situations in which attention is called to yourself, like seeing your reflection in a mirror or hearing your name called.

According to the diagnostic manual, you have Depersonalization Disorder if:

• You have the frequent experience of feeling detached from yourself, as if you are an outside observer watching yourself going through the motions of life.

• These experiences are very upsetting or significantly interfere with your life.

DIFFERENTIAL DIAGNOSIS

Especially when the episodes of depersonalization are long-lasting, you may worry that you are going crazy or losing your mind. Although depersonalization is certainly a strange and unsettling experience, it is not by itself evidence either of psychosis or severe mental illness. In fact, the difference between depersonalization and delusions is that the person retains the awareness that these are no more than uncomfortable feelings and does not actually believe he has been turned into a robot or in some other real way robbed of himself.

Depersonalization occurs as an associated symptom that accompanies many psychiatric disorders—40 percent of hospitalized psychiatric patients and one third of people with Posttraumatic Stress Disorder (page 110) have experienced it. Depersonalization is also common in Panic Disorder (page 79), phobias (page 86), Generalized Anxiety Disorder (page 95), Schizophrenia (page 313), Major Depressive Disorder (page 33), Borderline Personality Disorder (page 224), after using drugs or alcohol (page 117), as a side effect of certain medications, and in association with certain kinds of seizures. However, the diagnosis Depersonalization Disorder is relatively uncommon and is to be used in a residual way only for those patients whose depersonalization symptoms are severe and persistent, but not due to one of the above conditions.

AM I OKAY?

Occasional episodes of depersonalization are frequent in the general population and do not mean that one has, or is at special risk for, a psychiatric problem. It has been estimated that half of all adults have experienced at least one brief episode of depersonalization at some time in their lives—usually when they are under stress. Adolescents may be especially likely to have depersonalization experiences, but then to grow out of them. Depersonalization and derealization are also important elements of meditation and self-induced trance states, and are part of religious or cultural rituals. Depersonalization is considered pathological only when episodes are persistent, particularly upsetting, or interfere with one's ability to work, study, or interact with other people.

TREATMENT OPTIONS

When depersonalization is part of another psychiatric problem, the treatment target is the primary disorder. For example, the depersonalization that occurs during panic attacks will go away when the panic attacks are cured. For people whose depersonalization is transient, just knowing that the episodes are "normal" and not indicative of mental illness can be very reassuring and is usually enough to allow the person to weather them with minimal distress. When depersonalization episodes are particularly frequent or long-lasting, psychotherapy, meditation, or self-hypnosis can be helpful. The basic idea is to have the person learn how to deliberately self-induce depersonalization symptoms so that he can gain a sense of mastery and control over the feelings rather than being victimized by them. One can also learn to associate pleasant feelings of floating in space to replace the out-of-control feelings of detachment.

Suggested Additional Readings

Becoming One: A Story of Triumph over Multiple Personality Disorder
Sarah E. Olson
Inbook, 1997

Hoax and Reality: The Bizarre World of Multiple Personality Disorder
August Piper, Jr., M.D.
Jason Aronson, 1997

Someone I Know Has Multiple Personalities: A Book for Significant Others—
Friends, Family, and Caring Professionals
Sandra J. Hocking
Launch Press, 1994

Silencing the Voices: One Woman's Triumph over Multiple Personality Disorder
Jean Darby Cline and Jeff Darby Cline
Berkley, 1997

Where to Go for Help
(Self-help, support, for more information)

HealingHopes, Inc.
(information and support for those with DID)

P.O. Box 134
Mansfield, MA 02048
Web: http://www.healinghopes.org/

Parents United International
(support group for those with a history
of childhood sexual abuse)

615 Fifteenth Street
Modesto, CA 95354
(209) 572-3446

CHAPTER 14

ADJUSTMENT DISORDER

The road of life inevitably has an occasional pothole that may cause us to stumble—at least temporarily. Some stressful events happen suddenly and unexpectedly, others may be more predictable and go on for years and years. Sometimes, stress is an inescapable part of our passage through the life cycle: starting school, getting married, having a child, or retirement. Sometimes, stress arises from a special challenge (a new job), a disruption (marital separation, job loss, homelessness after a fire), or a loss (death of a spouse or child).

How someone responds to stress—rolling easily with the punches versus developing troubling symptoms—depends on an interaction of the individual's personality, the nature of the stress, and the availability of support. Some people are constitutionally more resilient to stress than others—they bounce back as if nothing had happened no matter how often they are knocked down. Other, more vulnerable individuals find even seemingly minor problems unbearable. Some stressful situations are much more difficult to deal with than others. How severe is the stress, how unexpected, how prolonged, and how unmanageable all impact on one's ability to come through it all okay.

Also important is the level of social support. Having a well-developed network of understanding friends, colleagues, and family members can go a long way toward mitigating the negative emotional fallout caused by a stressful event—especially if you are good at accepting help from others when you need it. The fact that women are more likely than men to retain and nurture lifelong friendships probably explains the higher rates of post-divorce maladjustment in ex-husbands as compared to their ex-wives.

A given stressful event can have very varied effects on different people depending upon the way each person experiences it. For example, some people will be great at handling job stress but become very disturbed by an interpersonal loss—or vice versa. A person who previously despised his job but is insufficiently motivated to leave it voluntarily will almost certainly experience being laid off differently than someone who is downsized from a job that represents his lifelong aspiration. People are more able to handle stressful events if they have become "inoculated" to them owing to prior exposure to the same kind of stress. A policeman is likely to have a milder response to witnessing a car accident than will the average bystander. The degree of control in the situation is also a big factor. It is easier to accept a divorce if you see it coming and have been included in the decision-making. Sometimes a stressful event may represent the "straw that broke the camel's back." A person who has limped along but continues to function more or less adequately after weathering a series of difficult events (career change, death of elderly parents, being forced to move to a smaller house) may fall apart after a seemingly trivial fight with his spouse.

Adjustment Disorders are maladaptive reactions to stressful events that do not fit the description of any of the other mental disorders in this book. While the symptoms of Adjustment Disorder usually resolve over a period of weeks to months, often without treatment, in some cases they persist for a long time or evolve into a more serious condition.

According to the diagnostic manual, you have an Adjustment Disorder if:

- You have emotional or behavioral symptoms that have developed in response to a stressful event or to a chronically stressful situation.
- Your reaction is either abnormal (that is, is more extreme than what one would expect given the nature of the stressful event) or else significantly interferes with your ability to work, study, or interact with friends, colleagues, or family.
- Your symptoms are time-limited—that is, they last for no longer than six months after the stressful event (or its consequences) is over.

DESCRIPTION

The stress that leads to Adjustment Disorder can be either a one-shot deal or a chronic problem that casts a shadow over many years. Single events are things like being fired from a job, starting or ending school, relocating to another city, or a romantic disappointment. Whenever the stressor is so clearly delineated, there is a six-month time limit on the symptoms because it gets harder after that to be sure that the more persistent problems were indeed caused by the stressor. For example, if a person continues to remain significantly depressed two years after ending a relationship, it becomes less likely that the breakup was by itself responsible for the depression and more likely that the person may have an independent mental disorder, like Major Depressive Disorder (page 33) or Dysthymic Disorder (page 42).

Sometimes the stressful events do not have such a clear-cut endpoint. Examples of ongoing stressors include being physically abused on a regular basis by a violent spouse, or working in an unbearable job, or dealing with being HIV positive. Some stressful events may seem to be time-limited but have serious ongoing repercussions that are long-term, like the continuing financial hardship after a divorce or the loss of a job. A chronic form of Adjustment Disorder is present when there is a long-term maladaptive reaction to a chronic stress and the person does not develop the full-blown severity of symptoms that would meet the definitional requirements of another mental disorder in this book.

The most common problems that people develop in response to a stressful event are depression, anxiety, physical symptoms, a change in behavior, or some combination of these. After being fired from work, a woman falls into a funk, feeling depressed, drained of energy, and unable to get motivated to look for another job. Prior to an impending marriage, a man becomes so anxious, restless, and jumpy that he cannot concentrate at work or sleep through the night. Children may develop conduct problems that are completely out of character for them. After his parents' separation, a previously well-behaved seven-year-old starts beating up his younger sister and trashing her toys.

Adjustment Disorder occurring in the context of medical illness is a common and sometimes even a potentially deadly combination. There is a large body of evidence that a positive outlook about an illness can make a big difference in achieving a good outcome. The symptoms of Adjustment Disorder can place a serious roadblock on the path to recovery. For example, a middle-aged businessman becomes depressed and listless after having a heart attack, gives up hope for the future, and repeatedly forgets to take his medication or follow his exercise program. Successful management of his Adjustment Disorder may be the most crucial step in improving his chances of recovery from the heart attack.

Differential Diagnosis

Many psychiatric disorders are more likely to occur in someone who is under the gun of stressful life circumstances. The diagnosis of Adjustment Disorder is reserved for those situations in which the stress is causing significant problems but these have not crystallized into one of the more specific conditions described elsewhere in this book.

Suppose a fifty-five-year-old man becomes anxious and depressed after being fired from a managerial job, loses interest in his family, friends, and hobbies, has trouble sleeping, loses weight, and is tired all the time. If his symptoms persist for at least two weeks, and are sufficiently severe, this would conform to the description of Major Depressive Disorder that is presented starting on page 33. If the symptoms last only for a few days or are relatively mild, this would be Adjustment Disorder with depressed mood. Adjustment Disorder is diagnosed only when a more specific diagnosis is not appropriate.

Adjustment Disorder and Posttraumatic Stress Disorder (PTSD) (page 110) are alike in that these are the only two conditions in DSM-IV that require the presence of an external stressor. They differ, however, in the characteristic nature of the stressor and in the symptoms that result from it. In PTSD the stress is a life-threatening event (a natural disaster, or a serious accident, or being the victim of a violent crime), whereas in Adjustment Disorder the stressors are more everyday and not life-threatening. The characteristic symptoms in PTSD (nightmares, flashbacks, and avoidance of reminders) distinguish it from the milder and more general symptom presentation in Adjustment Disorder.

Also keep in mind that even when an emotional symptom develops immediately after a stressful event, there are possible explanations other than its being a psychological reaction to it. Consider a seventy-five-year-old woman who becomes depressed after suffering a stroke that paralyzes the right side of her body. Although her depression could be a psychological reaction to her incapacity, it is equally possible that the stroke has caused it by damaging a part of her brain responsible for regulating mood. A college student, upset over the breakup of a romantic relationship, starts drinking heavily and then becomes alternately agitated, irritable, and weepy. Assuming a cause-and-effect relationship between the breakup and the mood changes ignores the alternative explanation that his unstable mood is a direct result of his heavy drinking.

AM I OKAY?

Having an unpleasant reaction to a stressful event is entirely "normal." In fact, the complete lack of any emotional response is probably a less adaptive and more abnormal approach in dealing with life's problems. The essence of Adjustment Disorder is an inappropriate or excessive emotional or behavioral response that is maladaptive, far exceeds what would be expected given the severity of the stressful event, and makes a bad situation worse. A student who develops depression and misses a week of school after being rejected on a first date has an Adjustment Disorder because the severity of his reaction seems out of proportion to the stress and is getting him into trouble. The same behavior occurring after hearing the unexpected news that his father had a heart attack or that his parents are divorcing would be well within the bounds of normality. Because it is also entirely "normal" for anyone to develop a fairly severe but time-limited reaction to the death of a loved one, a diagnosis of Adjustment Disorder does not usually make sense for someone who is grieving.

TREATMENT OPTIONS

Not everyone with an Adjustment Disorder needs treatment for it. Most people figure out a way to weather the storm. Time and circumstances can be great healers. Unfortunately, not all Adjustment Disorders are so mild or so fleeting. Even though the severity, duration, and number of symptoms in Adjustment Disorders are usually less than in other mental disorders, people with this diagnosis can sometimes be in real trouble. The symptoms can drag on for months (especially when the stressful situation is ongoing); can be extremely upsetting, painful, or self-destructive; can cause major league disruptions in one's life; and may interfere with one's ability to appropriately follow recommended treatment for an associated medical condition. In fact, there are people, especially teenagers, who succeed in killing themselves with no diagnosis other than Adjustment Disorder.

Treatment for Adjustment Disorder is meant to contain and relieve the symptoms, minimize their disruptive effects, and nip the problem in the bud before it evolves into a more serious or persistent condition. Brief, time-limited psychotherapy that focuses on the here-and-now problem is usually the most helpful. Adjustment Disorder can be viewed as a temporary breakdown in a person's ability to cope effectively with the stressors.

The therapy is a way of supporting the person's existing coping mechanisms and helping him to find some new ones. The person's negative reaction to the stressful situation often results from an exaggerated view of its significance and its implications for the future. A romantic breakup means that you will never get married; failing a test means you will never get into professional school; a diagnosis of multiple sclerosis means never being able to walk again. Therapy encourages the person to identify such all-or-nothing thinking for what it is—an irrational catastrophization that can make a very difficult situation much worse than it needs to be. The therapist helps the patient to counter such thoughts with more realistic responses ("although the loss of this relationship is very upsetting to me and I will grieve for a while, I am still young and there are many other suitable people out there—if I just look hard enough I'll eventually find the right one").

Therapy can also provide a cathartic outlet releasing the feelings of anger, sadness, giving up, or fear that so often accompany a stressful experience. The expression of such feelings in a safe therapeutic environment reduces the likelihood that they will emerge inappropriately in the person's relationships and can help prevent the development of more severe symptoms of depression or anxiety.

Often the focus of therapy is to help the person take concrete steps to overcome the negative effects of the stressful event—exploring what are the alternatives, the advantages and disadvantages of each, and how to judge what is working best. For example, someone who is depressed and shies away from all contact with friends and family after being left by his wife would be helped to seek out their emotional support.

Therapy for Adjustment Disorder usually lasts weeks rather than months and can often be done in stress-management groups. Occasionally the temporary use of sleeping or antianxiety medication can be helpful (in addition to psychotherapy) to control the particularly disruptive symptoms of insomnia or agitation. But this should be done cautiously and only for a short time—particularly if the person has ever had a substance abuse problem—since these medicines can become addicting.

Suggested Additional Readings

Adaptation to Life
George E. Vaillant
Harvard University Press, 1995

The Art of Coping
    Fredrica R. Halligan
    Crossroad, 1995

Free Yourself from Harmful Stress
    Trevor J. Powell et al.
    Dorling-Kindersley, 1997

Where to Go for Help
(Self-help, support, for more information)

American Institute of Stress
(clearinghouse for information about stress)

124 Park Avenue
Yonkers, NY 10703
(914) 963-1200
Web: http://www.stress.org/

CHAPTER 15

LOSS OF REALITY TESTING

A fundamental aspect of normal mental functioning is the ability to distinguish between thoughts and perceptions that originate from within our minds versus the stimuli that come from the outside world. This ongoing process is called "reality testing." Most of us maintain a fairly strong grasp on reality, except when we dream at night or if we take a psychedelic drug. In contrast, someone suffering from psychosis has lost the ability to distinguish fact from fantasy, reality from imagination, and internal fears from actual threats.

Most psychiatric disorders do cause at least some distortion in a person's perception and understanding of reality. A man with Major Depressive Disorder (page 33) may contemplate suicide as the only way of atoning for his imagined sins. A skin-and-bones woman with Anorexia Nervosa (page 157) starves herself further because she is convinced her thighs are still flabby. A man with Alcohol Dependence (page 120) denies that his excessive drinking is the cause of his cirrhosis of the liver. A man with Narcissistic Personality Disorder (page 222) is repeatedly fired for insubordination when he insists that his bosses give him special treatment because of his unique talents. Although these twisted perspectives can certainly cause serious trouble, in each of these situations the person's overall ability to discern real from imagined remains intact. However, when distortions in thinking, perception, and behavior become so extreme that there is a complete break with reality, that person is considered to be "psychotic." (In common speech, synonyms might be "mad," "insane," "out of one's mind," "lost one's marbles," or "crazy.")

It is impossible to adapt well to the reality of our world if we experience it in a markedly distorted way. Trouble inevitably follows whenever someone bases his acts on an idiosyncratic and personalized experience of reality, rather than on the sure footing of the real thing. A man who hears voices warning of an imminent apocalypse stands on a street corner screaming out his urgent message to the studied indifference of the passing traffic. A woman convinced that radio waves beamed from the television set control her thoughts threatens to kill the TV anchorman. A man who believes that foreign agents monitor his thoughts from overhead satellites goes outside only if his head is covered with aluminum foil. A teenage boy refuses to eat unpackaged food because he is convinced his parents are trying to poison him. The diverse contents of psychotic thoughts are a tribute to the creative range of the human imagination and display our darkest fears and most troubling preoccupations.

There are several specific symptoms of psychosis. A *delusion* is a fixed, false belief that is firmly held even in the face of overwhelming evidence to the contrary. For example, a man convinced that a metal receiver has been implanted in his head insists on the absolute certainty of this implausible belief despite repeated negative X-rays ("I know it's there—they are using stealth technology and an X-ray-proof metal to hide it!"). He disparages all suggestions that his imagination might be getting out of hand or that the return of this belief signals a recurrence of illness caused by his having discontinued medications last month. Although alternative explanations for delusional convictions ("Is it even remotely within the realm of possibility that the clicks on your telephone could be caused by line noise rather than the sound of a wiretap?") are usually dismissed out of hand, offering them can sometimes lead to an interesting debate and at least partial insight.

Although virtually any false idea can be held with delusional intensity, certain themes arise particularly often. A person with a persecutory delusion believes that some particular person, group of people, organization, or institution is conspiring to "get" him. For example, an elderly woman living alone is convinced that an upstairs neighbor is intentionally playing loud music and banging on the walls in order to harass and drive her to suicide. A twenty-three-year-old computer software designer believes that programming "bugs" have been planted purposely in his software by co-workers as part of a company-wide plot to get him fired. Delusional jealousy is a related theme. A thirty-five-year-old married woman is absolutely convinced that her husband is having a sexual liaison during his morning runs and offers as compelling proof that he is out of breath and perspiring upon return.

Another common theme involves the grandiose delusion of having extraordinary power, fame, or religious mission. A man in his twenties suddenly develops the conviction that he can read other people's minds. A thirty-five-year-old lawyer is convinced that he has developed a scheme that will instantly reverse the effects of global warming. A formerly nonreligious man in his twenties believes that he will be divinely anointed to save the entire world from the designs of Satan if only he can say the proper prayers in the proper order.

An erotomanic delusion involves the fixed false belief that you have an admirer who is secretly in love with you, although reluctant to declare it openly. Usually the person is someone you know, but sometimes it may be a stranger or a celebrity. You see hidden romantic messages buried in casual comments, the contents of books or TV programs, or coincidental meetings. Some celebrity stalkers are motivated by an erotomanic delusion—for example, John Hinckley, who shot then-president Reagan in order to impress his imagined love, Jodie Foster.

Sometimes delusional beliefs are focused on one's body. An elderly man is convinced that maggots are eating up his vitals. A nineteen-year-old man is sure that he has AIDS despite repeated negative HIV testing and a complete lack of risk factors. A thirty-three-year-old woman demands a hysterectomy for uterine cancer despite repeated negative biopsies.

Many delusions involve bizarre beliefs that defy the basic laws of nature and mental functioning. A person believes that his ideas are being broadcast on the Internet, or that his actions are being controlled by extraterrestrials, or that thoughts are inserted into, or removed from, his mind by some powerful and malignant force, or that body parts have been stolen without surgery.

Hallucinations are a perceptual break with reality. Our five senses are the windows that connect the external world with our internal experience of it. Under normal circumstances, we register a sensory perception only when the relevant sensory organ is stimulated by an appropriate external stimulus. We hear things only when our eardrums pick up sound waves. We see images only after light rays stimulate the rods and cones on the surface of the retina. Similarly, there are tangible external stimuli that trigger the senses of touch, taste, and smell. During hallucinations, you have sensory perceptions that seem to reflect the physical reality but which occur in the absence of any actual stimulus.

Hallucinations can affect any of our senses. *Auditory hallucinations* involve voices, music, buzzing, or other sounds that seem to come from an external source that simply does not exist. Don't confuse hallucinations with the companionable internal "voice" that expresses conscious thoughts or with having a tune that you can't get out of your head. Auditory hallucinations are experienced as genuine sounds coming from outside the head, rather than as a thought originating from within. The voices usually have distinct vocal characteristics (male versus female, high versus deep-pitched) and are sometimes recognizable as voices from the person's present or past (sounding like a boss, a teacher, or a relative). The voices may be critical ("you are a good-for-nothing lowlife"), reassuring ("I'm there for you always"), or neutral (calling your name or repeating a nonsensical phrase like "forest fire"). An especially worrisome type is a "command hallucination"—a voice that issues direct and often forceful instructions that the person is supposed to follow ("go jump out of the window, you scum!"). Psychotic patients are sometimes unable to appreciate that the voice is a manifestation of illness and may carry out the commands with occasional disastrous results.

Hallucinations occurring in the other sensory modalities are much more likely to be associated with substance use or having a medical illness rather than with a psychiatric condition such as Schizophrenia or Mood Disorder. Visual hallucinations may consist of fully formed images (of people, animals, or other objects) or may contain only a single visual element such as a flash of light or a splash of color. A person with tactile hallucinations feels something under his skin or on it, like crawling bugs, electric shocks, or vibrations. Hallucinated tastes and smells are usually extremely unpleasant, like the smell of burning rubber or the taste of metal or rotting fish.

Psychosis is sometimes expressed as an extreme disturbance in movement, speech, or behavior that indicates a gross break with reality. Patients with *catatonia* move strangely, fail to move at all, or assume bizarre body positions that suggest they are oblivious to the environment. A twenty-five-year-old man sits for hours, mute and motionless, staring straight ahead, ignoring all attempts at communication. Another young man who believes he is Jesus stands against the wall with his arms outstretched as if he were on a cross and resists all efforts to end his crucifixion. A young woman runs around the psychiatric unit in aimless circles and flails her arms for no apparent reason until she drops from exhaustion. Since it is often difficult to get patients with catatonia to drink fluids or eat food, there is a risk of dehydration or starvation if it persists for long.

DSM-IV classifies the psychotic disorders according to specific cause, the nature of the symptom mix, and the overall duration. Psychotic symptoms caused by substances or a medical illness have the best prognosis—the person's break with reality generally disappears once the drug effects wear off or when the medical condition is treated successfully. Psychotic symptoms that occur only as part of a severe depression or mania also usually disappear completely when the Mood Disorder is successfully treated. Brief

Psychotic Disorder describes transient psychotic symptoms that come and go within days or weeks, usually when a person is under an extraordinary stress. This has a good chance of never returning. Schizophreniform Disorder is a characteristic mixture of psychotic symptoms that lasts between one and six months. It has an intermediate prognosis. Schizophrenia has the same psychotic symptoms lasting for six months or longer and has the worst prognosis among the psychotic disorders (although even here things are looking up because there are very promising new treatments that have recently become available). Patients with Delusional Disorder can appear perfectly normal so long as one steers clear of their delusional preoccupation (for example, not mentioning the wife of a person with delusional jealousy). We conclude this chapter with the description of Shared Psychotic Disorder, a fascinating but relatively rare condition in which psychotic symptoms spread by contagion among closely bound individuals who are isolated from the outside world. We will go through all of these in some detail.

PSYCHOTIC SYMPTOMS CAUSED BY SUBSTANCES OR MEDICINES

The first thing to consider whenever someone is delusional, hallucinating, or behaving strangely is what they are taking. There are many mind-altering substances that produce transient psychotic symptoms, either during intoxication or withdrawal. Even some prescription medicines can cause psychotic symptoms as a side effect, especially when taken beyond recommended doses, in combination with other medicines, or in the elderly, who metabolize drugs more slowly.

LSD, PCP, certain mushrooms, and mescaline are known as "hallucinogens" because they are taken expressly for the purpose of triggering "psychedelic" phenomena. The experience is not really "psychotic" whenever the user maintains awareness that he is hallucinating and that the hallucinations were self-induced—because there is no loss of reality testing. More often, however, when psychotic symptoms occur as part of drug use they are an unintentional, unanticipated, and often a terrifying result of taking too high a dose or of abruptly stopping something that had been taken regularly for a long time. For example, high doses of cocaine, speed, angel dust, or marijuana make some people extremely paranoid, convinced that the police have them under surveillance or that family members are conspiring to hurt them. Especially striking is their often complete lack of insight that the paranoia is drug-induced. They may become agitated or even violent in an effort to "protect" themselves from imagined oppressors.

Many patients with long-standing psychotic disorders use street drugs, either in an attempt to self-medicate or to counteract the "deadening" effects of their prescribed antipsychotic medications. This leads to a potentially confusing chicken-and-egg problem: Are the psychotic symptoms a result of the person's drug-taking or is the drug-taking a result of having an underlying psychotic disorder? Often the only way to tease this apart is to have the person abstain from drugs and see what happens to the psychotic symptoms. If the delusions or hallucinations go away when the person is off drugs, then the psychosis was most likely drug-induced. If the psychosis continues past the time when the drugs are out of the person's system, then he most certainly has one of the psychotic disorders we will discuss in the rest of this chapter.

According to the diagnostic manual, you have Substance-Induced Psychotic Disorder if:
- You have had delusions or hallucinations that have developed:
    (1) after taking high doses of a street drug; or
    (2) after stopping a drug that you have been taking for a long time; or
    (3) as a side effect of taking a prescribed medication; or
    (4) after exposure to a toxin
- The psychotic symptoms were not already present before you took the drugs and go away within a month or so after you have stopped taking them.

PSYCHOTIC SYMPTOMS
DUE TO A MEDICAL CONDITION

Any medical condition that directly or indirectly impairs brain functioning can loosen our fragile grasp on reality. Neurological diseases like stroke, brain tumor, epilepsy, and head trauma cause psychotic symptoms through their direct damaging effect on the brain. Many other medical illnesses exert a system-wide effect on the body, which then has a negative secondary impact on the brain. For example, the failure of the kidneys to filter out harmful waste products from the blood can lead to a buildup of natural toxins that cause hallucinations. Other medical conditions that can secondarily influence the brain in this way include liver failure, overactivity or underactivity of certain hormone-secreting glands, imbalances in body fluid chemistry, heart and lung diseases, and dehydration. Psychotic symptoms are also a very common associated feature of Delirium (page 336) and Dementia (page 339).

The risk that a medical illness is the underlying cause of psychotic symptoms varies greatly depending on the age of the patient, when the symptoms begin, and the nature of the symptoms. Psychotic symptoms associated with Schizophrenia or Mood Disorders usually start in late adolescence or by early adulthood. It is possible, but fairly unusual, for a medical condition to cause psychotic symptoms in this age group and an intensive medical evaluation is necessary only when the person also has some accompanying neurological complaint, disorientation, or head trauma. In contrast, the new onset of psychotic symptoms in someone over the age of forty always raises the concern that some as-yet-undiagnosed medical problem may be responsible. In such situations, a much more thorough medical evaluation is necessary, including a careful physical examination, batteries of blood tests, and a brain scan. Furthermore, certain types of psychotic symptoms are especially likely to be caused by a medical condition—specifically hallucinations affecting the sensations other than hearing (vision, taste, smell, and skin sensations)—and are only rarely caused by Schizophrenia or Mood Disorder.

Delusions and hallucinations are more common in people who have developed hearing or visual impairments as they age. The mechanism is probably related to sensory deprivation. If our senses don't get stimulation from external sources they seem to take off on a life of their own. A normal person placed in a totally dark, completely soundless sensory deprivation float tank is likely to begin having visual and auditory hallucinations within a few hours.

The third criterion listed below suggests that a close temporal relationship between the medical illness and the psychiatric symptom provides a clue that the former is causing the latter. This is usually very helpful advice, but keep an important caveat in mind—sometimes the psychotic symptoms start first as an early harbinger of a medical condition (like Dementia) that may take months to years to fully declare itself.

According to the diagnostic manual, you have Psychotic Disorder Due to a Medical Condition if:
- You have delusions or hallucinations.
- You have a type of medical condition that can affect the brain directly (like metastatic brain cancer) or causes systemic problems in your body that affect the brain indirectly (like kidney or liver failure).
- The delusions or hallucinations have developed only since the medical condition started and/or they go away once the medical condition is treated.

DEPRESSION OR MANIA
WITH PSYCHOTIC FEATURES

Psychotic symptoms (delusions, hallucinations, and catatonia) sometimes occur as part of a very severe major depressive episode (page 33) or manic episode (page 61). Most often, but not always, the content of the delusions or hallucinations matches the mood of the episode. If you are depressed, you are likely to have delusions of unreasonable worthlessness and guilt (you are the worst person in the world and deserve to be punished for some unspeakable transgression); or delusions of hopelessness (you have a terminal illness that will kill you in a year); or nihilistic delusions (the world, or at least your world, is about to collapse). A clinically depressed mother develops the conviction that she is responsible for her daughter's multiple sclerosis because she remembers eating some bad-tasting meat while she was breast-feeding. Auditory hallucinations in depression commonly consist of an accusatory or critical voice chiding the person for deficiencies, defects, and past crimes. Manic patients, on the other hand, characteristically develop grandiose or persecutory delusions, and often both together. For example, a manic woman is so convinced that the screenplay she has written will be a surefire hit she runs up enormous credit card bills in advance of her anticipated multimillion-dollar deal. When no producer offers to buy the screenplay, she discovers there is a Hollywood plot to keep her outside the inner circle. Grandiose hallucinations may involve a direct visual or auditory communication with God, the Pope, the President, or some other famous person alive or dead.

Occasionally, Psychotic Mood Disorder is accompanied by "mood incongruent" delusions, so named because their content is bizarre and unrelated to the depressed or manic mood. For example, a depressed man believes an influencing machine has been installed in his head to control his behavior; or a manic woman believes that her ovaries were removed by extraterrestrials; or an immobile catatonic woman believes that if she moves her finger (even the slightest bit) her daughter in a distant city will die of mysterious causes. When the psychotic symptoms are mood incongruent, the Mood Disorder may be especially persistent and difficult to treat.

According to the diagnostic manual, you have Depression with Psychotic Features or Mania with Psychotic Features if:
- You have a depression severe enough to conform to the criteria for Major Depressive Disorder (page 33) or a mania severe enough to conform to the criteria for Bipolar I Disorder (page 61).
- Your delusions, hallucinations, or catatonic behavior occur *only* during the times when you are depressed or manic and these symptoms disappear when you recover from the Mood Disorder.

BRIEF PSYCHOTIC DISORDER

By its very definition, this psychotic disorder has a terrific prognosis. There must be a complete recovery within one month after the symptoms begin. Almost always, the duration of the psychotic symptoms is only a few days and the person recovers as if he were awakening from a bad dream. This usually happens to people who are experiencing an extraordinary stress, most commonly in the military, in prisons, while moving to an unfamiliar environment, or when starting a new job or school situation. A shy eighteen-year-old student from a small town begins his freshman year at a large state university and is increasingly overwhelmed by the workload in his grueling premed courses. Prior to his first set of midterms, he becomes extremely distraught and agitated, develops the delusion that his roommates are plotting to murder him in his sleep, and is found on the main quadrangle running naked to escape from them. After he is sent home, his psychotic symptoms disappear completely and with little medication in just five days. He is fuzzy about what happened, but realizes that he flipped out.

Before making this diagnosis, it is very important to remember the alternative causes that must always be first ruled out—he has never used drugs, has no history of head trauma or physical illness, and has no evidence of Mood Disorder. Brief Psychotic Disorder is relatively rare since most brief bouts of psychosis indeed turn out to be substance-, illness-, or Mood Disorder-related. Having a preexisting Personality Disorder may sometimes be a vulnerability factor (particularly Borderline, Paranoid, Schizotypal, Histrionic, or Narcissistic—see Chapter 10, page 207, for descriptions). Individuals with Mental Retardation (page 355) may also be prone to brief and quickly reversible psychotic episodes when they are confronted by environmental changes or complexities that are beyond their coping capacities.

Childbirth is another important stressor that can trigger Brief Psychotic Disorder. It has been estimated that one or two deliveries out of every thousand are complicated by postpartum psychoses. Unlike postpartum mood disturbances, which start a couple of days after delivery, postpartum psychosis may not be apparent until two or three weeks later. This is not a good time to be psychotic, either for the mother or for the child. The symptoms may impair the mother's ability to care for her newborn infant or, worse yet, may result in her acting violently against the child. For example, a mother who developed the delusion that her child was possessed by the devil (à la *Rosemary's Baby*) successfully strangled the baby in order to "save the world from the Antichrist." She was ultimately acquitted by reason of insanity.

According to the diagnostic manual, you have Brief Psychotic Disorder if:
- You have delusions or hallucinations or bizarre behavior.
- These symptoms last a least a day but get better within a month.
- All other causes (particularly Mood Disorder, substance use, medication side effect, and medical condition) have been considered and ruled out.

SCHIZOPHRENIA
AND SCHIZOPHRENIFORM DISORDER

Popular usage to the contrary, Schizophrenia is *not* synonymous with split personality (which falls closest to Dissociative Identity Disorder, page 286). Schizophrenia is a brain disorder that causes severe problems in thinking, feeling, and behavior. People with Schizophrenia experience difficulty distinguishing reality from fantasy. They also have trouble relating to other people, communicating through language, controlling their emotions, and making everyday decisions. Schizophrenia affects approximately two million Americans, or almost 1 percent of the entire U.S. population, with men and women represented in equal numbers. The illness usually strikes at a relatively young age—the early twenties for men and the late twenties for women. As compared to men, women with Schizophrenia generally display more mood symptoms and have a better lifetime course and response to treatment.

If left untreated, Schizophrenia is one of the most disabling of the mental illnesses. Fortunately, ongoing treatment combining antipsychotic medications with support, rehabilitation, and psychotherapy is increasingly effective in controlling the illness and helping the person to lead an independent and productive life. Early diagnosis and treatment will dramatically improve the overall course of the illness. Being psychotic is bad for the brain. The more episodes you have the harder it is to treat each subsequent episode and the more likely that your overall functioning will eventually deteriorate. Early treatment helps prevent more severe and more frequent relapses and also reduces the risk of suicide, which is highest during the earliest years of the illness.

According to the diagnostic manual, you have Schizophrenia if:
- You have periods lasting at least six months in which at least two of the following are prominent and cause serious problems for you:
  (1) Delusions: You hold on to strange beliefs with complete conviction—for example, that there is a conspiracy to harm you; that strangers are always talking about or laughing at you; that your thoughts are being broadcast out loud; that a bugging device has been implanted in your head.
  (2) Hallucinations: You hear voices that no one else can hear—for example, a voice continually commenting on your behavior, calling you bad names, or telling you to do things.

(3) Disorganized Thinking or Speech: Other people have commented that your speech is extremely hard to follow because your thoughts keep sliding off the track and do not seem to connect.

(4) Disorganized or Catatonic Behavior: Other people have told you that you act strangely and in a way that does not make sense.

(5) Negative Symptoms: You are not motivated to do anything, take no pleasure in things, hardly speak at all, and show very little or no emotion.

- These problems very seriously affect your ability to work, study, deal with other people, or take care of yourself.
- All other causes (particularly Mood Disorder, substance use, medication side effects, and medical conditions) have been considered and ruled out.

DESCRIPTION

The five symptoms of Schizophrenia can be divided into three categories: psychotic symptoms (delusions and hallucinations), disorganized symptoms (bizarre speech and behavior), and negative symptoms (loss of pleasure, emotion, and motivation). Remember that for a diagnosis of Schizophrenia you must have at least two of the five symptoms and that these must last at least for six months. Schizophreniform Disorder looks just like Schizophrenia but lasts a shorter time (one to six months) and has a better prognosis for an eventual complete recovery.

Although the content of the delusions experienced in Schizophrenia varies from person to person, certain themes are very frequently observed. The most common are paranoid delusions of being persecuted, followed, monitored, tormented, or poisoned. Feeling you are the victim of a conspiracy is terrifying and can be dangerous for you and others. Under the influence of a paranoid delusion you may feel the urge to jump out a window to avoid the imagined attackers at the door or may strike out preemptively at an innocent bystander who you think is tailing you. Closely related to paranoid delusions are delusions of reference in which you are convinced that random comments, song lyrics, words spoken on television or radio, or passages from books or newspapers are being directed specifically toward you. Walking down the street becomes difficult because it feels as if everyone is looking at you, commenting on your behavior, making jokes at your expense, and laughing at you. Everything seems to have cosmic significance and everything is directed at you.

Grandiose delusions are more characteristic of a manic episode (page 61), but also occur in Schizophrenia. The person thinks he has some special power, most commonly the ability to read the minds of others or control their thoughts. Religious delusions also occur. The individual may believe he has a special relationship with God or Satan, a unique religious mission, or that he has become a prophet. Delusions often have a somatic theme that certain organs have ceased functioning or that a specific body part has been tampered with. Nihilistic delusions of being dead or that the world has died are also observed, but less commonly than in Mood Disorders. Delusions that express feelings of a loss of control over one's mind or actions are particularly common. This is not surprising since an essential aspect of Schizophrenia is having less control of thinking and behavior and the delusions may be the patient's way of trying to explain this. You may believe that your thoughts are either being inserted or taken away by some outside force or that some power is controlling your actions and making you do things you do not want to do. It feels as if you are a puppet whose thoughts and actions are jerked out of sequence by someone pulling whimsically on your string.

Hallucinations are usually auditory but, in about 5 percent of cases, may also be visual. Much more rarely, there may be tactile, olfactory (smell), or gustatory (taste) hallucinations, but these are much more commonly caused by substances or medical illness. The voices may sound familiar or unfamiliar, may consist of a single voice or several voices, may converse or argue with one another, or provide a running commentary on your actions and thoughts. While the content of the voices varies from individual to individual, they are usually negative or threatening and sometimes command you to perform aggressive or self-destructive acts. If you have voices telling you to do bad things, it is important that you identify them as no more than hallucinations and learn to resist following the instructions. Alice in Wonderland has a crystallizing insight like this when she recognizes that the terrifying Queen and her entire court are no more than a "bunch of cards." Sticks and stones can break your bones but words can never harm you.

The second characteristic group of Schizophrenia symptoms include disorganized thinking, behavior, and speech. The disorganized thinking results in speech patterns that are constantly slipping off one track and onto another so that phrases are often unrelated and very difficult or impossible to follow. This constant shifting of the conversational thread from one frame of reference to another is known as "derailment" or a "loosening of associations." In its most severe form, derailment results in completely incoherent speech in which the words are strung together meaninglessly (known as "word salad"). Disorganized behavior can include purposeless movements in which the person appears oblivious to his environment (catatonic excitement); a complete cessation of movement or conversation for extended periods of time (catatonic withdrawal); assuming bizarre, rigid, and extremely uncomfortable positions for hours at a time like keeping one arm raised in a Nazi-like salute (catatonic posturing), or the parrotlike repetition of others' words or imitation of their actions (echolalia or echopraxia). The patient may also engage in unusual and sometimes socially inappropriate activities, such as wearing numerous overcoats on a hot summer day, directing traffic, screaming obscenities, or masturbating in public.

In contrast to these psychotic and disorganized symptoms (often called "positive" symptoms because of their outwardly florid nature), negative symptoms reflect the loss of normal functioning. The most prominent of the negative symptoms is the inability to feel and express emotion and to experience pleasure. Life feels empty, and lackluster, like watching TV in black and white with no sound. Other people's emotions are hard to read and impossible to respond to. You lack facial expression, maintain poor eye contact, and have diminished body language. You frequently withdraw from other people and isolate yourself. Speech is limited to vague and brief replies. It is an uphill struggle to plan, initiate, and follow through with the activities of daily life. In extreme cases, the individual may even lack the motivation to bathe or change clothes. There is one important thing to keep in mind—negative symptoms may occur as a side effect of the antipsychotic medications and sometimes adjusting the dose downward or changing the type of medicine can be very helpful. But don't do this on your own and certainly don't stop medication altogether because this will almost certainly lead to a relapse of the psychotic symptoms within weeks or months.

DELUSIONAL DISORDER

People with Delusional Disorder also suffer from long-standing delusions that have a profound impact on their lives. In contrast to Schizophrenia, however, they do not have any of the other psychotic symptoms we just discussed. There are no hallucinations, disorganized thinking, disorganized behavior, or negative symptoms. You can function reasonably well in those parts of life that can be kept apart from your delusional preoccupations. For example, a bank cashier develops the delusion that the well-known surgeon who occasionally stops by her window is secretly madly in love with her. Although she sends him letters, repeatedly fills his answering machine to capacity with her messages, and spends her weekends spying on him from afar, she continues to work, maintain her apartment, and socialize with her friends. A lawyer becomes convinced that his estranged wife is trying to kill him. He spends two hours each day getting to work because he must take a circuitous route to avoid the detectives he imagines she has employed to follow him. Once at work, he functions at his usual high level and no one would suspect that anything was out of the ordinary or that he is living in a private hell imposed by his delusions. Similarly, a doctor who is delusionally jealous of his wife to the point of keeping her virtually a prisoner in their house continues to do just fine in his practice.

According to the diagnostic manual, you have Delusional Disorder if:

- You hold on with complete conviction to strange beliefs that everyone else says are just simply not true—for example, that there is a conspiracy to harm you; that strangers are always talking about or laughing at you; that you are being followed; that someone famous loves you; or that you have a serious illness that can't be picked up with extensive testing.
- Unlike Schizophrenia, these beliefs are not accompanied by hallucinations, disorganized speech, disorganized behavior, or loss of emotions or motivation.
- Aside from any problems related to your strange beliefs, you are still able to function fairly well.
- All other causes (particularly Mood Disorder, substance use, medication side effects, and medical conditions) have been considered and ruled out.

SCHIZOAFFECTIVE DISORDER

Many patients with psychotic symptoms are neither classically mood disordered nor classically schizophrenic, but instead have features of both.

Schizoaffective Disorder resembles a psychotic Mood Disorder at certain times during its course (that is, when mood symptoms and psychotic symptoms occur together) and Schizophrenia at other times (when the psychotic symptoms occur by themselves). From a prognostic perspective, people with Schizoaffective Disorder do better than those with Schizophrenia, but do worse than those with Major Depressive Disorder or Bipolar Disorder. The treatment is also often hybrid—using the medications employed to treat both illnesses. Schizoaffective Disorder can be unipolar if the symptoms are restricted to depression or bipolar if the person has also had manic or hypomanic episodes.

According to the diagnostic manual, you have Schizoaffective Disorder if:

• You have had a period of time in which you had a combination of severe mood symptoms (either depression or mania) and psychotic symptoms occurring simultaneously.
• You have had other periods of time in which you had delusions or hallucinations when your mood was fine.

SHARED PSYCHOTIC DISORDER (FOLIE À DEUX)

A person who would otherwise not be psychotic can very occasionally come to share someone else's delusional beliefs. Several ingredients are necessary for the development of this folie à deux. First, two parties must be very intimately involved with one another. Second, one of the two holds strong psychotic convictions. Third, the psychotic person has a powerfully dominant position in the relationship. And fourth, the parties must be cut off from the outside influences that could subject the beliefs to the fresh air of reality. Often the shared delusions include the need to stick together in response to a perceived threat from the outside world. This further intensifies the self-imposed isolation and solidifies the enmeshment ("you and me against the world").

Shared Psychotic Disorder most typically occurs in related pairs of a parent and child or a husband and wife. In some instances, entire families can share a delusion imposed by the dominant psychotic parent. There have also been a number of tragic instances in which cult members so fervently adopted the psychotic beliefs of a dominant charismatic leader they were willing to commit mass suicide. Jim Jones's followers willingly drinking cyanide-laced Kool-Aid and the San Diego UFO cult mass suicide are recent examples of group-inspired paranoid delusion. Fortunately, the delusions weaken and eventually resolve once the person is removed from the influence of the psychotic family member or the cult leader.

According to the diagnostic manual, you have Shared Psychotic Disorder if:
• You have accepted as real the delusional beliefs of someone who has a dominating influence on you.
• When you are removed from this person's influence, your belief in the delusion goes away.

AM I OKAY?

In most clinical situations, the boundary between psychosis and normality is straightforward and easy to draw. Occasionally, however, each of the psychotic symptoms (delusions, hallucinations, catatonia, and disorganized speech) can blend into normal so that distinctions are not so clear-cut as might be expected.

Each of us operates according to an explicit or implicit set of assumptions about the meaning of life, what happens after death, how the world began, how we expect others to behave, and how we view ourselves. Undoubtedly, many of our most cherished beliefs are "false" or at least debatable and are based on very incomplete knowledge and possibly mistaken conceptions. One person's religious belief or strongly held political conviction might be someone else's delusion. A false belief is considered to be a delusion (and hence "psychotic") only if the person believes it so strongly, uncritically, and single-mindedly as to lose his grip on reality. For example, a person who harbors a mildly paranoid worldview ("people are not to be trusted") may lead an isolated existence but would not be considered delusional unless his distortions are severe enough to impair his day-to-day sense of reality. On the other hand, someone who refuses to leave his house because he is convinced that there is a conspiracy to have him killed has crossed the line from distortion to delusion.

Philosophers and epistemologists have pondered for thousands of years on what is "reality," what is truth, how do we know them, and how do we know when we know them. For our more practical purposes, it is clear that reality and truth are relative and very much influenced by social, cultural, and religious context. This is especially important if you are trying to decide whether someone else's convictions are delusional. We caution you against using your own belief system as the absolute yardstick for measuring everyone else's. Cultural and religious mores play a tremendous role in laying the groundwork for one's sense of reality. In many cultures, it is completely "normal" to hear the voice of a deceased loved one following that person's death. It would be a mistake to consider this evidence of psychosis simply because one comes from a cultural background where such phenomena are not an expectable part of life and death. It is often impossible to distinguish a crisis of religious faith from a religious delusion unless you follow the person over time and see how things turn out.

All of us can be very wrong about things (and even hold highly unusual beliefs) and still not be considered delusional. Being in touch with reality does not require capturing truth—this would be far too high a standard that few if any could attain. Instead, the question is whether the beliefs are sustained by a consensual validation from others. To a large degree, reality depends on the social context—a false belief is not delusional if it joins you to others rather than rendering you a minority of one or a member of a small lunatic fringe. It is often helpful to get the advice of someone in or closer to the person's cultural context in determining whether the beliefs or experiences make sense when corrected for cultural differences.

The presence or absence of hallucinations is usually, but not always, clear-cut. Our five senses continually flood our brains with a bubbling brew of stimuli that must be received, processed, and put into context. Occasional perceptual errors and misinterpretations are inevitable. This is especially true for ambiguous input that forces our minds to fill in the missing elements. The child's game Whisper Down the Lane is a good illustration of how we add our own idiosyncratic interpretation to garbled language. Anyone who has ever been spooked by what appeared to be an intruder in a darkened room can attest to the apparent "reality" of a misinterpreted image. Most of us have had the fleeting experience of hearing our name called, only to find that no one is there. And one's state of mind can affect perceptual experiences. Sleep deprivation, drug intoxication, and medical illness can all lead to distorted perceptions, misinterpretations, and even hallucinations. Visual hallucinations during the transitional period from wakefulness to sleep (and vice versa) are especially common and have no pathological significance.

Disorganized behavior is also on a continuum that goes from the creative to the disturbingly weird. The disorganization of psychosis is meant to be unmistakable and of major league proportions. Signs of social awkwardness, making poor eye contact, eccentricity, and mild illogicality of speech do not mean you have a psychotic disorder.

TREATMENT OPTIONS

The first step in treating psychotic symptoms is to pin down their cause. If the psychosis is due to substance intoxication or substance withdrawal, the treatment recommendation will necessarily be very different than if the diagnosis is Schizophrenia or Mood Disorder. Antipsychotic medications are effective in managing symptoms across the variety of different diagnoses, but their dosage and duration vary widely depending on the particular condition being treated.

Psychotic symptoms caused by substance intoxication are usually transient and self-limited, and disappear spontaneously. The best treatment is usually as simple as reassurance, talking the person down, providing reality cues and corrections, and ensuring a structured, safe, and quiet environment. Occasionally, an antipsychotic or a sedative medicine is helpful, especially if the person is severely agitated or sleepless. On rare occasions, a brief hospitalization or prolonged emergency room stay may be necessary.

Things get much more complicated if the psychotic symptoms triggered by substance intoxication don't disappear as expected within days or weeks of stopping the drug. In these instances, it is impossible to know for sure what is happening. Did the cocaine cause an unusually prolonged cocaine psychosis; or did it merely trigger a psychosis in someone who was already vulnerable and might have had the problem anyway; or was the cocaine taken secondarily after the person was well on the way to becoming psychotic? If psychotic symptoms persist beyond a few days, antipsychotics should be started and the person needs careful observation in a structured environment to avoid the risks of suicide, violence, or accidents. Usually these episodes respond well to medication and the patient can be gradually tapered off the antipsychotic medicine and advised strongly to stay forever away from mind-altering drugs because they have proven to be so destructive. If the psychotic symptoms persist, you might wonder about whether the person has really stopped the street drug and also whether he is really taking the prescribed medicine. The longer the symptoms persist, the less likely they were due exclusively to the substance intoxication and the more likely that the correct diagnosis may be a Mood Disorder or Schizophrenia—unless the person is still using the drug.

If psychotic symptoms occur during substance withdrawal, this will usually indicate that the person had been dependent on alcohol or on a sedative hypnotic medication, or both. The withdrawal syndrome can constitute a medical emergency with appreciable risks for *delirium tremens* (page 338), seizures, and even death. Active detoxification, establishing electrolytic balance with intravenous fluids, and vitamin replacement are crucial. Symptomatic treatment may also be necessary with antipsychotic medication directed toward the psychotic symptoms and agitation.

If the psychotic symptoms are due to a general medical condition, the obvious necessary first step is diagnosing which specific condition is causing the problem and then treating it. Very often in this context the patient is also delirious, disoriented, and agitated and this may also require medication management (see page 350).

If the psychotic symptoms are part of a unipolar depression, the treatment will be either the combination of an antipsychotic medication and an antidepressant medication or electroconvulsive therapy. The combined medication treatment is usually tried first. ECT works faster and more effectively but has a relapse rate of about 20 percent and provides fewer clues about what will be the best long-term treatment. If the psychotic symptoms are part of a depression in Bipolar Disorder, the medication regimen will also include a mood stabilizer. If the psychotic symptoms occur during a manic episode, the treatment will be a mood stabilizer and usually an antipsychotic. Sometimes ECT is also used to treat mania if medication has failed or if a particularly rapid response is necessary because the patient is on a destructive rampage.

Brief psychotic episodes are usually treated with a short course of antipsychotic medication; removal from the stressful situation; the provision of a structured and safe environment; and finally psychotherapy to identify the stressors, teach new coping skills for dealing with them, and to help you deal with the painful fact that you had a psychotic episode.

Delusional Disorder is usually treated with antipsychotic medications. Psychotherapy can also be helpful to sharpen reality testing and call into question the certainty with which the patient holds the delusional belief.

Some useful questions might go like this: "Can you really be absolutely one hundred percent sure your wife is being unfaithful?" "I am never that sure about anything." "Isn't there a possibility she is telling the truth?" "How high would you rate that possibility—5 percent, 10 percent, 25 percent, more?" "What evidence could sway your certainty or raise the percentages?" "Are you determined to believe this in the face of any amount of overwhelming contradictory evidence?" "Let's figure out how we can test your concerns and find out what is really happening."

The treatment of Schizoaffective Disorder has not been studied systematically because clinicians have such difficulty making the diagnosis reliably that it is hard to generalize the results of any one study. In practice, most patients receive treatments that combine what works for Schizophrenia with what works for Mood Disorders. For a manic episode in Schizoaffective Disorder, the person would receive a mood stabilizer and an antipsychotic. For depressed episodes, an antidepressant and an antipsychotic would be given with the addition of a mood stabilizer if the person has ever had previous manic or hypomanic episodes.

The rest of this chapter will consist of a somewhat more detailed discussion of the treatment of Schizophrenia. Schizophrenia is a chronic illness and like other chronic illnesses, such as diabetes and high blood pressure, it almost always requires lifelong treatment. The treatment options and goals differ depending on whether the patient is currently having an acute psychotic break or whether he is in a maintenance phase between episodes. The main goal in the treatment of a psychotic break is to eliminate the florid psychotic symptoms and to protect the patient (and potentially others) from their sometimes dangerous consequences. The main goal of long-term treatment is to prevent future relapses and to improve quality of life, productivity, and happiness.

Antipsychotic medications are quite effective for treating delusions, hallucinations, and thinking problems and have allowed the vast majority of people with Schizophrenia to function well enough to live in the community. It is extremely important to stay on medications for the long haul to reduce the risk of relapse. Most people will have a new episode within one year if medication is discontinued. Other steps to prevent relapses include reducing stress in your life, staying off alcohol and other drugs, learning skills for coping with the difficulties of the illness, recognizing early warning signs of a recurrence, and having a good place to live and supportive people to be with.

Although continuing to take medication regularly is the most important step you can take to keep on the right track, it is often easier said than done. Antipsychotic medications commonly have side effects. These include feeling terrible, being slowed down or stiff, getting restless or being unable to sit still, developing tremors in the hands or feet, gaining weight, and having sexual problems. Unfortunately, many patients deal with such problems by stopping their medication, usually without telling the doctor. This is always a bad idea. Most side effects can be reversed either by lowering the dose, switching to a different medication, or adding an "antidote" (like Cogentin or Artane). Fortunately, a whole new class of "atypical" antipsychotics (Risperdal, Zyprexa, Seroquel, Zeldoc, and Clozapine) has recently become available. These have much fewer side effects than the older medicines and may be more effective for many patients. The new medicines are often a godsend and may help you feel "awakened."

Substance use is a huge problem that complicates the lives and treatment of most patients with Schizophrenia. No other group of people in the United States has such a high rate of addiction to nicotine (approximately 85 percent) or smokes so intensely (more than two and a half packs per day per person). Caffeine is also used in large quantities. The favorite drugs of abuse are cocaine and amphetamines. The reasons for the pattern of use seem clear. All of these are activating substances that help the person with Schizophrenia deal both with the negative symptoms of the illness and with the sedating side effects caused by antipsychotic medication. It is also of great interest that nicotine, cocaine, and amphetamines all exert their major effects by increasing the levels of the brain neurotransmitter dopamine, which is responsible for pleasure and stimulus seeking. Dopamine is also implicated in causing psychotic symptoms and all medicines given to treat Schizophrenia work by reducing it in the brain. Here lies a paradox responsible for many relapses. Doctors give patients with Schizophrenia a dopamine-receptor-blocking medicine to reduce the longer-term risk of psychosis, but patients will often take a dopamine-enhancing street drug to reduce their current discomfort.

Everyone with this diagnosis needs to have a thorough evaluation for possible substance use and the treatment plan often needs to include interventions that will help contain it. Detoxification may sometimes be necessary. Lowering the dose of the antipsychotic medicine or switching to one of the newer medicines with fewer side effects can be very helpful. It is a good idea to select an AA group that includes other people who are on medicines and understand the necessity for taking them; however, some AA groups have an antimedicine bias and may not be useful in meeting your special needs.

Medication alone is not enough to effectively treat Schizophrenia. Some combination of individual, group, and family therapy is usually crucial in helping the patient and his family cope with the vicissitudes of the illness. Psychoeducation focuses on teaching everyone about the illness, what causes it, the characteristic symptoms, and how to deal with them. A longer-term goal is to help you return to usual activities and responsibilities and learn new social and vocational skills. Drop-in clinics with a casual and friendly clubhouse atmosphere provide a comfortable low-stress environment to encourage getting involved with people again. Vocational rehabilitation can help you sharpen job skills and find gainful employment. Support groups for family members provide a great setting to share experiences and suggestions with others who are facing many of the same problems.

There used to be a lot of pessimism about the treatment of Schizophrenia. This is no longer the case. Long-term studies show that many people do surprisingly well. Moreover, the new medications for Schizophrenia are having a profound impact on the symptoms and quality of life of many people who were previously nonresponders or who had terrible side effects. The new models of psychoeducation and community care are also making it much easier for patients to stick with the long-term treatment that is necessary to beat the illness. Most encouraging, scientific research is making really remarkable strides in understanding the basic problems that cause the illness. Within the next decade there should be a breakthrough in knowledge that is bound to result in even better-tolerated and more effective treatments.

Suggested Additional Readings

When the Music's Over: My Journey into Schizophrenia
    Ross Burke, Dr. Richard Gates (editor), Robin Hammond (editor),
    and David Burke
    Plume, 1996

My Mother's Keeper: A Daughter's Memoir of Growing Up
    in the Shadow of Schizophrenia
    Tara Elgin Holley and Joe Holley
    Morrow, 1997

Surviving Schizophrenia: A Manual for Families, Consumers and Providers
    E. Fuller Torrey
    Harperperennial, 1995

Understanding Schizophrenia: A Guide to the New Research on Causes and Treatment
Richard S. E. Keefe and Philip D. Harvey
Free Press, 1994

Whispers: The Voices of Paranoia
Ronald K. Siegel
Crown, 1994

Where to Go for Help
(Self-help, support, for more information)

National Alliance for the Mentally Ill (NAMI)

200 North Glebe Road
Suite 1015
Arlington, VA 22203-3754
(703) 524-7600
(800) 950-NAMI
Web: http://www.nami.org/

National Alliance for Research on Schizophrenia and Depression (NARSAD)

60 Cutter Mill Road
Suite 404
Great Neck, NY 11021
(516) 829-0091
Web: http://www.mhsource.com/narsad.html

National Mental Health Association

1021 Prince Street
Alexandria, VA 22314-2971
(703) 684-7722
Web: http://www.nmha.org/

National Mental Health Consumer's Association
(information about chronic mental illness)

Suite 1100
1211 Chestnut Street
Philadelphia, PA 19107
(215) 735-2465

Center for Psychiatric Rehabilitation
(resource center for information about chronic mental illness)

Boston University
930 Commonwealth Avenue
Boston, MA 02215
(617) 353-3549
E-mail: kfurlong@bu.edu
Web: http://web.bu.edu/SARPSYCH

COGNITIVE DIFFICULTIES

The term "cognition" refers to the many intellectual processes that allow us to "know" our environment and structure responses to it. These include the ability to focus attention, recall events, stay oriented, do calculations, coordinate motor activity, plan ahead, speak and understand language, process perceptions and information, and finally to be aware of all of these wonderful mental activities through that mysterious thing called consciousness. Recent observation suggests that animals are much smarter (and less instinctual) than we ever imagined and that humans are more instinctual (and perhaps less smart) than we would have hoped. Nonetheless, human intellectual skills are perhaps our most precious possession and most distinguish us from our closest animal relatives. The higher cognitive functions are so much the jewels in our human crown that it is always painful when they become diminished.

The three cognitive disorders described in this chapter (Delirium, Dementia, and Amnestic Disorder) share two features. All three involve severe disturbances in the ability to think clearly, learn new information, remember past information, and interact effectively with the environment. And all three are caused by an attack on brain functioning that arises from a medical condition, a medication, drug abuse, or toxin exposure. Once it has been identified that a cognitive problem is present, the next job is to determine the underlying cause as quickly as possible. This is necessary so that treatment can be started soon enough to reduce further brain damage.

The ten questions of the following Mini-Mental State Examination provide a quick test to determine if someone's cognition is seriously enough disturbed to warrant a more intensive medical evaluation. We've included it in this book to give you an idea of the types of cognitive abilities that are affected by the disorders in this chapter. Just about everyone who can follow this book will likely score in the "normal" or perfect range.

The "Mini-Mental State"
(adapted with permission from the *Journal of Psychiatric Research*)

Orientation

1. Ask the person the following questions about the current time: What is the (year) (season) (date) (day of the week) (month)? *(Score 1 for each correct answer; 5 points possible.)*
2. Ask the person the following questions regarding current location: Where are we (state) (country) (city) (hospital or clinic) (floor)? *(Score 1 for each correct answer; 5 points possible.)*

Registration

3. Ask the person if you can test his or her memory. Then say the names of three unrelated things (e.g., red rubber ball, black Cadillac, honesty); say them clearly and slowly at a rate of 1 word per second. Ask the person to repeat all three after you have finished saying them. *(Score 1 for each correct answer; 3 points possible.)* If incorrect, repeat them until the person is able to relate all three correctly—this is to lay the groundwork for question 5.

Attention and Calculation

4. Ask the person to begin with 100 and count backward by 7 (i.e., 100, 93, 86, 79, 72). Stop after five subtractions. *(Score 1 for each correct result; 5 points possible.)* Alternatively, if the person is not schooled to do such calculations, have the person spell the word "world" backward. *(Score the number of letters in correct order; for example, dlrow = 5; dlorw = 4.)*

Recall

5. Ask the person to recall the three things you previously asked him or her to remember in question 3. *(Score 1 point for each correct answer; 3 points possible.)*

Language and Performance

6. Show the person a pencil and a wristwatch and ask the person to name them. *(Score 1 point for each correct answer; 2 points possible.)*
7. Ask the person to repeat the following phrase: "No ifs, ands, or buts." *(Score 1 point if correct.)*

8. Give the person a blank piece of paper and ask him or her to perform the following three-stage command: "Take this paper in your right hand, fold it in half, and put it on the floor." *(Score 1 point for each command correctly carried out; 3 points possible.)*

9. On a blank piece of paper, print the sentence "Close your eyes" in letters large enough for the person to see clearly. Have the person read it and do what it says. *(Score 1 point if and only if he or she actually closes his or her eyes.)*

   Give the person a blank piece of paper and ask him or her to write a sentence for you. Do not dictate the sentence—it should be written spontaneously. *(Score 1 point if it contains a subject and verb and is sensible—correct grammar and punctuation are not necessary.)*

10. Instruct the person to copy this design exactly as it is:

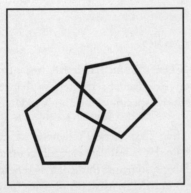

(Score 1 point only if all ten angles are present and two of them intersect. Unsteadiness due to tremor and rotation of the object—e.g., by 90 degrees—should not affect the scoring.)

Scoring: add up total score, 30 points are possible; 25–30 is considered normal in older adults; 18–24 reflects mild impairment; and less than 18 moderate to severe impairment.

ORIENTATION

Orientation to the environment and oneself is so automatic and so crucial to survival that we usually take it for granted. Without it, we would be lost. Problems in orientation are assessed in three domains: time, place, and person (hence, in medical charts, a fully oriented person is noted to be "oriented times 3"). Even if we are not always fully cognizant of the precise time or exact date (especially when on a vacation!), an oriented person should at least be aware of the month, season, year, the approximate date, and whether it is morning, afternoon, or night. Disorientation to time is an early indicator of the presence of possible brain damage. Orientation to place refers to the awareness of where one is at any moment—not necessarily the exact address, but whether the location is a home, place of work, a classroom, or doctor's office, and why you are there. Orientation to person refers to knowledge of who you are—your name, occupation, and place in your family. Most people are able to hang on to orientation to place and person until they have the most serious of cognitive deficits. The loss of orientation to person is a great personal and family tragedy—you literally don't know who you are and experience your loved ones as strangers.

MEMORY

Memory has three separable components: immediate recall, recent memory, and remote memory. Each may be affected separately so that testing them individually may help indicate the specific cause and location of the brain injury.

Immediate recall is the frontline filter of experience. Whenever we are presented with an image or a sound, we hold it in immediate recall for up to several seconds. This can be tested by having someone immediately repeat a list of numbers or objects (see question 3 in MMS). Most people with "normal" immediate recall should be able to repeat all three objects without a problem.

All information subject to future retrieval is then transferred from our immediate recall to our recent memory. We keep in passive storage at least some of the day's events (for example, where is my wallet, is there food cooking on the stove, where is my car parked, yesterday's weather) and also have available some information we are actively trying to save for later retrieval (for example, my appointments for the day, a mental list of groceries to buy at the store, or memorizing facts for a test). Recent memory can be checked by asking the person to recall something that has been learned or experienced recently, like last evening's sports scores or what was eaten for lunch. On more formal testing (see question 5 in MMS), a person with intact recent memory should be able to correctly recall three unrelated objects after a five-minute delay.

Remote memory acts as a more or less permanent storage for the grab bag of previous happenings that become part of our personal legacy. Our memory banks hold on to things that are of particular personal significance (anniversary dates, the ages of our children; what we were doing when JFK was shot or the *Challenger* exploded); facts that are part of common knowledge (past presidents, the state capital, who are the characters in *The Wizard of Oz*, who starred in *Gone With the Wind*); and details related to familiar activities (how to get to the store and back again, how to perform one's job, the sequence of steps in baking a cake). Remote memory can be tested by checking the person's general knowledge about historical facts ("Name the past five presidents."), geography ("What is the capital of the United States?"), or personal history ("Where did you grow up?" "What kind of work did your father do?" "How many children do you have?").

ABILITY TO FOCUS ATTENTION

Brain injury can result in a clouding of consciousness that limits the ability to focus or shift attention. The tasks presented in question 4 (subtracting serial 7's from 100 or spelling a word backward) require a certain clearheadedness and serve as a rough test of attention. You need to keep the goal of the task in mind, remember where you are in the sequence, and keep moving on until you have completed it. Someone with clouding of consciousness is likely to get stuck in the middle of a calculation, repeat it over and over again, or forget what he was supposed to be doing in the first place.

LANGUAGE AND PERFORMANCE

Language is an integral part of cognitive functioning and the most distinctly human of brain activities. Language provides us with the means of forming internal representations of reality, manipulating ideas to solve problems, planning for the future, and communicating abstract concepts. Numerous interacting cognitive functions are involved in language processing. Consider the seemingly simple act of answering the telephone, taking a message, confirming that you got it right, and saying good-bye. In order for this sequence of events to occur, you must be able to recognize the sound of the telephone, comprehend the spoken request, convert the message to written language, read it back to the caller, and then terminate the call with the appropriate "good-bye."

Because the different aspects of language functioning can be separately impaired, four questions in the Mini-Mental State Examination are devoted to its assessment: Question 6 tests one's ability to recognize familiar objects and then summon up the appropriate name; question 7 tests one's ability to repeat phrases; and questions 8 and 9 test comprehension of both verbal and written commands.

MOTOR AND SENSORY FUNCTION

Another critically important intellectual skill is the ability to move one's body in order to get things done. This requires hand-eye coordination and the ability to carry out sequential movements toward a goal. Questions 8 and 9 specifically test one's ability to convert language and thought into meaningful action. One must understand the instruction (both by hearing and reading), translate the language into a concept, and then apply a complex set of sequential hand, arm, and body movements to get the task done. Question 10 tests the ability to integrate complex visual stimuli and to integrate the motor functions required to write and copy figures.

OTHER INTELLECTUAL FUNCTIONS: PROBLEM SOLVING, ABSTRACT THINKING, INSIGHT, AND JUDGMENT

The ability to think abstractly is assessed by asking the person how two objects are either similar or different ("How are a bus and train alike?") or to interpret the meaning of a proverb or saying. For example, when presented with the proverb "People who live in glass houses shouldn't throw stones," a person who previously taught college English but now has Dementia may give a very concrete and literal interpretation rather than considering the metaphorical implications of the statement. "It means that you have to be careful because the stone may fall out of your hand and smash the window."

Judgment and insight are two higher-order intellectual functions that reflect a person's self-awareness and awareness of social conventions and expectations. Standard questions used to assess judgment include: "What should you do if you are in a theater and you see a fire?" or "Why are laws necessary?" It is probably more relevant to tailor questions about judgment to the person's actual living situation. For example, asking a retired businessman how to deal with a phone solicitation asking for money; or asking a grandmother who baby-sits with two young children what she would do if she had to leave them to go to the doctor; or asking an elderly woman why it is not a good idea to go out alone at night. Assessment of insight usually focuses on whether the person knows he is ill: "Why do you think you have been brought in to see a doctor?" A person with little insight might respond, "Because my wife needs help; I'm perfectly okay."

Be cautious when considering the significance of a cognitive problem: Anyone can have an unrepresentative bad day in mental performance based on fatigue, physical discomfort, performance anxiety, lack of motivation, or inattentiveness. Moreover, many other psychiatric disturbances, such as depression, mania, Attention-Deficit/Hyperactivity Disorder, or Schizophrenia may exert a negative impact on cognitive functioning that translates into poor performance on cognitive tests. The person may be on medications that impair memory or attention. Finally, it can be difficult to know how to interpret a cognitive assessment without having the results of a prior baseline evaluation for comparison. For example, two calculation errors in subtracting sevens would be much more indicative of a problem when it occurs with a mathematics professor than it would for a person with a sixth-grade education. People who started with superior intelligence may continue to do well on fairly simple testing but have difficulties performing complex tasks that previously were a snap for them.

The three disorders in this chapter (Delirium, Dementia, and Amnestic Disorder) differ in onset and course, the nature of the cognitive impairments, and in their most likely specific causes. Delirium is the most fluid of the three, with cognitive symptoms that start abruptly, fluctuate over time, and cause gross confusion and interference with a panoply of intellectual functions. Delirium is a medical emergency that is caused by an acute medical illness or by an intoxication or withdrawal from a medication, street drug, or alcohol. Dementia and Amnestic Disorder usually come on more gradually, are more stable (or steadily progressive), and are caused by ongoing and long-standing medical conditions (like Alzheimer's disease, strokes, chronic HIV infection, or vitamin deficiencies) or long-term exposure to toxic substances (chronic alcohol abuse, occupational exposure to toxins). They are usually, but not always, irreversible. Dementia differs from Amnestic Disorder in that many more cognitive difficulties are involved beyond the loss of memory.

DELIRIUM

The term "delirious" (from the Latin "deviating from a straight line") conjures up the image of someone who is wild and out of control. This is extremely misleading. Although some people with Delirium do become temporarily agitated and difficult to contain, there are many others who develop confusion and disorientation in a quiet, unobtrusive way that will be missed unless Delirium is considered as a possible reason for their changed behavior. The experience of Delirium is like being in a fuzzy dream or a dense fog that is clouding your awareness of the outside world. You lose the ability to keep track of what is going on and feel frightened, agitated, or even combative. You may become disoriented and feel confused as to where you are, the time of day, the season of the year, who the people are around you, or even (at the extreme) who you are. Delirium is usually a short-term problem that arises suddenly. Within days, it either disappears completely with no permanent damage or more tragically may be a precursor to irreversible Dementia, Amnestic Disorder, or even death. Delirium is one of the few problems described in this book for which prompt diagnosis and treatment is a medical, not just a psychiatric, emergency.

According to the diagnostic manual, you have Delirium if:
- Your awareness of the external environment has been seriously compromised—you are unable to pay attention to or keep up with what's going on around you.
- You have at least one additional and serious problem in the way your mind is working. These include:
  (1) You are disoriented—you do not know where you are, what day it is, or who other people are around you.
  (2) You are having hallucinations—you see, hear, feel, smell things that are not really there.
  (3) You have serious problems remembering things like what happened earlier that day.
  (4) Other people have trouble following your speech because it is rambling or disorganized.
- Your symptoms have started up abruptly and fluctuate during the day.

DESCRIPTION

Virtually all brain functions become disturbed during Delirium. Recent memory is almost always affected. Who visited earlier that day, what was served for breakfast, what the doctor said during morning rounds (or five minutes ago) all fade away quickly in a cloud of confusion. It is difficult to communicate. The person's attention keeps wandering to the other things that are going on in the room, the distractions of TV or radio, or someone walking by. You probably will have to repeat your questions over and over again. The person has trouble understanding and responding to you, and may keep saying the same thing over and over again.

Disorientation and confusion can result in accidental injuries, tearing out intravenous lines, falling out of bed or down the stairs, or running in front of traffic. Hallucinatory experiences with accusing voices, frightening visions, unpleasant smells or tastes, and touch sensations like bugs crawling are much more common in Delirium than in Schizophrenia or Mood Disorder. Hallucinations are particularly common in people who have hearing or visual impairments. One tip that sensory deprivation is a problem is that the patient is screaming at the top of his lungs—a hearing aid may make all the difference. In Delirium, the daily rhythm of sleep and wakefulness often becomes mixed up—the person is likely to keep drifting off during the day, but to become hyper-alert even to the point of agitation in the dead of night. This characteristic sleep-wake pattern is called "sundowning" since the trouble usually begins as evening progresses.

One of the striking things about Delirium is how abruptly it starts and ends and how much the cloudiness can fluctuate over brief periods of time. The person may slip from tranquil restfulness to confused agitation in just a matter of minutes. Sometimes, during the course of a conversation the person's level of consciousness can switch in front of your eyes. Mood can also be surprisingly labile—apathetic or depressed one minute, angry, terrified, agitated, or paranoid the next.

CAUSES OF DELIRIUM

Delirium Due to Medical Illness

Many medical illnesses can upset brain functioning and cause Delirium. These include strokes, heart failure, brain tumor, head trauma, low blood sugar, infections, vitamin deficiencies. Some patients develop Delirium after surgery due to the lingering effects of anesthesia, blood clots, and post-operative infections or some combination of these.

People admitted to a hospital often have many problems that in combination can lead to Delirium. They must have quite a serious medical illness or they wouldn't be hospitalized in the first place. They are often also receiving hefty doses of medication—often several different ones, all of which have the potential to cause confusion. The hospital also tends to bring out the worst in someone who is already compromised cognitively. The structure and regularity of everyday routine helps to provide us with constant orienting reminders. The unfamiliar environment (simultaneously both over-stimulating and understimulating) of a hospital room or intensive care unit may be enough to push someone who already has marginal cognitive functioning over the edge into a full-blown Delirium. Being sick and stuck in a strange place is a doubly stressful challenge that often exceeds the resources of someone whose ability to deal with unfamiliarity is already severely impaired. Hospital-induced sleep deprivation can make all of this worse. If a relative is admitted to the hospital, try to provide orienting stimuli. A night light, pictures of family members, a prominently displayed clock or calendar, and regular visits from a familiar face all offer helpful reminders of what is happening and why. This can make a great deal of difference.

Substance-Induced Delirium

Many medications and most recreational drugs, if taken in large enough doses or if withdrawn abruptly, can wreak havoc on brain functioning. Someone who consistently drinks a large amount of alcohol or takes high doses of tranquilizers cannot suddenly stop them without risking a potentially life-threatening form of Delirium called "D.T.'s" (for *delirium tremens*). Instead, they must be detoxified slowly to allow gradual weaning. The abrupt change in drinking habits imposed by hospitalization for a medical condition can put an alcoholic at grave risk for D.T.'s. The unexpected withdrawal may result from his reluctance to inform the hospital staff of his large daily alcohol intake—so you have to do this for him. It is also important to remember that there is a lag of several days after someone stops drinking before withdrawal begins. Don't have a false sense of security if there is no problem in the first day or two off alcohol.

Delirium Due to Multiple Etiologies

More often than not, a combination of factors conspire to bring on Delirium. This can be dangerous. Sometimes, one cause of Delirium is successfully identified and treated but the patient goes on to death or Dementia because a second cause lurking in the background was never picked up. People with a physical illness and a substance problem have a particularly risky combination. Many medical illnesses lower the brain's ability to withstand the intoxicating or withdrawal effects of drugs or alcohol and this predisposes to severe Delirium. It is, therefore, wise to keep searching for other causes of Delirium even after one possible culprit has been identified and dealt with.

One of the authors had a chilling experience with this in his very first medical school rotation. A man was brought to the hospital with obvious Alcohol Withdrawal Delirium and "rum fits" seizures, both of which were treated very successfully. Unfortunately, he died four days later from a bleed into his brain that resulted from a fistfight that no one knew about or took into account. Delirium can be deadly and requires the most active of diagnostic and treatment efforts.

DEMENTIA

The most characteristic impairment in Dementia is severe memory loss. All three types of memory functioning may be affected: immediate, recent, and remote. In early Dementia, recent memory is most severely affected with immediate and remote memory remaining relatively intact. You may be able to repeat a telephone number right after you hear it and remember the telephone number of your childhood home, but cannot remember your son's current telephone number, no matter how many times you struggle to learn it. As the Dementia advances, no aspect of memory is spared. The person may forget even the most basic personal facts like what line of work he previously performed, or the city in which he was born, or the ages of his children. Eventually, and most tragically, he may be unable to figure out his relationships to his wife and children and regards them as strangers.

Although severe memory problems are invariably present in Dementia, many other intellectual functions are affected as well. "Aphasia" is an impairment in the ability to understand and produce language, both written and spoken. Speech may become empty of content or irrelevant to the topic being discussed. The difficulty in finding words and framing sentences can become so severe that speech or writing is littered with vague references and the frequent use of nondescript words like "thing" and "it" in place of specific words or names. Communication with others gets limited, slow, and difficult.

Dementia also eventually affects the ability to coordinate and integrate sensory and motor activity—functions usually so automatic that we appreciate their great importance only when they are not working very well. Whenever our senses are confronted with a sight, sound, taste, smell, or feel, the raw perceptual experience must be processed and assigned a meaning. The term "agnosia" refers to an inability to recognize and categorize a pattern of sensations that previously would have been familiar. The peripheral perceptual system is working just fine, but the person's brain cannot make sense of the perceptions it is receiving. The loss in pattern recognition may occur with any mode of sensory input. For example, you are unable to place what had previously been a familiar face; identify a quarter by the feel of it; recognize the sound of a ringing telephone; or associate that a particular smell arises from a rose, a cup of coffee, or horse manure. When Dementia is at its most severe, the loss of recognition renders the person unable to recognize the faces of even the closest family members. In the extreme, the person may find his own reflection in the mirror to be completely unfamiliar.

Dementia also affects the ability to organize and carry out any sequence of movements—like handwriting, tying shoes, brushing teeth, getting dressed, waving good-bye, or chopping onions. This deficit (technically called "apraxia") reflects both a difficulty in overall coordination of motor activity and a confusion regarding the body's spatial orientation (for example, knowing left from right or judging how far to move one's hand in order to grasp an object). Apraxia can deprive the person of the ability to get dressed, wash up, or even feed himself. When apraxia becomes severe, nursing home placement or very close supervision is required to provide basic assistance with necessary daily activities.

Finally, Dementia reduces the person's "executive functioning"—the higher-level, most characteristically human intellectual activities that are anatomically localized mostly in the frontal lobes of the brain. These include the ability to plan and implement projects; think abstractly; solve problems; do calculations; and exercise appropriate discretion, impulse control, and judgment. Activities requiring multiple steps, like balancing a checkbook or preparing a meal, become difficult. Often the person "adapts" to these problems by avoiding new activities and situations that may tax his impaired ability to think and reason. Declines in executive functioning are most difficult to evaluate in someone who started out with a very high baseline and may still be doing well compared to most folks even when there is a clear decline from previous superb functioning.

The lack of judgment and insight can lead to accidents. The person often has little or no awareness of the nature or extent of the problems, may grossly overestimate his abilities, and make plans to do things that he is clearly incapable of safely carrying out. For example, he may plan to take a bus by himself to see his doctor, ignoring his propensity to get lost once he leaves the immediate confines of his home. He may cross streets without caution and may drive a car for many years past his real competence to do so. Pacers and wanderers are at special risk for falls and hip fractures, especially if they are overmedicated. The complications of hip fractures are a major cause of death in elderly patients with Dementia.

Denial of illness is very common in Dementia and arises from both psychological and biological factors. Rather than admitting to memory gaps, the person will make up cover stories (this is called "confabulation"). He may complain that others are stealing his wallet, keys, or other misplaced items. Forgotten appointment times are blamed on external circumstances (my car wouldn't start) or to miscommunication (you told me the wrong time). The erosion of one's mental faculties is such a terrifying prospect that many people handle it by denying, to others and to themselves, the full scope of their cognitive decline. Denial may also result directly from the damage to the specific parts of the brain that are self-monitoring.

Dementia robs the person of the cognitive and emotional resources needed to cope effectively with stresses in his environment. Agitation is often the result. Mild agitation is marked by irritability, confrontations, and low frustration tolerance. In more severe forms, there is wandering away, screaming, spitting, biting, or lashing out at caregivers. Severe agitation is the number-one reason for having to place loved ones in nursing homes. Be aware, however, that the sudden onset of agitation may indicate that a Delirium or medical discomfort has become superimposed on the Dementia. The fragility of patients with Dementia makes them especially prone to develop agitation in response to medication changes, urinary tract or other infections, pain, sleep deprivation, sensory impairments, dehydration, or sudden changes in the environment (like being moved to a new room). A thorough medical evaluation is essential to determine the medical and environmental causes of the agitation and to start appropriate treatment.

A number of other symptoms can occur in Dementia. A "catastrophic reaction" is an extreme form of emotional liability with heart-rending crying, striking out, or severe anxiety resulting from what would seem to be relatively trivial triggers. These emotional outbursts start and stop abruptly—the patient may be easily distracted out of the intense emotions. Difficulty falling asleep or staying asleep are especially common. The insomnia may stem from depression, pain, taking too many daytime naps, or a disturbance in the brain's timekeeper. Paranoid delusions may arise— most commonly that possessions are being pilfered; that one is being threatened by criminals, family members, or hospital staff; that one's spouse is unfaithful; or that food is being tampered with. Depression is a particularly common problem and is often severe enough to meet the definition of Major Depressive Disorder (page 33).

According to the diagnostic manual, you have Dementia if:
- You have a serious memory impairment—you are unable to learn new things, or recall facts or events, or recognize people you previously knew.
- You also have at least one of the following problems:
  (1) difficulty understanding other people's speech or in being understood by them ("aphasia")
  (2) inability to recognize objects despite being able to see, hear, touch, taste, or smell them ("agnosia")
  (3) inability to integrate complex motor activities despite having the muscular strength and coordination to do them ("apraxia")
  (4) other disturbances in intellectual functioning—like planning events, organizing your affairs, and thinking abstractly
- These problems seriously interfere with your daily functioning.

CAUSES OF DEMENTIA

Dementia always has as its underlying cause either a medical condition or the impact of a substance. Don't make the mistake of attributing severe memory problems and other serious intellectual deficits occurring in an elderly family member to the inevitable ravages of time. A thorough medical evaluation is always essential to see if the underlying problem can be corrected.

Alzheimer's Disease

Alzheimer's disease is the most common cause of Dementia. Solving the puzzle of Alzheimer's is currently one of the most exciting areas of research in medicine. There is great promise that we will soon both understand why and how it happens and have much more powerful tools to prevent and treat it. This is a huge public health problem. As many as 10 percent of people aged sixty-five or older suffer from Alzheimer's disease and the risk continually goes up as one gets older so that 50 percent of those over age eighty-five are afflicted. People who have a strong family history of Alzheimer's disease are at greater risk, but at least half of those who develop the condition have no significant family history.

Dementia of the Alzheimer's type progresses at different rates in different people. For a very rare few, the decline happens with alarming rapidity (going from the initial diagnosis to almost complete helplessness within just a year), whereas most people have a much slower, but still inexorably downhill course for about ten to fifteen years before death. Onset before age sixty-five is often associated with a more rapid decline.

People with Alzheimer's disease often have profound changes in personality, behavior, and mood—sometimes preceding by years the appearance of the clear-cut cognitive deficits. This means you have to consider the diagnosis whenever there is an unexplained first appearance of any psychiatric symptoms or unusual behavior in elderly people who previously did not have a psychiatric disorder. A garrulous, aggressive, and extroverted businessman gradually becomes passive and apathetic; a shy, retiring, extra-proper former schoolteacher becomes loud, belligerent, and bawdy. Only much later is the Dementia recognized. There may be the new onset of paranoid fears that result either from the memory loss (for example, misplacing credit cards and then claiming that a caretaker has stolen them), or directly from brain damage caused by the disease.

Currently, the only definitive way to make the diagnosis of Alzheimer's disease is by examining brain tissue under the microscope, something that is rarely done before death because of the danger involved in obtaining a brain biopsy from a living person. This may change very soon. Promising new diagnostic tests are now being evaluated in research settings that should be available before long for clinical use. Until then, Alzheimer's remains mostly a "diagnosis of exclusion" to be considered after making sure that other possible causes have been eliminated.

Vascular Dementia

When a person has a stroke, one or more blood vessels in the brain become blocked or rupture, damaging the part of the brain supplied by that vessel. Which neurological and cognitive brain functions are lost depends on which side and which part of the brain are affected. For example, a stroke affecting the left side of the brain often results in right-sided paralysis and a difficulty with speech. Multiple small strokes (or one or two very large strokes) affecting those areas of the brain involved in memory, language, and other intellectual functions can result in Vascular Dementia.

Unlike Alzheimer's, which evolves slowly over time and affects a broad range of intellectual functions simultaneously, the symptoms in Vascular Dementia come on abruptly and develop in stages, each new problem signaling that another stroke has occurred. For example, a fifty-nine-year-old man with high blood pressure suddenly develops difficulties with short-term memory after a stroke. After a year of struggling to compensate for his memory, he suddenly develops a host of new problems, like getting lost in his own neighborhood, being unable to recognize faces of friends, and being unable to write legibly. Since the brain areas affected by small strokes are well circumscribed, certain intellectual functions are impaired while others are left untouched.

People most at risk for having a stroke (and thus, at risk for Vascular Dementia) include those with high blood pressure, high cholesterol, obesity, diabetes, heart rhythm abnormalities, and heavy smoking. Reducing these risk factors (carefully controlling the high blood pressure, losing weight, stopping smoking, lowering cholesterol, improving diet or increasing exercise) can reduce your risk of stroke and the subsequent development of Dementia and paralysis. Since people who have already suffered a stroke are likely to have more strokes over time (potentially resulting in an additional loss of intellectual functions), it is especially important for them to do everything possible, and right away, to minimize risk factors. One aspirin taken on a daily basis as a preventive is also often helpful.

Dementia Related to AIDS

Up to 40 percent of people infected with the virus responsible for AIDS will eventually experience symptoms of Dementia. For as many as one in ten people, cognitive problems are the first signs of AIDS. Sometimes the virus has directly infected brain cells, leading to symptoms of forgetfulness, slowed thinking, difficulty in problem solving, or problems with concentration. Sometimes, the Dementia arises as a more indirect result of the HIV infection. People with AIDS are more susceptible to certain types of infections (like toxoplasmosis and cytomegalovirus) and to tumors (like lymphoma or metastatic Kaposi's sarcoma), which can affect the brain and result in Dementia. Finally, the medications used to treat AIDS (like AZT) can sometimes cause confusion and cognitive problems. Teasing apart these potentially interacting factors is important in order to ensure that the treatment is directed to the appropriate problem.

Dementia Due to Parkinson's Disease or Huntington's Disease

Both of these neurological conditions are caused by a degeneration of certain parts of the brain resulting in abnormal movements, mood changes, and Dementia. Parkinson's disease usually starts after age fifty and affects one in one thousand people over age sixty-five. The main motor symptoms in Parkinson's disease include shaking and rigidity of the extremities, slowed movements, and lack of facial expressions. Up to 60 percent of Parkinson's patients eventually develop at least mild Dementia as they get older. Usually the Dementia involves problems in spatial orientation, slowed memory recall, and difficulty in problem solving. Treatments that are targeted for the movement problems (like L-dopa, which increases brain dopamine) are sometimes also effective for the cognitive symptoms.

Huntington's disease is much less frequently encountered than Parkinson's disease (affecting around five per hundred thousand) and is characterized by abnormal jerking and writhing movements of the arms and legs. Unlike Parkinson's, in which most cases are sporadic, Huntington's disease is a clearly genetic disease always inherited from an afflicted parent. If one parent has Huntington's disease, the odds are fifty-fifty that each child will also get the disease. The symptoms usually first become evident between ages thirty-five and forty-five. Often, Dementia and depression emerge before the arrival of the abnormal movements. There is now a genetic test to identify who will develop the disease and treatments or methods of prevention may soon emerge from our rapidly increasing understanding.

Other Medical Causes of Dementia

Although we usually think of Dementia as an irreversible process, this is not always the case. A number of the less common causes of Dementia can be resolved if the underlying medical problem is treated promptly. These potentially reversible causes include vitamin deficiencies, accumulations of blood in the brain as a result of a blow to the head (subdural hematoma), a buildup of fluid pressure in the brain (normal pressure hydrocephalus), and hormone deficiencies or excesses (such as low thyroid hormone). A prompt and thorough medical evaluation to rule out these conditions is essential.

Dementia Caused by Alcohol

Alcohol is just as poisonous to the brain as it is to the liver and constitutes the third most common cause of Dementia (after Alzheimer's and strokes). Most people with Alcohol-Induced Dementia have been drinking heavily for at least fifteen to twenty years. Slowly but surely, the death of brain cells causes the insidious development of memory loss, apathy, personality changes, slowed thinking, and various other intellectual impairments. If you are a heavy drinker, think about this the next time you mix a cocktail. The amount of deterioration is related to age (the older one is, the more likely one is to be demented), the amount consumed, nutritional and vitamin status, and episodes of head trauma.

Abstinence is crucial to preventing further progression of the Dementia. Although the Dementia is not completely reversible, those who protect their brains from alcohol will experience some improvement in cognitive abilities over time. An additional contributing factor to memory loss is the nutritional deficiencies that go hand-in-hand with heavy drinking. Chronic thiamin (a B vitamin) deficiency can by itself lead to a severe memory impairment (called Korsakoff's syndrome) or to episodes of Delirium (Wernicke's encephalopathy). Since it is often not clear how much of the memory problem is due to the toxic effects of alcohol versus thiamin deficiency, it usually is a good idea for alcoholics to take high doses of thiamin (at least 100 mg a day) as a precaution.

Dementia Caused by Other Substances

Many of the substances that adolescents use for a cheap high can lead to permanent brain damage. Organic solvents (like airplane glue, paint thinner, gasoline, and other substances found in paints and cleaning fluids) are the most commonly used and most dangerous. They produce a whole host of other medical problems besides Dementia, including kidney damage, suppression of bone marrow, seizures, impairment in motor coordination, and other nervous system damage. Heavy metals are also poisonous to the nervous system. Lead poisoning continues to be a serious problem for children exposed to lead-containing paint chips or dust. It causes poor concentration, memory loss, speech problems, deafness, headaches, and joint pain. Dementia related to heavy metal exposure can also result from long-term occupational contact by workers (for example, mercury exposure among photoengravers).

AMNESTIC DISORDER

Amnestic Disorder differs from Dementia in that the cognitive difficulties are confined to a loss of memory. There are no problems with any other type of cognitive functioning—for example, language, abstraction abilities, motor functioning, and sensory interpretation are all fine. Amnestic Disorder differs from Delirium because attention and orientation are intact. Some people have a circumscribed amnesia ("blackout") only for a specific period of time—their ability to learn new information remains unaffected. Others suffer from an ongoing inability to lay down new memories and develop an increasingly long period for which they have no memory. As with Dementia, immediate recall and remote memory for events long past are generally much more available than recent memory.

According to the diagnostic manual, you have Amnestic Disorder if:
- You have a serious memory impairment—either you are unable to learn new things, or to recall facts or events, or to recognize people you previously knew.
- Unlike Dementia or Delirium, your intellectual functioning is otherwise unimpaired.

CAUSES OF AMNESTIC DISORDER

The range of medical conditions and substances that cause an Amnestic Disorder is narrower than those causing Dementia and Delirium. These are limited to those medical conditions and substances that can selectively affect that part of the brain involved in laying down new memories and recalling previously saved memories.

Head Injury

This can lead to transient or permanent memory loss usually for events immediately preceding the traumatic event. A wide variety of other psychiatric symptoms can also result from head injury including depression, personality changes, Dementia, and Delirium.

Thiamin Deficiency (Korsakoff's Syndrome)

Thiamin (vitamin B_1) deficiency selectively affects parts of the brain responsible for laying down new memories. It usually occurs in severe alcoholics who drink all their meals and have limited caloric intake from other sources. To protect against Amnestic Disorder, alcoholics are often automatically given thiamin injections in emergency rooms. Thiamin deficiency can also occur in people suffering from severe malnutrition because of starvation or stomach cancer. Although prompt administration of vitamins can result in some improvement, complete return of memory is rare.

Substances Causing Amnesia

Heavy drinking and sedatives can temporarily impair the laying down of memory, thus leading to "blackouts." For this reason, using sedatives to help you relax or sleep the night before an examination is unwise since it may impair your ability to remember what you have been studying.

DIFFERENTIAL DIAGNOSIS

Delirium and Dementia both cause severe cognitive problems affecting multiple intellectual abilities, but there are several ways to distinguish them. The most important difference is the clarity of the person's consciousness. People with Delirium act as if they are in a cloud—it is almost impossible to sustain more than a brief conversation with them without getting the feeling that they have drifted off elsewhere. In contrast, even though the person with Dementia may not know what day it is or even recognize who you are, he is able to remain relatively alert and will stay connected with you during a conversation. Another important difference is in the way the symptoms change over time. A person with Delirium often has a fluctuating Jekyll-and-Hyde quality—whereas the cognitive problems in Dementia are more stable from day to day.

Delirium often occurs on top of a preexisting long-standing Dementia. People with Dementia are the most likely to develop Delirium when confronted with a new infection (urinary tract or respiratory); dehydration; metabolic or electrolyte imbalance; or a change in medication. Therefore, if a loved one with a relatively stable pattern of deficits suddenly becomes severely confused, agitated, and disoriented, you should not necessarily chalk it up to a bad day. A medical evaluation and review of medications may help to determine what may have precipitated the new impairments.

One must also be on the lookout for other psychiatric conditions that compromise intellectual performance. Major Depressive Disorder (page 33) especially in the elderly can produce severe cognitive impairments that are virtually identical to a Dementia (in fact this is called "pseudodementia"). Successful treatment with antidepressant medications can sometimes result in a complete resolution of what appeared to be an irreversible Dementia. There are several clues to help differentiate depression and Dementia. Are depressive symptoms present? People with pseudodementia are also much more likely to be distressed by their cognitive problems than those with Dementia, who are often blasé or unaware of the extent of the difficulties. A careful history usually indicates that the person functioned well cognitively prior to the depression, as opposed to the typically gradual onset of symptoms in Dementia. Sometimes, however, the late onset of a first depression is a signal that the person may ultimately go on to have a full-blown Dementia in several years.

Other disorders that can negatively affect cognitive performance include Schizophrenia (page 313), Bipolar Disorder (page 61), Attention-Deficit/ Hyperactivity Disorder (page 387), and Mental Retardation (page 355).

AM I OKAY?

All of us lose something cognitively as we age and start having trouble remembering everyday names, facts, faces, and words the way we could when we were younger. This is no more abnormal than having to wear reading glasses. In order to make a diagnosis of any of the cognitive conditions covered in this chapter, the difficulties must be abnormal for your age and they must significantly interfere with your ability to function in your usual activities. For example, the memory problems are so bad that you keep losing your wallet and repeatedly burn dinner because the food is left in the oven. Lost skill in calculation makes it impossible for you to balance your checkbook. Things that you have done for years at work now seem unfamiliar and beyond your grasp. Your ability to organize and plan activities is so compromised that you can no longer manage your finances. Your word-finding problems are so frequent that your speech becomes halting or hard for others to understand. You keep getting lost when driving to what were familiar locations. If you are in doubt about what is "normal" for your age and are having serious problems, a medical examination and neuropsychological assessment may be helpful.

TREATMENT OPTIONS

Delirium is a medical emergency that requires immediate efforts at diagnosis and treatment. More often than not a combination of factors is involved—each of which must be addressed in order to bring the Delirium under control and prevent further brain damage. If the problem is caused by a substance intoxication or a medication side effect, the substance should be stopped or the medication reduced under close medical supervision. Substance withdrawal symptoms need to be treated in a detoxification program or hospital. If the problem is infection, it should be treated aggressively with the appropriate antibiotic or antiviral medication. Dehydration and malnutrition must be reversed. And always consider the possibility of head trauma.

People with Dementia are sensitive to daily stresses (emotional, environmental, and physical) and are especially prone to develop Delirium. The best "treatment" for Delirium is to prevent its occurrence. Delirium prevention includes making sure that people with Dementia are healthy, well nourished, and well hydrated; live in a quiet, well-lit, uncrowded, safe, well-structured environment with orienting clues such as windows, clocks, calendars, and pictures of family members; and take their medications regularly and at doses that reflect age, size, medical status, and other medicines that are also being taken. Checking orientation on a regular basis helps to ensure that Delirium will be picked up early and treated before it gets out of hand. If the patient's agitation, confusion, or distorted thinking might lead to self-harm, it is necessary to ensure a safe environment and to use medications. Depending on the situation, antipsychotic medications or antianxiety medications are most helpful.

Although Dementia and Amnestic Disorder are less likely to be reversible, it is no less important to track down their cause. Timely intervention is needed to prevent a reversible Dementia from turning into an irreversible one and to reduce the further progression of cognitive impairments. Although there are no treatments for the underlying cause of Alzheimer's Dementia, there are two medications (Cognex and Aricept) that may be helpful in temporarily slowing the loss of memory. There is also some evidence that high doses of vitamin E may reduce damage to brain cells. Researchers are currently hard at work in their search for a medication that will address the underlying cause and stop this ravaging disease in its tracks.

A number of treatments are available to address the associated symptoms that often go along with the Dementia. Depression is an especially common complication and can be markedly improved with antidepressant medication, usually at much lower doses than used in younger and healthier patients (see page 49). Although people with Dementia often have trouble falling asleep and staying asleep, sleeping pills should be used not at all or only very briefly because of their potential for triggering memory loss, falls, or Delirium. The use of low doses of trazodone (a very sedating antidepressant) seems to be the least risky of the available choices. The agitation and psychotic symptoms that sometimes accompany Dementia respond well to antipsychotic medications. Mood stabilizing drugs are also sometimes useful in reducing aggressive behavior and agitation.

The often-forgotten victim of Dementia is the person who is responsible for taking care of the minute-to-minute needs of the patient, which can become a year-after-year drudgery. Often it feels as if you are losing your loved one a day and one step at a time. Not surprisingly, there is a high rate of depression among family members and other caregivers—even higher than for those taking care of relatives who have cancer. The tasks can be thankless, exhausting, frustrating, and sometimes even frightening. It is hard enough sometimes having to change the diapers of a frisky infant—imagine what it is like to deal with a two-hundred-pounder who is incontinent and flailing out at anyone who is bothering him. It is no surprise that the three symptoms most disturbing to family members taking care of loved ones with Dementia are violence, memory loss, and incontinence.

Providing education can teach specific techniques and reduce the sense of isolation and guilt about never doing enough. Understanding what is causing the behavior and what might be done to help alleviate it give the caregiver a greater sense of control over what is otherwise an overwhelming situation. There are a variety of ways of improving the environment that may enhance cognitive functioning, improve quality of life, and reduce the risk of agitation. Try to establish stable routines and work around any particular times of day that seem to be consistently difficult. Provide frequent snacks and drinks. Be sensitive to bathroom needs. Use Velcro to simplify dressing. Make the living area dangerproof.

It may be useful to develop an activity program that emphasizes pleasant activities. Even if the person's cerebral cortex is not working very well, he can still enjoy most of the basic pleasures—music, dancing, pets, TV, sorting coins, having a massage or perm can all be relaxing. Reassure and soothe to prevent difficulties and distract and redirect once they begin. Find helpful substitutes for troublesome behaviors. Create a safe walking track for pacers, give a job sweeping to someone who is agitated, encourage a rummager to sort laundry. Break all tasks into the simplest component parts and encourage repetition of a few familiar activities. Never expect too much and don't be too put off by embarrassing behavior that doesn't really cause that much trouble or expose anyone to danger.

Difficulties and misunderstandings often occur because the patient has problems communicating. For example, he may reach out, flail, or scream in frustration because he has no other way of expressing his need to go to the bathroom. Developing simple signals for the most important functions can sometimes make a world of difference. Communication can be improved if the focus is on the essentials. Don't argue or get frustrated if your loved one blames you for not visiting enough even if you have been there every day for the past seven years. Instead, say how nice it is to be together now. Keep identifying yourself and providing orienting cues. Always give the patient room, approach from the front, keep eye contact, and provide a gentle touch. Speak slowly, simply, and at a volume the patient can hear. Structure simple questions so that a yes or no or nods will suffice as answers. Learn shared gestures that can substitute for words. Avoid painful topics, conflictual themes, or confrontations.

It is especially important always to keep in mind that the indifferent, difficult, or combative behavior comes from the disease and is not a willful act on the part of the patient. Support groups are a very helpful forum for family and caregivers to meet and share their experiences with others who are grappling with the same problems. If families are given lots of support, some people can be handled at home who would otherwise require nursing home care.

Suggested Additional Readings

The 36-Hour Day: A Family Guide to Caring for Persons
    with Alzheimer's Disease, Related Dementing Illnesses
    and Memory Loss in Later Life
    Nancy L. Mace and Peter V. Rabins
    Warner Books, 1994

Alzheimer's & Dementia: Questions You Have . . . Answers You Need
    Jennifer Hay
    Peoples Medical Society, 1996

The Vanishing Mind: A Practical Guide to Alzheimer's Disease
    and Other Dementias
    Leonard L. Heston and June A. White
    W. H. Freeman, 1991

Where to Go for Help
(Self-help, support, for more information)

Alzheimer's Disease and Related Disorders Association

919 North Michigan Avenue
Suite 1000
Chicago, IL 60611-1676
(312) 335-8700
(800) 272-3900
(800) 572-6037 (in Illinois)
E-mail: info@alz.org
Web: http://www.alz.org/

Stroke Connection—Council on Stroke—American Heart Association
(information for stroke survivors and referrals to support groups)

7320 Greenville Avenue
Dallas, TX 75231
(214) 373-6300
(800) 553-6321
FAX: (214) 706-5231
E-mail: strokaha@amhrt.org
Web: http://www.amhrt.org/

National Stroke Association

96 Inverness Drive East
Suite I
Englewood, CO 80112-5112
(303) 649-9299
FAX: (303) 649-1328
E-mail: info@stroke.org
Web: http://www.stroke.org/

The Brain Injury Association, Inc.

105 North Alfred Street
Alexandria, VA 22314
(703) 236-6000
FAX: (703) 236-6001
Web: http://www.biausa.org/

CHAPTER 17

DELAYS IN DEVELOPMENT

The maturation of the human brain is so remarkably complicated a process that it is something of an evolutionary miracle that it ever turns out right. Undoubtedly, nature is a brilliantly successful engineer, but also a very implausible one. Brain development requires billions of intricate synaptic interactions coordinated temporally and geographically in a tightly choreographed neuronal dance. Murphy's law would suggest that lots of things should go wrong in anything so complicated. No government advisory committee sitting in judgment would have approved the feasibility of these blueprints. Nonetheless, natural selection developed these specifications and they usually work beautifully to produce a well-functioning brain.

Unfortunately, however, things do not always go so smoothly. This chapter describes several of the scenarios in which brain development goes awry. Problems in brain development can result in Mental Retardation, which affects virtually all aspects of the child's cognitive function. In Autistic Disorder, basic psychological functions, like social interaction and language, are not just delayed—they are severely distorted. At the other end of the severity spectrum, the Learning Disorders reflect a compartmentalized wiring problem that usually affects just one specific mode of information processing, leaving overall intellectual and emotional functioning intact (the excellent student with exceptionally poor spelling skills).

MENTAL RETARDATION

A diagnosis of Mental Retardation requires that the child's "intelligence quotient" (IQ) be significantly below normal. Measuring IQ is a highly controversial topic that raises many educational, clinical, cultural, and political questions for which there are no simple answers. IQ testing is so widely performed because it identifies special cognitive problems and gifts, predicts performance, sets reasonable expectations, and determines special educational needs at both ends of the intelligence spectrum. Intelligence testing also gains credibility because IQ is about 70 percent predicted by genetic endowment, can be measured in very young children, and is remarkably consistent throughout life. That's the good news. The bad news is that IQ testing can be culturally biased, influenced by motivation and test-taking skills, and does not necessarily correlate with the other adaptive and social skills that are also very important in life.

An IQ score of 70 is used in DSM-IV, and by most experts in the field, to separate normal from below normal intelligence. This suggested boundary must be put into context and not be given more veneration than it deserves. First off, to be meaningful the IQ test must be administered in a one-to-one situation because group-administered tests are much less valid. Second, even under ideal testing conditions, IQ scores are considered to be accurate only to within five points up or down (for example, a measured IQ of 61 is in "reality" somewhere in the range of 56 to 66). Thus the lower cut-off for defining Mental Retardation really ranges from 65 to 75 and should take into account how well the person is adapting to the various situational demands of life. A child with an IQ score of 74 who has considerable trouble getting dressed, finding his way home from school, and knowing how to interact appropriately with peers might qualify for a diagnosis of Mental Retardation that would allow him to qualify for treatment services. The diagnosis makes much less sense for someone with an IQ of 66 but good adaptive functioning. Third, many people score well below their real intelligence if the language in which the test is administered is not their first language, if they have received a substandard education or failed to work in school; if they have specific learning disabilities for reading, writing, or arithmetic; if they have deficits in communication or eye-hand coordination; or if they are poor test takers out of indifference or anxiety. Remember that a low score on an IQ test is not by itself enough to justify a diagnosis of Mental Retardation. There must also be clearly demonstrated impairments in the person's adaptive capacity. Does he have problems in communication, self-care, school performance, social skills, and in dealing with the complexities of everyday life?

According to the diagnostic manual, your child has Mental Retardation if:
- Your child has an IQ of approximately 70 to 75 or below as measured on an IQ test that has been administered by a psychologist.
- Your child's low intelligence has made it difficult for him or her to communicate or interact with others, take care of himself or herself, do things on his or her own, work, study, or spend leisure time.

DESCRIPTION

The diagnosis of Mental Retardation does not necessarily last a lifetime. Although the IQ score is not likely to change much, the person's level of adaptive functioning may very well improve with age and with the changing demands in different parts of the life cycle. As time goes by, the person's IQ remains below 70, but his adaptive skills may be enhanced through education, rehabilitation, maturation, and a change in the tasks required by the environment. Someone who could not handle the academic work required in school may do well working in a factory or gas station. In fact, nearly two thirds of children diagnosed with mild Mental Retardation (IQ 55 to 70) no longer qualify for the diagnosis by the time they reach adulthood because of a significant improvement in their adaptive aptitudes.

The evaluation of adaptive functioning is difficult and changes as the person grows up and faces different challenges. The manner in which someone copes with the dynamic demands of life is influenced not only by mental capacity but also by educational background, level of motivation, and personality characteristics. It may be useful to have the child tested with one or another of the several available standardized assessments that have been designed to measure adaptive capacity and social skills. In creating a composite of adaptive performance, it is also useful to gather as much information as possible from all sources, including teacher evaluations, parental interviews, and medical history. Remember that adaptive ability will change and probably will improve with time.

The etiology of Mental Retardation is heterogeneous. Even after thorough evaluations, the specific cause is never determined in about 40 percent of cases—especially for milder retardation. Mild retardation runs in families and probably results from both biological and environmental influences in proportions that are unknown and controversial. There is an ongoing, often bitter, educational and political debate concerning the degree to which the low IQ scores in mild Mental Retardation may reflect culturally biased testing, poor education, economic and social deprivation, reduced early verbal stimulation, inherent biological factors, or some combination of all of these. Mild Mental Retardation may not be diagnosed until the child has reached school age and faces the increased intellectual demands of the classroom. Documenting the diagnosis is often necessary for the child to acquire the special services that may help improve both academic and other adaptive functioning.

In contrast, the more severe forms of Mental Retardation are usually detected during infancy or early childhood, are more likely to have a clear etiology, and are less subject to controversy regarding the potential for subtle cultural biases. The most commonly encountered predisposing factors to the more severe forms of Mental Retardation are genetic or chromosomal abnormalities and perinatal problems (such as lead poisoning and head trauma).

The most frequent chromosomal cause of Mental Retardation is Down syndrome resulting from the presence of an extra twenty-first chromosome. Persons with Down syndrome usually have moderate levels of Mental Retardation as well as a broad, flat face, slanted eyes, a short neck, low-set ears, and an enlarged tongue. The incidence of this congenital disorder increases with maternal age from one in one thousand in young women to about one in forty in women over the age of forty. Down syndrome can be diagnosed prenatally by identifying the abnormal chromosome in samples of fetal cells taken from amniotic fluid.

Fragile X syndrome is the second most common identifiable genetic cause of moderate and severe forms of Mental Retardation, occurring in approximately one in one thousand males. Because this is caused by a fragile site on the end of the X chromosome, females are partially protected by virtue of their having a second "backup" X chromosome, as compared to males, who only have one copy.

Individuals with Mental Retardation can and do experience any and all of the problems we have described elsewhere in this book and a thorough evaluation must therefore include a psychiatric as well as a medical assessment. The rates of psychiatric illness among those with Mental Retardation are about the same as in the general population and the treatments are also the same. There may be a greater incidence of brief reactive agitation or transient psychotic symptoms when the person with Mental Retardation is faced with an interpersonal loss, a change in environment, overstimulation (noise or crowding), or any other stressor that requires a complex response beyond his adaptive capacity. Fortunately, these episodes are usually short-lived and respond to structure, simplifying the problems, improvements in the environment, reassurance and support, and medication.

Whether the Mental Retardation is of the milder less clearly understood form or is the product of a serious birth defect, the course and outcome can be very much influenced by providing appropriate educational opportunities as well as parental and social support.

Differential Diagnosis

Children with Mental Retardation have a general impairment in intellectual functioning that affects all aspects of learning. When the impairment is limited only to a specific area, like reading, writing, or mathematical ability, the child is considered to have a specific learning disability (page 366). Children diagnosed with Autistic Disorder (page 361) have developmental problems in a number of areas, usually, but not always, including intellectual functioning. Autistic Disorder differs from Mental Retardation in that social and language development is not just delayed but is distorted. Whereas a ten-year-old child with Mental Retardation may act as if he had a chronological age of three when interacting with a stranger, the child with Autistic Disorder acts in a bizarre way, like repeatedly reciting train schedules, oblivious to the disinterest of the listener. Most children with Autistic Disorder also have Mental Retardation and they should be given both diagnoses. Most children with Mental Retardation do not have Autistic Disorder.

Treatment Options

Perhaps the most important goal of treatment is "normalization"—providing an environment, living conditions, educational, occupational, and social opportunities that are, as much as possible, close to the norms of mainstream society. Historically, people with Mental Retardation have often been abused and neglected. The ill-treatment stemmed from the pessimistic view that they were hopelessly untreatable and difficult to manage.

They were warehoused in understaffed institutions where they languished with virtually nothing to do and were often overmedicated to make their behavior more manageable.

Several factors turned this around in the 1960s and 1970s. The civil rights movement sent the loud and clear message that all forms of segregation are both unjust and harmful. Parents' organizations became more powerful and filed lawsuits on behalf of maltreated children. People became more aware of the severely negative effects of chronic institutionalization. Finally, research showed that providing stimulating educational, vocational, and other opportunities can have a profound positive effect on the course of Mental Retardation. Even people with more severe Mental Retardation can often under the proper circumstances learn to participate in self-care, food preparation, and leisure activities and can enjoy a significantly improved quality of life.

Each and every person with Mental Retardation needs to be carefully evaluated so that his living situation, vocational opportunities, and leisure activities can be tailored in accordance with intellectual capacity, emotional needs, and personal preferences. Many behavioral problems (aggression, frustration, withdrawal) result from being in environments that are either too noisy, overtaxing, and overstimulating or conversely too boring, repetitive, and understimulating.

One of the main objectives in treatment is to provide the person with new skills to improve his ability to interact with others and to take more control of his life and environment. These might include educational programs that concentrate on developing leisure skills (teaching the person how to play group sports and games); self-help skills (how to cook and go to the bank); communication skills (using gestures to augment speech); and social skills (making conversation).

Even under the best of circumstances, people with Mental Retardation can have occasional behavioral disturbances particularly when they are under stress and have to deal with overly complex problems. The first step in management is to simplify and structure their environment. Behavior modification techniques are also very effective in controlling aggression, self-injury, property destruction, and noncompliance. Desirable behavior can be promoted and suppression of negative behavior rewarded through positive reinforcement (gold stars, verbal approval, awarding of points or tokens that can be exchanged for candy). Problematic behavior can be discouraged through negative reinforcement (time out, no TV, loss of previously earned rewards). Distraction and getting away from conflicts are very important ways of defusing difficult situations.

The role of medication in the treatment of people with Mental Retardation is controversial. The deplorable history of indiscriminate overuse of antipsychotic medication in institutional settings for the purpose of manageability has resulted in the pendulum swinging too far in the opposite direction, leading many clinicians and families to avoid medication at all costs. This is unfortunate since it is clear that medicine is often necessary, at least from time to time, and that each person should be evaluated on an individual basis to determine whether and which medication may be potentially helpful. It has been estimated that about 30 percent of people with Mental Retardation suffer from a psychiatric disorder, like Major Depressive Disorder (page 33), Anxiety Disorder (see Chapters 3, 4, and 5), Attention-Deficit/Hyperactivity Disorder (page 387, and Brief Psychotic Disorder (page 311). These conditions should not be explained away as unavoidable consequences of the Mental Retardation. Instead, they should be addressed and treated in their own right in the same way one would treat a person without Mental Retardation.

Medications are also used specifically to treat the aggressiveness and self-injurious behavior that occasionally occurs in people with Mental Retardation. Although conventional antipsychotic medications (Haldol and Thorazine) are most commonly used, the availability of the newer atypical antipsychotics (Risperdal, Zyprexa, Seroquel, Clozapine) shows great promise. Because of the potential side effects, medication should be used judiciously in the lowest possible doses and, if possible, for limited periods of time.

AUTISTIC DISORDER
(PERVASIVE DEVELOPMENTAL DISORDER)

This is undoubtedly one of the most heartbreaking problems ever to confront a family. The birth of a child is usually the happiest and most expectant of moments—unless the baby fails to develop the usual behaviors that will attach him to the world. There is no social smile, no desire to cuddle or be held, a seeming disinterest in human interaction, and a failure to acknowledge caregivers. It seems as if the baby is in a world of its own, so unresponsive that you wonder if it has been born deaf. Language fails to develop altogether or is much delayed, strange in syntax, and hard to follow. There is a lack of emotional reactivity, spontaneity, and joy. Behaviors are stereotyped, rigid, repetitive, bizarre, and purposeless. It is virtually impossible to communicate in any meaningful way through words, gestures, or expressions. And on top of all this, there is likely to be some Mental Retardation, with about a third of autistic children having an IQ below 50, a third between 50 and 70, and a third with an IQ of 70 or above. Although the child will likely experience some improvement with maturation and intense educational and psychotherapeutic interventions, the quality of his life will always be tragically limited.

When Autistic Disorder was first described in the medical literature more than a half century ago, there was a good deal of nonsense written about its possibly being caused by cold or indifferent mothering. We now understand that autism is completely the result of a failure of normal brain development. The "cold" mothering that was observed was an understandable result, not at all the cause, of having a baby who is cold and indifferent and impossible to cuddle and nurture. Autistic Disorder is more common in males than females, with a ratio of about five to one. Thankfully, Autistic Disorder is rare—two to five cases per ten thousand children.

According to the diagnostic manual, your child has an Autistic Disorder if:
- Your child has very serious problems interacting appropriately in social situations. For example, he or she:
  (1) fails to develop socially appropriate nonverbal behaviors such as eye-to-eye gaze, facial expressions, and body language
  (2) fails to develop friendships with other children
  (3) is uninterested in sharing with other people
  (4) does not develop a give-and-take of emotions
- Your child has very serious problems communicating. For example, he or she:
  (1) has a delay in, or total lack of, spoken language
  (2) is unable to start or sustain conversations
  (3) tends to use the same word over and over again or use words in a strange way
- Your child's behavior, interests, and activities are repetitive and very limited in range. For example, he or she:
  (1) becomes preoccupied with one topic or activity to the exclusion of virtually everything else
  (2) requires that the environment be organized according to a rigid routine

(3) engages in repetitive motor mannerisms—for example, hand or finger flapping or twisting, or complex whole body movements

(4) focuses on parts of objects rather than the whole

• These problems started in infancy or very early childhood.

_____

Description

Individuals with Autistic Disorder exhibit severe and sustained developmental impairments that start shortly after birth and remain profoundly disabling throughout life. The child is disinterested in social interactions, indifferent to human warmth and affection, and rarely takes notice of other children. He is unable to form peer relationships, seldom engages in play with children, and prefers solitary games that involve other people only to the extent they serve as a tool or aid. He may view adults as interchangeable or be excessively clinging to a specific individual. He avoids eye contact, rarely smiles, has few facial expressions or gestures, and expresses little or no emotion. Older individuals with Autistic Disorder may come to have more interest in social interaction, but they remain strange, lack interpersonal understanding, and have difficulty respecting other people's boundaries.

There is little attempt to compensate for a lack of spoken language with gesturing and other modes of nonverbal communication. If the child does develop speech, it may consist mostly of an idiosyncratic repetition of words or phrases, with odd pitch and rhythm, strange grammatical structure, or the use of made-up words. Only those caregivers who are most accustomed to the child's style of communicating will be really good at understanding it, and even they will often have difficulty. The child also has trouble understanding the language of others and often does not understand directions, questions, or jokes.

The most frequent behavioral stereotypes are constantly repetitive rocking, clapping, swaying, finger flicking, and odd hand movements—done over and over and over again. Forms of self-mutilation (head banging and wrist biting) are present in severe cases. There may be a preoccupation with a few areas of very specific interest such as baseball statistics, train schedules, memorizing phone numbers, stacking toys, or mimicking the actions of someone on television. He will often recite this information numerous times, regardless of its lack of relevance to the situation. *Idiot savant* skills may very rarely be present. These individuals can perform extraordinary, but very circumscribed feats of memory, calculation, drawing, or music, but remain at the Mental Retardation level of intelligence for all other cognitive abilities. This is a kind of Learning Disorder in reverse.

A person with Autistic Disorder is ultrasensitive and resistant to environmental changes and will insist that things be done repetitively following just exactly the same routine day after day for an entire lifetime. He eats only a few select foods prepared and served in a particular way at a particular time on a particular dish. The routine may include an obsessive attachment to a specific inanimate object, such as a blanket, a piece of string, or a rubber band. He may be fascinated with moving objects and spend endless hours turning a light switch on and off, spinning wheels, opening and closing doors, or watching an electric fan. He becomes agitated if any deviation occurs from the usual pattern. This problem was poignantly illustrated in the movie *Rain Man* in the scene in which the Dustin Hoffman character becomes extremely agitated about the prospect that the pancakes will arrive on the table before the syrup.

Asperger's Disorder is a milder variant of Autistic Disorder. It has similar social and behavioral problems, but the child preserves significantly more language, cognitive development, and age-appropriate self-help skills. (Although commonly assumed to have Autistic Disorder, the character portrayed in *Rain Man* suffered from Asperger's Disorder given his superior language skills.) Even though individuals with Asperger's Disorder experience great difficulty with peer interaction, they often develop close relationships with family members.

DIFFERENTIAL DIAGNOSIS

Autistic Disorder and Mental Retardation are not at all synonymous. Like autistic children, children with Mental Retardation often have problems with the delayed development of language and often do not know how to act appropriately in social situations. They do not, however, have the characteristically odd pattern of interactions, behavior, and communication. On the other hand, most autistic children (75 to 80 percent) do also suffer from Mental Retardation and require the services provided for this.

Schizophrenia (page 313) most often begins in adolescence or adulthood whereas Autistic Disorder begins in infancy. Both disorders are characterized by strange behaviors, bizarre preoccupations, and extreme social withdrawal, but children with Schizophrenia also have delusions and hallucinations, both of which are absent in Autistic Disorder.

Am I Okay?

There is great variety in the normal distribution of developmental skills. Children smile, walk, talk, wave, kiss, and interact with peers at very different paces. Don't jump to the conclusion that your child is autistic if any one or all of these skills takes a bit longer than usual to develop or your child seems to be a bit behind the rest of the play group. Most kids will catch up and eventually do just fine. It is also not uncommon for normal children to become transiently fixated on one or two things, such as singing the jingle from a particular commercial or wanting to eat cereal from a certain Mickey Mouse bowl. Mercifully these temporary passions will usually soon pass. Some normal children are just not by nature very affectionate and cuddly—this does not mean they are autistic. Autistic Disorder describes really marked delays in developmental milestones combined with severe behavioral oddities and a lack of communication skills. Social interaction in autism is so impaired that the child lacks any substantial interest or enjoyment in relationships with others. The repetitive behavior patterns occur over and over and for a lifetime, almost to the exclusion of all other things.

Treatment Options

Unfortunately, there are no treatments available that will predictably bring an autistic child out of his shell. Treatments tend to focus on reducing the harmful behaviors (like self-injury or aggressive outbursts) and educational efforts promoting learning and language development so that the child can function to the best of his abilities.

Because of the wide individual variability in autism, special educational opportunities must be specifically tailored to each child's strengths and weaknesses. Structured learning settings help reduce the child's retreat into solitary activities. A predictable schedule enhances the child's feeling of control. Language teaching focuses on the practical—how to effectively communicate with others to get needs met rather than the abstract study of vocabulary and grammar. Computer learning may be helpful. Alternative modes of communication can also be taught, such as sign language or gestures. Social skills training focuses on real world situations such as how to ask for change from a cashier or how to conduct a simple conversation with a new friend. Behavior therapy is used to reduce problematic behaviors.

Medication may be needed if the child has violent temper tantrums, aggressive outbursts, hyperactivity, and self-injurious behavior such as head banging or picking at parts of the body. Antipsychotic medications are most helpful. Since the frequency of and predilection to such behaviors change over the course of Autistic Disorder, the medication therapy should be viewed as a temporary measure and should periodically be reevaluated (perhaps every six months) to see if it remains necessary.

Medication used for Obsessive-Compulsive Disorder (page 101), like Luvox, Anafranil, Prozac, Zoloft, and Paxil, can be helpful in reducing the repetitive stereotyped movements that often go along with Autistic Disorder, suggesting that there may be some similarity between these behaviors and obsessions/compulsions. Unfortunately, these medications seem to be effective only in adolescents or adults.

LEARNING DISORDERS

Among all the problems in the human condition that are described in this book, the Learning Disorders constitute by far the most modern and recent acquisition. It is very safe to say that no human being ever had a disorder in reading, writing, or arithmetic until as recently as fifteen thousand or so years ago for the very simple reason that man had not until then gotten around to inventing these fine arts. In contrast, it is quite likely that most of the other problems described in this book originated during the infancy or early childhood of our species.

The Learning Disorders are not psychiatric problems and are not often treated by mental health clinicians. Instead, they are within the province of the educational system. Nonetheless, many children seen in mental health settings (especially those with Attention Deficit or Conduct Disorder) are especially likely also to have a learning disability that may have an impact on their psychiatric status. The Learning Disorders are included in DSM-IV only to encourage mental health workers to be comprehensive in their evaluations.

Another fascinating, and in some ways telling, aspect of the Learning Disorders is the selection of the specific skills whose deficit has been the subject of most attention. Clearly, the choice of reading, writing, and arithmetic suggests that these abilities are considered most fundamental to "civilization," literacy, and proper schooling. One of the authors who gets on reasonably well with these three "R's" feels quite grateful that there are no defined Learning Disorders for deficits in musical skills, drawing, map reading, woodworking, changing flat tires, or putting together the complex jumble of parts that needs assembling whenever you buy a gadget in a department store. For whatever reason, our society provides its highest rewards and sets its clearest standards for the left brain cognitive activities. We demand that these be present at least to the point of literacy for someone to get promoted from grade to grade. We have very systematic screening for these skills so that problems are identified by the time a child reaches the second or third grade. In contrast, the right brain skills, which are still very important in day-to-day life (and were ever so much more important to survival before civilization), are now relegated to a somewhat secondary position. If mechanical skills were equally emphasized in elementary education (as perhaps they should be), a different group of children might be diagnosed as having learning disabilities.

According to the diagnostic manual, your child has a Learning Disorder if:
- Your child's ability to read, do math, or write is far below what would be expected given his or her age, IQ, and schooling. This should be confirmed by a standardized test individually administered by a special education teacher or psychologist.
- Your child's learning problems have a significantly negative impact on school performance.

DESCRIPTION

Approximately 5 percent of students in public schools are identified as having some type of Learning Disorder. The diagnosis is usually made in the early grades of elementary school when the specific deficits in acquiring basic skills first become apparent. Learning Disorders may not be identified until the later grades in children with especially high IQs whose intelligence may provide something of a buffer until they are faced with more advanced learning tasks.

The child's ability to acquire and perform the skills of reading, writing, or arithmetic is very significantly below what is expected given his age, measured intelligence, and educational level. Reading Disorder, also known as Dyslexia, is characterized by slow reading speed and problems with comprehension and reading accuracy. Someone with Dyslexia may omit words, reverse letters, or distort meanings. The Disorder of Written Expression is characterized by difficulties with spelling, grammar, and paragraph organization. It is common for someone with this type of Learning Disorder to spend an excessive amount of time on writing assignments with many erasures and rewriting, only to finally turn out a sparse product with numerous errors. Individuals with Mathematics Disorder have problems learning to count, copy numbers, perform simple calculations, and think spatially. They often have difficulty in comprehending or recognizing mathematical symbols and in conceptualizing sets of objects.

Learning Disorders are specific and circumscribed deficits as opposed to Mental Retardation, which includes problems in most of the intellectual functions that reflect general intelligence. It is, however, possible for someone with Mental Retardation also to have a specific Learning Disorder if the deficit in any one area is substantially worse than you would expect given his IQ. The DSM-IV differentiates each Learning Disorder based on the problem area. However, it is important to realize that deficits in more than one skill can occur simultaneously. It is also not uncommon for Learning Disorders to co-occur with other childhood disorders, such as Attention Deficit/Hyperactivity Disorder (page 387) and Conduct Disorder (page 377).

Differential Diagnosis

When a child does poorly on a standardized reading, writing, or mathematics test, all possible causes should be considered before assuming that the problem is a Learning Disorder. For starters, test scores that are significantly below par can result from inadequate schooling, whether it is due to overcrowding, poor teaching, inappropriate classroom placement, or being in an unsafe school environment that is not conducive to learning. Environmental factors such as family disruption or neglect, sleep deprivation, malnutrition, or living in a chaotic neighborhood can also have a negative impact on learning. Children from other cultural or ethnic backgrounds have an obvious disadvantage when taking a test in English. Because hearing or visual impairments can interfere with learning, all children who fall behind in school should be evaluated with audiometric testing and eye charts. Medical problems that affect the brain, such as head trauma or lead poisoning, can sometimes cause a child to have problems in school. Other psychiatric disorders, like Major Depressive Disorder (page 33), Schizophrenia (page 313), Anxiety Disorder (Chapters 3, 4, and 5), and Attention-Deficit/Hyperactivity Disorder (page 387) can interfere with a child's ability to learn effectively.

Am I Okay?

No one is perfect in reading, writing, or arithmetic. Learning Disorders must be differentiated from normal variations in academic achievement as well as from scholastic difficulties due to a lack of educational opportunity, poor motivation, or inadequate teaching. Learning Disorder does not refer to the expectable range of strengths and weaknesses in various school subjects that all of us have. For instance, a child who is a math whiz but relatively less excellent at reading does not have a Reading Disorder. Parents and kids sometimes put too much pressure on themselves to be perfect at everything and may assume that anything less than great performance must constitute a problem.

The recent emphasis on Learning Disorders has been useful in identifying children who require special services in school and who might otherwise fall through the cracks. Early detection and remedial education can help correct many learning disabilities and reduce the child's tendency to become demoralized, feel dumb, have low frustration tolerance, and lose interest in school. However, the label is sometimes loosely applied to children who are doing just fine but not well enough to fill their own or their parents' perfectionist expectations. The diagnosis should be made only after careful individualized testing, especially in borderline cases.

Treatment Options

Learning disabilities usually require intensive educational remediation. Until recently, children with learning problems were often taught in segregated special education classes with the unfortunate side effect of stigmatizing them. Remedial education now uses more of an "inclusion" approach—special education teachers come to the classroom and work with the entire class while devoting special attention to the learning-disabled children.

It is crucial that the teaching approach be flexible and designed to match the strengths and weaknesses of the child. It does not make sense to teach reading by focusing on phonics for a child who has the most difficulty with auditory processing. Educational programs surmount specific processing problems by integrating several sensory modalities simultaneously. For example, the child learning the alphabet would be encouraged to read, feel, speak aloud, write, and mime the letters. Supplementing school by providing a language-rich environment at home can be very helpful for children with reading problems. Reading each day with your child can lead to improved reading skills.

Suggested Additional Readings

Hope for the Families: New Directions for Parents of Persons with Retardation and Other Disabilities
Robert Perske
Abingdon Press, 1981

Leslie's Story: A Book About a Girl with Mental Retardation
Martha McNey and Leslie Fish
Lerner, 1996

Nobody Nowhere: The Extraordinary Autobiography of an Autistic
Donna Williams
Avon Books, 1994

A Parent's Guide to Autism
Charles A. Hart
Pocket Books, 1993

Turning Around the Upside Down Kids: Helping Dyslexic Kids Overcome Their Disorder
Harold N. Levinson, M.D., and Addie Sanders
M. Evans, 1992

Smart but Feeling Dumb: The Challenging New Research on Dyslexia—and How It May Help You
Harold N. Levinson, M.D.
Warner Books, 1994

Where to Go for Help
(Self-help, support, for more information)

The Arc of the United States
(largest advocacy group for individuals
with Mental Retardation)

500 East Border Street
Suite 300
Arlington, TX 76010-7444
(817) 261-6003
FAX: (817) 277-3491
TDD: (817) 277-0553
E-mail: thearc@metronet.com
Web: http://TheArc.org/

National Association for the Dually Diagnosed
(resources for persons with Mental Retardation
and mental illness)

132 Fair Street
Kingston, NY 12401
(914) 331-4336
FAX: (914) 331-4569

Sibling Information Network
(information related to siblings and families of individuals
with developmental disabilities)

c/o A. J. Pappenikou Center
249 Glenbrook Road
U-64
Storrs, CT 06269-2064
(860) 486-4985

National Down Syndrome Society

666 Broadway
Eighth Floor
New York, NY 10012-2317
(212) 460-9330
(800) 221-4602
Web: http://www.ndss.org/

National Down Syndrome Congress
(support, information, and advocacy for families affected by Down syndrome)

1605 Chantilly Drive
Suite 250
Atlanta, GA 30324-3269
(800) 232-NDSC
(404) 633-1555
FAX: (404) 633-2817

The National Fragile X Foundation
(provides information, phone support, referrals)

1441 York Street
Suite 303
Denver, CO 80206-2127
(800) 688-8765
(303) 333-6155
FAX: (303) 333-4369

FRAXA Research Foundation
(provides literature on Fragile X syndrome)

P.O. Box 935
West Newbury, MA 01985
(508) 462-1990
FAX: (508) 463-9985
E-mail: fraxa@seacoast.com
Web: http://www.FRAXA.org/

Learning Disabilities Association of America
(information and referrals)

4156 Library Road
Pittsburgh, PA 15234
(412) 341-1515

TALK (Taking Action Against Language Disorders for Kids)
(resource network for parents of children
with speech and language impairments)

Donna Lane
Bend, OR 97701
(503) 389-0004

Autism Society of America
(education and advocacy group)

7910 Woodmont Avenue
Suite 650
Bethesda, MD 20814
(301) 657-0881
(800) 3-AUTISM (information and referral only)
FAX: (301) 657-0869
Web: http://www.autism-society.org/

Autism Network International
(autistic-run self-help and advocacy organization)

P.O. Box 448
Syracuse, NY 13210-0448
(315) 476-2462 (long-distance calls will be returned collect)
FAX: (315) 425-1978
E-mail: jisincla@mailbox.syr.edu
Web: http://www.students.uiuc.edu/~bordner/ani.html

Center for the Study of Autism
(provides information about autism)

P.O. Box 4538
Salem, OR 97302
Web: http://www.autism.org/

Asperger Syndrome Support Group
(online support network for
parents of children with Asperger's Disorder)

E-mail:bkirby914@aol.com
Web: http://www.udel.edu/bkirby/asperger

CHAPTER 18

CHILDHOOD BEHAVIOR
PROBLEMS

Puppies are playful—whether they be puppy dogs, puppy whales, puppy dolphins, puppy elephants, puppy humans, or the puppy members of most of the other higher species. The behavior of juveniles is always more active, disruptive, law breaking, and risk taking than it will be when they grow up and eventually wise up. Particularly, this is true for young males, who across almost all species earn a well-deserved reputation for rambunctiousness and troublemaking. The disruptive behaviors described in this chapter go well beyond normal mischief and carry serious and destructive consequences for the child, his family, and the larger society.

Nurture and nature both play a role in either discouraging or encouraging disruptive behavior. Young male elephants on one of the African game preserves were recently found to be teasing, bullying, torturing, and sometimes even killing white rhinos for no apparent reason other than the raw fun of it. This was surprising because elephants are usually among the best behaved of animals, accustomed to comporting themselves with punctilious manners and exquisite discretion. The explanation for their unusual behavior provides a fascinating illustration of how social organization helps to keep us all in line. It happens that the young bucks in question had just been moved from another game preserve because it had become overcrowded. In the process, they had been inadvertently removed from the tutelage and social restraint usually provided by the senior bulls and the wise matriarchs. Although previously well behaved, the sudden lack of structure allowed the youngsters to act like juvenile delinquents off the set of *West Side Story.*

The tendency toward misbehavior also has strong biological roots. The proclivity for male disruptiveness is probably mediated mostly through testosterone. Shortly after birth, males across most species display much more exploratory, risk-taking, and aggressive behavior—so much so, that they are much more likely than females to be killed off before adulthood by predators or by their own kind. And within the brotherhood of any given species, individual males are born with marked differences in aggressiveness that determine their place in the dominance hierarchy. All of this seems to be equally true among humans, who have great innate variability in aggressive and exploratory tendencies. Early differences in aggressiveness measured in infancy remain pretty good predictors of how the child will turn out later in adolescence and adulthood—although most people do quiet down at least a bit with aging.

Nature and nurture interact. Just as with the delinquent elephants, the presence or lack of parental and social structure can play an important role. At the margins, appropriate discipline influences whether a high-spirited human youngster eventually becomes the socialized leader of the tribe (or corporation); the unsocialized leader of an outcast gang; a solitary rogue criminal; or the early victim of fatal violence.

All of this has recently been made even more complicated by two very powerful social forces that seem to increase the rates of behavioral disturbance among the young. The first is the rapid decline of the moderating influences exerted by the family. During the first half of this century, the development of extraordinarily convenient means of travel and long-distance communication resulted in a remarkable job mobility that virtually eliminated the extended family as a powerful influence in the lives of most children. In the second half of this century, the nuclear family has been threatened by rising divorce rates and an increase in single mothers. There is much truth to the cliché that takes it a village to raise a child. Increasingly, that village has become the teenage peer group or gang rather than a nurturing and controlling family. And the worship of violence on TV does not help teach behavioral restraint.

The second social force is the unprecedented availability of illegal drugs. Substance abuse promotes disruptive behavior in any number of different ways that reinforce one another. The direct intoxicating effect of drugs causes accidents, crimes, assaults, murders, suicides, and every other form of human mayhem. The high cost of drugs requires the young addict to work illegally to earn the money necessary to finance his habit. The high profitability of the drug trade creates a criminal business bureaucracy with job opportunities that are so unbelievably lucrative that ordinary jobs seem almost silly or quaint. Finally, the widespread flouting of the nation's drug prohibitions evaporates any sense of awe or respect that our children might otherwise have had for other laws.

Boys display Conduct Disorder at least three or four times as often as do girls. The rising rates of Conduct Disorder appear to be occurring in both genders, but take different forms in each. Among boys, the most distinctive disruptive acts include violence toward people and the destruction of property. Girls with Conduct Disorder can occasionally also be aggressive or destructive, but most often they indulge in more nonconfrontational behaviors such as lying, running away, truancy, prostitution, unsafe sex, theft, drug use, and drug dealing.

There are two types of disruptive behavior described in DSM-IV: Conduct Disorder and Oppositional Defiant Disorder. These probably form a severity continuum with Conduct Disorder at one extreme end, Oppositional Defiant Disorder in the middle, and nonpathological "boys will be boys" mischief at the mildest end.

CONDUCT DISORDER

Conduct Disorder describes an especially severe, pervasive, and destructive pattern of disruptive behavior that occurs in childhood and adolescence. There may be aggressive actions toward people, cruelty to animals, vandalism, stealing, and serious infractions of rules.

The age of onset of Conduct Disorder may be a tip-off to its ultimate outcome. When the trouble starts early (before age ten), it is usually an indication of a very strong biological contribution to the bad behavior with a family history of criminal activity, violence, and substance use. The child usually has poor peer relationships and acts as a solitary lone wolf, rather than in response to peer pressure. The disruptive behaviors will often include aggression and destructiveness. Early onset predicts a long, difficult, recidivist course that may not respond even to the best parenting, schooling, psychiatric treatment, or correctional interventions. Most of the adults who display Antisocial Personality Disorder (page 228) are drawn from the children who began their careers early. Early onset Conduct Disorder is even more likely to be restricted to boys.

Later onset Conduct Disorder is certainly no cup of tea, but it has a much better chance of being self-limited. The troublesome behavior usually starts between puberty and age sixteen and often represents a departure from family norms. Peer relationships tend to be stronger—unfortunately with the wrong peers—and the delinquent behavior is likely to occur as a group activity. The later the onset the more likely this will be a temporary aberration that the child will outgrow with maturity, different friends, or getting off drugs—although there are some late onset kids who will also go on to disastrous future lives that fill all the criteria for Antisocial Personality Disorder.

A major question challenging the scope of psychiatric diagnosis is whether the detrimental and injurious behaviors that typify Conduct Disorder are better considered to be clinical or criminal—"mad" or "bad." Those who argue that Conduct Disorder should be considered a mental disorder cite evidence that disruptive behavior often has a genetic component and a biological underpinning. Furthermore, Conduct Disorder is often associated with the presence of other mental disorders (Attention-Deficit/Hyperactivity Disorder, Major Depressive Disorder, or Dependence or Abuse), suggesting that it is in some way of the same ilk. It is also associated with drinking, smoking, substance use, and early sexual behavior—all of which can lead to health problems. Conduct Disorder is the most common diagnosis of children and adolescents in both outpatient and hospital mental health settings. Adolescents with Conduct Disorder have a much higher than expected rate of suicide attempts and completed suicides.

Those who argue against "medicalizing" Conduct Disorder believe it is better kept within the moral, legal, or socio-environmental realm. They raise concerns that applying a psychiatric diagnosis and assigning a sick role to such behavior will inappropriately relieve personal and parental responsibility. Proponents of this second position maintain that those who favor "medicalizing" this type of behavior are soft on the individual and also fail to consider the socio-cultural contexts which encourage the egregious behavior. Whatever the cause, society certainly does need to be protected from the actions of raging youth. The diagnosis of Conduct Disorder should not be used as an excuse to reduce anyone's responsibility for doing the right thing, especially until we develop an effective treatment.

According to the diagnostic manual, your child has Conduct Disorder if:
- Your child consistently violates important rules and disregards the basic rights of others, as demonstrated by at least three of the following patterns of behavior:

Aggression toward People and Animals

(1) Your child often bullies, threatens, or intimidates other children.
(2) Your child often starts physical fights.
(3) Your child has used a dangerous weapon in a fight (like a bat, brick, broken bottle, knife, or gun).
(4) Your child has been physically cruel to people.
(5) Your child has been physically cruel to animals.
(6) Your child has forced someone into sexual activity.

Destruction of Property

(7) Your child has deliberately set fires with the intention of causing damage.
(8) Your child has deliberately destroyed other people's property.
(9) Your child has broken into a house, building, or car.

Deceitfulness or Theft

(10) Your child has stolen from other people by mugging, purse snatching, blackmail, or armed robbery.
(11) Your child has committed other forms of theft (e.g., shoplifting, forgery, burglary).
(12) Your child often cons others to obtain goods or favors or to avoid obligations.

Serious Violations of Rules

(13) Your child often stays out at night past curfew without your permission.
(14) Your child runs away from home and stays away overnight.
(15) Your child often skips school.

DESCRIPTION

Individuals with Conduct Disorder exhibit a startling disregard for the feelings, desires, and safety of other people. They misinterpret the actions of others as being much more antagonistic and threatening than is really the case and may strike out preemptively in situations that might really be benign. They callously treat others in an aggressive and malicious manner that they perceive to be justified and reasonable and lack appropriate feelings of remorse for the harm that is inflicted. The aggressive behavior can include bullying, intimidating, initiating physical fights, forcing sexual activity, torturing people and animals, using a weapon, and even homicide.

Destroying property may take the form of fire setting, breaking into houses and cars, smashing car windows, writing graffiti, or defacing school property. Theft and deception are the coin of the realm. The child is a natural-born liar who will say whatever will further his current interests, promising the world to exploit other people's gullibility. The stealing may include shaking down classmates, shoplifting, burglarizing, and mugging, and even armed robbery. The child will do what he wants and violates the rules with defiant insouciance or bland indifference. This usually starts with staying out late at night, running away from home, and truancy, and then progresses to more aggressive and illegal activities.

AM I OKAY?

Occasional mischief making and the testing of limits are a part of childhood. Not every modern-day Huck Finn has Conduct Disorder. The pattern of antisocial behavior must be well beyond the scope, severity, and persistence of what would be considered naughty but normal behavior. The diagnosis of Conduct Disorder may be especially ambiguous in social contexts where aggressive and illegal behaviors are seen as an adaptive rite of passage that may even be essential for self-protection. If everyone else is carrying a weapon, can you stay on the sidelines? The relationship between Conduct Disorder and Substance Abuse is also hard to sort out. Conduct Disorder predisposes to early Substance Abuse, but substance use also predisposes to bad conduct. It is often impossible to determine whether the problem is more the kid or more the drug until the course develops over time. Certainly, Substance Abuse is usually the most feasible treatment target—more likely to respond to our available interventions than are the conduct problems.

It is most likely to be Conduct Disorder when the misbehavior starts early, involves aggression or destruction of property, is done alone and without peer pressure, persists over time, and does not respond to appropriate discipline and structure. A history of antisocial or substance problems in biological relatives also suggests that there may be genetic loading for problem behaviors and that these are not totally explainable based on a difficult environment.

OPPOSITIONAL DEFIANT DISORDER

Oppositional Defiant Disorder (ODD) describes a much less severe and less disruptive level of hostility and defiance. These children have more respect for the rights of others and do not get into serious trouble with the law, but they are a terrific nuisance to their parents, teachers, camp counselors, and others who function in the role of authority figures. Disobedience and verbal aggression are common, but the more antisocial behaviors associated with Conduct Disorder do not occur. Although most children with Conduct Disorder will have previously passed through an oppositional defiant stage before going on to bigger and more outrageous behavior, most children with this diagnosis do not go on to develop Conduct Disorder. Instead, they either outgrow their oppositional behavior or eventually develop a Personality Disorder diagnosis. ODD has a gradual onset usually before age eight and rarely makes an initial appearance if it is not present by early adolescence. These children are likely to have a somewhat earlier use of alcohol, tobacco, and drugs than does the average teenager.

According to the diagnostic manual, your child has Oppositional Defiant Disorder if:
- Your child has a long-standing pattern of negativistic, hostile, and defiant behavior as demonstrated by at least four of the following behaviors.
  (1) Your child often loses his temper.
  (2) Your child often argues with adults.
  (3) Your child often actively defies your requests or rules.
  (4) Your child often deliberately does things to annoy others.
  (5) Your child often blames others for mistakes or misbehavior.
  (6) Your child is often touchy, sensitive, or easily annoyed.
  (7) Your child is often angry and resentful.
  (8) Your child often does things just out of spite or to be vindictive.
- Since all of these can be "normal" during certain ages, they count as evidence for this disorder only if they cause serious problems, persist for at least six months, and are not what would be considered appropriate for your child's developmental stage.

DESCRIPTION

Kids with Oppositional Defiant Disorder engage in a recurrent pattern of disobedient, argumentative, and hostile behavior. The defiant actions include temper tantrums, constant arguments with adults, defying requests, failing to follow rules, intentionally annoying others, blaming others, touchiness, anger, and vindictiveness. The hostility is most often aimed at parents, teachers, or other authority figures and only to a much lesser degree toward peers. The child is stubborn, resistant to compromise, and persistently tests the limits that are set by adults.

A vicious cycle often develops in the relationship between the parent and the child with each side feeding off each other's escalating anger and frustration. Before long, every interaction brings out the worst in everyone. In the midst of oppositional struggling, the child is willing to take a self-defeating stand and sacrifice privileges and love rather than lose the struggle. The parent feels called upon to show who is boss. "Winning" the confrontation becomes a do or die for the child (and perhaps also for the parent) and the process of struggle becomes more important than what is being argued about or preserving harmony in the relationship. No one ever gets to win.

DIFFERENTIAL DIAGNOSIS

Among children referred to mental health professionals, up to one half are evaluated because of aggressive or antisocial behaviors. Since disruptive behavior can be indicative of many other conditions besides Conduct Disorder and Oppositional Defiant Disorder, it is important to first consider possible alternative explanations.

Children born with Mental Retardation (page 355) or who later develop brain damage (for example, from head trauma or infection) may have difficulty controlling aggressive impulses, especially when they are angry, frustrated, or confronted by an overly complex or stimulating environment. An adolescent in the midst of a manic episode (page 63) may experience extreme irritability and aggressivity, or engage in antisocial acts for the thrill of it (stealing, vandalism, reckless driving). Aggressive or antisocial behavior may also occur as a consequence of a break with reality in an adolescent who has developed Schizophrenia (page 313). Children with Attention-Deficit/Hyperactivity Disorder (page 387) can be disruptive in school and at home but do so because of impulsivity rather than a disregard for the rights of others.

Some children react to difficult situations in their lives by developing transient conduct problems. For example, after his parents separate, a previously well-behaved child starts stealing money from them and getting into fights at school. After her family moves to a new city, a usually compliant ten-year-old girl throws temper tantrums, refuses to do her homework or her chores, torments her younger brother, and curses at her parents. A diagnosis of Adjustment Disorder (page 295) would best describe these transient problems. About one third of kids with Conduct Disorder continue their pattern of disruptive behavior into adulthood and go on to receive the diagnosis of Antisocial Personality Disorder (see Chapter 10).

More often than not, children with Conduct Disorder have other psychiatric symptoms in addition to their behavioral problems. If your child has Conduct Disorder, you should also review the chapters covering Substance Abuse (starting on page 117), depression (starting on page 31), anxiety (starting on page 79), developmental delay (starting on page 355), attention deficit (starting on page 387), and tics (page 399).

AM I OKAY?

Taken one by one, it is impossible to distinguish each of the behaviors associated with Oppositional Defiant Disorder from the normal behavior of any bossy toddler or blue-haired, tattooed seventeen-year-old about to become a freshman at Yale. Isolated or transient oppositional behaviors can occur in perfectly healthy children especially when they reach the "terrible twos" and the terrible teenage years. To qualify for this diagnosis, there must be a pattern of multiple and varied oppositional behaviors that are much more persistent and severe than those exhibited by other children of the same age and maturity level. These behaviors must be causing significant problems that are far beyond the average expectable family tussle.

Children and adolescents being considered for a diagnosis of ODD are usually brought to the clinician by harried parents at their wits' end because of the increasing strains in the family relationships. Oppositionalism can be a two-way street however. Some parents make unrealistic demands for submission or performance that go beyond what even a normally complacent child can deliver. It is often a tough call whether the child's problematic behavior stems from his own inherent ODD tendencies, from a relational problem at least in part instigated by the family, or from both. Everyone is probably acting more unreasonably than they would be if not in the heat of battle. One clue is how the child does with other authority figures. If the battles are only with the parents, but the child does well at school and in a part-time job, it is much more likely to be a relational problem within the family than Oppositional Defiant Disorder within the child. Another clue is how the parties participate in a family evaluation. If the family dynamics are dominated by a can-you-top-this struggle to win every point at all costs, the odds point to a relational problem as the primary cause. King Solomon would be interested in finding out who has to win every point at all costs and who is most prepared to compromise in an argument to make things better for the family.

Treatment Options

First off, let's admit that there is no treatment with proven efficacy for either Conduct Disorder or Oppositional Defiant Disorder. Probably the best hope for many kids is that they will mature and outgrow their disruptiveness, or develop friendships that are less destructive, or get over the drug problem that may be fueling their bad behavior. Providing strong, constant, and consistent parental and school discipline that is fair and not harsh is necessary and often helpful. Sometimes the child's having to endure the disciplinary consequences of his disruptive acts has a powerful sobering effect and does wonders in changing behavior.

Cognitive/behavioral treatment for Conduct Disorder is directed at reducing or eliminating the pattern of disruptive behaviors and modifying the child's attitude toward responsibilities, rules, and other people. The child is taught to identify the triggers that set off temper tantrums and aggressive acts. Rather than striking out immediately in frustration, he practices the anger control strategies of time out, distraction, and walking away. There is an attempt to correct misperceptions that others are ganging up against him and that he has to strike first. It is not easy to teach empathy and to instill more altruistic values, but it is worth the try. Sometimes the focus is on the negative consequences of the aggression and disruptive behavior. Unfortunately, scaring the kids into "going straight" is rarely successful since it requires an admission of weakness and vulnerability. A better strategy is to appeal to the child's selfish interests by pointing out how ineffective the disruptive behavior has been in actually getting needs met. Substance abuse prevention and treatment can also play a crucial role. The treatment usually needs to be directed not only at the child but also at the family and the school. Consistency of discipline and expectations across the various parts of the child's environment are crucial for success.

It is also important to focus treatment on the complications of Conduct Disorder—particularly depression and Substance Abuse. Suicide attempts and completed suicide are surprisingly common, particularly in the context of a romantic disappointment or a legal confrontation. Hospitalizations, when they are necessary, should usually be brief and targeted to control suicidal and aggressive impulses. It is not wise to provide the child with too much of a sick role as this may serve as an excuse and further reduce his sense of responsibility.

There is no research on the treatment of Oppositional Defiant Disorder. The most common approach is a family therapy directed at improving communication, clarifying expectations, and establishing fair and clear limits. Each member of the family needs to realize that no one has ever, or will ever really win an argument. The ability to compromise in the family's best interest is far nobler than stubborn insistence or defiant triumph. Assertiveness training for the child and parent training in setting consistent limits may both be helpful.

Suggested Additional Readings

Leave Me Alone! Helping Your Troubled Teenager
Belinda Terro Mooney
Human Services Institute, 1993

Behavior Management: Applications for Teachers and Parents
Thomas J. Zirpoli and Kristine J. Melloy
Prentice Hall, 1996

Where to Go for Help
(Self-help, support, for more information)

Toughlove
(support group for parents of teenagers with behavior problems)
P.O. Box 1069
Doylestown, PA 18901
(800) 333-1069
FAX: (215) 348-9874
E-mail: service@toughlove.org
Web: http://www.toughlove.org/

Federation of Families for Children's Mental Health
(information and advocacy)

1021 Prince Street
Alexandria, VA 22314-2971
(703) 684-7710

Families Anonymous World Service Office
(self-help group for family or friends of children with behavior problems)

P.O. Box 3475
Culver City, CA 90231-3475
(818) 989-7841
(800) 736-9805

CHAPTER 19

HYPERACTIVITY
OR DISTRACTIBILITY

This is undoubtedly the most controversial of all the psychiatric diagnoses with implications that touch on major public health and educational concerns. More than two million schoolchildren in the United States are taking stimulant medication intended to help their concentration and/or to reduce their hyperactivity. For many children, this results in a dramatic improvement in performance, self-esteem, and interpersonal relationships. Nonetheless, there is a serious disagreement even among the best experts in the field on the optimal threshold for defining Attention-Deficit/Hyperactivity Disorder (ADHD or sometimes shortened to ADD) and how to decide which and how many kids to treat. Many parents, and some experts, believe that the diagnosis of ADHD is being made too liberally and that stimulants are being used indiscriminately as a quick fix for more complex educational, family, or social problems. It is impossible to know with any degree of certainty how many children are being needlessly exposed to the potentially harmful side effects of the stimulant medications. It is equally unclear how many kids who would benefit from the medication are not yet receiving it.

The debate arises because there is no precise way to draw the line between normal distractibility and hyperactivity and the pathological levels that require treatment. Perfectly normal children are inherently fairly distractible and hyperactive—especially during certain stages of their development.

There are many psychiatrists, pediatricians, psychologists, teachers, and parents who believe that the early diagnosis and treatment of ADHD has been enormously beneficial both to the individual child and to their classroom colleagues. They point out that without a diagnosis of ADHD, many of these children would have been just labeled as lazy, spacey, unintelligent, or poorly behaved, with the inevitable negative effects on their self-esteem. On the other hand, there are many other psychiatrists, pediatricians, psychologists, teachers, and parents who believe that the diagnosis is sometimes being given too readily to children who are really well within normal limits of hyperactivity and poor focus. Interestingly, there is clear difference between U.S. and European views on the subject. The diagnosis of ADHD (and the consequent prescribing of stimulants to children) is much more common on this side of the ocean. Either there is something that U.S. children are being exposed to that is causing increased rates of ADHD or, much more likely, clinicians and parents here are more likely to seek medical cures for behavioral problems.

Because ADHD has become something of a media darling, many adults have come to wonder whether it is responsible for their perceived difficulty in concentrating. The flood of publicity has been both helpful and detrimental. On the plus side, it has exploded the myth that everyone grows out of ADHD—in fact fully 65 percent of children continue to have some symptoms into their adulthood. Increased awareness helps identify cases that were previously missed and encourages long-term treatment for those who need it. On the negative side, adult ADHD has become almost the diagnosis *du jour*—broadly misapplied both to normal people who aspire to supernormal powers of concentration and to people whose poor concentration is caused by any one of a number of other psychiatric and substance use problems.

According to the diagnostic manual, you (or your child) has Attention-Deficit/Hyperactivity Disorder if:
- Your child (or you, if you are an adult) has a serious problem with inattention, hyperactivity, or both. Since all of these behaviors can be "normal" during certain ages, they should count as evidence for this disorder only if they cause serious problems, persist for at least six months, and are not what would be considered appropriate for your child's developmental stage.
  (1) Evidence for an *attention-deficit component* would be the presence of at least six of the following:
    (a) Your child often makes careless mistakes.
    (b) Your child often has trouble sustaining attention when engaging in tasks or play activities.
    (c) Your child often does not seem to be listening to what is being said.

388

(d) Your child often leaves schoolwork or chores unfinished.

(e) Your child often has difficulty organizing tasks and activities.

(f) Your child often avoids tasks that require sustained mental effort and concentration.

(g) Your child often loses things that he or she needs for tasks or activities.

(h) Your child is easily distracted by extraneous stimuli.

(i) Your child is often forgetful in daily activities.

(2) Evidence for a *hyperactivity component* would be the presence of at least six of the following:

(a) Your child often fidgets with his hands or feet or squirms in his seat.

(b) Your child often leaves his seat when he is not supposed to.

(c) Your child often runs about or climbs excessively.

(d) Your child often has difficulty playing quietly.

(e) Your child is always "on the go" or acts as if "driven by a motor."

(f) Your child talks excessively.

(g) Your child often blurts out the answer before the question has been completed.

(h) Your child often has difficulty waiting in lines or awaiting his turn.

(i) Your child often interrupts or intrudes on others (e.g., butts into others' conversations or games).

• The problems started before age seven.

• The problems are not limited to just one setting (e.g., only at home or only at school).

• The difficulties are severe enough to cause marked problems in school, work, or relationships.

The diagnostic manual recognizes three types:

Attention-Deficit/Hyperactivity Disorder, Predominantly Inattentive Type

Attention-Deficit/Hyperactivity Disorder, Predominantly Hyperactive-Impulsive Type

Attention-Deficit/Hyperactivity Disorder, Combined Type

Description

The diagnosis of ADHD is tough because the symptoms of inattention and hyperactivity are so ubiquitous in the general population. The fact is that most people would love to calm down and concentrate better. The diagnostic criteria set therefore include a number of built-in protections intended to reduce the risk of overdiagnosis. Please pay careful attention to them in order to avoid false positive diagnoses and unnecessary treatment. Perhaps most important is the requirement that the symptoms have an onset before age seven. ADHD is a problem that necessarily starts in toddlers and in very young children—there is no such thing as a new onset of ADHD in adolescence or adulthood. This helps to narrow the diagnosis by eliminating all of the many other psychiatric disorders that may be confused with ADHD but have a later onset (see the Differential Diagnosis section on page 392). Of course, long after the fact it is not always easy to get a clear history of what you were like in the first seven years of your life and whether your behavior then would have met the criteria for ADHD. Parents and other people who were around to see you as a small child may have useful insights. Report cards from preschool on up can also be very illuminating. Comments such as "never sits still," "always interrupts other children," and "can't follow instructions" are highly suggestive of ADHD.

The second caveat to reduce overdiagnosis is that the symptoms must be severe, persistent, beyond what is expected at the particular age level, and must cause considerable distress and impairment in functioning. Some hyperactive people may get a whole lot accomplished and not be the least impaired. The issue for them may be more one of temperament than disease. We would suggest withholding diagnosis and treatment in marginal cases where impairment has not been established.

As a final check on overdiagnosis, the distractible and hyperactive behaviors must occur in multiple (perhaps most) contexts and settings. If a kid is fidgety only in one setting or with one person, this probably represents a specific and transient reaction to that setting or that person and is not an indication of ADHD. The symptoms must be really pervasive, something the child brings with him almost everywhere he goes. Of course, some situations will bring out the worst—especially those that require long-sustained mental exertion and physical immobility, particularly in a group setting that has the potential for numerous tempting distractions. Inattention and hyperactivity are likely to be most evident when the child must sit through a class, take a test, attend Sunday school, or do homework in a study section.

The situations that bring out the best in the child's ability to focus are those that have strict limits and a one-on-one relationship, like the doctor's office for an ADHD evaluation. Some stimuli are so intense and engrossing that they capture the attention even of children who have great difficulty focusing on most other things. TV and video games fall in this category and may therefore be useful for educational purposes.

The symptoms of ADHD are divided into the three categories of inattentiveness, impulsivity, and hyperactivity. How these look will vary depending on the person's developmental stage. For example, hyperactivity in children may be manifested by excessive motor activity, such as running, climbing, and difficulty remaining seated. In adolescents and adults, hyperactivity may be more subtle and take the form of restlessness or difficulty engaging in stationary activities, such as reading or doing paperwork.

Perhaps most characteristic of ADHD is distractibility. As a child you were a space cadet, now you are an absentminded professor. You can't keep your attention focused on a specific task, school assignment, household chore, or the rules of a game. This results in careless mistakes, quick shifts from one unfinished thing to the next, and numerous uncompleted tasks. You are very easily distracted by even the most minor and irrelevant of noises or events (a car honking down the street or a conversation taking place in another room). It is hard to follow directions, and often it appears as if you were not listening or that your mind was wandering someplace else. In social scenarios, you experience difficulty sustaining conversation, often shifting topics rapidly and not really listening to what other people are saying. You have disorganized work habits and often lose or damage the materials needed for a project (homework assignments rarely make it to and from school in one piece).

The hyperactivity of ADHD can assume heroic proportions that are daunting for those charged with containing the child. Parents often describe him as a whirlwind of energy, a blur, always on the go, constantly getting into everything, rampaging through the house like a tornado, leaving a trail of toys and a clutter of unfinished activities. The child runs, talks, and climbs excessively and in inappropriate situations. He is everywhere and rarely engages in more sedate activities, such as playing board games, listening to stories, or doing puzzles. He can't stay in one place and has to jump up from his seat while eating, during class, doing homework, or while watching television. In classroom situations when absolutely forced to remain seated, he will fidget, tap hands, squirm, or shake his feet and legs.

The characteristic impulsivity of ADHD is evident in interruptions, intrusions, difficulty waiting in line, grabbing things, and blurting out answers when not called upon or before the question has been asked. The child is accident prone, knocks things over, runs into people, gets stuck on sharp objects, and takes needless daredevil risks—riding a bicycle with no hands down a busy street, or climbing a steep wall, or swimming across a lake without first considering the possible consequences.

Although most individuals with ADHD display all the defining symptoms of hyperactivity, impulsivity, and inattention (the "Combined Type"), there are some people in whom one or the other pattern of behavior is far more pronounced—the "Predominantly Inattentive Type" versus the "Predominantly Hyperactive-Impulsive Type." A child at a younger age is likely to have the Combined Type and then grow into the Inattentive Type as maturation mellows out the hyperactivity.

DIFFERENTIAL DIAGNOSIS

Inattention, hyperactivity, and impulsivity are not at all specific to Attention-Deficit/Hyperactivity Disorder and occur also in a wide variety of other psychiatric disorders. Several medications that are prescribed for young children can cause hyperactivity as a side effect (especially the bronchodilators that are prescribed for asthma and decongestants for colds). Children with Mental Retardation who are in school settings that are above their intellectual ability may be inattentive or hyperactive because they are overwhelmed by the situation.

Problems with focusing attention, excessive distractibility, and increased motor activity can be seen in Major Depressive Disorder (page 33), in manic and hypomanic episodes in Bipolar Disorder (pages 61 and 66), in Panic Disorder (page 79) or Generalized Anxiety Disorder (page 95), as part of a psychotic disorder (see Chapter 15, starting on page 303), in Autistic Disorder (page 361), in any of the Dissociative Disorders (see Chapter 13, starting on page 281), and as a result of brain damage (see Chapter 16, starting on page 329). Before settling in on ADHD (especially the controversial diagnosis of residual ADHD in an adult), each of these competing possibilities should be looked at to see if they offer a better fit.

Adult ADHD is a relatively "new" phenomenon. It used to be thought that children with ADHD outgrew their attentional and hyperactive problems when they reached adulthood. However, studies that carefully follow children with ADHD as they have grown up reveal that the majority do continue to have residual symptoms that persist into adulthood. Unfortunately, recent news coverage has suggested that undiagnosed ADHD is a major public health problem. This media spotlighting has led most people with poor concentration, job and marital instability, or difficulty in controlling anger and other impulses to wonder whether they are in fact suffering from a previously undiagnosed ADHD. If you think you might have ADHD because you have always had trouble paying attention and focusing your mind on what you need to do, it is more likely either that you are completely normal, or are drinking too much alcohol, or are suffering instead from a chronic low-level depression or anxiety. Keep in mind that simply reviewing the diagnostic criteria for ADHD to see if you have the required symptoms is not enough—because inattention and/or hyperactivity occur in too many other psychiatric conditions. The clincher for making the diagnosis in adults is being able to document that you had a *childhood history of ADHD* with clear symptoms before age seven. There should be a history of poor school performance or significant disruptive behavior that was inappropriately attributed to such factors as "underachieving," "poor study skills," and "chronic misbehavior." A nonproblematic school history thus virtually rules out a diagnosis of adult ADHD.

It is not necessarily always an "either/or" proposition. A number of studies have suggested that ADHD more commonly occurs in conjunction with other psychiatric conditions than it does in isolation. For example, it has been estimated that up to 50 percent of ADHD cases have co-occurring Conduct Disorder (page 377), up to 75 percent may also have a mood disorder (see Chapters 1 and 2), and up to 90 percent may also have learning disabilities (page 366). Although Tourette's Disorder (page 399) is uncommon in children with ADHD, up to 50 percent of children with Tourette's Disorder also have ADHD. Make sure you review the twenty questions section beginning on page 17 to check whether any of these disorders may also be a part of your symptom picture.

AM I OKAY?

In assessing yourself or your child for ADHD, it is important to recognize that the behaviors that typify the disorder are normal for children at certain ages and developmental levels. No one should get the diagnosis of ADHD merely because he is distractible and hyperactive. The symptoms have to have started early in life; be severe, persistent, and disabling; occur in multiple contexts; and not be due to another psychiatric disorder. Judgment calls at the boundary should probably default to no diagnosis and watchful waiting unless more severe and characteristic symptoms or impairments emerge. The diagnosis should be considered only if the behavior is very inappropriate for the child's developmental age. For example, one would not consider a two-year-old's difficulty sitting through a TV program as evidence of ADHD, since a short attention span is characteristic of children at that age. Furthermore, the symptoms must be present in several settings. For instance, fidgeting in an unstimulating environment is context specific and does not indicate a problem. Classroom inattention may occur when exceptionally bright children are placed in academically understimulating environments. A child who does not pay attention to his parents but can concentrate well in school is more likely to be having a relational problem than ADHD.

TREATMENT OPTIONS

Over the years, many different treatments for ADHD have been advocated, including medication, behavioral therapy, dietary restrictions and supplements, biofeedback, and even eye exercises wearing colored glasses. One reason for this proliferation is that no single treatment is completely effective in all children with ADHD. But some are clearly superior to others: The only two types of treatment that have consistently and conclusively been shown to work are medication and behavior therapy.

Although it is counterintuitive that stimulants would exert a calming effect on hyperactivity, studies going back to 1937 prove absolutely conclusively that they do. The stimulants specifically target the main ADHD symptoms, helping the person to better focus attention on tasks, control errant impulses, reduce motor overactivity and aggressiveness, and improve overall academic performance. The different stimulants used to treat ADHD on average work about equally well and have similar potential for side effects, but people may respond better to one medication than another so that a certain amount of trial and error is sometimes necessary before deciding on the right choice. The most common side effects are loss of appetite, sleep difficulty, and mild growth suppression. The side effects often go away by themselves, but they can also be addressed by adjusting the timing and amount of medication. For example, the effects on appetite can be reduced by having the child take the medication after meals or eating a bedtime snack after the last dose wears off. Interference with sleep is avoided by not giving the medication after 5 P.M. Because growth suppression is somewhat less likely with Ritalin, it is often the medication tried first. Limiting the use of stimulants to the school year allows the child to catch up for lost growth during summer, winter, and spring breaks. Antidepressant medications are helpful in treating hyperactivity but may not work as well on problems with attention and aggression.

Behavior therapy aims to reduce problematic behaviors and substitute more desirable ones through a combination of positive and negative reinforcement. This is usually a family affair with considerable parent training. The parent is taught how to provide rewards to encourage positive behavior (gold stars on a daily chart) and mete out limit setting (time-out periods) to deter negative behavior. In order to keep the behavioral program consistent throughout the day, the teacher should also be included as part of the team. For example, a "daily report card" can be used to set up specific behavioral goals—like sitting still for fifteen straight minutes at least five times a day. The child shows the report card to his parents at the end of the day, is rewarded for meeting the goals, and new goals are then set for the next day.

The treatment plan should be specifically designed for each individual person, taking into account specific needs and environmental situations. For example, some children with severe inattention problems can probably benefit from medication alone if they are identified early, before they have secondary problems like school failure and chronic low self-esteem. Other children, who have been struggling with ADHD for years, will often need a combination of medication to treat the inattention, behavioral therapy to learn alternative ways of behaving in the classroom and with friends, and remedial education to help get back to speed academically.

Over the years, a variety of dietary "cures" for ADHD have been touted as alternatives to medication. Initial glowing reports of efficacy always wither when the treatment is subjected to more careful scientific scrutiny. Because of the enormous effect that positive expectation can exert on outcome, the effectiveness of a treatment can be determined only if a patient is unaware whether he is receiving the "new" treatment or a placebo alternative. The Feingold diet of the 1970s was based on the belief that ADHD is caused by food allergies to naturally occurring and artificially added chemicals such as colorings and preservatives. Unfortunately, carefully controlled studies have found it to be effective in fewer than 5 percent of children with ADHD. Another popular theory proposed that hyperactivity is caused by an abnormal reaction to refined sugars and suggested treating ADHD by strict avoidance of these in favor of protein and starches. This has not survived close scientific scrutiny. Also not supported are megavitamin therapy and using caffeine as a stimulant in place of Ritalin.

As we discussed at the beginning of this chapter, the medication treatment of Attention-Deficit/Hyperactivity Disorder is probably the single most controversial question in all of psychiatry and pediatrics. How is an individual parent to react when the experts disagree? The commonsense approach is definitely to go with the use of stimulants for clear-cut and severe instances of ADHD. Here the evidence is overwhelming that stimulants help a great deal and often make all the difference. In borderline cases, stimulant use is much more up to the parents' and child's discretion. It can be withheld altogether in favor of behavior therapy or just watching and waiting, or it can be tried on a very brief trial basis to see if the benefits outweigh possible side effects.

Suggested Additional Readings

Taking Charge of ADHD: The Complete, Authoritative Guide for Parents
Russell A. Barkley, Ph.D.
Guilford Press, 1995

Distant Drums, Different Drummers: A Guide for Young People with ADHD
Barbara D. Ingersoll
Cape, 1995

Driven to Distraction: Recognizing and Coping with Attention Deficit Disorder from Childhood Through Adulthood
Edward M. Hallowell and John J. Ratey
Simon & Schuster, 1995

Learning Disabilities and A.D.D.: A Family Guide to Living and Learning Together
Betty B. Osman
John Wiley, 1997

Where to Go for Help
(Self-help, support, for more information)

National ADDA
(information and referrals for adults and children with ADHD)

1070 Rosewood Avenue
Suite #A
Ann Arbor, MI 48104
(800) 487-2282 (recording)
(800) 975-0004 (free resource catalog)
(440) 350-9595
FAX: (440) 350-2334
E-mail: natladda@aol.com
Web: http://www.add.org/

Children and Adults with Attention Deficit Disorders (CHADD)

499 N.W. Seventieth Avenue
Suite 109
Plantation, FL 33317
(800) 233-4060
(954) 587-3700
Web: http://www.chadd.org/

ADD Anonymous
(twelve-step program)

P.O. Box 421227
San Diego, CA 92142-1227
E-mail: addanon@aol.com

AD-IN (Attention Deficit Information Network), Inc.
(network of support groups)

475 Hillside Avenue
Needham, MA 02194-1207
(617) 455-9895 (Tuesday and Thursday, 10 A.M. to 12 noon)
FAX: (617) 444-5466

CHAPTER 20

OTHER CHILDHOOD PROBLEMS

A Miscellany of Other Disorders
That First Arise in Childhood or Adolescence

We have come finally to the very last of our twenty diagnostic questions. In this chapter, we will cover several miscellaneous diagnoses that have no special relationship to one another except for the fact that each is usually first diagnosed in childhood or adolescence.

TIC DISORDER/TOURETTE'S DISORDER

You can usually tell tics when you see or hear them, but they are not so easy to define concisely in words. Tics are involuntary, sudden, recurrent, quick, and stereotypical motor movements or vocalizations. Tics can be simple or complex. Typical simple motor tics are eye blinking, shoulder shrugging, facial grimacing, and limb jerking. Complex motor tics include jumping, facial gestures, bending, foot stomping, touching, grooming behaviors, and echokinesis (imitating someone else's movements). Simple vocal tics are grunting, coughing, barking, throat clearing, and snorting. Complex vocal tics include repeating irrelevant words or phrases; echolalia (repeating the last heard sound or word); and coprolalia (using inappropriate or obscene language).

Tourette's Disorder is characterized by the presence of multiple motor and multiple vocal tics. Tourette's is more common in males than females and usually starts early in childhood. It is lifelong, but the severity, frequency, and anatomical location of the tics can vary over time and with treatment. There may also be periods of remission lasting from weeks to years. Motor tics are usually the first to appear, beginning with the head and then progressing to involve the trunk and limbs. Vocal tics usually start as a simple, single sound and can progress to longer phrases and more complex vocalizations.

Obsessions and compulsions are commonly associated with Tourette's Disorder and usually begin about five years after the first simple tics. There may also be problems with hyperactivity, inattention, and impulsivity. In some cases, the tics interfere with daily activities, such as reading and writing. Performance in academic or social situations may also be impaired because of self-consciousness and rejection by peers. If you have Tourette's Disorder you also likely suffer from low self-esteem as a result of being constantly teased and ridiculed by unsympathetic people who believe you are doing these things on purpose.

According to the diagnostic manual, you (or your child) have Tic Disorder if:

- You (or your child) have tics. A tic is a sudden, rapid, recurrent, stereotyped body movement or vocalization. When tics involve *both* body movements (blinks, shrugs) *and* vocalizations (grunts, words) and have been present for at least a year, this is called Tourette's Disorder. If tics last for less than a year, this is called Transient Tic Disorder.
- The tics occur many times a day (usually in bouts), nearly every day or intermittently, and start before age eighteen.
- The movements are not caused by a drug, medication, or medical condition.

DESCRIPTION

The urge to perform the tic is irresistible and out of conscious control. At best, a person can voluntarily suppress a tic for a brief period of time until the tension builds to an ultimately irresistible point. Once you perform the tic, there is a release of tension. You are likely to be embarrassed by the tics and have found ways to cover them up by incorporating the movement into what appears to be a purposeful behavior, such as scratching your head, yawning, or fixing your hair. Tics vary in intensity over time and are usually made worse by stress, conflict, excitement, and fatigue. They are less likely to occur during focused mental activities, such as reading or working at a computer screen. Tics usually attenuate greatly during sleep, but may not fully disappear.

DIFFERENTIAL DIAGNOSIS

It is important to distinguish tics from other types of abnormal movements that may be caused by medications, medical disorders, or other psychiatric disorders. Stimulant medications can cause tics or make tics worse in someone who already has Tic Disorder. The repetitions and stereotypical movements associated with Autistic Disorder (page 361) are more rhythmic and intentional in nature. There is also a difference between tics and the compulsions seen in Obsessive-Compulsive Disorder (page 101). Compulsions are complex rituals that are rigidly performed to neutralize the extreme anxiety caused by an obsession. In contrast, tics tend to be more simple motor behaviors that are not primarily aimed at reducing anxiety, although there is often a reduction of tension afterward. It is common, however, for individuals with Tourette's Disorder to experience both tics and compulsions (in which case both Tourette's and Obsessive-Compulsive Disorder are diagnosed).

TREATMENT OPTIONS

The first step, and perhaps the most important, is educating yourself and your family about Tic Disorders. Everyone will be greatly relieved to learn that tics are not indicative of a progressively debilitating condition. On the contrary, most children experience significant improvement with treatment and as they become adults. The many examples of professional sports figures who have publicly acknowledged having tics underscores that this does not have to be impairing. An invaluable source of support for both patients and their families is the Tourette Syndrome Association, a self-help group with both national and local chapters.

The goals of therapy are to eliminate tics and treat the conditions most commonly associated with them, like the inattention, hyperactivity, and impulsivity in Attention-Deficit/Hyperactivity Disorder (page 387) and the obsessions and compulsions in Obsessive-Compulsive Disorder (page 101). There are a number of medications that can reduce the frequency of tics, if not get rid of them altogether. It turns out that many of the medications used to treat psychosis (see Chapter 15, starting on page 303) are also effective at suppressing tics—Haldol, Prolixin, and Orap are the most commonly used. Medication side effects, like sedation, muscle spasms, and feelings of restlessness are unfortunately also quite common, to some degree limiting their usefulness. It will be interesting to see whether the newer atypical antipsychotic medications (Clozapine, Zyprexa, etc.) are helpful without the side effects. Clonidine, a medication used to treat high blood pressure, and Klonopin, a medication used to treat anxiety and seizures, are less likely to cause side effects but are also often less effective.

A behavioral therapy technique called habit reversal training can be used as an alternative or supplement to medication. The person is taught to actively use an opposing muscle group to counteract the tic movement. For example, someone with a shoulder-shrugging tic can actively do the opposite, lower his shoulders, when he feels that the tic is about to happen. Since tics often get worse when the person is in a stressful environment, interventions that teach stress management can indirectly lower tic frequency. A structured and predictable environment with clear expectations both at home and at school is also helpful. Family therapy may address the strains on the family imposed by the illness.

Up to 60 percent of children with Tourette's have symptoms of ADHD. Tics and the ADHD symptoms must each be addressed in treatment. One wrinkle is that the most commonly used treatment for ADHD, namely stimulants, often makes tics worse. For such children, behavioral approaches to ADHD may be preferred.

ENCOPRESIS

Luckily, toilet training is usually a very natural activity that is built into the instinctual repertoire of most higher animals, including man. Animals are born knowing that you don't defecate where you eat. Shortly after birth, they develop toilet rituals that help ensure reasonably sanitary conditions for the den.

Encopresis is characterized by frequent intentional or unintentional defecations that are dropped into inappropriate places. The accidents keep occurring beyond the age of four when better bowel control is expected. Most often the child soils his clothing or defecates on the floor or is the last in his play group to still require diapers. The child may smear the feces in an attempt to clean or hide the excrement.

Most cases of Encopresis are unintentional. Some children suffer from constipation and stool retention that is then accompanied by a more or less continuous leaking of feces. The cause of the constipation can be physiological (such as dehydration or medication side effect) or psychological (such as anxiety about defecating in a toilet), or may be a symptom of oppositional behavior that is triggered by the battle of the potty.

Encopresis not associated with constipation and overflow may result from poor sphincter control. More commonly, however, it is deliberate behavior that reflects premature, inconsistent, or hostile toilet training on the part of the parents or oppositional, hostile, and/or impulsive behavior on the part of the child—or an interactive power struggle between them.

There are two types of Encopresis, the "primary type" and the "secondary type"—and these are about equally common. In the primary type, the child has never fully established bowel control. In the secondary type, the child has been successfully toilet trained but reverts to fecal incontinence usually beginning around age eight. Encopresis is more common in males than females. It can persist intermittently for years and become a source of low self-esteem for the child, extreme irritation for parents, and colossal battles between them. Fortunately, however, Encopresis is rarely chronic and the child and family generally outgrow it together.

According to the diagnostic manual, your child has Encopresis if:
- Your child repeatedly moves his bowels inappropriately into clothing or on the floor.
- This happens at least once a month for at least three months.
- Your child is old enough to have acquired bowel control (usually by age four).
- Medical causes have been considered and ruled out.

AM I OKAY?

It is essential first to consider what would be developmentally appropriate for a child at this age and stage of development. There is no absolute age at which failure to be properly toilet trained crosses the line and becomes pathological. An occasional accident is usually no big deal. The DSM-IV convention suggests that Encopresis requires a mental age of four, and that fecal incontinence must occur at least once a month, and must persist for a minimum of three months. It is important to rule out general medical conditions and to treat whatever may be causing constipation.

TREATMENT OPTIONS

Behavior modification is very effective in treating Encopresis. The therapy focuses on having the child incorporate toilet use into his daily routine. Typically, the child is instructed to sit on the toilet for up to fifteen minutes after every meal, in an attempt to take advantage of the natural reflex for post-meal defecation. Rewards for both compliance to the schedule and successful defecation provide positive reinforcement. Keeping a chart of scheduled toileting behavior and using gold stars to denote success can provide an ongoing encouragement. For those with the constipated type of Encopresis, it is usually necessary to take daily laxatives in conjunction with the behavioral therapy. After an extended period of regularity, the child can be gradually weaned from the laxatives.

ENURESIS

What we just said about the built-in inevitability of toilet training in Encopresis applies to an even greater degree in Enuresis. Here the instinctual aspect of the urinary control is even more evident since it has to become ingrained in the sleeping brain. Enuresis is the recurrent voiding of urine into inappropriate places (usually the child's clothing or bed) occurring after an age at which urinary continence is customarily expected. The incontinence is usually involuntary, but may sometimes be intentional.

"Bed-wetting" most commonly occurs during rapid eye movement (REM) sleep in the first half of the night. The child may dream that he is urinating while he is actually doing so. Daytime Enuresis may occur when the child is too embarrassed to ask to use the rest room at school—a scenario that is more common in girls than boys. Children with daytime Enuresis often also experience nighttime bed-wetting. Approximately 80 percent of these children have primary Enuresis—urinary continence has never been established. The 20 percent with secondary Enuresis have managed to attain bladder control, but have later regressed for some reason that is often related to stress or to the birth of a sibling.

The impairment and distress associated with Enuresis often results less from the symptom itself than from the battles it causes with parents or caregivers and from the child's avoidance of desirable activities (such as school, camp, or sleepover parties). Self-esteem is usually impaired due to social rejection by peers and punishment by caregivers. Interestingly, approximately 75 percent of children with Enuresis have a first-degree biological relative who also had the disorder.

According to the diagnostic manual, your child has Enuresis if:
- Your child repeatedly urinates into bed or clothes.
- This happens at least twice a week for at least three consecutive months or otherwise causes significant embarrassment or interferes with activities.
- Your child is old enough to have acquired adequate bladder control (usually by age five).
- Medical causes have been considered and ruled out.

AM I OKAY?

The developmental level of the child is crucial in making the diagnosis of Enuresis. Obviously, urinary continence is not expected in a two-year-old, but should have kicked in by age five. The voiding of urine must occur at least twice a week, persist for a minimum of three months, and cause substantial impairment. It is also crucial to first rule out possible medical etiologies, such as diabetes, urinary tract infections, spina bifida, or seizure disorders.

TREATMENT OPTIONS

Only a small minority of children suffering from Enuresis are ever brought to a clinician for evaluation and treatment, suggesting that many families consider bed-wetting a "normal" part of childhood. This is often unfortunate because there are a number of simple and effective treatments for Enuresis that can help reduce the embarrassment, frustration, and low self-esteem that these children often experience.

Nighttime Enuresis is most effectively treated using a simple device known as a night alarm. When the device detects urine in the bedsheets (by completing a circuit between two electrodes placed in the bed), a bell or buzzer is sounded (or alternatively, a pad starts vibrating). A full cessation of Enuresis can be expected in over 80 percent of cases, with long-standing remission (off the alarm) occurring in the majority. The main disadvantage of using the night alarm is that improvement often does not occur until the second month of treatment. Unfortunately, this delayed effect limits its use since most evaluations for Enuresis are prompted by an impending event like a family vacation or an overnight stay at someone's house where immediate relief is needed.

Medication can be helpful. The synthetic antidiuretic hormone DDAVP, given as a nose spray or pill, can completely stop bed-wetting in up to 50 percent of children (and reduce the frequency in another 40 percent). The antidepressant imipramine, given in much lower doses than used in treating depression, is effective in up to 85 percent of bed-wetters. However, both medications have side effects (DDAVP can cause headache, nausea, and abdominal pain; imipramine can cause dry mouth, dizziness, and constipation) and the Enuresis may return quickly when the medication is stopped.

The treatment of daytime Enuresis is similar to the treatment of Encopresis and depends primarily on behavior modification. This usually occurs in children who are so excessively shy at school that they are unwilling to ask to be excused to use the bathroom. The teacher can help by periodically reminding the child to use the bathroom and by finding subtle ways of excusing her that will avoid embarrassment. Other children with daytime Enuresis either ignore the sensation of needing to urinate or else have too short a lead time between when they experience the urge and have to pass urine. Treatment for these children focuses on establishing a regular pattern of daytime use of the toilet, regardless of whether or not they feel the need. Interestingly, the medications used for nocturnal Enuresis (DDAVP and imipramine) are ineffective for daytime problems.

SEPARATION ANXIETY DISORDER

The ability to experience separation anxiety derives from the fundamental mammalian trait of needing to be attached. Like all mammals, we are born in a helpless state and would not survive were it not for innate attachment behaviors triggering maternal instincts that ensure we will be well cared for.

Any infant who can be easily separated from his mother without a storm of protest is not long for this world. Nature is too smart to let this happen very often and has built in all sorts of remarkably effective ways for infants to anticipate dangerous separations and ensure that they are prevented altogether or last only for the very shortest time. However, it is equally important for mammals to grow up, individuate, and leave the den. Separation Anxiety Disorder reflects major problems in this natural evolution of parent/child attachment behavior.

Children with this disorder experience excessive anxiety and distress in response to real or anticipated separations from home or parents. When away from home, the child is usually completely preoccupied with thoughts of getting back and reuniting with the missing and sorely missed parent. He insists on knowing his parent's exact whereabouts and may need frequent telephone contacts. If his parent is late picking him up, the child becomes worried, depressed, and agitated. He is obsessed with fears about the possible harmful occurrences, accidents, or even death that may befall him or his parents whenever they are apart. He is afraid of getting forever lost or separated from his parents. The level of distress is so severe that the child refuses to go places alone. He misses out on age-appropriate experiences of school, camp, or going to a friend's house. He has difficulty concentrating on work or play and becomes withdrawn when away from his parents. Social relations are severely restricted because of his reluctance to play at friends' houses and because other kids tease him for being a baby. Academic performance may deteriorate because of missed school days and trouble paying attention in class.

When at home, the child is likely to be excessively clinging and may follow his parent around like a shadow. It is very common for him to have difficulty going to bed unless someone stays and reads stories interminably. He may fight violently against sleep for fear that his parents will use the occasion to leave him alone. Troubling nightmares are common, most likely with themes of harm or catastrophe befalling members of the family (kidnapping, burglary, monsters, scary animals, or car accidents).

The anxiety over separation, or anticipated separation, often results in physical symptoms such as nausea, headaches, and even vomiting. Body symptoms that may also occur in older children include heart palpitation, feeling faint, and dizziness. The child may use these physical ailments as an excuse to stay home from school. When at school, he may insist he is sick and needs to go home.

Many parents report that their child seemed to be anxious and worried almost since birth. These children are demanding and in need of constant reassurance and attention, but also tend to be compliant, perfectionistic, and eager to please. The separation fears get worse during periods of stress, such as when changing schools, upon the death of a pet or loved one, or at the birth of a sibling. Some kids grow out of separation anxiety, others grow into a full-fledged adult anxiety disorder. Many adults with an Anxiety Disorder initially had Separation Anxiety Disorder as a child, suggesting that it may have been a precursor. Separation Anxiety Disorder is not uncommon, affecting about 4 percent of all children.

According to the diagnostic manual, your child has Separation Anxiety Disorder if:
- Your child is excessively anxious when separated from home or from you, as evidenced by three or more of the following, lasting for at least four weeks:
  (1) Your child is excessively upset when separations happen or are anticipated.
  (2) Your child is excessively worried about losing you or that something bad will happen to you.
  (3) Your child is excessively worried that something bad will happen to him that will result in being separated from you (like getting lost or being kidnapped).
  (4) Your child persistently refuses to go to school or other places because of separation fears.
  (5) Your child is excessively scared to be home alone.
  (6) Your child refuses to go to sleep without you being near or to sleep away from home.
  (7) Your child has repeated nightmares involving the theme of separation.
  (8) Your child complains of physical symptoms (stomachaches, headaches, nausea) when separation is anticipated.
- Your child's fears and worries cause problems in school or home, lead to serious restrictions on what he can and cannot do, or seriously affect the way he interacts with other people.

AM I OKAY?

Separation anxiety is a normal and adaptive developmental phenomenon when it occurs at the right time and to the right degree. In contrast, Separation Anxiety Disorder occasions a level of distress that is very far beyond what is developmentally appropriate or expectable under the circumstances. The severe separation anxiety must persist for at least a month and cause significant impairment that may take the form of school refusal, academic underachievement, problems with peers, and a failure to develop an appropriate sense of autonomy.

For example, a three-year-old who is hesitant to stay away from home overnight and is preoccupied with knowing his mother's whereabouts is completely normal and does not demonstrate any evidence of a disorder. In contrast, the same behavior in an eight-year-old may be considered problematic because a higher degree of autonomy is expected at that age and transient separations from caregivers should occur with relative ease. The same behavior in a seventeen-year-old meant to leave soon for college is obvious evidence of Separation Anxiety Disorder.

It is also important to consider the child's cultural context when evaluating for a possible diagnosis of Separation Anxiety Disorder. There is a great deal of variation from culture to culture in the value placed on autonomy. Independence and autonomy are especially encouraged and expected in the United States. There are many other cultures throughout the world that place a much greater emphasis on interdependence among family members. Girls may also be expected to have a higher ambient level of separation anxiety than boys.

DIFFERENTIAL DIAGNOSIS

Anxiety about being separated from others is not at all specific to Separation Anxiety Disorder. If your child experiences excessive fear of being separated from you, other possible diagnoses should also be considered. People with Generalized Anxiety Disorder (page 95) are plagued by severe anxieties and worry about a whole range of situations, which may include separation fears. Some people with Panic Disorder (page 79) may have difficulty being left alone because they are afraid that nobody will be there to help them in case they have a panic attack. Skipping school is also common in Conduct Disorder (page 377) but for very different reasons.

Some autistic children (page 361) are intolerant of being away from caregivers.

TREATMENT OPTIONS

There have been no controlled trials regarding the treatment of Separation Anxiety Disorder. In practice, behavior therapy is most commonly done using the same techniques as for phobias (see page 94). These usually involve desensitizing the child to the anxiety through graded exposure of feared situations. For example, the child would start the therapy by learning to tolerate an image of his parents going out of the house for the evening. Exposure continues with progressively more difficult situations until the child can tolerate being away from attachment figures for extended periods of time. Medications can also be used in conjunction with the behavioral therapy to reduce the overall levels of anxiety. Although studies documenting effectiveness are lacking, medications that are used most often include Buspar (a nonaddictive medication used primarily for the treatment of Generalized Anxiety Disorder), SSRI antidepressants such as Prozac, Zoloft, Paxil, and Luvox, and low doses of Klonopin, an antianxiety medication chemically related to Valium.

Suggested Additional Readings

Bedwetting: A Guide for Parents and Children
Arthur C. Houts and Robert M. Liebert
Charles C. Thomas, 1985

Getting to Dry: How to Help Your Child Overcome Bedwetting
Max Maizels, Diane Rosenbaum, and Barbara Keating
Harvard Common Press, 1997

Clouds and Clocks: A Story for Children Who Soil
Matthew R. Galvin
Magination, 1991

A Mind of Its Own: Tourette's Syndrome: A Story and a Guide
Ruth Dowling Bruun and Bertel Bruun
Oxford University Press, 1994

Children with Tourette Syndrome: A Parent's Guide
Tracy Haerle (editor)
Woodbine House, 1992

Living with Tourette Syndrome
Elaine Fantle Shimberg
Fireside, 1995

Mommy, Don't Go (Children's Problem Solving Book)
Elizabeth Crary
Marina Megale (illustrator)
Parenting Press, 1996

Where to Go for Help
(Self-help, support, for more information)

National Enuresis Society
(information and support)

7777 Forest Lane
Suite C-737
Dallas, TX 75230-2518
(800) NES-8080
Web: http://www.peds.umn.edu/Centers/NES/

Tourette Syndrome Association
(education and services)

42-40 Bell Boulevard
Suite 205
Bayside, NY 11361
(888) 4-TOURET
Web: http://neuro-www2.mgh.harvard.edu/TSA/tsamain.nclk

Conclusion:

Ten Take-Home Messages

Our goal in this book has been to provide you with a comprehensive summary of the various psychiatric disorders that have become a part of the human condition. By now, you should know which disorders you definitely don't have and which (if any) may apply to you. What should you do next? In this last chapter we will answer the ten questions that are most often asked by patients and their families.

1. How can I know for sure that I have a psychiatric problem that needs treatment?

The simple answer is that you can never be completely sure unless you check out your own first impressions with a well-trained and experienced clinician. Although self-diagnosis is a very helpful first step, it is inherently limited by your possible biases and misunderstandings. You cannot expect to have mastered all the nuances of psychiatric diagnosis after reading one book. And, even if you happen to be a skilled clinician, we would always recommend against practicing on yourself. As the saying goes, "A lawyer who represents himself has a fool for a client."

It is hard to decide whether someone qualifies for a psychiatric diagnosis precisely because most people occasionally have at least some mild psychiatric symptoms. If you add up everyone who has had a few days of depression, or a few weeks of anxiety, or an occasional panic attack, or periodic eating binges, or misuses a substance from time to time—you would include at least 80 percent of the entire population. But fewer than one quarter of these have a diagnosable psychiatric condition that needs treatment. Unfortunately, there is no clear line marking the boundary distinguishing those with psychiatric disorders from those who are suffering from no more than the average expectable aches and pains of everyday life. Deciding whether or not you are okay is a cinch at the polar extremes—if you have no symptoms at all or if your symptoms are really a crusher—but it is much more difficult if you are one of the many people who are somewhere in the middle. Remember that one symptom does not a disorder make. Each psychiatric disorder has its very own characteristic pattern of symptoms and course. Before jumping to conclusions, refer back to the pertinent chapter and make sure that your symptoms conform pretty closely to the requirements of the appropriate diagnostic criteria set. Remember that your problems must also be really interfering with your life in a major way, not just be causing a bit of discomfort.

Because this boundary between mental health and mental illness is not easy to define, it is important that you guard against both under- and over-diagnosis in thinking about where you stand. The biggest problem is underdiagnosis. It is a startling fact that fully three fourths of the people with a treatable psychiatric disorder never get the help they need. We hope that reading this book will alert some of these folks so that they can get started in a timely fashion and on the right foot. Overdiagnosis is much less common—but it does occur in people who are emotional hypochondriacs and magnify run-of-the-mill problems into imagined psychiatric catastrophes (this might be called the Woody Allen syndrome). Not every imperfection in life is a psychiatric disorder, nor is every symptom or quirk amenable to psychiatric treatment. When in doubt, always check it out. Getting a diagnostic consultation requires no large expenditure of either time or money and does not mean that you have committed yourself to an ongoing treatment. You will almost certainly learn a lot about where things stand and what, if anything, you should do next.

2. What is causing my psychiatric problem?

This is much better worked out for some disorders than for others, but there are a few general principles that probably apply pretty much across the board. Most psychiatric disorders result from an inborn genetic vulnerability that then interacts with all the many challenges our environment throws at us. Our genes are just as powerful in increasing the odds that we will get depressed, experience panic attacks, become an alcoholic, or have a paranoid temperament as they are in raising the risk for diabetes, heart disease, or cancer. But genes never work in a vacuum. How they are expressed depends on the stress and support we experience in our lives—so much so that identical twins born with the very same package of DNA usually have no more than a fifty-fifty chance of getting the same disorder.

Scientific research is now hot on the trail tracking down which specific genes are involved in which psychiatric disorders and determining how they exert their influence. Within a decade we may well unlock at least some of the basic secrets of Schizophrenia, Bipolar Disorder, and Obsessive-Compulsive Disorder. It won't be a simple story. Many genes are probably involved in producing each disorder and the precise patterns of causation will undoubtedly differ in different people. The environmental factors that promote illness are remarkably varied and include complications related to childbirth, infections, physical trauma, family stressors, and all the other difficulties that must be faced in a long lifetime. In contrast, a strongly supportive environment may help to protect against illness, particularly if the genetic loading is not all that strong to start with.

The tremendous advances in neuroscience, brain imaging, and genetics are almost every day giving us a clearer picture of how the brain works to produce behavior—in both illness and health. It is a source of wonder that we live at a time when it will be possible to have answers to questions that have puzzled physicians and philosophers for at least the last five millennia. The practical return from the neuroscience revolution will lead to more specific and effective treatments and hopefully also improved methods of prevention.

There is another fascinating question that is related to the specific factors that cause psychiatric disorders. Why do they happen at all? If natural selection is so keen on promoting successful adaptation, why has it tolerated the survival of all of these seemingly maladaptive patterns in our genetic repertoire? The most obvious answer is that natural selection is far from perfect—witness the many physical ailments our species remains prey to. But beyond this, it is likely that all of the psychiatric disorders represent an exaggerated expression of the tendencies that in much more muted form confer adaptive advantages. This is most obvious in the tendency toward the personality disorders—being paranoid fosters alertness in a dangerous world; being antisocial is an extension of human predatory behavior; being narcissistic confers dominance leadership skills; being histrionic is an exaggeration of normal courtship behavior; and so on.

Somewhat less obviously, the same principle applies also to the other psychiatric disorders. Depression is an extreme form of the natural mammalian reaction to grief, stress, or loss of status. Panic attacks are a "fight or flight" response that occurs in the absence of an appropriately dangerous trigger. Inborn phobias protect us from the things that were most dangerous to our ancestors two hundred thousand years ago—heights, drowning, fire, dogs, snakes, and being smothered. Humans have a built-in taste for binge eating because no one was ever quite sure where the next meal was coming from before the species got around to inventing the agricultural revolution and refrigeration. Psychiatric disorders survive because they represent a much too concentrated form of what in small doses has been a very good thing.

3. Is having a psychiatric disorder my fault?

The answer is a resounding no—but most people with a psychiatric problem tend to blame themselves for having it. And, unfortunately, rigid social attitudes often reinforce this misconception by piling on unfair stigmatization. No one holds anyone responsible for having diabetes or hypertension or heart disease or cancer, but there is a tendency to look down on someone for being depressed, anxious, or addicted to a substance. We somehow expect ourselves to have much more control over the illnesses of the mind than over the illnesses of the body.

This is illogical, unfair, unhelpful, and counterproductive. Having a psychiatric illness may be a sign of lousy luck, but it is no more an indication of personal or moral weakness than having any one of a hundred medical illnesses. Never blame yourself for having the problem. Only blame yourself if you don't deal with it in the prudent way we suggest in the answer to the next question.

There is one crucial caveat that limits this seemingly blanket release from blame for mental illness. Having a psychiatric problem almost never relieves someone from responsibility for criminal or immoral behavior. There has been a recent ludicrous tendency to claim mental illness and victimhood as an excuse for all sorts of illegal and vile acts. Fortunately, this strategy usually fails in the courtroom and hopefully it will gradually fade from the talk shows. Most people who do terrible things do not have a psychiatric problem; most people who do have a psychiatric problem never do terrible things. If you are in the small minority of people with a psychiatric problem who do something terrible, you are not responsible for having the psychiatric problem but you are almost surely going to be held responsible for the terrible behavior. People with psychiatric problems sometimes have to work extra hard to control impulses and be considerate of others, but this is part of the responsibility of being a patient.

4. What can I do to get better?

From this moment onward, take control of the problem—rather than having it control you. Knowledge really does bring power. Become an informed consumer. Learn everything you can. Reading this book constitutes a good beginning, but go far beyond this first step and try to become a studious scholar about your disorder. The reference resources and support groups listed at the end of each chapter will assist in your research efforts. Your work of staying informed will have to be ongoing because new research findings are constantly increasing our knowledge and you should try to stay up to date.

It is also important to work with a clinician who can teach you more about your problems and help put them in their proper context. Be discerning in this. The most common complaint patients have about their doctors in both medical and psychiatric settings is that they don't tell them enough about what is going on. An important beginning of any treatment should be the clinician teaching you about what is happening and the different ways it can be treated. If your therapist is not a good and willing teacher, find another therapist.

Finally, it is all-important that you know yourself. Human beings are remarkably keen observers of just about everything that happens on this planet—except themselves. Self-knowledge is the first and necessary step to self-improvement, but it is easy for us to have big blind spots when we are looking at the one thing we can never really see straight on—ourselves. Take the time and make the effort to learn more about your characteristic behaviors, likes, dislikes, strengths, weaknesses, propensities, attitudes, biases, and fears. It helps to round out your subjective introspective picture by getting objective feedback from people you trust.

Getting over a psychiatric problem means really putting your heart into it. Motivation and hard work are crucial. When it comes to being a successful patient, perspiration is usually much more valuable than inspiration. Unlike Hollywood-style therapy in which complete remissions regularly occur after pivotal therapeutic epiphanies, real-life improvement in therapy is a much more gradual process. Only rarely are there giddy moments of sudden, profound, and earth-shaking insight. And very often these are fool's gold. Gains are made piecemeal, by doing some small mundane thing you previously would have avoided, or by achieving a quiet sense of self-acceptance, or by taking your medicine even when you don't like the side effects. Homework is usually more important than the work you do in the sessions. You have to put into action the things you come to understand and expose yourself to situations you might normally avoid.

Many of the disorders described in this book have a course that is either chronic or frequently recurrent. If you already have had many episodes, it is a good bet you are going to have many more unless you get a firm grip on this problem. This usually means achieving a very long-term view of your illness and taking the steps needed to keep it in check. Don't stop treatment suddenly just because you temporarily feel better. This is very likely to lead to a recurrence—usually not right away, but after several months. Even when you are doing perfectly fine, you may need to be on medication at least for months or years (and in some cases a lifetime). Maintenance visits to the therapist every six months or every year may help prevent the recurrences, allow for careful monitoring of medication, and keep everyone alert to any early signs of stress or recurrences before they can do real damage. The intensity and duration of the necessary treatment will depend on the particular illness, how long you have had it, the previous frequency of episodes, and the risk of recurrence versus the cost and difficulty of doing everything possible to prevent them.

Perhaps most important, you have to follow good general principles of mental hygiene. Avoid using substances—these are the single most frequent trigger for the relapse of psychiatric problems. Keep regular hours of work, play, and sleep. Don't overextend yourself or take on excessive stress. Stop and smell the roses. Remember that love (for yourself and others) is ultimately more satisfying than worldly triumph or accumulating more things than you will ever really need. And take your medicine as prescribed.

5. Why do I have to start treatment now—can't I wait to see if I will really need it?

There are huge advantages to identifying and treating psychiatric problems in the earliest stages, before they can become a deeply ingrained part of your life and brain functioning. It is very much akin to fixing a leak in your roof. Early on, especially if the leak hasn't penetrated into the house, the temptation is almost irresistible to let well enough alone and go about your business. Eventually, however, the leak will rot out the shingles and wallboard. What would have been a cheap and simple repair now instead requires a major and costly overhaul. Preventive maintenance and early intervention provide a stitch in time, eventually saving nine.

Psychiatric problems behave the same way. The more time you spend being depressed, or panicked, or compulsive the more the parts of your brain responsible for these symptoms become practiced at generating them. This is called "kindling." It is much easier to douse the flame before it becomes a conflagration. Studies show that many psychiatric illnesses respond much faster and more completely when the treatment has been started early in the course before the symptoms have become a way of life for you and your brain. Prompt treatment also reduces the risk of later relapses and improves the overall lifetime course. However tempting, watchful waiting is almost always a bad idea unless your psychiatric symptoms are extremely mild, brief, equivocal, or related to a transient stress. It also usually takes a period of about three to six weeks for treatment to begin working, so that the earlier you get started the sooner you will feel better.

6. What should I tell my family, fiancé(e), friends, or boss?

This is a tough question that has no simple and universal answer. In a totally enlightened world, one might enjoy the luxury of being totally open in discussing psychiatric problems—but it is quite clear that we don't yet live in such a world. The great desirability of being honest must be balanced against the need to protect privacy and the risk that the listener may harbor negative biases against psychological problems. What to do in any given situation is context specific and very much a question of your individual judgment of the dynamics of the moment.

Let us take the easiest situation first. You should probably always confide in your family and get their help—unless you have been very alienated from them or your problem is too trivial or temporary to require their being involved. Blood is thicker than water and families are usually much more accepting and useful than you might imagine they could ever be. In almost all instances, you will sooner or later need their support so you might as well get them on board early.

What and how much to tell your friends depends on the intimacy, longevity, and meaningfulness of the relationship. Avoid deep confidences with casual acquaintances but you may want to open up with your closest friends, especially if they have opened up to you and you are reasonably sure that they can be discreet. Social withdrawal is often an unfortunate consequence of having a psychiatric problem. You can avoid this to the extent that you have understanding friends who know what you are going through and are ready to pitch in and help.

How about romantic interests? It doesn't make much sense to tell all on a first date, but gradually sharing aspects of yourself is part of the getting-to-know-you process as intimacy begins to develop. Discussing a psychiatric problem is not too different than deciding when to tell someone that you have diabetes or some other medical illness. Truth in advertising and promoting intimacy require that you be open, but not before you care about the other person and feel confident enough about the relationship to share something very personal about yourself. The reaction you get from a potential partner will also tell you a great deal about whether he or she is the right soul mate for you.

The decision about degrees of openness is especially tough in the work environment. Should you be completely forthcoming on a job application when doing so may well mean that you won't get the job but not doing so feels dishonest and may get you into trouble later if you are found out? No one can tell you what to do in a situation like this and you will have to use your own judgment. Certainly, you should not volunteer any more information, or be any more specific, than is called for.

What if your psychiatric problem is affecting your work? Again this is a judgment call that depends on the problems you are having, how evident they are, what your boss and company are like, and your own comfort discussing personal issues. It is much easier if you work for a larger corporation that has an Employee Assistance Program whose job it is to help you in this situation. If not, what to do next will be greatly influenced by your relationship with your boss. You will probably want to keep things to yourself unless the problem is showing or you need time off for doctors' appointments or to recuperate. However, it may sometimes be better for your boss to know at least a little bit of what is troubling you rather than having her assume that you are being lazy, irresponsible, or difficult to deal with. This is a good topic to discuss with your therapist, who probably has had lots of experience advising people about it.

7. How do I decide what treatment to get?

For most psychiatric disorders, there are any number of different effective treatments from which to choose. This is a wonderful state of affairs offering you an extensive menu from which to select the treatment or treatments that provide the best custom fit to your specific needs, wants, preferences, and pocketbook. It is also nice to know that if the first treatment you try does not work sufficiently, there is almost always a second or third or fourth or fifth alternative. Hopefully sooner, but eventually later, you will almost certainly find something that works well for you.

The wealth of available treatments sometimes leads to an embarrassment of riches and a sense of confusion about all the possible choices. Should I be in psychotherapy or taking medicine or both? What kind of psychotherapy? What kind of medicine?

When medicines and psychotherapy are both effective for a particular condition, we recommend making the choice between them based on the severity and urgency of the problem. If the symptoms are mild to moderate and

CONCLUSION: TEN TAKE-HOME MESSAGES

not urgent, it is good to begin first with psychotherapy and see how far you get with it in curing the problem. There should be some clear improvement within a month or so and a dramatic improvement within a few months—if this does not happen, medication can then be added to the therapy. For moderate to severe symptoms and those that are more urgent, medications should be started immediately, usually along with psychotherapy. Some conditions—Schizophrenia, Bipolar Disorder, frequently recurring depressions—always require medicines, usually for years and often for a lifetime.

How about choosing from among all the different psychotherapies—psychodynamic, cognitive, behavioral, and interpersonal? We think that the best therapists are the ones who are most flexible and versatile and use all of the available techniques rather than sticking rigidly to any one of them. For many problems, a cognitive/behavioral approach is essential for efficient treatment but this is usually best delivered by someone who is also keenly aware of, and sensitive to, your psychological conflicts, interpersonal relationships, and environmental situation. Pick a psychotherapist who says things that make immediate sense to you rather than someone who mouths platitudes from any one school of psychotherapy.

The choice among medications may seem to be at least as bewildering. There are close to thirty different antidepressant medicines, more than a dozen antipsychotics, and another dozen antianxiety drugs. The names of the classes of medicines are also incredibly misleading. The "antidepressants" also work well for Panic Disorder, Obsessive-Compulsive Disorder, eating disorder, sleep problems, and even Enuresis. The "antipsychotics" work well for anxiety and agitation in many patients who are not psychotic. And anticonvulsants are often effective for Bipolar Disorder.

Although medicines must always be prescribed by a doctor and are never chosen by you alone, it is crucial that you understand their target symptoms, how they work, and the most common side effects. The more involved you are in selecting the regimen and the more knowledgeable you are about it, the more likely that you will take the medicine in the consistent way that is necessary if it is to be effective. There is about a two-thirds chance that the first medicine you try will work for you and it usually takes six to eight weeks to find out. If the first trial doesn't work, you have to move on patiently to the second or third choice until you find the right match. The choice among medicines will also be greatly influenced by how their side effect profiles match your preferences and needs. But don't just stop a medicine if you don't like the side effects—it may be possible to take in lower doses or at a different time of the day without a loss of effectiveness. Decisions about the next steps always should be made together with your doctor.

8. How do I pick the right clinician to work with?

There are two things to think about—chemistry and competence. Studies show that the best predictor of good outcome in treatment is that the people involved in it like and respect each other and work well together. Don't stay with a therapist you really don't like as a test of your endurance or in the hope that resolving the problem with him will somehow make you a better person. Every therapeutic relationship will have its occasional ups and downs (which you are likely to be contributing to in ways that may be enlightening), but these must occur on a foundation of trust and engagement if they are to be weathered well. It is probably a good idea to interview several clinicians before picking the one you want to work with and to go with your gut in choosing among them.

Competence is much more difficult to determine. There is an ever-growing array of different professional disciplines offering treatment for psychiatric problems. Competence varies widely both within and across disciplines. Many mental health clinicians are the best people our species is capable of producing—among the most competent and most caring of individuals. But there are also many well meaning but incompetent therapists, some outright charlatans, and even a fair share of the mean-spirited who have mistakenly wandered into the most helping of professions.

There is no surefire way of finding someone who knows what he is doing, but a few tips may help. First off, get personal recommendations from your friends who have been helped as well as suggestions from medical schools, professional associations, and patient support groups. The fact that someone comes highly recommended does not always prove that he is competent or right for you, but it is better than a complete shot in the dark picking at random from the yellow pages. Next, ask questions and expect good answers. Most of what mental health clinicians do is pretty straightforward and can be stated in commonsense language. If the clinician cannot articulate a plausible diagnostic assessment, treatment plan, and clear answers to your questions, this may reveal a fuzziness of thinking that you can do without. And you can check the answers you get by going to references, the Internet, or getting a second or third opinion from other clinicians. Again, by all means possible, be an informed consumer.

Selecting the discipline of your clinician creates its own set of issues. If you need medication, it will have to be prescribed by an M.D.—usually either a psychiatrist or a primary care physician. There are some primary care physicians who are terrific with psychiatric problems and medications—but these constitute a tiny minority. Most primary care physicians have had little training, experience, or interest in dealing with mental health problems, and tend to prescribe psychiatric medications in a haphazard way that ignores their indications, risks, interactions, and side effects. For example, beware any primary care doctor who prescribes an antidepressant for you without asking if you have ever had manic or hypomanic episodes or if you have a family history of Bipolar Disorder.

Psychiatrists are more experienced with the use of psychotropic medications and are more likely to individualize the treatment regimen (both with respect to specific choice of medicine and the dosing strategy) to meet your particular needs. For example, the dosing regimen for antidepressants recommended by pharmaceutical companies has been simplified in order to make using them a "no-brainer" for the primary care doctor. While easy to learn, this one-size-fits-all strategy often leads to problems. The standardized starting doses may be too high for you, resulting in a torrent of unwanted side effects. On the other hand, the recommended upper doses are usually overly conservative, leading to some people being undermedicated. Many of the initial side effects (agitation, sedation, dizziness) can be minimized by a more gradual increase in dosage. Psychiatrists are more able to manage unwanted side effects and have more experience in adding additional medications to augment the effects of the first medicine. Finally, as trained mental health professionals, they are able to incorporate psychotherapeutic strategies into the treatment.

While most psychiatrists have had extensive training in medications and are usually good at prescribing them, there are some (especially the older guard) who may be more comfortable with psychotherapy and may be less knowledgeable as psychopharmacologists than is desirable. On average, however, we believe that you are much better off having a psychiatrist prescribe your medications than relying on a primary care doctor.

How about choosing a psychotherapist? Beyond the crucial issue of getting the right interpersonal matchup, some therapists are much smarter, better-trained, practical, sensible, and experienced than others. To some degree this is related to the person's discipline—psychiatrists, psychologists, and social workers usually have more training and experience in psychotherapy than do other professional counselors—but there are terrific and terrible therapists in each discipline. We would recommend avoiding any therapist with an ideological ax to grind who is trying to fit you into a favorite theory. Beware especially of experts who specialize in Dissociative Identity Disorder/Multiple Personality Disorder, the recovering of repressed early memories of sexual abuse, hypnosis, sand play, or crystal gazing—all of these are likely to do you much more harm than good.

Stick to a mainstream person whom you like, who you can tell likes you, and who makes sense to you. Most of the therapy should probably focus on your here-and-now problems and on finding a better way of dealing with them. Discussing the past may be important in determining the enduring patterns of your behavior and how they may interfere with your current relationships—but this exploration should not become an end in itself or an excuse for settling for what you have got. If you are in therapy and have any doubts about it, a second opinion consultation is almost always helpful.

9. How can this bring my family together rather than tearing us apart?

It is likely that your psychiatric symptoms have created a good deal of tension and misunderstanding between you and your family. It is especially important, but often difficult, for everyone in the family to take a no-blame approach toward one another. Keep in mind that a psychiatric problem can make you difficult to live with. It is no fun being around someone who is constantly depressed, or high, or angry, or terrified, or engaged in unnecessary rituals, and so on. Your family may understandably lose patience and become reciprocally angry, disappointed, and impatient with you. This is not what they bargained for or have come to expect.

The more your family learns about your problem the less likely they are to criticize you for it or for the behaviors it causes. Otherwise, they may think that you are being willful, hostile, irresponsible, selfish, or unloving. With education about the illness, they will understand better what you are going through and blame the illness rather than blaming you. This will help them accept and respond better to aspects of your behavior that have been puzzling to them. The hope is that everyone can pull together, provide mutual support, and become even closer than before the illness announced itself. Having a shared problem can focus everyone's attention on what is really important in life.

It is usually a good idea to have your family join you for at least some sessions with your therapist. This is a chance to get everyone on the same page about the illness and to jointly find ways of dealing with it. They need to know what the treatments will be and how they can help you stick with them. It will be reassuring for them to learn that you will get better and return to being yourself. Getting your family on your side as a strong support makes it much more likely that things will work out well for you and for them—and that your relationship will improve.

If you are the family member, please keep in mind that it is the illness talking, not your loved one. Blame the psychiatric disorder and do whatever you can to help your partner or parent or child or sibling get over it. It may be useful to remember that the illness is the dragon, and that your loved one is the damsel or knight in distress who has been temporarily captured by it.

10. How do I deal with feeling ashamed and bitter about my problem?

Having a psychiatric problem is certainly no fun and can often be a pretty bad break. But no one ever said life was meant to be fair and lots of people have much worse physical and psychiatric problems than you can ever imagine. The best attitude is to gracefully accept the cards that you have been dealt and make the very best play you can with them. Of course, it may take some time before you come to this level of acceptance and achieve full resiliency in the face of adversity. The crucial step is realizing that you can have a richly rewarding life if you take charge of your illness and work hard to limit its complications—or that you can have a simply terrible life if you let the illness take charge of you and eat away at your center.

The many available support groups listed at the end of each chapter can provide tremendous help for you and your family. Attending a support group makes it crystal clear that you are not alone, uniquely damned, or condemned to a life of impairment. The first overwhelmingly successful support group was Alcoholics Anonymous and its twelve-step model has spread to similarly designed programs for other substance addictions, sexual problems, gambling, and many other problems. You are never very far away from an AA group. More recently, advocacy organizations have achieved enormous success in helping people deal with Schizophrenia (National Alliance for the Mentally Ill); Mood Disorders (National Depressive and Manic Depressive Association); anxiety disorders (Anxiety Disorders Association of America); and Obsessive-Compulsive Disorder (Obsessive Compulsive Foundation, Inc.). These groups have also had tremendous influence on the national and state political scene in gaining increasing resources and benefits for mental illness and in reducing the discrimination against it. They have also joined with professional organizations in stimulating research and improving treatment facilities.

The advocacy organizations provide extensive and readily accessible print and Internet information on each disorder and advice on how to get help for it. Most important, they provide loving and compassionate support. In most parts of the country, you can find a support group of people and family members who have been through, or are still living with, the same problem you have. They can provide a treasure trove of practical advice on things that have helped them and those that haven't. They can recommend clinicians. They can help you access resources. And, most important, they can be there when you need a sympathetic listener and friendly encouragement. Join a support group and bring your family. Eventually, when things get better for you, you will be able to return the favor and have the satisfaction of helping others get through this tough time on the road to recovery.

Well, that is it. Our book now finally comes to its end. Writing it has been a labor of love for us and we hope that it has been useful for you. The great thing about being a psychiatrist is that most of our patients get better or at least make tremendous progress. Whatever your problem—take heart, get help, and push onward.

INDEX

ABIL, Inc., 100
Abstract thinking, 334, 340
ADD. *See* Attention Deficit/Hyperactivity Disorder (ADHD)
ADD Anonymous, 397
Addiction
  detoxification in, 145–47
  Substance Dependence and, 120
  See also Alcohol use; Nicotine use; Substance Abuse; Substance Dependence; Substance use
ADHD. *See* Attention Deficit/Hyperactivity Disorder
AD-IN (Attention Deficit Information Network), 397
Adjustment Disorder, 295–300
  description of, 296–97
  differential diagnosis in, 298, 383
  questionnaire on, 27
  symptoms of, 296
  treatment of, 299–300
Adrenal problems, Panic Disorder and, 83
Advocacy organizations, 425–26
  See also the listings under specific illnesses
African-American women, idealized body shape of, 157
Aggression, in Intermittent Explosive Disorder, 264–67
Agitation
  in Dementia, 341
  in depression, 36
Agnosia, 340, 342
Agoraphobia, 82–83, 86–88, 95
  symptoms of, 88
  support group for, 100
Agoraphobics in Motion (AIM), 100
AIDS
  delusion about, 305

Dementia Related to, 344–45
  preoccupation with having, 256
  See also HIV infection
Al-Anon, 149, 153
Alcohol Dependence, 119, 120, 128–29, 143, 303
  information group for, 154
  support groups for families in, 153
  treatment of, 144–49
Alcoholics Anonymous (AA), 118, 124, 144, 145, 147–49, 151
  as first successful support group, 425
  groups with people on medicines, 324
Alcohol-Induced Dementia, 346, 348
Alcohol use, 117–29
  antianxiety agents and, 130
  danger of sedatives with, 131
  depression caused by, 44, 298
  dissociation from, 281
  effects of, 128–29, 175, 191
  Posttraumatic Stress Disorder and, 115
  psychiatric symptoms caused by, 127
  questionnaire on, 21–22
  sleepwalking and, 199
  thiamin recommended in, 346
  withdrawal from, 97, 123, 128–29, 146
    by hospitalization, 338, 339
Allen, Woody, 171, 414
Alzheimer's disease, 192, 283, 343, 353
Alzheimer's Disease and Related Disorders Association, 353
Ambien, 202
American Anorexia/Bulimia Association, 169
American Association of Sex Education, 188
American Chronic Pain Association, 262
American Heart Association, 354
American Institute of Stress, 301

American Narcolepsy Association, 204
American Sleep Disorders Association, 204
Amnesia
  alcohol use and, 346, 348
  in Alzheimer's disease, 283–84
  feigning of, 284
  medication as cause of, 140, 335
  from medications or drugs, 284
  protective nature of, 282
  substances causing, 127, 136, 202, 348, 351
  after trauma, 26, 281
  See also Amnestic Disorder; Dissociative Amnesia
Amnestic Disorder, 347–48
  differential diagnosis in, 335
  symptoms of, 347
  treatment of, 351
Amotivational syndrome, 134
Amphetamines, 83, 123, 146, 161, 175, 190
  description of use of, 131–32
  dopamines released by, 119
  in Schizophrenia, 324
Amytal, 129
Anafranil, 106, 279, 366
Angel dust. See PCP
Anger, loss of control of, 264–67
Animals
  depression in, 31, 32
  fertility and starvation in, 160
  intelligence of, 329
  misbehavior by young of, 375
Annie Hall (film), 171
Anorexia Nervosa, 157–64, 303
  description of, 158–60
  differential diagnosis in, 156, 161
  fear and avoidance in, 93
  low weight in, 156
  support groups for, 169–70
  symptoms of, 158
  treatment in, 162–64
Antabuse, 149
Antianxiety drugs, 84–85, 95, 98
  problems of use of, 129–31
Anticancer agents, depression from, 45
Anticonvulsants, 76
Antidepressants, 40, 41, 49–51, 191
  in Anorexia Nervosa, 164
  anxiety as possible side effect of, 97
  best prescribed by a psychiatrist, 423
  in Bulimia Nervosa (binge eating), 167–68
  in Dementia, 351

in Dysthymic Disorder, 55–56
in Generalized Anxiety Disorder, 99
mania from, 62, 67, 71, 76
newer, 51
in Panic Disorder, 84, 95
for Pathological Gambling, 276–77
in Posttraumatic Stress Disorder, 115
in pregnancy, 42
sexual side effects of, 175
as sleeping pills, 202
in Substance Abuse, 149
for unexplained physical complaints, 261
used in many disorders, 167
vs. violent behavior, 267
weight gain from, 156
Antidiarrheal drugs, 137
Antihistamines, 191, 202, 203
Antihypertensive drugs
  anxiety from, 97
  depression from, 45
  Sexual Dysfunction from, 176
Antipsychotics, 321
  in Autistic Disorder, 366
  in Bipolar Disorder, 76
  in depression with psychosis, 40
  for managing institutional patients, 361
  new class of, 324, 325, 361, 402
  in Schizophrenia, 316, 323–24
  side effects of, 97, 324
  vs. violent behavior, 267
  weight gain from, 156
Antiseizure medications, 267
Antisocial Personality Disorder, 211, 228–30, 268
  Conduct Disorder and, 377, 378, 383
  evolutionary context of, 12
  impulse-control problems in, 228–29, 264
  in mesomorphs, 208
  symptoms of, 229
  no treatment of, 241
Anxiety, 79–99
  conversion of, 251
  in Obsessive-Compulsive Disorder, 103–4, 106
  questionnaire on, 19–20
  substances causing, 127, 129, 130, 133, 140
  support groups in cases of, 99–100
  weight change from, 156
Anxiety Disorders, 79–115
  with Mental Retardation, 361
  See also Anxiety; Generalized Anxiety Disorder; Panic Disorder; Phobias; Separation Anxiety Disorder

Anxiety Disorders Association of America, 99, 425
Aphasia, in Dementia, 339–40, 342
Apraxia, 340, 342
Arc of the United States, The, 371
Aricept, 351
Aristotle, 208
Aromatic hydrocarbons, 138
Artane, 324
As Good As It Gets (film), 105
Asperger's Disorder, 364
Asperger Syndrome Support Group, 374
Asthma
  drugs for, side effects of, 97, 392
  Panic Disorder and, 83
Ativan, 76, 84, 98, 129, 146, 202
Attention and calculation, 333, 335, 340
  examination on, 330
Attention Deficit/Hyperactivity Disorder
  (ADHD), 387–96
  adult, 392–93
  Conduct Disorder and, 378
  description of, 390–92
  differential diagnosis in, 71, 335, 349,
    369, 382, 392–93, 402
  Learning Disorders with, 366, 368
  with Mental Retardation, 361
  questionnaire on, 29–30
  support groups for, 397
  symptoms of, 388–89
  three recognized categories of, 389, 391
  treatment in, 394–96
Auditory hallucinations, 305–6, 310, 315
Autism Network International, 374
Autism Society of America, 374
Autistic Disorder, 361–66
  description of, 363–64
  differential diagnosis in, 359, 364–65,
    392, 401
  support groups for, 373
  symptoms of, 362–63
  treatment in, 365–66
Avoidance, 79–99
  questionnaire on, 19–20
  See also Panic Disorder; Phobias
Avoidant Personality Disorder, 211, 217–19
  symptoms of, 218
  treatment of, 238
AZT, 345

Barbiturates, 129, 146
Bed, staying in, 40
  See also Sleep

Bed-wetting. See Enuresis
Behavioral changes
  in Alzheimer's disease, 343
  in Bipolar Disorder, 63–65
  See also Criminal behavior
Behavioral therapy
  ADHD, 395
  Anorexia Nervosa, 163
  Bulimia Nervosa, 168
  Conduct Disorder, 384
  depression, 53–54
  Encopresis, 404
  Enuresis, 406
  Gender Identity Disorder, 187
  Generalized Anxiety Disorder, 98
  Kleptomania, 269
  Mental Retardation, 360
  Panic Disorder, 85
  Paraphilia, 182–83
  phobias, 94
  Separation Anxiety Disorder, 410
  Sexual Dysfunction, 178
  Tic Disorder (Tourette's Disorder), 402
  Trichotillomania, 278–79
Behavior problems of children. See
  Children, behavior problems of
Benadryl, 203
Benzodiazepines, 129, 202
Beta blockers, 95
  vs. violent behavior, 267
Binge eating. See Bulimia Nervosa
Bipolar Disorder, 32, 59–66
  differential diagnosis in, 46, 70–73, 156,
    193, 288, 349, 392
  incidence of, 60–61
  seasonal depression in, 42, 62
  substance use in, 74
  support groups for, 58, 77–78, 145
  treatment for, 74–77, 322
  types of, 61, 65–66
Bipolar I Disorder, 61–66
  description of, 63–65, 72
  rapid cycling in, 62, 76
  symptoms of, 62–63
  typical pattern in, 66
Bipolar II Disorder, 66–69
  description of, 68–59, 72–73
  symptoms of, 67–68
  typical pattern in, 66
Bipolar Spectrum Disorders, 65–66
Bisexuality, 185
Blackouts, 284, 347, 348
Blindness, in Conversion Disorder, 250

Blood-brain barrier, 119
Blood sugar, low, 337–38
"Blues," the. *See* Depression
Body Dysmorphic Disorder, 246, 254,
    256–57, 260
  differential diagnosis in, 104
  symptoms of, 257
Body hair, fine (lanugo), 159
Body image, women's, 156–57, 161
Body Mass Index (BMI), 162
Borderline Personality Disorder, 70,
    224–26
  depersonalization in, 291
  differential diagnosis in, 166, 312
  impulse-control problems in, 225, 264
  symptoms of, 225
  treatment of, 239–40
Boss, what to tell to, 420
Brain
  development of, 355
  distractibility from damage to, 392
  frontal lobes of
    Dementia and, 340
    impulse-control problems and, 266
  normal pressure hydrocephalus of, 346
  organic solvents' damage to, 347
  subdural hematoma in, 346
  tumors of, 62, 72, 308, 337
    in AIDS, 345
  See also Head injury (trauma)
Brain Injury Association, 354
Breathing, rapid chest, 82, 85
Brief Psychotic Disorder, 306–7, 311–12
  with Mental Retardation, 361
  symptoms of, 312
  treatment for, 322
Bright light therapy. *See* Light therapy
Bronchodilators, 392
Bulimia Nervosa (binge eating), 156,
    164–68, 415–16
  description of, 165–66
  differential diagnosis in, 156, 160, 166
  evolutionary context of, 12
  questionnaire on, 22–23
  support groups for, 169–70
  symptoms of, 164–65, 167
  treatment of, 167–68
Burning oneself, 225, 240
Buspar, 98, 410

Caffeine, 117, 190
  in anxiety disorders, 83, 96
  in Bipolar Disorder, 74, 77

dependence on, 132–33
  psychiatric symptoms caused by, 127
  in Schizophrenia, 324
  in treatment of ADHD, 396
Caffeine intoxication, 133
CAGE questionnaire, 141–42
Calculation, 333, 335, 340
  examination on, 330
Cannabis. *See* Marijuana
Cannibalism, 181
Carbamazepine, 76
Carpenter, Karen, 158
Cataplexy, 192
Catastrophe reaction, 341–42
Catatonia, 306, 314, 315
Celebrity stalkers, 305
Celexa, 106
Center for Psychiatric Rehabilitation, 327
Center for the Study of Autism, 374
Central nervous system depressants, 129–31
Character and fate, 209, 211
Chemically Dependent Anonymous, 152
Childbirth
  Brief Psychotic Disorder after, 312
  depression after. *See* Postpartum
    depression
Children
  behavior problems of, 375–85
    questionnaire on, 29
    support groups for, 385–86
  developmental delays of, 355–70
    questionnaire on, 28–29
    support groups for, 371–73
    See also Autistic Disorder; Learning
      Disorders; Mental Retardation
  Dissociative Identity Disorder and, 287
  with Gender Identity Disorder, 184–87
  hair pulling in, 278
  hyperactivity or distractibility in. *See*
    Attention Deficit/Hyperactivity
    Disorder (ADHD)
  interest in fire by, 271
  miscellaneous problems of
    questionnaire on, 30
    See also Encopresis; Enuresis;
      Separation Anxiety Disorder
  nightmares in, 200
  Obsessive-Compulsive Disorder in, 104
  phobias learned by, 91
  sexual abuse of
    Dissociative Identity Disorder and, 287
    memories of, 284–85
    in Pedophilia, 179, 180–81

Sexual Dysfunction after, 175
support group, 293
sleep-related problems of, 24
Sleep Terror Disorders in, 198, 200
sleepwalking in, 199, 200, 203
stressful events for, 297
temperamental differences of, 208–9
Tic Disorder (Tourette's Disorder) in,
399–402
Children and Adults with Attention Deficit
Disorders (CHADD), 397
Chloral hydrate, 129
Chocolate, 41
"Choleric" temperament, 208
Cholesterol, high, 344
Chromosomal abnormalities in Mental
Retardation, 358
Chronic fatigue syndrome, 258
Circadian Rhythm Sleep Disorder, 190,
194–95
symptoms of, 195
treatment of, 203
Classification of mental disorders, 10
Clinics, drop-in, 325
Clonazepam, 76
Clonidine, 402
Clozapine, 324, 361, 402
Co-Anon's World Service Office, 153
Cocaine, 120, 121, 124, 131–32, 175, 190
antidepressants compared to, 49–50
in anxiety disorders, 83, 96
crack, 131
depression after crash following, 44
dopamine release by, 118
long-term use of, 126
paranoia from, 307
psychiatric symptoms caused by, 127, 321
in Schizophrenia, 324
weight change from use of, 156
withdrawal from, 123, 146
Cocaine Anonymous World Services, 151
Codeine, 121, 123, 137
Co-Dependents Anonymous (CoDA), 153,
242
Cogentin, 324
Cognex, 351
Cognition, definition of, 329
Cognitive difficulties, 329–53
differential diagnosis in, 349
lead poisoning to, 347
Mini-Mental State Examination on,
329–31
questionnaire on, 28

treatment in, 350–53
See also Amnestic Disorder; Delirium;
Dementia
Cognitive therapy, 48, 53, 85, 94, 98, 163,
168, 178, 238, 384
Cold preparations. See Decongestants
Combat fatigue, 111
Compulsions
definition of, 102
in Obsessive-Compulsive Personality
Disorder (OCPD), 214
questionnaire on, 20–21
See also Obsessive-Compulsive Disorder
Concentration camps, 113
Conduct Disorder, 377–80
description of, 379–80
differential diagnosis in, 383, 393, 409
Learning Disorders with, 366, 368
sex differences in, 377
symptoms of, 378–79
treatment of, 384–85
Confabulation, 341
Constipation, encopresis and, 403
Contamination, obsession with, 103, 106
Control, need for, 236–37
Conversion Disorder, 246, 250–52
Coprophilia, 181
Cough suppressants, 137
Council on Stroke, 354
Counting, 20
Crack, 131
Creativity, mania and, 65, 73–74
Criminal behavior
alcohol and, 128
in Antisocial Personality Disorder, 228, 230
in Bipolar I Disorder, 65
drug use and, 131, 132, 136–38, 144,
376–77
Kleptomania and, 268–69
memory loss and, 284
misguided justification of, 11, 181, 378,
416
in Paraphilia, 180–83
in Pyromania, 271
whether Conduct Disorder is, 378
Cross-dressing, 184–85
Cults, 319
Culture
behavior and, 235
delusions in context of, 320
in IQ testing, 356, 358
pain as influenced by, 253
Separation Anxiety Disorder and, 409

Cushing's disease, 72
Cutting oneself, 225, 240
Cyclothymic Disorder
  symptoms of, 69–70
  typical pattern in, 66
Cylert, 203

D.T.'s. *See Delirium tremens*
Dahmer, Jeffrey, 181
Dalmane, 129, 202
Darwin, Charles, 208
Daytime Enuresis, 404, 406
DDAVP, 406
Deafness, in Conversion Disorder, 250
Dean Foundation for Health Research and
  Education, 77
Decongestants, 83, 141, 191, 392
Defoliant exposure, 141
Dehydration, 306, 309, 349, 403
Delirium, 336–39
  causes of, 337–39
  differential diagnosis in, 335, 337, 349
  prevention of, 350–51
  psychosis in, 309
  Substance-Induced, 338
  substances causing, 127, 136
  symptoms of, 336
  treatment in, 350
Delirium Due to Medical Illness, 337–38
Delirium Due to Multiple Etiologies, 339
Delirium tremens (D.T.'s), 129, 322, 338
Delusional Disorder, 307, 316–17
  symptoms of, 317
  treatment of, 322–23
Delusions
  from alcohol, 129
  arson from, 270
  in Bipolar Disorder, 42, 71
  common themes of, 304–5
  definition of, 304
  in depression, 39, 42
  erotomanic, 305
  from marijuana, 134
  medication as cause of, 140
  mood incongruent, 311
  reality compared to, 319–20
  in Schizoactive Disorder, 71
  in Schizophrenia, 313–17
  in Shared Psychotic Disorder, 318
Dementia, 339–47
  causes of, 342–47
  depression caused by, 45
  description of, 334

differential diagnosis in, 335, 349
impulse-control problems in, 263, 266
psychosis in, 309
substances causing, 127, 347
support groups for, 353–54
symptoms of, 342
treatment of, 350–53
Vascular, 344
See also Alzheimer's disease
Dementia Caused by Alcohol, 346, 348
Dementia Caused by Other Substances, 347
Dementia Due to Parkinson's Disease or
  Huntington's Disease, 345
Dementia Related to AIDS, 344–45
Demerol, 137
Depakote, 75, 76
Dependent Personality Disorder, 211,
  215–17
  symptoms of, 216
  treatment of, 237–38
Depersonalization, 135, 136
Depersonalization Disorder, 290–92
  differential diagnosis in, 291, 392
  symptoms of, 291
  treatment of, 292
Depressed Anonymous, 57
Depression, 31–58, 415
  in Anorexia Nervosa, 160
  bipolar. *See* Bipolar Disorder
  with Dementia, 351
  differential diagnosis of, 44–46, 104, 156,
    166, 176–78, 193, 258–59, 268,
    297, 298, 335, 349, 369, 392
  evolutionary context of, 12
  four triggers of, 31
  impulse-control problems in, 266
  incidence of, 32
  medical illness and, 45–46
  pain and, 253–54
  questionnaire on, 17–18
  Sexual Dysfunction from, 176
  support groups for, 56–58
  treatment in, 48–56
  unipolar. *See* Dysthymic Disorder; Major
    Depressive Disorder
Depression after Delivery, 57
Depression and Related Affective
  Disorders Association (DRADA), 57
Derailment, 315–16
Derealization, 292
Desedrine, 203
Desensitization, 269
See also Phobic desensitization

Desipramine, 41
Despair, in depression, 37–39
Desyrel, 202
Dexatrim, 141
Diabetes, 176, 344, 405
Diagnosis
    criteria of. *See* DSM-IV
    differential, 13–14
    of exclusion, 247, 343
    self-, 11, 14, 413
    as sophisticated name calling, 11
    whether you need, 413–14
*Diagnostic and Statistical Manual of Mental
    Disorders, Fourth Edition. See*
    DSM-IV
Diet pills, 83, 96, 191
Diet therapy for ADHD, 395–96
Disorder of Written Expression, 368
Disorientation
    in Delirium, 336, 337
    See also Orientation
Dissociative Amnesia, 282–86
    differential diagnosis in, 283–85, 392
    in sexual abuse, 284
    symptoms of, 283
    treatment of, 285–86
Dissociative experiences, 281–92
    incidence of, 282
    questionnaire on, 26–27
Dissociative Identity Disorder (DID), 27,
    286–90, 313
    description of, 287–88
    differential diagnosis in, 288
    Multiple Personality Disorder as other
        name for, 282, 289
    support group for, 293
    symptoms of, 287
    treatment of, 289–90
Distractibility, 391
Distraction therapy, in Kleptomania, 269
Dopamine, 118, 324, 345
Doral, 202
Down syndrome, 358
    support groups for, 371–72
Dreams, 190, 192
    Nightmare Disorder, 197–98
Drugs
    classes of, 119
    tolerance of, 120, 122
    See also specific drugs; Medication
Drugstore Cowboy (film), 123
DSM-IV, 10, 12–14, 17, 21
    drug classification by, 119

Durning, Charles, 129
Dyslexia (Reading Disorder), 368, 369
Dyspareunia, 174
Dysthymic Disorder, 42–44
    description of, 43–44, 48
    differential diagnosis in, 44–46, 166, 297
    Major Depressive Disorder with, 44
    symptoms of, 43
    treatment in, 55–56

Eating disorders, 155–68
    differential diagnosis in, 104–5
    evolutionary context of, 12, 155
    questionnaire on, 22–23
    support groups for, 169–70
    See also Anorexia Nervosa; Bulimia
        Nervosa; Overeating
Eccentricity, in Schizotypal Personality
        Disorder, 232–33
Echolalia, 316
Echopraxia, 316
"Ecstasy" (MDMA), 135
Ectomorphs, 208
Effexor, 98
Elavil, 202
Elderly people. *See* Older people
Electroconvulsive therapy (ECT)
    in depression, 40–41, 51–52, 55, 322
    mania after, 71
Emotions Anonymous, 57, 242
Encopresis, 402–4
    symptoms of, 403
    treatment of, 404
Endomorphs, 208
Enuresis, 404–6
    Daytime, 404, 406
    support group for, 411
    symptoms of, 405
    treatment of, 405–6
Environmental factors in mental disorders, 415
Erotomanic delusions, 305
Ethnocentrism, 235
    See also Culture
Euphoric mood. *See* Mania
Exhibitionism, 179, 180
Explosive behavior. *See* Intermittent Explo-
        sive Disorder
Exposure therapy. *See* Phobic desensitization
Eyebrow-plucking. *See* Trichotillomania

Families and loved ones
    in Bipolar Disorder, 60, 61, 77
    in Dementia, 339, 340, 351–53

Families and loved ones (*cont.*)
depression after loss of, 31, 34, 47, 54, 297–300
Gender Identity Disorder and, 187
joint psychiatric sessions with, 424–25
Obsessive-Compulsive Disorder (OCD) and, 106
in Paranoid Personality Disorder, 226, 227
in Pathological Gambling, 273, 276
phobias and, 94–95
in Separation Anxiety Disorder, 407
in Shared Psychotic Disorder, 318–19
sharing your problem with, 419–20, 424–25
in Substance Dependence, 119, 144–49
support groups, 153–54
suicide and, 38–39
See also Rejection
Families Anonymous, 154
Families Anonymous World Service Office, 386
Family, decline of, 376
Fatigue, in depression, 36–37, 43
Fear, 79–99
questionnaire on, 19–20
See also Panic Disorder; Phobias
Fearlessness, 20
Fear of success, 224
Fear of Success Anonymous, 243
Federation of Families for Children's Mental Health, 386
Feeling
lack of
in Schizoid Personality Disorder, 231
in Schizophrenia, 316
loss of, in depression, 35–36
Feingold diet, 395
Fetishism, 179, 180
Fibromyalgia, 258
Fields, W. C., 269
"Fight or flight" response, 81–82, 92
Fiorinal, 129
Fire setting. *See* Pyromania
Flashbacks, 136, 298
Folie à Deux. *See* Shared Psychotic Disorder
Food allergies, 395
Foster, Jodie, 305
Fragile X syndrome, 358
support groups for, 372
Freud, Sigmund, 46, 179, 181, 208, 250–51

Friends, what to tell about your problem to, 419
Frotteurism, 179, 180

Gall, Franz Joseph, 208
Gam-Anon International Service Office, 279
Gamblers Anonymous, 272, 276, 279
Gambling, 26, 105
See also Pathological Gambling
Gasoline, 138, 347
Gender Identity Disorder, 183–87
definition of, 172
description of, 184–85
questionnaire on, 23
symptoms of, 184
treatment of, 186–87
Generalized Anxiety Disorder, 95–99
depersonalization in, 291
differential diagnosis of, 96–97, 104, 193, 392, 409
symptoms of, 96
treatment of, 98–99
Genetic vulnerability to mental disorders, 414–15
Glass Menagerie, The (Williams), 89
Glue, 121, 138, 347
Glue sniffer's rash, 139
Gone With the Wind (book and film), 219, 333
Grandiose delusions, 304–5, 315
Grandiose hallucinations, 110
Greece, ancient
personality theories in, 207–8
tragedy in, 211
Grief, depression and, 31, 34, 47–48, 54
Grieving, 31
Gulf War Syndrome, 141

Habit reversal training, 278–79, 402
Hair pulling. *See* Trichotillomania
Halcion, 129, 202
Haldol, 361, 402
Hallucinations
arson from, 270
auditory, 305–6, 310, 315
command, 306, 315
definition of, 305
in Delirium, 336, 337
in depression, 39
from marijuana, 134
medication as cause of, 140
misinterpretations compared to, 320–21

in postpartum depression, 42
in Schizophrenia, 313, 315
from sensory deprivation, 309
tactile, 306
visual, 306, 315, 321
in withdrawal from alcohol or depressants, 129
Hallucinogens, 121, 123, 135–36, 307
psychiatric symptoms caused by, 127
Haloperidol, 76
Hand-washing, 20, 103
Hashish, 133, 134
Head banging, 363, 366
Head injury (trauma)
amnesia from, 284, 348
Dementia from, 346, 348, 350
dissociation after, 281
impulse-control problems after, 263, 266
Learning Disorders from, 369
Mental Retardation from, 358
psychosis after, 308
support group for, 354
Health-store treatments, 52–53
Heart problems
Adjustment Disorder and, 297
Delirium with, 337
Dementia with, 344
Panic Disorder and, 83
psychosis from, 309
Heavy metal exposure, 347
Herbal medicine, 141
Heroin, 120, 121, 123, 131, 137
antidepressants compared to, 49–50
methadone treatment for, 149–50
support groups for users of, 151–52
Heterosexuality, 185
High blood pressure
Vascular Dementia with, 344
See also Antihypertensive drugs
Hinckley, John, 305
Hip fractures, 341
Hippocrates, 126, 207, 209
Histrionic Personality Disorder, 211, 219–22, 235
symptoms of, 221
treatment of, 238–39
HIV infection
of heroin addicts, 138, 150
See also AIDS
Hoffman, Dustin, 364
Hog. See PCP
Homeopathic treatments, 52
Homosexuality, 185

Hospitals
Delirium from conditions in, 338
fire setting in, 271
inpatient detoxification in, 145–47
overuse of antipsychotics in, 361
Huntington's Disease, Dementia Due to, 345
Hydrocephalus, 346
Hyperactivity
in ADHD, 391
various causes of, 392
Hyperactivity Disorder. See Attention Deficit/Hyperactivity Disorder (ADHD)
Hypersomnia
Primary, 196–97
See also Oversleeping
Hypertension, 176
Hyperventilation, 82, 85
Hypnosis
for Dissociative Amnesia, 284, 286
memories "recovered" under, 284–86
in Trichotillomania, 278
Hypnotics, 202
Hypoactive Sexual Desire Disorder, 173
Hypochondriasis, 246, 254–56, 260, 414
differential diagnosis in, 104
symptoms of, 256
Hypoglycemia, 258
Hypomania, 67, 68, 70, 72–73

"Ice," 131–32
Idiot savant, 363–64
Illness (general medical condition)
Adjustment Disorder as result of, 297
Delirium Due to, 337–38
delusions about, 305
Psychotic Disorder Due to a Medical Condition, 306, 308–10, 322
terminal, undermedication in, 138
See also Unexplained physical complaints; specific illnesses
Imipramine, 41, 406
Impotence, 173, 178
Impotence Information Center, 188
Impotence Institute of America, 188
Impotents Anonymous (IA) and I-Anon, 188
Impulse-control problems, 263–79
in ADHD, 392
evolutionary context of, 263
in mania, 65, 75
questionnaire on, 26

Industrial exposures or accidents, 141, 142
Infections
    with AIDS, 345
    Delirium with, 338, 349, 350
    See also HIV infection
Inhalants, 121, 123, 124, 138–39
    psychiatric symptoms caused by, 127
Insight, 334–35
Insight-oriented therapy, 49, 54
Insomnia, 190, 200, 201
    in Dementia, 342
    in depression, 36, 40, 41, 43, 47
    medication as cause of, 140, 191
    Primary, 195–96
    questionnaire on, 24
    in shift work, 194–95, 203
Instinct, 329
Interest or pleasure in things, decreased, 35–36, 46
Intermittent Explosive Disorder, 264–67
    differential diagnosis in, 265–66
    symptoms of, 265
    treatment of, 266–67
Internet, 15
Interpersonal therapy, 48, 54
IQ, in Mental Retardation, 355–57
Irritable bowel syndrome, 258

Jamison, Kay, 35
Jekyll and Hyde quality, 265, 349
Jesus, belief that one is, 306
Jet lag, 194, 203
Jones, Jim, 319
Journal of Psychiatric Research, 330
Judgment, 334–35, 340

Kidney disease, hallucinations from, 309
Kindling, 60, 418
Kleptomania, 264, 267–69
    differential diagnosis of, 268–69
    symptoms of, 268
    treatment of, 269
Klonopin, 76, 84, 98, 129, 402, 419
Korsakoff's syndrome, 346, 348
Kretschmer, Ernst, 208

L-dopa, 345
Lamictal, 76
Lamotrigine, 76
Language, 333–34
    in Autistic Disorder, 361–63, 365
    examination on, 330–31
Lanugo, 159

Laxative abuse, 164–66
Lead poisoning, 141, 347, 358, 369
Learning Disabilities Association of
    America, 372
Learning Disorders, 366–70
    description of, 367–68
    differential diagnosis in, 368–69, 393
    incidence of, 367
    support groups for, 372
    symptoms of, 367
    treatment of, 369–70
Lethargy, in depression, 36
Libido, decreased, 160
Librium, 129, 146
Lighter fluid, 138
Light therapy
    Bipolar Disorder, 71
    Circadian Rhythm Sleep Disorder, 203
    Seasonal Depression, 42
    unipolar depression, 48
Linnaeus, 52
Lithium, 75–76, 156
Lithium Information Center, 77
Liver failure, 309
Loners
    with Schizoid Personality Disorder, 230–32
    with Schizotypal Personality Disorder, 232–33
Long Island Rail Road shooting, 114–15
Loosening of associations, 315–16
Loved ones. See Families and loved ones
LSD, 120, 135, 307
Luvox, 41, 51, 95, 106, 175, 191, 279, 366, 410

Major Depressive Disorder, 33–42, 303
    with atypical features, 41, 62
    Conduct Disorder and, 378
    Dementia with, 342
    depersonalization in, 291
    description of, 34–39, 46–48
    differential diagnosis of, 44–46, 104, 156, 166, 176–78, 193, 258–59, 268, 297, 298, 335, 349, 369, 392
    grief as trigger of, 47
    with melancholic features, 40–41
        treatment for, 55
    with Mental Retardation, 361
    postpartum. See Postpartum depression
    with psychotic features, 39–40, 310–11, 322
        treatment for, 40, 51, 55
    recurrence of, 33–34

seasonal. *See* Seasonal depression
symptoms of, 34
treatment in, 48–55, 322
Managed care of psychiatric disorders, 10,
  55, 247, 260–61
Mania, 59–61, 72
  differential diagnosis of, 268, 335, 382
  euphoric vs. dysphoric, 63
  evolutionary context of, 12, 59
  first, after ages forty to fifty, 62, 72
  impulse-control problems in, 60, 264,
    266
  Pathological Gambling and, 273, 275
  with Psychotic Features, 310–11
  questionnaire on, 18–19
  treatment for, 75, 322
  See also Bipolar Disorder
Manic-depression. *See* Bipolar Disorder
MAO (monoamine oxidase) inhibitors, 41,
  95
Marijuana (cannibis), 120, 121, 123,
    133–35, 143, 146
  incidence of use of, 133
  paranoia from, 307
  with PCP, 136
  psychiatric symptoms caused by, 127
Marijuana Anonymous, 151
Marriage
  attraction of opposites in, 235
  delusional jealousy in, 304, 307
  See also Families and loved ones
Masochism, sexual, 179, 180
Mathematics Disorder, 368
MDMA ("Ecstasy"), 135
Medical conditions. *See* Illness; *specific
  conditions*
Medication
  in ADHD, 394–95
  in AIDS, 345
  amnesia from, 284
  anxiety from, 97
  in Autistic Disorder, 366
  best prescribed by a psychiatrist, 423
  in Bipolar Disorder, 75–77
  children's growth suppression in, 394–95
  choice of, 421–22
  Dementia from change in, 349
  depression sometimes caused by, 45
  dissociation from, 281
  fluctuations in mood from, 71
  interactions and side effects of, 45,
    140–41, 392
  in Mental Retardation, 361

in Obsessive-Compulsive Disorder
  (OCD), 106
in older people, 45, 203
overeating as reaction to, 156
Panic Disorder from, 83
placebo groups in tests of, 50–51
in Posttraumatic Stress Disorder, 115
psychotic disorder induced by, 307–8
in Separation Anxiety Disorder, 410
for Sexual Dysfunction, 178
sexual side effects of, 175
sleep problems from, 191, 197
in Substance Abuse, 149
in Tic Disorder (Tourette's Disorder),
    401–2
vs. violent behavior, 267
See also specific drugs and types of drugs
Medicinal plants, 52–53
Meditation
  depersonalization in, 292
  dissociation from, 282
Megavitamin therapy, 396
Melancholia. *See* Major Depressive
    Disorder—with melancholic features
"Melancholic" temperament, 208
Melatonin, 141, 203
Memory
  of *idiots savants,* 363–64
  loss of
    in Dementia, 339–40
    medication to slow down, 351
    in older people, 350
    See also Amnesia; Amnestic Disorder
  normal imperfection of, 285
  remote, 332–33
  "repressed" or "false," 284–85
  three components of, 332–33
Men. *See* Sex differences
Menstruation
  in Anorexia Nervosa, 158–60, 163
  See also Premenstrual period
Mental disorders (psychiatric disorders)
  boundary between mental health and,
    414
  classification of, 10
  descriptions of, 13
  evolutionary context of, 12
  genetic vulnerability to, 414–15
  managed care and, 10, 55, 247, 260–61
  need for you to learn about, 416–18
  people not relieved of responsibility by,
    11, 181, 378, 416
  percentage of people with, 10

Mental disorders (psychiatric disorders) (*cont.*)
    picking right clinician in, 422–24
    second-opinion consultation in, 424
    should be treated at earliest stages,
        418–19
    what treatment to get in, 420–22
    whether you are responsible for, 416
Mental functioning, questionnaire on, 28
Mental Retardation, 355–61
    Autistic Disorder with, 362, 364
    description of, 357–59
    differential diagnosis in, 312, 349, 382,
        359
    psychiatric disorders in, 361
    support groups for, 371
    symptoms of, 357
    treatment in, 359–61
Mercury exposure, Dementia from, 347
Mescaline, 135, 307
Mesomorphs, 208
Methadone, 137, 149–50
Methadone Anonymous, 151
Methamphetamine, 131–32
Methaqualone, 129
Miltown, 129
Mini-Mental State Examination, 329–31
Mood
    depressed, 35
    euphoric. *See* Bipolar Disorder; Mania
    instable, 69–71
    irritable, 59, 61–63, 68
Mood Disorder, 32, 306, 309, 312, 315,
        322, 393
    differential diagnosis in, 337
    in endomorphs, 208
    Psychotic, 311
    substances causing, 127
Mood stabilizers, 75–76, 267, 277, 322,
        323, 351
Morning glory seeds, 135
Morphine, 123, 137
Motor and sensory functions, 334
    in Dementia, 340
Multiple Personality Disorder. *See* Dissocia-
    tive Identity Disorder
Multiple sclerosis, 176, 246, 251
Mushrooms, 135, 307

Nail polish remover, 138
Naltrexone, 149
Nar-Anon World Service Organization, 153
Narcissistic Personality Disorder, 211,
    222–24, 303

symptoms of, 223
treatment of, 239
Narcolepsy, 192, 197, 204, 205
Narcolepsy Network, 205
Narcotics
    withdrawal of, 97, 122–23
    See also Drugs; Substance Abuse; Sub-
    stance Dependence; *specific drugs*
Narcotics Anonymous, 152
Nardil, 41, 95
National ADDA, 397
National Alliance for Research on
    Schizophrenia and Depression
    (NARSAD), 58
National Alliance for the Mentally Ill
    (NAMI), 58, 145, 425
National Association for the Dually Diag-
    nosed, 371
National Association of Anorexia Nervosa
    and Associated Disorders (ANAD),
    169
National Chronic Pain Outreach Associa-
    tion (NCPOA), 262
National Council for Compulsive Gam-
    bling, 280
National Depressive and Manic-Depressive
    Association (NDMDA), 58, 145
National Down Syndrome Congress, 372
National Down Syndrome Society, 371
National Drug and Alcohol Abuse
    Information and Treatment
    Referral Hotline, 154
National Eating Disorders Organization, 169
National Enuresis Society, 411
National Foundation for Depressive Illness, 58
National Institute on Drug Abuse Helpline,
    154
National Mental Health Association, 58
National Mental Health Consumer's
    Association, 326
National Organization for Seasonal
    Affective Disorders (NOSAD), 57
National Organization for Victim
    Assistance, 116
National Sleep Foundation, 204
National Stroke Association, 354
National Victim Center, 116
Necrophilia, 181
Nembutal, 129
Nicholson, Jack, 52, 105
Nicotine use, 117, 124, 139–40, 344
    as most addictive substance, 139
    in Schizophrenia, 324

Night alarm, 406
Nightmare Disorder, 197–98
Nightmares, 298
Nortriptyline, 41
Numbness, 250, 251, 258

Obesity, 156, 344
Obsessions
definition of, 102
questionnaire on, 20–21
Obsessive-Compulsive Anonymous, 107
Obsessive-Compulsive Disorder (OCD),
101–15
description of, 102–4
differential diagnosis in, 84, 104–5, 401
fear and avoidance in, 92–93
incidence of, 101
support groups for, 107, 145
symptoms of, 101–2
treatment in, 106
Obsessive Compulsive Foundation, 107,
145, 425
Obsessive-Compulsive Information Center,
107
Obsessive-Compulsive Personality Disorder
(OCPD), 212–14, 235
differential diagnosis in, 105
symptoms of, 213–14
treatment of, 236–37
Older people
Alzheimer's disease in, 343
cognitive loss in, 350
with Dementia, 341, 346
hearing and visual impairments in, 309
mania in, 62
medications in, 45, 203
Parkinson's disease in, 345
sleep patterns in, 189, 200
Substance-Induced Psychotic Disorder in,
307
One Flew Over the Cuckoo's Nest (film), 52
O'Neill, Eugene, 73
Opioid Dependence, treatment of, 149–50
Opioids, 123, 124, 127, 131, 137–38, 191
psychiatric symptoms caused by, 127
Opium, 120
Oppositional Defiant Disorder (ODD),
381–85
description of, 382
differential diagnosis in, 382–83
symptoms of, 381
treatment of, 385
Oral contraceptives, depression from, 45

Orap, 402
Organic solvents, 347
Orgasm, 172, 174
Orientation, 331–32
examination on, 330
Overeaters Anonymous, 169
Overeating
in depression with atypical features, 41, 62
as reaction to medication, 156
Oversleeping, 190
in depression, 36, 41, 43, 62
Primary Hypersomnia, 196–97
treatment for, 203

Pain, acute vs. chronic, 253
Pain Disorder, 246, 252–54
support groups for, 262
symptoms of, 254
Painkillers, depression from, 45
Paint thinner, 121, 138, 347
Panic Disorder, 79–86, 415
depersonalization in, 291, 292
description of, 81–83
differential diagnosis in, 83–84, 97, 258,
392, 409
as leading to Agoraphobia, 83–84, 87, 95
support group for, 100
symptoms of, 80–81
treatment of, 84–86
Panic in Needle Park, The (film), 123
Paralysis
in Conversion Disorder, 250, 251
after stroke, 344
Paranoia
in Dementia, 342
drug-induced, 307–8
Paranoid delusions in Schizophrenia,
314–15
Paranoid Personality Disorder, 210, 226–28
symptoms of, 227
treatment of, 240–41
Paraphilia, 179–83
definition of, 171–72
differential diagnosis in, 105
symptoms of, 179
treatment of, 182–83
Parents United International, 293
Parkinson's disease, 97, 192
Dementia Due to, 345
Parnate, 41, 95
Pathological Gambling, 272–77
differential diagnosis in, 274–75
support groups for, 279–80

Pathological Gambling (*cont.*)
    symptoms of, 274
    treatment of, 276–77
    See also Gambling
Paxil, 41, 50, 51, 95, 106, 175, 191, 279,
    366, 410
PCP (phencyclidine), 120, 123, 124, 126,
    136, 146, 307
    psychiatric symptoms caused by, 127
Peace pill. *See* PCP
Pedophilia, 179, 180–81
Perfectionism, 236–37
Performance, 333–34
    examination on, 330–31
Persecutory delusions, 304
Personalities, multiple. *See* Dissociative
    Identity Disorder
Personality
    definition of, 207
    differences in, 207–9
    need for awareness of, 236
Personality Disorders, 181, 207–42, 415
    definition of, 234–35
    description of, 210–12
    differential diagnosis in, 233–34, 288,
        312
    impulse-control problems in, 266
    questionnaire on, 24–25
    support groups for, 242–43
    symptoms of, 209–10
    treatment of, 236–42
Pervasive Developmental Disorder. *See*
    Autistic Disorder
Perversions. *See* Paraphilia
Pessimistic personality, 48
Peyote, 135, 142
"Phlegmatic" temperament, 208
Phencyclidine. *See* PCP
Phobias, 86–95
    depersonalization in, 291
    differential diagnosis in, 84, 92–93, 97
    evolutionary context of, 12
    prevention of, 94
    support groups for, 100
    treatment of, 94–95
    types of, 86, 91–92
Phobic desensitization (exposure therapy),
    94, 163, 238, 261, 410
Phobics Anonymous, 100
Physical appearance
    dissatisfaction with, 26
    See also Body Dysmorphic Disorder; Body
        image

Physical symptoms, unexplained. *See*
    Unexplained physical complaints
Picking at parts of the body, 366
Placebo
    in drug tests, problem of, 50–51
    "side effects" from, 259
Placidyl, 129
Postpartum depression, 42, 62, 312
    support groups for, 56–57
Postpartum Support International, 56
Posttraumatic Stress Disorder (PTSD),
    110–15
    depersonalization in, 291
    description of, 111–13
    differential diagnosis in, 84, 193, 298
    fear and avoidance in, 92
    incidence of, 110
    support groups in, 116
    symptoms in, 111
    treatment in, 114–15
Praying, ritualistic, 20
Premature ejaculation, 173, 174, 178
Premenstrual period, caffeine and, 133
Preservatives, 395
Prevention Online: SAMHSA, 154
PRIDE (Patient's Resource Institute for
    Drug Education), 154
Primary care physicians, 50, 423
Primary Hypersomnia, 196–97, 203
    symptoms of, 197
Primary Insomnia, 195–96
    symptoms of, 196
    See also Insomnia
Progressive muscle relaxation, 278
Prolixin, 402
ProSom, 202
Prostate disease, 176
Prozac, 41, 50, 51, 95, 106, 129, 175, 191,
    279, 366, 410
Pseudoseizures, in Conversion Disorder,
    250, 252
Psilocybin, 135
Psychedelic drugs. *See* Hallucinogens
Psychiatric disorders. *See* Mental disorders
Psychodynamic psychotherapy. *See*
    Insight-oriented therapy
Psychoeducation
    in Anorexia Nervosa, 163
    in Schizophrenia, 325
    in unexplained physical complaints, 261
Psychosis, 303–25
    classification of, 306–7
    disorganized behavior in, 321

impulse-control problems from, 264
from psychedelic drugs, 135
support groups in, 326–27
See also Brief Psychotic Disorder;
  Delusions; Hallucinations; Major
  Depressive Disorder, with
  psychotic features; Schizophrenia;
  Schizoaffective Disorder; Shared
  Psychotic Disorder
Psychotherapists
  background and licensing of, 54–55
  choice of, 422–24
Psychotherapy
  in ADHD, 395
  in Adjustment Disorder, 299–300
  in Bipolar Disorder, 77
  choosing among various schools of, 421
  for Conduct Disorder, 384–85
  in depression, 41, 47, 48–49, 52–55
  in Dissociative Identity Disorder, 289–90
  in eating disorders, 163, 168
  Freud on, 46
  in Gender Identity Disorder, 187
  in Generalized Anxiety Disorder, 98
  in Intermittent Explosive Disorder, 266–67
  in Mental Retardation, 360
  in Obsessive-Compulsive Disorder
    (OCD), 106
  in Panic Disorder, 85–86
  in Paraphilia, 182–83
  in Pathological Gambling, 276–77
  in Personality Disorders, 238
  in phobias, 94
  in Posttraumatic Stress Disorder, 114–15
  in psychosis, 322–23, 325
  for Pyromania, 271
  in Sexual Dysfunction, 178
  therapist-patient "chemistry" in, 55
  in Trichotillomania, 278–79
  in unexplained physical complaints, 261
  when ineffective, 40
  when to start with, 420–21
Psychotic Disorder
  differential diagnosis in, 104
  Due to a Medical Condition, 308–10
    symptoms of, 310
  substances causing, 127
Psychotic Mood Disorder, 311
Public speaking, fear of, 88–89
Pyromania, 269–71
  differential diagnosis in, 270–71
  symptoms of, 270
  treatment of, 271

Quaalude, 129
Questionnaire, 11–12, 17–30
  CAGE, 141–42

Rain Man (film), 364
Rape
  Dissociative Amnesia in, 282–83
  Posttraumatic Stress Disorder after, 112
Rational Recovery Systems, 152
Reading Disorder (Dyslexia), 368, 369
Reagan, Ronald, 305
Reality testing, loss of, 303–25
  in Panic Disorder, 80–81
  questionnaire on, 27–28
Recall, 332
  examination on, 330
Registration, examination on, 330
Rejection
  in Borderline Personality Disorder, 224,
    240
  depression following, 41
Religious delusions, 315
Remedial education, 369–70
REM sleep, 190, 192, 197
Restoril, 129, 202
Reynolds, Burt, 129
Risperdal, 324, 361
Ritalin, 203, 395, 396
Rohypnol ("rophies"), 129

Sadism, sexual, 179–81
St.-John's wort, 52
San Diego UFO cult, 319
"Sanguine" temperament, 207
Schizoaffective Disorder, 317–18
  differential diagnosis in, 71
  symptoms of, 318
  treatment for, 323
Schizoid Personality Disorder, 230–32
  symptoms of, 231
  treatment of, 241
Schizophrenia, 313–16
  depersonalization in, 291
  description of, 314–16
  differential diagnosis in, 156, 193, 268,
    288, 309, 322, 335, 337, 349,
    364–65, 369, 382
  in ectomorphs, 208
  impulse-control problems in, 264, 266
  incidence of, 313
  prognosis of, 307, 323
  substance use in, 324
  support groups for, 58, 145, 325, 326

Schizophrenia (*cont.*)
  symptoms of, 313–14
  treatment of, 313, 323–25
Schizophreniform Disorder, 307, 314
Schizotypal Personality Disorder, 232–33
  symptoms of, 233
  treatment of, 241
Schubert, Franz, 73
Seasonal depression, 41–42, 52, 62
  support group for, 57
Seconal, 129
Second-opinion consultation, 424
Secret lovers, 305
Sedatives, 122–23, 129–31, 175, 191, 202
  amnesia from, 348
  in Bipolar Disorder, 76
Seizures
  grand mal, in depressant withdrawal, 130
  urinary incontinence in, 405
Self-diagnosis, 11, 14, 413
Self-hypnosis, 278, 292
Self-loathing, 46
Sensation, loss of, in Conversion Disorder, 250, 251
Sensory deprivation, 309
Sensory functions. *See* Motor and sensory functions
Separation Anxiety Disorder, 406–10
  differential diagnosis in, 409–10
  fear and avoidance in, 93
  incidence of, 408
  symptoms of, 408
  treatment of, 410
Seroquel, 324, 361
Serotonin reuptake inhibitors. *See* SSRI's
Sex change surgery, 187
Sex differences
  in aggressive behavior, 376
  in Antisocial Personality Disorder, 228
  in Bipolar I Disorder, 62
  caffeine and, 133
  in Conduct Disorder, 377
  in Dependence Personality Disorder, 215
  in drug dependence, 130
  in Encopresis, 403
  in evaluation of Personality Disorders, 235
  in fragile X syndrome, 358
  in gambling, 273–74
  in Histrionic Personality Disorder, 221
  in idealized body shape, 156–57
  in lifelong friendships, 295
  in Paraphilia, 179
  in Schizophrenia, 313

in Separation Anxiety Disorder, 409
in Sexual Dysfunction, 172–75
in sleep patterns, 189, 200
  See also Gender Identity Disorder
Sexual abuse. *See* Children, sexual abuse of
Sexual Aversion Disorder, 173
Sexual Dysfunction, 171–78
  differential diagnosis in, 175–77, 182
  medication as cause of, 140
  "normality" and, 177
  questionnaire on, 23
  substances causing, 127
  support groups for, 188
  treatment of, 177–78
Shaman, 9
Shared Psychotic Disorder (Folie à Deux), 307, 318–25
  symptoms of, 319
  treatment of, 321–25
Sheldon, W. H., 208
Shell shock, 111
Shift work, 194–95, 203
Shock therapy. *See* Electroconvulsive therapy (ECT)
Shuteye Helpline, 204
Shyness, 219
Sibling Information Network, 371
Sick building syndrome, 141
Sinequan, 202
Sleep, 189–203
  bed-wetting during. *See* Enuresis
  in Bipolar Disorder, 64, 74
  in Delirium, 337
  deprivation of, 189–90, 197, 338
  evolutionary context of, 201
  questionnaire on, 24
  stages of, 190
  substances causing problems with, 127
  support groups for problems with, 204–5
  treatment for disorders of, 200–3
  types of disorders of, 190
  See also Circadian Rhythm Sleep Disorder; Insomnia; Nightmare Disorder; Oversleeping
Sleep apnea, 192, 197
Sleep Disorder Due to a General Medical Condition, 191–92
Sleep Disorders Related to Another Mental Disorder, 193
Sleep drunkenness, 196
Sleeping pills, 97, 141, 146, 191, 202–3
  memory loss and, 351
  problems of use of, 129–31

Sleep restriction therapy, 202
Sleep Terror Disorders, 198
Sleepwalking Disorder, 24, 199, 203
S.M.A.R.T. Recovery Self-Help Network, 152
Smoking. *See* Nicotine use
Snoring, 192
Social Phobia, 88–89, 93, 95
  symptoms of, 89
Social withdrawal
  in Anorexia Nervosa, 160
  in Avoidant Personality Disorder, 217–18
Sodium valproate, 76
Somatization Disorder, 246, 249–50, 260
Soviet Union, Schizotypal Personality
    Disorder in, 233
Special education, 369–70
Specific Phobia, 90–92
  symptoms of, 92
Speech
  in Autistic Disorder, 361–63
  in Bipolar I Disorder, 64
  in Dementia, 339–40, 344
  in Schizophrenia, 314–16
Speed, 96, 127
  depression after crash following, 44
  paranoia from, 307
Spina bifida, 405
Spinal injuries, 176
Spray paint, 138
SSRI's, 41, 95, 106, 175, 191, 279, 410
Starting Over (film), 129
Status, loss of, depression from, 31–32, 54
Stealing. *See* Kleptomania
Steroids
  depression from, 45
  inappropriate use of, 141
  wild mood fluctuations from, 71
Stimulants, 123
  in ADHD, 388, 394–95, 396
Stimulus-control therapy, 201–2
Street Car Named Desire, A (play and movie),
    219
Stress
  Adjustment Disorder and, 295–300
  in Brief Psychotic Disorder, 311
  clearinghouse for information on, 301
  depressions related to, 31
  dissociation in, 281
  questionnaire on, 27
  in Somatization Disorder, 249
  See also Posttraumatic Stress Disorder
    (PTSD)
Stress-management techniques, 278, 402

Stroke Connection, 354
Strokes
  Delirium after, 337
  depression after, 45, 298
  impulse-control problems after, 263
  psychosis after, 308
  Vascular Dementia after, 344
Subdural hematoma, 346
Substance Abuse, 120, 125–26, 142
  in Antisocial Personality Disorder, 230,
    241
  Conduct Disorder and, 378, 385
  symptoms of, 125
  treatment for, 144–50, 321–22
Substance Dependence, 119–25, 143, 147,
    268
  Conduct Disorder and, 378, 380
  description of, 122–25
  support groups for, 151–54
  symptoms of, 121–22
Substance-Induced Delirium, 338
Substance-Induced Disorder, 120, 126–27
  symptoms of, 127
Substance-Induced Psychotic Disorder,
    307–8
  symptoms of, 308
Substance-Induced Sleep Disorder, 190–91
  symptoms of, 191
Substance use, 117–50
  behavior of young affected by, 376–77
  in Bipolar Disorder, 74
  cost-effectiveness of treatment for, 145
  depersonalization after, 291
  depression from, 45
  detoxification in, 145–47, 322, 324
  futility of war on, 144
  impulse-control problems from, 263, 266
  mania from, 70–71
  in psychosis, 308
  psychosis caused by, 306, 321–22
  psychotic symptoms in withdrawal from,
    322
  questionnaire on, 21–22
  in Schizophrenia, 324
  sleepwalking and, 199
  weight loss in, 161
Sugar, refined, 396
Suicide
  in Antisocial Personality Disorder, 224,
    228
  in Bipolar Disorder, 61, 67, 75
  in Borderline Personality Disorder, 225,
    240

Suicide (*cont.*)
   in Conduct Disorder, 378
   depression and, 37–39, 47
   in postpartum depression, 42
   in Schizophrenia, 313
Sundowning, 337
Superego, 54
Support and advocacy groups, 15
Support groups, 425
   in depression, 56–58
   See also listings under specific problems
Surgery
   Delirium after, 338
   sex change, 187
Sutton, Willie, 267
Sybil (book), 286
Symptoms. *See* Unexplained physical
   complaints; *specific disorders*
Synesthesia, 135

TALK (Taking Action Against Language
   Disorders for Kids), 372
Tantrums, 224, 366
Tegrerol, 75, 76
Telephone numbers, recall of, 339
Telephone scatologia, 181
Temperaments, in Hippocrates, 207
Terminal illness, undermedication in, 138
TERRAP, 100
Terror. *See* Anxiety
Testosterone, 376
THC, 133
Thiamin, 346, 348
Thorazine, 361
Three Faces of Eve, The (film), 286
Thyroid problems
   Dementia from, 346
   mania and, 72
   Panic Disorder and, 83
   rapid cycling with, 62
Tic Disorder (Tourette's Disorder), 393,
   399–402
   description of, 400–1
   differential diagnosis in, 401
   support group for, 401, 411
   symptoms of, 400
   treatment of, 401–2
Tobacco, 121
   See also Nicotine use
Toilet training. *See* Encopresis
Toughlove, 385
Tourette's Disorder. *See* Tic Disorder
Tourette Syndrome Association, 401, 411

Toxins, 141–42
Trances, depersonalization in, 292
Tranquilizers, 97, 129
   depression caused by, 44
   hospital withdrawal from, 338
Transexuals, 185
Transient Tic Disorder, 400
Transvestic fetishism, 179, 180
Trauma Survivors Anonymous, 116
Traumatic events, 109–15
   amnesia from, 26, 281–86
   questionnaire on, 21
Trazodone, 351
Treatment, options for, 14, 420–22
Trichophagia, 277
Trichotillomania, 277–79
   differential diagnosis in, 105
   support group for, 280
   symptoms of, 278
   treatment of, 278–79
Trichotillomania Learning Center, 280
Tricyclic antidepressants, 41, 51, 202
Twain, Mark, 21
Typewriter correction fluid, 138

Unconsciousness, in Conversion Disorder,
   250
Unexplained physical complaints, 245–61
   differential diagnosis in, 258–59
   questionnaire on, 25–26
   treatment in, 260–61
Unipolar depression. *See* Dysthymic
   Disorder; Major Depressive Disorder
Urinary tract infections, 405
Urophilia, 181

Vaginismus, 174
Valium, 95, 98, 129, 410
   amnestic effects of, 284
Van Gogh, Vincent, 73
Vascular Dementia, 344
Velcro, 352
Viagra, 178
Vietnam War, 112, 141
Violence in human nature, 265–66
Vitamin deficiency
   Delirium from, 338
   Dementia from, 346, 348
   of thiamin, 346, 348
Vitamin E, in Alzheimer's disease, 351
Vocational rehabilitation, in Schizophrenia,
   325
Voice, loss of, in Conversion Disorder, 250

Voices, hearing, 305–6, 313, 315
  as "normal" in some cultures, 320
Vomiting, self-induced, 156, 164–66
Voyeurism, 179, 180

War neurosis, 111
Weakness, in Conversion Disorder, 250
Weight change
  in depression, 36, 40, 41
  in drug abuse, 161
  See also Anorexia Nervosa; Overeating
Weight tables, 161–62
Wenicke's encephalopathy, 346
West Side Story (play and film), 375
Whisper Down the Lane, 320
Williams, Tennessee, The Glass Menagerie, 89
Winfrey, Oprah, 288
Winter depression. See Seasonal depression
Wizard of Oz, The (film), 333
Women. See Postpartum depression;
  Sex differences

Women for Sobriety, 153
Word salad, 316
Workaholics, 212
Workaholics Anonymous World Service
  Organization, 243
Work environment, what to tell about your
  problem in, 420
Worthlessness, feelings of, in depression, 37,
  43, 47
Wrist biting, 363

Xanax, 84, 95, 98, 129, 202

You Can't Cheat an Honest Man (film), 269

Zeldoc, 324
Zoloft, 41, 50, 51, 95, 106, 191, 279, 366,
  410
Zoophilia, 181
Zyban, 139
Zyprexa, 324, 361, 402

About the Authors

Allen Frances, M.D., is Professor of Psychiatry and former chairman of the Department of Psychiatry and Behavioral Science at Duke University. Dr. Frances was chairman of the DSM-IV Task Force and is currently leading an effort to develop expert consensus practice guidelines for the different psychiatric disorders.

Michael B. First, M.D., is Associate Professor of Clinical Psychiatry at Columbia University College of Physicians and Surgeons and is a research psychiatrist in the Biometrics Research Department at New York State Psychiatric Institute. He was the editor of the DSM-IV text and criteria, and now maintains a private practice in Manhattan.